Revolutions in Communication

Revolutions in Communication

Media History from Gutenberg to the Digital Age

Bill Kovarik

continuum

The Continuum International Publishing Group
80 Maiden Lane, New York, NY 10038
The Tower Building, 11 York Road, London SE1 7NX

www.continuumbooks.com

Library of Congress Cataloging-in-Publication Data
Kovarik, Bill.
  Revolutions in communication : media history from Gutenberg
to the digital age / Bill Kovarik.
    p. cm.
  Includes bibliographical references and index.
  ISBN 978-1-4411-9495-4 (hardback : alk. paper) – ISBN 978-1-4411-1460-0 (pbk. : alk. paper)
1. Mass media—History. 2. Communication—History. I. Title.

P90.K666 2011
302.2309--dc22

                                                                                                    2011004240

ISBN: HB: 978-1-4411-9495-4
       PB: 978-1-4411-1460-0

Typeset by Newgen Imaging Systems Pvt Ltd, Chennai, India
Printed and bound in the United States of America

Visit the companion website at www.revolutionsincommunication.com

Contents

Preface

Working on the copy desk of newspapers in the 1980s, late into the evening hours, we would sip coffee and sift through news reports and wire service photos from all over the world. Occasionally, as Atlanta editor Ralph McGill once said, we'd get a sense of our world, wheeling again towards the sun, alive with joys, struggling with sorrows, and all reflected in the photos and news reports that poured into the newsroom. We wished everyone could see what we were seeing, but in those days we could only print a tiny fraction of the day's intelligence.

Those were the last days of hot lead typesetting and Western Union telegrams. We were glad that it was the end of an era. We were all too aware of the media's constraints, and we wondered how things would look on the other side of the digital revolution that we knew was coming. We pretty much figured that, as with any revolution, there would be both ennobling and corrosive impacts.

What made the digital revolution so interesting was that it did not spring from the technology developed by media institutions, computer corporations or the defense department. Instead, to paraphrase John Adams, we saw the digital revolution first taking place in the hearts and minds of a global community of scientists, engineers, writers, philosophers, artists and visionaries. The technology emerged as part of the vision, not the other way around.

A look at media history tells us that a similar sense of community animated most of the great communications revolutions in history. Gutenberg's printing press spread rapidly across Europe in the 1400s thanks to a community of craftsmen; Daguerre literally gave away photographic patents in 1839 and created a world community of photographers almost overnight; and Morse's Code became the first universal software in the 1840s, even if, to his dismay, his telegraphic patents ended up in the hands of a monopoly. Even so, a community of critics who fought the telegraph monopoly funded Alexander Graham Bell's work to create the telephone, and the global community of scientists investigating electromagnetic phenomena were the ones who created radio, television and satellite communications.

The benefits of these communication revolutions are well known to those of us living in the early twenty-first century; they include instant free global messaging; instant access to information and entertainment; cell phones and community-building applications; and the communications networks that support medical, scientific, cultural and political information exchanges around the globe.

Every revolution comes at an unexpected price. Printing triggered centuries of religious and political struggle; visual communication diluted and (some say) degraded political discourse; electronic communication submerged unique cultures and sometimes fostered xenophobia; and the digital revolution seems to be undermining the political culture that was created by the printing press while pulling the world closer together.

To understand these interesting times, a sense of history is a basic requirement. Without history, we are blind and powerless. With history, at the very least, we are not blind, and occasionally, we may perceive an opening for a real contribution to our common destiny.

Bill Kovarik, PhD Floyd, Virginia
www.revolutionsincommunication.org
bill.kovarik@gmail.com

Acknowledgments

Revolutions in Communication is dedicated to my father, David Kovarik, who inspired a love of history, and to my wife, Linda Burton, who helped me box the compass of issues when I would get lost in the mass of details. Also I'd like to express deep appreciate to family members who deserve more mention than possible here: Ben Kovarik, Nick Kovarik, Karen Kovarik, Daniel Kovarik, Kitty Kovarik, Ken Kovarik, Lisa Kovarik, David Burton, Sue Burton, Mary Wise, Joe Flynn, Kim and Andy Acres, and George and Joanne Guess.

A major debt is also owed to friends and colleagues Maurine Beasley, Jim and Laurie Grunig, Reese Cleghorn, Jon Franklin and Robert Friedel at the University of Maryland; Glen Martin, Phyllis Turk, Lynn Zoch, Bob Stepno, Roland Lazenby, Tricia Easterling, Vince Hazelton, Chris Carter, Rhonda McCrosky, Theresa Burriss, Denis Grady, Joe Flickinger, Joe Staniunis, Kristin Froemling, Richard Worringham, Sherry Carr, Basel Saleh and Buddy Timberg at Radford University; William Emerson, Mark Ethridge and Rick Stevens at the University of South Carolina; Sam Riley and Skip Garner at Virginia Tech; Tom Carmichael, David Spencer and Nick Witheford at the University of Western Ontario; Steven Berry at Howard University; Venise Berry at University of Iowa; Cathy Jackson at Norfolk State; and Ivanka Knezevic at the University of Toronto.

Colleagues and friends in the Society of Environmental Journalists, the Society of Professional Journalists and the Association for Education in Journalism and Mass Communication require special mention as well: Bill Allen, Gary Braasch, James Bruggers, Jeff Burnside, Saul Chernos, Marla Cone, Osha Gray Davidson, Lynn Davis, Rob Davis, Peter Dykstra, Bill Eby, Dan Fagin, Peter Fairley, Douglas Fischer, Christy George, Steve Goldstein, Pauli Hayes, Tom Henry, Don Hopey, Cheryl Hogue, Marsha Johnston, Bill Johnston, Wilford Kale, Jamie Kitman, Jay Letto, Randy Loftis, Mike Mansur, Sally McClure, Robert McClure, Jim Motavalli, Mark Neuzil, Sharon Oosterhook, Beth Parke, Chris Rigel, Bruce Ritchie, Judith Robinson, David Sachsman, Craig Saunders, Debra Schwarz, Mark Schleifstein, Peter Thompson, Rae Tyson, JoAnne Valenti, Ken Ward, Bud Ward, Tim Wheeler, Carolyn Whetzel, Dale Willman, Roger Witherspoon, Bob Wyss, Tom Yulsman and many others.

Special thanks are also due to Mary Anne Hitt, Matt Wasson, Jamie Goodman, Jeff Deal, Benji Burrell, Shay Boyd, Judy Bonds, Maria Gunnoe, Willa Mays and Leny Kohm; and to fellow historians Wess Harris, Roland Schnell, John Carter, Hal Bernton, Scott Sklar, George Krimsky, Tewfik Mishlawi, Bill Holmberg, Richard Flynn, R. James Woolsey, Boyd Griffin, Amanda Mecke and Howard Zinn.

Teachers also learn from their students, and some who have particularly helpful include: Chamonix Berry, Sierra Jones, Holly Collins, Camden Brown, Saskia Snuffer, Brandon Farthing, Katie Frank, Anne Lindsey, Tyler Bird, Lora Caster, Stephen Clark, Wes White, Brittany Keenan, Megan Van Patten, Brittany Case, Taylor Faw, Sean Burrows, Jeff French, Lindsey Mead, Andrea Carlston, April Gray and many others.

Finally, much of this publication would not have been possible without countless unknown people in the community of scholars who made vital information accessible through the internet and web. Their sense of community fosters hope for the prospects for humankind.

About the cover illustration

It may look like a giant satellite dish and an old computer, but in fact, the illustration depicts a demonstration of solar energy technology by French engineer Able Pifre in the Tuileries Garden of Paris in 1883. The conical concentrating solar collector is powering a steam engine that is running a printing press. Like many people engaged in political and social revolutions, Pifre used new media technology to advance new ideas.

Introduction

Revolutions in Communication

We are riding the crest of a great communications revolution that is visibly transforming daily life. Old institutions are falling and new ones rise overnight. Individuals now have unprecedented publishing technologies at their fingertips. Cultures that
have long been isolated from each other have been unexpectedly thrown together,
generating new kinds of social friction.

We often call it "the" communications revolution, but it is at least four separate
mass media revolutions—printing, imaging, electronic and digital—and each had its
own internal developments, external contexts and social impacts. Each of these has
swept through the world in succession over the centuries, not only having primary
effects but also refocusing the previous communications revolutions with secondary
and tertiary effects.

It no longer seems sufficient to simply present an isolated, progressive, narrative
history of American journalism. This is not to be critical of previous textbook
authors but rather to say that times are changing and, as usual, media historians are
struggling to catch up. Surely the fact that new media has broken down international
barriers must be part of any serious topical treatment of media history today. Surely,
also, the interdependent nation-state / print media institution, with a relationship
now over five centuries old, is only one thread of the story of an emerging global
media.

As Mitchell Stephens said in "A Call for an International History of Journalism":

> To attempt to separate the history of American journalism from developments
> overseas seems . . . as foolish as attempting to separate the history of journalism
> in Ohio or Kansas from what was happening in Boston, Philadelphia and New
> York. . . . A kind of ignorance—which would not be tolerated in literature depart-
> ments, in theater departments, in art departments, in science departments—is

routinely accepted in journalism departments. American journalism history is dangerously and unflaggingly parochial. (Stephens, 2011)

The same parochial nationalism is even more evident in public relations, advertising, broadcasting, and other communications fields, partly because in the past, communications history was valued as preparation for students aiming for careers in media. Historians who hope to inspire future generations by honoring the heroes of the past often oversimplify and omit the mistakes and connections that provide historical lessons and paths for ongoing inquiry.

Constructing a history that approaches a broad professional and international scope presents an interesting problem of scale. One solution is to take advantage of the new media that this book describes. We might see this book as a focal point for an international history of the media that is already begun on a variety of collaborative websites such as Wikipedia. Since we live in revolutionary times, we ought to reflect and model those revolutionary new modes of communication in the way communication history is taught—and written. With that in mind, scholars and students can turn to this book's website—www.revolutionsincommunication.com—for links to wikis, timelines and other resources that can enhance understanding of media.

It's best to read history with some idea of what history is all about, and we begin with two items as part of a conceptual toolkit. The first is a quick overview of historians who exemplify different approaches to historical research and writing. The second is a glimpse at how historians have seen technology in general and media history in particular. This book then proceeds on a mostly chronological basis through the four mass media revolutions: print, visual, electronic and digital.

Understanding history

History is never above the melee. It is not allowed to be neutral, but forced to enlist in every army. (Allan Nevins, 1938)

To begin with, recorded history represents our collective memory. It is an attempt to understand how and why history is made, and it is the best guide to the possibilities of the future.

History is the discipline that allows us to examine both small events and sweeping trends, and to ask the broadest possible questions. Historians are free to explore without an expectation of exact answers. In this sense, history is not science, nor is it social science. It is a separate discipline that plays by its own rules and answers very much to its own muse.

Above all, history has a duty to accuracy and truth. It is a powerful tool, not only in terms of analytical ability and scope, but also in terms of how it can be used to legitimize present day political agendas and projects. In that sense, history has been called "the dressing room of politics" (Weber, 1972). Perhaps the most important first lesson about history, then, is that historians have motivations—that is to say, they usually write with a purpose in mind.

Why do historians write history?

Two of the highest purposes of history might be summarized as (1) to remember and honor the heroes and (2) to learn the lessons of history. These were expressed very early in classical Greece.

Herodotus (484–420 BC) said he wrote history ". . . in the hope of . . . preserving from decay the remembrance of what men have done, and of preventing the great and wonderful actions of the Greeks and the Barbarians from losing their due meed (reward) of glory . . ."

On the other hand, Thucydides (460–400 BC) hoped *The History of the Peloponnesian War* would "be judged useful by those inquirers who desire an exact knowledge of the past as an aid to the interpretation of the future . . . I have written my work, not as an essay which is to win the applause of the moment, but as a possession for all time."

These two motivations are often at cross purposes. Heroic nationalistic history often omits the blemishes and controversies. When students are first introduced to history in secondary school, the heroics usually get far more attention than the controversial perspectives that help us appreciate the lessons of history.

The best-known idea about history comes from George Santayana (1863–1952), who echoed Thucydides when he said: "Those who cannot remember the past are condemned to repeat it." But those "lessons of history" are not just static collections of established facts any more than science is an unchanging description of the physical world. History includes perspectives and motivations; it serves modern interests; and it may change, grow and coalesce around facts that may only become available decades after events in question.

As James W. Loewen said:

> History is furious debate informed by evidence and reason, not just answers to be learned. Textbooks encourage students to believe that history is learning facts. "We have not avoided controversial issues" announces one set of textbook authors; "instead, we have tried to offer reasoned judgments" on them—thus removing the controversy! No wonder their text turns students off!

And so, in the end, the capacity to think through historical issues and understand historical evidence is key to understanding history.

Is history objective?
How should history be written?

Another important set of ideas about history has to do with objectivity and the way history is written. Objectivity is a question that has dogged the historical profession as much as it has challenged the news media.

One famous German historian, Leopold Von Ranke (1795–1886) said that historians should take a "scientific" approach and report "the way things really were." But by that he meant that an account of the battle of Waterloo should be based on facts commonly accredited by French, German and English historians. But few would suggest that the rise of Napoleon would be seen in the same objective light by all nationalities.

It's no surprise, then, that the quest for objectivity is often seen as quixotic. In *That Noble Dream*, Peter Novick describes American historians' attempts to first incorporate and then move away from Von Ranke's ideas about objectivity (Novik, 1988). Many historians abandoned this constricted view of objectivity and devoted their histories to nationalistic purposes, he notes. They disliked the idea of holding up a string of cold facts without an attempt at meaning, and focused on making history moral, or progressive, or more relevant to the present. These historians included Charles Beard (1874–1948) in the United States and Lord John Edward Emerich Acton (1834–1902) in Britain. Acton believed in a moral approach to history. His most famous aphorism is: "Power tends to corrupt, and absolute power corrupts absolutely."

Objectivity wasn't the real problem, according to other historians such as Herbert Butterfield (1900–1979). It was, instead, the tendency of historians to take sides. Butterfield objected to the way historians would "write on the side of Protestants and Whigs, to praise revolutions, provided they have been successful, to emphasize certain principles of progress in the past, and to produce a story which is the ratification if not the glorification of the present." This is often called "Whig" history. It's not always such a bad thing—in fact, the focus on democratic reform was designed rather deliberately to keep that historical frame in view as an aid to present-day political growth and reform. Yet Whig history was designed to honor the heroes and tended to present history in a linear form and omit irregularities.

In recent years, many historians have moved away from objective and progressive national histories, focusing instead on cultural history or other smaller topics. Cultural history involves the history of ideas, history of technology, women's history, black history, environmental history and many others not yet explored. Yet history as a discipline, as Novick has noted, has not moved any closer toward a resolution of the fragmentation.

To some, such as Francis Fukuyama (1952–present) and Jean Baudrillard (1929–2007), the collapse of ideology or even the end of an *idea* of historical progress represents the "end of history" (Fukuyama, 1992). According to Baudrillard, this comes from the abandonment of utopian visions shared by both the right- and left-wing political ideologies (Baudrillard, 1994).

And yet, not all ideas about utopian futures have been lost. Recent ideas along those lines have focused, as we shall see, on the advance of communications technologies and of the way they enabled social networks and free cultures.

How is media history different?

Historians have always seen a strong role for media in the larger sphere of national histories, and it would be unlikely that any historian would overlook the role of printers like Benjamin Franklin in spurring the American Revolution of the 1770s, or of radio news as a catalyst of public opinion during the 1940s, or of television images to bring home the suffering of Civil Rights demonstrators during the 1960s.

Among early American media histories are Isaiah Thomas' *History of Printing in America* (Thomas, 1810) and James Parton's *Life of Horace Greeley* (Parton, 1855). Like many subsequent histories, both took a "whiggish" approach that presumed a history of progress toward freedom. The same idea remained in the heart of the narrative until the 1970s, when the foundations of objectivity were shaken to the core by events inside and outside the world of the news media (Carey, 1992). Communications scholar James W. Carey challenged journalism historians to go beyond their identification with the press and, as one suggestion, to focus on the development of consciousness as expressed in the news report. One example was Mitchell Stephens' book, *A History of News* (Stephens, 2007).

Social theories of the media

Another part of our theoretical toolkit involves normative social theories that have critiqued and challenged the mass media. On the one hand, liberal democrats have seen the mass media as an agent of progressive social change, a self-righting component of a democracy. On the other hand, sociologists and critical theorists have seen the mass media's production of culture as a battleground for ideological conflict and an instrument of class control.

Illustrating this range of social theory, liberal democrats like Walter Lippmann held the press up against the idea that the press is part of a system of checks and balances ("the original dogma of democracy") in his 1922 book, *Public Opinion*. Lippmann also described four stages of media progress, from authoritative, to partisan, to commercial, and then to a state he called organized intelligence.

Other liberal media critics include:

- Upton Sinclair, who wrote *The Jungle* (about the Chicago meat industry) and *The Brass Check* (Sinclair, 1920)
- A. J. Liebling, a media critic with the New Yorker from the 1930s to the 1960s (Liebling, 1981)
- I. F. Stone and George Seldes, independent newsletter editors and press critics in the 1950s and 60s (Seldes, 1987; Stone, 2007)
- Ben Bagdikian, an American academic who criticized the "media monopoly" (Bagdikian, 1989)
- Niel Postman, an American academic who warned that we were "Amusing Ourselves to Death" with our use of media (Postman, 1985).

On the other side of the social theory of media are critical theorists. Sociologists like Max Weber and Michael Schudson used an ideational model as the focus for a critical examination of the media, observing, for example, the clash of ideas around effective social reform movements (Schudson, 1978).

Communications theorists like Michel Foucault used discourse analysis to understand the information content and structure of mainstream cultural products and "subjugated knowledges."

Critical theorists like Theodor W. Adorno, Walter Benjamin and Jürgen Habermas and others from the Frankfurt School saw the conflict of classes as the dominant theme and observed that mass media was structured to subvert identity and assimilate individuality into the dominant culture. Noam Chomsky, an academic expert in linguistics and self-described "libertarian socialist" is sometimes included in this group as a critic who sees media as little more than propaganda generation for the ruling elites.

Media technology in perspective

How much does the rapidly changing technology of mass media influence the world of the individual and the overall social structure? How has this influence been evident in the past? What is its likely path in the future? To begin grasping these issues, we will first introduce some basic concepts, then describe some recent debates, and consider the ideas and inspirations of a few important theorists.

The reason we study media technology, according to media theorist Marshall McLuhan, is that we need to be able to anticipate the process of social change it generates. McLuhan didn't believe that mass media is a neutral tool we can just take or leave:

> Because of today's terrific speed-up of information moving, we have a chance to apprehend, predict and influence the environmental forces shaping us—and thus win back control of our own destinies. The new extensions of man and the environment they generate are the central manifestations of the evolutionary process, and yet we still cannot free ourselves of the delusion that it is how a medium is used that counts, rather than what it does to us and with us. (*Playboy*, 1969)

Here McLuhan argues that technology has impacts, whether we like them or not. Because of this, McLuhan is in the "determinist" category of theorists. However, to the extent that we can influence technological changes, he sees a role for social responses to technology.

Technological determinism

Determinism involves the question of inherent freedom. For some religious traditions, determinism is a central issue, and the question is whether people have free will or whether our fates are predetermined. The stakes are not quite so high in technology,

Figure 0.1 The medium and the message: Marshall McLuhan (1911–1980), a Canadian media theorist, saw communications technology at the center of human psychology and the historical process. (Photo courtesy of Richard Worringham)

where determinism is the idea that a technology may have inherent characteristics that shape its impact on society.

Technological determinism is often contrasted with the idea that social processes (including politics, economics and culture) have more influence on a technology than a technology's own trajectory. The question can also focus on the social impact of technology: Is the social impact predetermined by a technology's inherent characteristics, or does society shape its response to technology?

These are historical and social questions with no fixed answers. They have been answered both ways, and neither side is right or wrong. Well-informed people frequently disagree about these kinds of issues, and in the give and take discussion, we learn to appreciate a variety of perspectives to complex issues.

For example, what is the impact of twenty-first-century high speed global satellite and fiber optic data networks? For columnist Thomas Friedman, these particular media technologies "flattened" the world, making it just as easy to process information or make phone calls from India as it would be in Europe or North America. The acceleration of information technology created this condition, he argues in his 2005 book, *The World is Flat*. While social institutions might buffer some of the impacts, the global sharing of semiskilled information work is inevitable and still expanding.

The idea of technological determinism was conceived by sociologist Thorstein Veblen (1857–1929), perhaps inspired by historian Charles Beard, who said: "Technology marches in seven-league boots from one ruthless, revolutionary conquest to another, tearing down old factories and industries, flinging up new processes with terrifying rapidity."

The possibility that the acceleration of technology could reach a point where no social process could exert any control is considered to be a technological singularity beyond which any future is opaque. For example, futurist Raymond Kurzweil posits a super-intelligent network of computers that could make decisions about ending all human existence (Kurzweil, 2005).

Social construction of technology

While some argue that the path and influence of some technologies seem more or less predetermined, there are examples of social and political controls holding back technology. Radio and television broadcasting industry technology and structure was largely a social construct, and examples include national and international telecommunications regulatory agencies, such as the Federal Communications Commission in the United States, and the technical standards for television screens, which were decided in board rooms and not in laboratories (Barnouw, 1970).

This experience meant that when the implications of the World Wide Web dawned in the mid-1990s, the push to regulate it like broadcasting was met with a strong counterargument to leave the Web unregulated, like print media (Rand, 1998).

Another perspective on social influence is that inventors themselves tend to infuse their own values into technology. For example, Steve Jobs of Apple computers wanted to make personal computing possible; Thomas Edison tried, through patent lawsuits, to retain control of the motion picture industry.

Sometimes the inventor's values come into conflict with powerful industrial or social forces. Brian Winston, for example, describes the emergence of some media technologies as influenced by what he calls the law of the suppression of radical potential (Winston, 2008).

No lone inventor, such as Samuel Morse, can today reinvent the Web or market a new spreadsheet application. But one could market an open source spreadsheet. What's different about the digital revolution, according to Jonathan Zittrain, is that the inventive values introduced in the mix have a different set of dimensions than the lone inventor in the lab. They are far larger than any idea of business or making money. In the more recent eras, among gaming companies and internet developers, the values of playfulness and creativity were far stronger than the desire to create well-made products or serve corporate loyalties. And in the process, they created an alternative economy, Zittrain said (Zittrain, 2006).

Luddites and utopians

When people reject technology in a pessimistic way, they are sometimes called Luddites. The term goes back to 1811, when thousands of British textile workers lost their jobs following the introduction of steam powered machinery. They broke the textile machinery and blamed it on a mythical figure named Ned Ludd, who according to legend was a simple-minded boy who accidentally broke textile machinery. The Luddite movement was nonviolent, or at least, the destruction was confined to steam powered textile mills. Still, 23 men were executed and a dozen more were exiled to Australia. This movement was very much on the mind of *London Times* owner John Walter II when he promised workers that they would keep their jobs even after steam printing presses were introduced in 1814.

Pessimism need not involve outright rejection of technology. Henry Adams, in his 1907 autobiography, said that civilization had left behind an old world concerned with religion and had entered a new one, a world concerned with science and technology but morally and philosophically adrift. His comparison of the two ages of civilization was between the Virgin and the Dynamo, an idea which has been often repeated in discussions about technology.

When people embrace technology in an extremely optimistic way, they are said to be technological utopians. A good deal of the rhetoric surrounding the development of the telegraph, the early years of radio, and the early years of the internet was influenced by this sort of enthusiasm (Czitrom, 1983).

It is possible for luddites and technological utopians to see technology as either deterministic or socially constructed. An example of a Luddite (or pessimistic) determinist would be Oswald Spengler, who saw technology inevitably leading to the decline of Western European civilization. An example of an optimistic determinism is evident in the rhetoric surrounding the 1933 Chicago World's Fair, where the motto was: "Science Finds, Industry Applies, Man Conforms."

An example of an optimistic view combined with a social construction of technology might be Thomas Friedman, mentioned above, or also Langdon Winner, who advocated more awareness of the social and political possibilities for control of technology.

Technological fallacies

Sometimes predictions for technological directions that do not occur are called technological fallacies. It was a fallacy, for instance, that computers would lead to a police state. It was a partial fallacy for Alexander Graham Bell and other inventors of the late nineteenth century to predict that the telephone would be used more or less as a medium for broadcasting, in the way that occurred with radio in the 1920s, carrying news and music. It was a complete fallacy for Guglielmo Marconi, inventor of the radio, to predict that radio waves could stimulate plants and act as a new kind of fertilizer. In the 1950s and 60s, comic book detectives carried "wrist televisions" like wrist watches to communicate with each other—again, something of a partial fallacy.

Envisioning the future has always been an interesting and sometimes productive pastime, but the future isn't what it used to be, as a variety of authors have noted. The atomic-powered airplane, the personal helicopter, the robot valet—all have been chalked up by now as technological fallacies (Barbrook, 2007; Eric and Jonathan Dregni, 2006).

McLuhan, Innis and media technology

One school of historical thought places communications history at the center of civilization. Two historians who explored this approach were:

- Harold Innis (1894–1952) an economic historian who explored the idea that cultures using durable media tended to be biased (oriented) toward time and religious orthodoxy (Egypt, Babylon), while, on the other hand, cultures with flexible media (Rome, Greece, modern) were biased toward control of space and a secular approach to life; and
- Marshall McLuhan (1911–1980) a media critic who was strongly influenced by Innis and also put communication at the center of history.

McLuhan foresaw international broadcast media connecting through satellites in the 1950s and 60s, and described the new media landscape in terms of a "global village." He also considered the idea of media as an extension of human thinking. He is probably most famous for the statement that "the medium is the message," which, in other words, means that the medium is has a strong influence on the message and the type of thinking that creates the message.

Communications theorist James W. Carey saw McLuhan's relatively optimistic ideas about media technology as something of a reaction to the pessimism expressed by others, especially British historian Lewis Mumford. McLuhan envisioned electronic media liberating users from the sensory limitations of the past, while Mumford "recognized the paradox of electrical communication: that the media of reflective thought—reading writing and drawing—could be weakened by television and radio; that closer contact did not necessarily mean greater peace; that the new inventions would be foolishly overused" (Carey, 1992).

Media are extensions of human perception, McLuhan observed. They are powerful influences, for good or bad, in helping us form our views of reality. (This idea was exaggerated in William Gibson's book *Neuromancer*, which then became the basis of a movie called *The Matrix*.)

But as communications theorists have pointed out over the decades, ascribing a great deal of power to a medium may be too deterministic. No matter how deeply they are steeped in media, people also have many non-media influences that help contextualize the media experience.

Hot and cool media

Media can be classified by their impacts on audiences, McLuhan said in his 1965 book *Understanding Media*. Some types of media tend to be "hot"—that is, they immerse audience members and allow less participation. Others tend to be "cool," allowing audience members to be detached from the message or requiring more participation in making sense of the message. The idea wasn't entirely new; for example, Enlightenment philosopher David Hume said in 1742 that a free press should not be feared because the medium could not incite rebellion. "A man reads a book or pamphlet alone, coolly. There is no one present from whom he can catch the passion by contagion" (Hume, 1742).

Just where each medium might fall on a hot-cool spectrum depends on its cultural and historical context. In the 1960s, McLuhan could say that cinema was "hot" because audiences were fully immersed in the medium, while television was "cool" because, at the time, it was a low-definition medium that required some effort to enjoy. Yet over time, as television technology improved, the medium became more and more immersive; today, McLuhan might see television as much hotter than it once was.

The categories are not really fixed, and McLuhan often said provocative things he called "probes" just to stir up conversation. For instance, he thought of radio as a "hot" medium since it immersed audiences, and yet many others have seen radio as requiring a sense of imagination to fill in the details of the story, which would make it a "cool" medium. Perhaps his most provocative idea was that "hot" new media technology could be so overwhelming that many people would go into a subtle state of shock, a "psychic rigor mortis," as they tried to "cool off" its effects. Modern concerns about addition to social media and online video gaming systems might be seen as examples of this idea.

In any event, it's useful to question whether a linear view of hot-cool media categories really helps us understand psychological reactions to media. Recent studies of brain activity using functional magnetic resonance imaging (fMRI), which was not available in McLuhan's time, show that reading books, watching movies or searching the internet all use very different portions of the brain in unique ways.

McLuhan's tetrad of technology change

New communications technologies change and grow in familiar patterns that McLuhan said could be mapped out in what he called a "tetrad" of four effects. A new medium can (1) enhance, (2) obsolete, (3) retrieve and (4) reverse. For example, the arrival of radio enhanced news and music, it obsolesced (or made less prominent) print and visual media; it retrieved the spoken word and music hall shows; and it reversed (when pushed to its limits) into television (McLuhan, 1992). We might also say that television enhanced the visual, obsolesced the audio, retrieved theatrical spectacle, and reversed into "500 channels with nothing on."

The comparison can help clarify and anticipate some of the social changes that technology creates. We ask:

- What does the new medium enhance or amplify?
- What becomes obsolete or driven out of prominence?
- What is retrieved that had nearly been forgotten from an earlier time?
- How does the medium "overheat" or warp under pressure?

The classic example is radio.

- Enhancement—news and music via sound.
- Obsolescence—reduces the importance of print media
- Retrieval—returns the spoken word to the forefront. For example, FDR's fireside chats, which for McLuhan were a form of "re-tribalization."
- Reversal—Radio becomes a medium for teenagers and rock and roll music.

As media revolutions continue to reverberate, McLuhan's tetrad is a useful way of making comparisons throughout the four media revolutions. Just as McLuhan argued that broadcast media made print less important, others have argued that images and digital media decreased the importance of print (Benjamin, 2008; Boorstin, 1961; Hedges, 2009).

While digital media may retrieve some elements of print media, such as letter writing, certainly the impact of digital media has been to obsolesce print media institutions such as newspapers and change the political culture of the press.

Conclusion

These concepts are part of our "toolbox" with which we consider the advance of new media technologies and we will use them in the coming chapters to consider the history of media revolutions.

A useful history of media and technology does not simply present a parade of gadgets strung together chronologically. Instead, we will try to view media revolutions as a series of technological waves, linked by communities of people and ideas, meeting and interacting with the structures of society.

Section 1

The Printing Revolution

Introduction to Section I

We should notice the force, effect, and consequences of inventions, which are nowhere more conspicuous than in those three which were unknown to the ancients; namely, printing, gunpowder, and the compass. For these three have changed the appearance and state of the whole world; first in literature, then in warfare, and lastly in navigation: and innumerable changes have been thence derived, so that no empire, sect, or star, appears to have exercised a greater power and influence on human affairs than these mechanical discoveries. (Francis Bacon—Novum Organum, 1620)

Introduction

The printing revolution was *the* pivotal development in history, the turning point in the transition between the Medieval and modern worlds.

Beginning in 1455, printing technology spread quickly over Europe and played a central role in the great sweep of events that followed—the rediscovery of classical cultures during the Renaissance, the Protestant Reformation, the Enlightenment and the political revolutions from the 1600s to the twenty-first century. Printing allowed the spread of knowledge and challenges to authority by enabling mass communication among people who had previously been linked only by personal and small group communication.

The industrialization of media technologies in the nineteenth century—including the telegraph and steam-powered printing—created the opportunity for larger audiences and new institutions to serve them. Publisher Joseph Medill once compared early newspapers to little sailboats along an almost empty shore. But he boasted that by the mid-1800s, the press had become very much like a large ocean-going ship, "a proud steamer, bidding defiance to the tempests, laden with the mails and commerce of the world" (Brendon, 1983).

Industrial media institutions continued in nearly the same form, if not always the same corporations, through the nineteenth and twentieth centuries. Digital media diminished their role during the twenty-first century by decreasing the cost of information and the relative value of the product as well, transforming the business so much that, by the early twenty-first century, the proud old steamers of the press were foundering in the digital typhoon.

The question, of course, is why. We study history not only to appreciate the people of the past, but also as a guide to the possibilities of the future, as Thucydides advised. We should approach the history of communication with this in mind, especially now that new earth-shaking communications revolutions are having force and effect today. According to a 1998 Rand Corp. report:

> The 21st century communications revolution may turn out to be every bit as dramatic, and entail similarly revolutionary and contradictory consequences, as the 15th century revolution. Some of these consequences may be just as beneficial, some just as unintended, and some just as socially damaging. Most will be well upon us before they are fully appreciated. (Dewar, 1998)

In this section on the Printing Revolution, we will compress over 500 years of publishing into three chapters in order to take the broadest possible view of media history. Chapter 1 covers the early printing revolution up to 1814. Chapter 2 describes the industrial media revolution in the nineteenth century and Chapter 3 describes the rise and fall of print media in the twentieth century. Naturally, there will be omissions, and readers are encouraged to use this as a starting point, and to follow links and suggestions for further reading, or to make their own suggestions for further exploration online at this book's website.

Before the printing revolution: pre-wired for oral culture

Printing was the first *mass* medium in human history, but long before printing, and even long before writing, people communicated in what is called an oral culture.

We know that humans had language skills for hundreds of thousands of years. Psychologists have shown that humans are born with a natural capacity for language while most other species have little capacity for anything beyond a few basic signals. (Cetaceans may be an exception; see Mercado, 2005.) Even the language abilities of primates such as chimpanzees and apes have been limited to several hundred idea symbols, as opposed to the virtually unlimited horizon of communication we enjoy. Studies comparing human and primate language abilities using functional Magnetic Resonance Imaging (fMRI) have shown that the human brain has special segments devoted to language (Wolf, 2008). In other words, we are "pre-wired" to talk and communicate.

On the other hand, reading and writing have to be learned. Unlike language, reading is not pre-wired in the human brain, and until the printing revolution in the 1450s, most reading took place among a very narrow elite in scholarly, religious or government institutions. Thus, most human beings, for nearly all of their natural history, communicated their songs, folklore, history and traditions within an oral culture.

Oral cultures can accurately transmit important information from generation to generation, but these abilities are subject to the limitations of a culture and human memory. This is not well understood today, and a good example of our modern misunderstanding is the children's game called "telephone," in which a message is whispered from one person to another person until it goes around a room. The message invariably gets garbled—sometimes with hilarious results—when the starting message and the final message are compared. But when it is important, historical information can be accurately transmitted down through generations within oral cultures. For example, American author Alex Haley was able to discover an oral record of his ancestors in Africa, and his search is described in the now-classic book, *Roots: The Saga of an American Family*. Similarly, the Odyssey and Iliad were originally oral histories of Greek culture that were only written down many centuries after they were composed.

How storytellers and minstrels could memorize such elaborate and lengthy epic poems has always been a subject of controversy, but according to the "theory of oral composition" a storyteller can draw from taproot of millennia—old oral tradition by a combination of improvisation, mnemonic devices and rote memory.

This taproot runs deep in human psychology. Most people need a sense of community, exemplified in oral culture, and some of the world's most poignant literature has shown the impact of its loss. Oliver Goldsmith's 1770 *The Deserted Village* lamented rural virtues lost to the English enclosure acts; Chinua Achebe's 1958 *Things Fall Apart* described the impacts of European colonialism in Africa; Anne Pancake's 2008 *Strange as This Weather Has Been* revealed the social disintegration that accompanies Appalachian mountaintop mining.

This sense of community can be seen as a kind of "tribalism," although that term seems derogatory in a modern context. However, Marshall McLuhan believed that radio created a new oral culture that recovered some of this lost sense of community, for example through the "fireside chats" of national leaders, and that this was a "re-tribalization" of a culture that longed for an older and more community-oriented communications system. Digital visual and aural media may be a relatively new extension of that concept.

Another link to the old oral culture might be the popularity of the "fantasy" genre in cinema, such as *Harry Potter* or *Lord of the Rings*. These movies help recover this sense of connection that was once served by the heroic epics of oral culture (Drout, 2006).

Before the printing revolution: the development of writing

Theorists believe that the step-by-step progression from symbols to a written language was the first real communications revolution because it was a leap forward from a natural ability to a revolutionary new ability. Since this book is focused on mass media, we will not spend a large amount of time on the writing revolution, but we do need to at least take note of what is arguably the first communication revolution in order to set the stage for the profound changes that mass media revolutions have wrought.

Figure I.1 Monk—writing changed history—Monks and scribes hand-copied books from the dawn of writing 6,000 years ago to the invention of the moveable type and printing in the 1450s. (Illustration by William Blades, 1891, Wikimedia Commons)

Writing was the first human communications revolution, but confined to social elites. Historian and media theorist Harold Innis argued that the combination of writing and flexible communications made it possible to build empires. Still, most people in most civilizations lived within the context of an oral culture (Innis, 1950).

The introduction of writing brought about a change in thinking. Historian Walter Ong noted that writing and printing introduced a more linear, sequential and homogeneous approach to thinking, and the old "oral culture" of heroic epics, songs and tales told by firelight was part of a more connected and ritualistic life (Ong, 2002). Similarly, theorist Walter Benjamin saw mechanical reproduction of writing and art as contributing to a loss of social ritual and personal identity (Benjamin et al., 2008).

Writing grew naturally from the elite in early cultures to the upper and then middle classes in the Greek and Roman empires. Although literacy faded in Europe during what is called the "dark ages," literacy was nearly universal in other cultures, for example, in Arab nations in the 900–1500 period when great centers of learning flourished from Timbuktu, Mali to Baghdad, Iraq.

Writing, said media scholar Wilbur Schramm, allowed humans to conserve their intellectual resources, save what needed to be saved without having to keep all the details in their heads, and devote their major energies to advancing knowledge. This had enormous effect on human life (Schramm, 1988).

"With language and writing in hand, humans had paid the tuition for their own education," Schramm said. Mass media, beginning with the printing revolution, would become their open university.

For additional reading, discussion questions, links to video and other suggestions, see www.revolutionsincommunication.com.

1   The printing revolution: from 1455 to 1814

Although the few had books before John Gutenberg gave us our art, not until printing could come learning, yes and wisdom also, knocking at every man's door. (Latin of Cardelius, 1546)

Foundations of the printing revolution

The printing revolution transformed Europe. It "changed the appearance and state of the whole world," as Francis Bacon said, by providing cheaper, quicker and more accurate communication across once-formidable boundaries of space and time. It was the turning point in the transformation of a backward Medieval region into modern Europe.

Rising literacy, expanding knowledge and growing expectations of Renaissance Europe during the 1400s were the wellsprings of the printing revolution, and the religious and political revolutions that followed were some of the effects.

By accelerating the exchange of ideas and removing the barriers to communication that existed in Medieval society, printing contributed to dialogue as well as confrontation. Like other new communications media, printing helped release the best, and the worst, in human nature.

As a consequence, the European world emerged, in the 1700s, with a new commitment to reason, to tolerance and to freedom—ideals that would emerge again and again in subsequent media revolutions and are still being contested.

Technological context of printing

Most of the technologies involved in printing were already known and being employed in various ways when the printing revolution took place in the 1450s.

Stamps in soft clay had been used as part of the ancient Babylonian accounting system, and metal seals were often impressed into wax to validate official documents in classical Rome. Wood block printing was widely used in China from the sixth century onward for sacred Buddhist scrolls. Impressions on textiles were known in Europe as early as the 1100s, and the first known woodcuts on paper appeared in Europe around 1400 (Hind, 1963). Presses had been used on farms for centuries to make olive oil and to press grapes into wine.

The increased availability of cheap, portable paper was another factor. Earlier cultures used clay or stone, which tended to be cheap and durable but not flexible or portable. In Asia, silk was available for transmitting and preserving important religious and civil texts, while in Europe, vellum (treated calf hide) and parchment (from sheep or goats) served elite readers. Papyrus, a paper made from plants native to the Nile River in Egypt, was widely used as a less expensive medium, but it was brittle and not as durable as paper.

The technique for making paper from wood or linen rags is said to have originated with Ts'ai Lun, a Chinese monk who observed paper wasps making a nest around 105 CE (Common Era/AD). Cheap paper became widely available around 1400 in Europe and was apparently in surplus by the mid-1400s. One contributing factor may have been the increased number of linen rags from cast-off clothing, which people needed to weather the winters in the Little Ice Age (c.1315–1800).

Historians have observed a small technical leap forward when monasteries began using presses to make impressions on paper or parchment from blocks of wood with raised areas to hold the ink. These woodcut impressions, mostly of religious icons, were offered for sale at fairs and pilgrimages. Books laboriously hand lettered were also becoming more common, and a thriving trade employed thousands of scribes, paper makers, illuminators, leather workers and bookbinders by the early 1400s.

And so, the printing revolution did not occur because one person invented one technology. It occurred when a key technical problem was solved within a supportive business and cultural context. In other words, Gutenberg found the right technology at the right time.

Gutenberg's insight: the original "matrix"

Johannes Gutenberg was a well-educated goldsmith from a politically active family in Mainz, Germany who planned to announce some kind of secret, probably a typesetting technique, at a religious fair in 1439. However, Gutenberg's plans went awry, and a long record of court documents and lawsuits by his investors gives us a somewhat cryptic record of his activities in the years leading up to the printing of the first Bible in 1454. During what was apparently a 15-year period of development, Gutenberg worked on perfecting the key technical problem of mass producing books.

The problem was that wood blocks did not hold up well to thousands of impressions. Although movable type made from wood blocks was widely used in China as early as 1297, Europeans did not adopt wood block type. One reason is that the monastic system of hand copying religious and classical texts served the market well in the early years of the Renaissance. The growing demand for books of all kinds led Gutenberg to consider how to serve the expanding market and make a profit.

Figure 1.1 Johannes Gutenberg: a goldsmith from Mainz, Germany, Gutenberg invented moveable metal type, which could be used many times in the process of mass producing books. (Engraving by Johnson, Fry & Co., 1869, Library of Congress)

Gutenberg's key insight was that individual pieces of "moveable" type could be made from an alloy of lead with tin and antimony. The alloy could be melted using conventional foundries and poured into a "matrix" that held the blanks for the different letters of the alphabet. The type could then be arranged face-up on a form and inked to make an impression on paper. Once the pages were printed, the type could be re-arranged for another set of pages. When the type eventually wore out, it could be melted and recast in the same type foundries.

The secret of movable type may have been discovered elsewhere in Europe around the same time. For example, Laurens Coster of Holland apparently used wooden type and was experimenting with lead type before his death in 1440. But it was Gutenberg who assembled all the necessary ingredients into a workshop that could quickly produce thousands of books.

The very first book printed—the Gutenberg Bible—looked very much like the hand-lettered manuscript books in terms of typographic style, column size, number of lines, selection of initials for decoration and other features (Eisenstein, 1980; Fussel, 2005). However, Gutenberg's printing method meant that the cost was far lower, and that other innovations were now possible.

The drop in the price of making a book gives an idea of the impact of moveable type. In Venice before the advent of printing, a monk might charge one florin for copying 80 pages of Plato's Dialogues. In 1483, the Ripoli press charged three florins for printing 1,025 copies of the same number of pages.

The secret of moveable type spread quickly as Gutenberg's associates set up printing shops in other cities. By the 1470s, every city in Europe had printing companies. Like other media revolutions to come, the printing revolution regrouped people with older skills and new skills. The older skills included paper making, ink manufacturing, leather working, book binding and book marketing; and the new skills included press work, type setting and foundry type casting. (Similar re-groupings of skills would be seen, for example, in the visual revolution, when portrait painters like Samuel Morse became daguerrotype photographers; in the broadcasting revolution, when theatrical performers and broadcast engineers created radio drama; and in the digital revolution, when journalists and computer hackers created blogs and collaborative civic information systems.)

By 1500s, an estimated four million books were printed and sold, and by 1533, another 18 million more (Smiles, 1867). Among the best sellers were the Bible (with dozens of editions in major cities), Christopher Columbus' reports on his explorations, medical and scientific works, and ancient literary classics from Greece and Rome.

The immediate effect of printing was to allow a rapid expanse of exact duplicates of information that had been laboriously (and often inaccurately) copied by hand. Where knowledge was once difficult to preserve and share, printing allowed standardized knowledge that could be preserved and disseminated rapidly. Old ideas could be contrasted, contradictions revealed and new ideas developed.

At first, the low price of printed books alarmed book retailers who had been selling expensive manuscripts to an elite clientele in the mid-1400s. But then business accelerated, turning retailers into wholesalers, street vendors into bookstore owners, and copiers into publishers.

The significance of Gutenberg's insight into the key technical problem of communication in the Renaissance cannot be overstated, nor can the impacts. He is often considered the most influential figure in modern history (Gottlieb, 2006).

"The printing press precipitated 200 years of chaos, moving from a world where the Catholic church was the organizing political force to the Treaty of Westphalia, where we finally knew what the new unit was—the nation state," said Clay Shirky, a sociologist who has described a close connection between communications revolutions and the collapse of institutions. The digital revolution, considered in Section IV of this book, would lead to similar decades of chaos, Shirky predicted (Shirkey, 2010).

Printing and the Protestant Reformation

Every day in the well-ordered Medieval world, priests in churches would read from the Latin Gospels and interpret the readings in a sermon. Usually there were only a few Bibles in a church, chained to a pulpit, closely guarded as their most valuable possessions. Many ordinary people could read a little, but they did not have much access to books; libraries were usually for scholars or monks. Only a very rich person could afford to own a Bible, let alone read one regularly. The church had an exclusive monopoly on information, and enforced it efficiently and ruthlessly.

It is significant that the Bible was the first book Gutenberg printed, since scripture was at the center of the Medieval world. Gutenburg's Bibles were printed in Latin, and printing was initially welcomed as a divine gift, not only for the dissemination of religious knowledge, but also to print pamphlets to rally Christians against invading Turks in the 1450s. Printing also accelerated the church's ability to trade cash for the forgiveness of sins—a practice known as selling "indulgences"—as churches ordered thousands to be printed for the use of priests.

At first, printing seemed to be nothing short of divine intervention, but that impression quickly changed. "There is considerable irony about the enthusiastic reception accorded printing by the church," said historian Elizabeth Eisenstein. "Heralded on all sides as a 'peaceful art,' Gutenberg's invention probably contributed more to destroying Christian accord and inflaming religious warfare than any of the so-called arts of war ever did" (Eisenstein, 1980).

This "destruction of Christian accord" began to occur when printers translated Latin Bibles into the "vernacular" languages of German, French, English and many other languages. This sudden removal of barriers to religious knowledge had an enormous and unexpected impact. For the first time, ordinary people could read the Bible for themselves. They soon noticed that there was no scriptural support for the idea of the infallibility of the Pope or the sale of indulgences. The spread of low-cost Bibles did not only mean that more religious knowledge would be disseminated, but also that the church lost the exclusive power over that process. With printing, ordinary people could be their own priests and reformers could spark far more serious opposition.

Conflict between the church and reformers was not unusual before the invention of printing. The most significant examples include the Lollard movement of John Wycliffe in England in the late 1300s and the Hussite Movement in the central European city of Prague a generation later. Wycliffe managed to survive until a natural death, but Jan Hus, dean at the University of Prague, was tricked into a meeting with church authorities, arrested and executed in 1415. Books by Wycliffe and Hus were banned, and although their ideas survived, it was only because they were copied by hand and passed from scholar to scholar. (Similar hand made copies would emerge in modern times, such as "samizdats" in the Soviet Union in the 1960s–80s.)

Martin Luther and printing

The impact of the printing press became clear when a monk named Martin Luther famously nailed his "95 Theses" to a church door in Wittenberg, Germany on October 31, 1517. There was nothing terribly dramatic about the act itself—the practice of posting notices by nailing them to doors of churches or other buildings was common—but the 95 Theses were quickly printed and widely distributed. Within a month they were a subject of controversy throughout Europe, and within a few years, an estimated 300,000 copies had been printed. Had the call for reform been copied by hand, as it was for Wycliffe and Hus, it could have been easily suppressed by the church.

Figure 1.2 Printing sparks Reformation—Martin Luther's calls for church reforms were nothing new to Europe, but they were amplified by the power of the printing revolution.

The printing press amplified Luther's voice to an extent that astonished everyone—including Luther. The 95 Theses were in such demand that crowds surged around printing shops, grabbing for pages still wet from the press (Smiles, 1867). "For the first time in history, a great reading public judged the validity of revolutionary ideas through a mass medium which used the vernacular language," Eisenstein wrote (Eisenstein, 1974).

"Printing was recognized as a new power and publicity came into its own," said Maurice Gravier. "The printing presses transformed the field of communications and fathered an international revolt" (Eisenstein, 1974). Luther himself described printing as "God's highest and extremest act of grace," and his followers began to see the printing press as an agent of freedom, delivering them from bondage to the Roman church and delivering the light of true religion to Germany.

The religious revolt sprang from a few sparks to a fire fanned by the power of the press, spreading rapidly across Europe. A decade after the Lutheran revolt started, the Reformation was well underway across Europe. Under John Calvin's leadership, Switzerland became something of the European capital of Protestantism, and in England, starting in 1529, King Henry VIII relied on the press to gather public support for a new Protestant church.

The danger of the spreading chaos eventually became clear to church officials. The Catholic Church confronted the Protestant Reformation with a ruthless Counter-Reformation. Thousands were executed simply for owning the wrong version of the Bible. Religious warfare broke out across Europe. In Germany, 25 to 40 percent of the population perished.

In England, as power see-sawed between Protestants and Catholics, cardinal Reginal Pole warned Londoners against reading scripture for themselves: "You should not be your owne masters," he said. "Household religion" would be "a seed bed of sedition." The English throne returned to a Catholic in 1553 and "Bloody" Queen Mary I ordered hundreds of executions. When Mary died in 1558, Protestant Queen Elizabeth I took the throne with a promise of religious tolerance. Protestants solidified power with the publication of John Foxe's Book of Martyrs a few years later. The book's strong emphasis on the cruelties of "Bloody" Mary's reign, including the execution of Protestant Bishop Thomas Cranmer (Figure 1.3), was designed to turn public opinion away from the Catholic Church and toward the Church of England.

To give an idea of how ordinary people fared during the Counter-Reformation, historian Carlo Ginzburg described the trial of one relatively ordinary but outspoken Italian miller named Menocchio. He was tried and executed for the simple heresy of openly expressing his doubts about religious dogma in 1584 (Ginzburg, 1992). Millions of such cases emerged on both sides of the widening chasm between the Catholic and Protestant churches.

Protestant reformers dogmatically referred to "sola scriptura" as the the only authority and then often insisted that they were the only ones who could interpret scripture. All too often "the rich an varied communal religious experiences of the Middle Ages" were lost as the new authorities demanded obedience. "Open books, in some instances, led to closed minds," Eisenstein observed (Eisenstein, 1980).

Even the dissidents surpressed other dissidents. The breakaway Church of England attempted to suppress Puritan and Scottish Presbyterian dissent well into the mid-1600s, sparking the "Bishops War" in Scotland and encouraging emigration to the new colonies of North America.

By the mid-1600s, religious fervor faded, while contests between emerging nation states accelerated. A turning point occurred when French Catholic Cardinal Richelieu formed a political alliance between France and the Protestant states to check the power of the Catholic Spanish-Austrian Hapsburg dynasty in the 1620s. Religious warfare simmered down after the Treaty of Westphalia in 1648, where the major powers of Europe agreed that each king would determine the religion of his own nation.

Figure 1.3 Execution of Thomas Cranmer—Archibishop Thomas Cranmer was burned at the stake at Oxford, England on March 21, 1556 as part of an attempt to stamp out the English Protestant cause. Cranmer was one of the three bishops of Oxford who were executed around this time. Catholic Queen Mary I earned the popular title of "bloody Mary" from the era of repression. (Illustration from Foxe's Book of Martyrs, Library of Congress)

Religion continued to be an important element in conflicts that continued to plague Europe in the late twentieth century, for example, in Ireland and the Balkans. As Elizabeth Eisenstein said,

> We still seem to be experiencing the contradictory effects of a process which fanned the flames of religious zeal and bigotry while fostering a new concern for ecumenical concord and toleration, which fixed linguistic and national divisions more permanently while creating a cosmopolitan Commonwealth of Learning and extending communications networks which have encompassed the entire world. (Eisenstein, 1980)

As the horror of religious warfare declined, the need for religious tolerance became a primary ideal in the minds of Enlightenment thinkers.

The slow emergence of religious tolerance

Although printing plunged Europe into centuries of religious warfare, it also amplified calls for tolerance and reason. In France, Sebastian Castellio (1515–1563) became one of the first proponents of freedom of conscience. "It is unchristian to use arms against those who have been expelled from the Church, and to deny them rights common to all mankind," he wrote in "Whether heretics should be persecuted," a response to the intolerance of Protestant reformer John Calvin.

A British poet famed for writing *Paradise Lost*, John Milton (1608–1674) matched the idea of religious tolerance to the historical touchstone of the Athenian marketplace, arguing for a "marketplace of ideas" in his 1644 *Areopagitica*.

> And though all the winds of doctrine were let loose to play on the earth, so Truth be in the field, we do injuriously by licensing and prohibiting misdoubt her strength. Let her and Falsehood grapple; who ever knew Truth put to the worse in a free and open encounter?

Figure 1.4 Milton's marketplace of ideas—John Milton argued for tolerance and free speech since, he said, truth would win in the marketplace of ideas. (Library of Congress)

Milton insisted that Truth would win out in a free and fair fight, yet his argument for freedom of conscience did not include "popery" (Catholicism), blasphemy or impiety. In France, Francois Voltaire (1694–1788) railed against "the dreadful folly of religious wars."

From the outset, the North American Protestant colonies of Virginia, Massachusetts and New York were notoriously intolerant of religious deviance, but at the surprisingly early date of 1649, the Catholic colony of Maryland made religious toleration the official position. Although Maryland's official tolerance only applied to Christians, and was something of a pragmatic approach for a minority religion in a mostly Protestant set of English colonies, the act is still considered a leap forward for human rights:

> Whereas the inforceing of the conscience in matters of Religion hath frequently fallen out to be of dangerous Consequence in those commonwealthes where it hath been practised . . . Be it Therefore . . . enacted . . . that noe person or persons whatsoever within this Province . . . shall from henceforth bee any waies troubled, Molested or discountenanced for, or in respect of, his or her religion nor in the free exercise thereof . . . nor any way compelled to the beliefe or exercise of any other Religion against his or her consent . . .

Figure 1.5 Printer and scientist—Benjamin Franklin believed that all sides ought to be heard in the marketplace of ideas. (Library of Congress)

Tolerance was a large part of the new creed of printing, and it was within this cultural ferment that the Renaissance gave way to the Enlightenment. "From the days of Castellio to those of Voltaire, the printing industry was the principal natural ally of libertarian, heterodox and ecumenical philosophers," Eisenstein said (Eisenstein, 1980). Printers naturally wanted to expand markets, but the capitalistic motive was not the central point. All Europe was on the move, and "the enterprising publisher was the natural enemy of narrow minds."

Printers themselves could be instruments of tolerance, as Benjamin Franklin said in his 1731 "Apology for Printers," when Pennsylvania Quakers reacted to his handling of religious controversy.

> Printers are educated in the Belief, that when Men differ in Opinion, both Sides ought equally to have the Advantage of being heard by the Publick; and that when Truth and Error have fair Play, the former is always an overmatch for the latter: Hence they chearfully serve all contending Writers that pay them well, without regarding on which side they are of the Question in Dispute. (Franklin, 1731)

In his 1787 Notes on the State of Virginia, Thomas Jefferson said: "Millions of innocent men, women and children . . . have been burnt, tortured, fined, imprisoned; yet we have not advanced one inch towards uniformity. What has been the effect of (religious) coercion? To make half the world fools, and the other half hypocrites."

Scientific and technical impacts of the printing revolution

Printing was "the most obvious and probably the most important" element in capturing the scientific and technological revolution from the Renaissance forward. Printing spread news of exploration, descriptions of new technologies, improvements in medicine, insights into astronomy and a host of other discoveries.

"The world before printing was one in which the whole pattern of learning, communicating and storing information was defined by what could be written down or drawn or spoken in a singular and immediate fashion," wrote historian Robert Friedel. After printing, it was the exact and repeatable message that "carried authority and influence" (Friedel, 2007).

Printing spurred the exploration of physical and mental horizons with the publication of exact maps, charts and astronomical tables. For instance, news of Columbus' explorations spread rapidly with printing in the 1490s, making him one of the first international heroes, at least, until the genocide in the West Indies was understood (Zinn, 1980). In contrast, the folkloric accounts of Viking landings in North America were little known outside the oral culture of Scandinavian nations.

The power of the press also influenced the way geographic discoveries were understood. The travel journals of Amerigo Vespucci were read by mapmaker Martin Waldseemüller, who believed Vespucci's idea that the land to the west could not be India, as Columbus claimed. In 1507, a world map called the new

Figure 1.6 Information spread rapidly— a letter by Christopher Columbus, with this engraving, spread rapidly across Europe in the 1490s providing an early demonstration of the power of the press.

continent America. The name, amplified by the new power of the printing press, continues to be used.

The printing press was not as much of an agent of change in the early years of the scientific revolution as it had been in the Protestant Reformation. At first, the focus on publishing books from classical Greek and Roman authorities may have delayed the acceptance of emerging new ideas. Religious intolerance was another factor, and the church's suppression of the heliocentric theories of Nicholas Copernicus and Galileo Gallilei (1564–1642) is an example.

A new trend was evident in a 1556 book by Georgius Agricola (1494–1555), *De Re Mettalica*, an exploration of geology, mining and metallurgy, lavishly illustrated. The book set a standard for scientific and technical books that were to come.

Gradually, scientists adopted the printing press as part of their educational and research efforts. For example in Denmark, the astronomical observatory established by Tycho Brahe (1546–1601) included a printing shop to help spread new scientific knowledge. While the church continued suppressing many new ideas, its rear-guard defense of an old way of thinking was doomed by the new media revolution.

As the horizon of knowledge expanded, the role of printing in forming communities became appreciated. Publishers of all kinds of books encouraged readers to help amend the next edition. For instance, mapmakers and medicinal herbalists called on readers to submit notes about plants and coastlines, and send seeds and maps to the publishers. They "called upon the unlearned to contribute to the knowledge of natural history, geography and physics by communicating their observations on birds and flowers, on ebb and flood tide, on celestial phenomena . . . Travellers and mariners especially were invited to do so" (Eisenstein, 1980, p. 236).

Eisenstein attributes the advent of participatory media to both idealistic and commercial motives, but there are parallels to crowdsourcing in the digital age, such as the Wikipedia online encyclopedia with thousandands of volunteer writers. "A new form of data collection was launched in which everyman could play a supporting role," she wrote.

Political impacts of the printing revolution

One early consequence of the printing revolution was to consolidate the wildly divergent dialects that eventually merged to form modern French, German, English, Italian and other languages. Along with the Bible, many other works were translated into vernacular, leading to a standardized national language.

William Caxton, the first English printer, set up shop at Westminster in 1476 and, among his first efforts were Geoffrey Chaucer's *Canterbury Tales*, excerpts from the Bible and various philosophical tracts, all in English. More translations of the Bible quickly followed: William Tyndale's 1525 New Testament, Henry VIII's Great Bible and the King James I Bible of 1604.

The wide circulation of printed books in the home language created a standard for writing and speaking a language that was, at the time, still highly unsettled. As a result, printing also "created a new instrument of political centralism (that was) previously unknown," according to Marshall McLuhan (McLuhan, 1962). Although many other forces combined to create the idea of the modern nation-state, printing was a factor in the mix.

However, just as the printing revolution first enhanced and then challenged the central control of religion, printing also helped amplify challenges to established political thought. "Printing was an active force in history," said historian Robert Darnton, "when the struggle for power was a struggle for the mastery of public opinion" (Darnton, 1989).

News in print

The need to hear and share news is universal in human cultures and a central part of what defines a community (Stephens, 2007). Personal news is the first thing most people discuss when they haven't seen each other in a while. People also want to know the latest events in politics, religion, finance and other areas, whether they are in an oral culture or a literate culture or some blend of the two.

Figure 1.7 Printing in 1560s— this view of a print shop a century after Gutenberg shows a printer placing paper into the tympan, another printer inking the type with soft leather "beaters," and two typesetters in the background. Printing technology barely changed until the early 1800s.

In ancient Rome and China, bureaucrats wrote of political events in the capitals and sent the news out to the provinces. Commercial news letters were produced as early as 131 BCE, and "armies of scribes" were employed to copy, publish and sell books by the thousands (Schramm, 1988). A daily newsletter called the "Acta Diurna" conveyed not only official acts of the Senate but also news of crime, divorce and other items of general interest (Ward, 1996). Intended for both a wide general audience and the upper classes, the Acta Diurna is usually considered the first example of a mass media publication.

Aside from individual correspondence and oral communication, there are few known examples of mass communication in Europe between the fall of the Roman Empire in the 400 AD period to the early Renaissance. Around the 1380s, the emergence of banks and international trading made small group communication necessary, and regular hand written newsletters were copied and sent by messenger.

Book publishing dominated the printing trade after Gutenberg's invention caught on, but a wide variety of small publications were also available. Book merchants offered a variety of woodblocks and engravings, religious tracts and sermons, exhortations to join a cause, or speeches by monarchs and other public figures.

Four basic kinds of news publications emerged between the late 1500s and early 1700s (Schramm, 1988, p. 153):

- The "relation" was a one-time publication about a single event, for example a battle or a coronation, usually printed on a small single sheet.
- The "coronto," often sold as a small bound book about news from a foreign country.

- The "diurnal" was a regular publication that covered one subject, typically events in government.
- The "mercury" was a small bound book that would cover events from a single country for six months at a time.

Each of these types of publication can still be found in various forms. For example, a modern day "diurnal" might be the Congressional Record or Federal Register, published by the US government. Industry newsletters from groups like the Bureau of National Affairs might be considered modern day "mercury," in that they can be assembled, bound by volume and used as reference books in specific industry and regulatory areas.

First newspapers

Johann Carolus, the owner of a French book printing company in Strasbourg, France, had grown tired of copying business newsletters by hand. In 1605, he decided to use the new media to save himself some time and began publishing the first newspaper.

> "The copying has been slow and has necessarily taken much time, and since, moreover, I have recently purchased at a high and costly price (a) former printing workshop . . . I have set, printed and published the said advice in my printing workshop." (Weber, 2006)

Another early newspaper that was closer in form to the modern newspaper was the Dutch *Courante uyt Italien, Duytslandt, &c.* first published in 1618. Holland's printing industry introduced many other innovations around this time, including the first newspaper advertisements, the first woodcuts in a newspaper, and the first English and French-language newspapers, printed in Amsterdam to evade strict censorship in England and France.

The spread of newspapers and the relationships between printers of various nations is also illustrated by the career of Benjamin Harris, a publisher of small textbooks and Whig reformist tracts in London in the 1670s. From 1679 to 1681, Harris published *Domestick Intelligence, Or News from Both City and Country* in London. He moved to Boston in 1686 and stared the London Coffee House, modeled on the coffee houses that were becoming popular in England. He also began publishing small almanacs and text-books and the first newspaper in the United States, *Publick Occurrences, Both Foreign and Domestick,* in 1690. The newspaper reported on a smallpox epidemic, on atrocities by Indians allied with the British, and some local news items. It had no license and was closed after the first edition. Harris took on some Massachusetts government printing work but decided to return London in 1695, where he founded the *London Post.*

Censorship and freedom of the press

Like most new media, printing was considered dangerous by the political rulers of Europe, and four basic approaches to censorship were put into effect:

- licensing of a printing company itself;
- pre-press approval of each book or edition of a publication;
- taxation and stamps on regular publications; and
- prosecution for sedition against the government or libel of individuals.

In Catholic countries, both state and church censored publications, and in most European nations, no book could be printed or distributed without permission of both the church and the king. The church issued the first Index of Prohibited Books in 1559, and through its control of universities such as the Sorbonne, also controlled all other kinds of publications. The dual system of censorship was widely used in Catholic nations around the world, for example, to prevent the invasion of Protestant ideas in Latin America in subsequent centuries (Newth, 2001).

Protestant nations were also engaged in political censorship. In sixteenth-century England, printing was controlled by licensing through the Stationers Company, and punishment for printing unlicensed material was meted out by the Star Chamber. The punishments included the death penalty for printing treasonous articles, for questioning the Church of England or advocating (or even envisioning) the death of the king.

Naturally, talented printers often moved to nations where they were free to publish, such as Holland and Switzerland, and later, Britain and the United States. Freedom of the press drew thinkers like Rene Descartes, John Locke and many others of the early Enlightenment to the publishing houses of Holland. As astronomer Carl Sagan noted: "Because of its tolerance for unorthodox opinions (Holland) was a haven for intellectuals who were refugees from censorship and thought control elsewhere in Europe—much as the United States benefited enormously by the exodus of intellectuals in the 1930s from . . . Europe" (Sagan, 1980).

Press freedom and the Enlightenment

The ideas that took hold in the new marketplace of ideas came from people like John Locke, Jean Jacques Rousseau, Benjamin Franklin, Thomas Paine and Thomas Jefferson. They insisted that human rights were natural, and not simply handed down by governments or kings. The very structure of government ought to be balanced to allow people to act according to these natural rights, said French philosopher Baron de Montesquieu in arguing for separation of government powers into executive, legislative and judicial branches. This idea, published in *The Spirit of the Laws*, was to form the basis of most nineteenth and twentieth century governments.

In Scotland, philsopher David Hume defended freedom of the press with this logic: "Press freedom can not excite popular tumults or rebellions . . . A man reads a book or pamphlet alone coolly. There is none present from whom he can catch the passion by contagion."

Sentiment in favor of free speech and free press echoed back and forth across the English Channel and the Atlantic. In London, on February 15, 1721, popular newspaper columnists John Trenchard and Thomas Gordon, writing under the name of Cato, said:

> Without freedom of thought, there can be no such thing as wisdom; and no such thing as publick liberty, without freedom of speech: Which is the right of every man, as far as by it he does not hurt and control the right of another; and this is the only check which it ought to suffer, the only bounds which it ought to know. (Trenchard, 1721)

Benjamin Franklin, in his personna as "Silas Dogood," made the identical comment a year later: "Without Freedom of Thought, there can be no such Thing as Wisdom; and no such Thing as publick Liberty, without Freedom of Speech." This motto, emblazoned across an entryway to the US Senate, differs only in the placement of a comma from the original by Trenchard and Gordon.

Figure 1.8 Think for yourselves and let others enjoy the privilege—that was the advice of Francois Voltaire, one of the most colorful and insightful of the philsophers from the French Enlightenment period.

The strongest voice of the French Enlightenment was Francois Voltaire (1694–1778), author of *Candide*, who believed, more than anything else, in toleration, the rule of law and freedom of opinion. In his *Essay on Tolerance*, Voltaire said: "Think for yourselves and let others enjoy the privilege to do so too." Voltaire also said, in a 1770 letter: "I detest what you write, but I would give my life to make it possible for you to continue to write." (The idea was later paraphrased as: "I disapprove of what you say, but I shall defend to the death your right to say it.") (Tallentyre, 1907).

Freedom of the press was among the natural freedoms, and it was among the "first freedoms" that also included religion, speech and assembly to be recognized during the American revolution with the *Virginia Declaration of Rights, of June 12, 1776*, followed by the *Declaration of the Rights of Man and of Citizen*, France, August 26, 1789.

Freedom of the press and religion were also included in the First Amendment of the federal US Constitution, one of ten amendments that were also called the *Bill of Rights,* in 1791. These formed the basis of a modern international understanding of human rights, guaranteed in the United Nations *Universal Declaration of Human Rights, of December. 10, 1948* and the European *Convention for the Protection of Human Rights and Fundamental Freedoms* of *May 5, 1963*.

Political revolutions

"A tumult of journalists"

The print media has a special relationship to political revolution, but aside from historians of the American revolution, only a few have investigated the idea on a broader basis. (Among these are Roger Chartier, Robert Darnton, Elizabeth Eisenstein, Jeremy D. Popkin and Rolf Reichardt.)

Every revolution had its own unique causes and effects, and historians usually make only weak claims about political revolutions being ignited by broadsides of the 1600s or printed newspapers of the 1700s. Yet, as a working historical hypothesis, the idea that revolutionary changes in media may be followed by changes in the entire structure of society is worth exploring (Billington, 1999).

Revolutionaries from the seventeenth to the twentieth centuries have advocated using the media of their day to advance the political revolutions they created, as historian Jeremy Popkin has pointed out. American revolutionary pamphleteers and publishers were well known as incendiaries. Observers of the French Revolution saw a rapid change in the media before and just after the revolution. Both Lenin and Gandhi began their revolutions by starting newspapers. And the role of various types of media in dozens of other revolutions has been well documented.

The printing press was not the cause of the political revolutions of England, America, France, Russia and other nations, but at the same time, it cannot be ignored as a vehicle. Clearly, the newspaper press, as a new system of communication in Europe, had been turned to the service of political revolution just as the printing of books and religious tracts had been turned to religious reform in previous centuries.

"If a great historical movement such as the Reformation can legitimately said to have started as a quarrel of monks, the (revolution of 1871) was also, in a certain sense, a tumult of journalists," said historian Aime Dupuy. The same point could have been made about any political revolution (Popkin, 1990).

Political change, as Habermas has argued, is not only marked by a clash of classes or cultures, but is often an outcome of changes in the way people exchange ideas. The period from the seventeenth to the twentieth century was marked by a shift away from authoritarian monopolies over public debate and toward the rise of public opinion, Habermas said. A major factor was the "explosive power" of the press (Habermas, 1991).

English Civil War and the marketplace of ideas

When England's Parliament broke with the monarchy, starting the English Civil War between 1641 and 1659, a small printing industry quickly expanded with more than 350 periodicals and tens of thousands of other one-off broadsheets, almanacs, ballads, broadsides and other publications (Friedman, 1992).

Both sides—the Royalists and the Parliamentary forces—had newspapers, some of them falsely designed to entrap supporters of the other side. Historian Hiley Ward tells the story of "Parliament Joan," a woman who pretended to be selling Royalist newspapers so that the buyers could be identified by their sympathies and turned over to Parliamentary forces (Ward, 1996).

John Milton's 1644 *Areopagitica* (noted above), was one of the few arguments for tolerance. While it had little contemporary impact, the concept of a marketplace of ideas was taken up by others arguing for freedom of conscience and press in the next century.

While both sides vehemently criticized the other, open discussion of political issues within each faction was not possible. Parliament continued the reign of censorship with the 1643 licensing act, which stayed in effect throughout the war. But the censorship was ineffective against the enormous pent-up demand for news, opinion and entertainment that had long been suppressed. As Jerome Friedman noted:

> The two tumultuous decades of the English revolution witnessed a virtual tidal wave of cheap pamphlet publication covering every conceivable topic from religion to pornography, from reports of apparitions and monsters to odes describing the beneficial effects of opium and marijuana, from hysterical reports of Ranter blasphemy to accounts of scandalous religious charlatans claiming they were Jesus, Mary, and a host of other Biblical personalities returned from the dead. (Friedman, 1992)

The end of censorship in England came in 1694, with the end for the formal licensing system, a result of the "Glorious Revolution" of 1688, when Parliament installed Dutch King William III and Queen Mary II as constitutional monarchs in England (Smith, 1988). The revolution marked the end of the English Civil War and the birth of a new period of religious tolerance and press freedom.

Voltaire compared the civil wars of Rome (49–45 BCE) to the English Civil War of the 1600s:

> The Romans never knew the dreadful folly of religious warfare . . . But here follows a more essential difference between Rome and England, which gives the advantage entirely to the later—viz., that the civil wars of Rome ended in slavery, and those of the English in liberty. The English are the only people upon earth who have been able to prescribe limits to the power of kings by resisting them . . . . (Voltaire, 1778)

Revolutionary press fights for American freedom

Meanwhile in the American colonies, governments initially punished even the mildest criticism with imprisonment. Many colonies still operated with absolute authority. Even though England was convulsed in Civil War at the time, Virginia governor William Berkeley said in 1648: "I thank God there are no free schools nor printing, and I hope we shall not have these hundred years; for learning has brought disobedience and heresy and sects into the world; and printing has divulged them, and libels against the best government. God keep us from both" (R. E. Brown and K. Brown, 1964).

Yet both were on the horizon. The 1693 establishment of the College of William and Mary, in honor of England's new Constitutional monarchs, indicated how far the colony had come since the days of Berkeley's absolute rule.

Governments continued to suppress printing in the American colonies, closing down *Publick Occurrences* after its first edition in 1690 in Boston. Coffee house owner Benjamin Harris had no license for his newspaper, and what's more, had slyly criticized the government. Prosecutions for libeling the government (called seditious libel) continued. Truth was not a defense in such cases, and in fact, truthful criticism was seen as even worse since it more credibly undermined authority. This changed when a New York jury overruled a judge and established truth as a defense in libel of government in 1735.

Seditious libel and John Peter Zenger

Figure 1.9 The cause of liberty—New York editor John Peter Zenger's lawyer argues before a colonial British court in New York. The Zenger decision was a landmark for freedom of the press in both the American colonies and Britain. (Library of Congress)

A landmark moment in American and British press freedom was the John Peter Zenger trial of 1735. Zenger's newspaper, the *New York Weekly Journal*, objected to electoral manipulation by an unpopular colonial governor, who responded by charging Zenger with seditious libel, which means defaming the government. At the trial, Andrew Hamilton, a Philadelphia lawyer, gave an eloquent argument to the jury, insisting that truth should be a defense against seditious libel and that the cause of freedom everywhere was at stake.

"The question before the court and you, gentlemen of the jury, is not of small or private concern. It is not the cause of one poor printer, nor of New York alone, which you are now trying. No! It may in its consequence affect every free man that lives under a British government on the main of America. It is the best cause. It is the cause of liberty. And I make no doubt but your upright conduct this day will not only entitle you to the love and esteem of your fellow citizens, but every man who prefers freedom to a life of slavery will bless and honor you as men who have baffled the attempt of tyranny . . . "

⇨

The Jury agreed with Hamilton and bravely returned a "not guilty" verdict. The judges, overruled by the jury, were powerless to continue the case since the jury had, in effect, changed the law. The case had far-reaching legal and psychological impact in colonies, to the extent that it was later seen as "the germ of American freedom, the morning star of that liberty which subsequently revolutionized America" (Linder, 2001). And the case was widely accepted as a precedent. Five years later, when *Virginia Gazette* publisher William Parks printed a story about the conviction of a House of Burgesses member for stealing sheep, he was arrested on criminal libel charges. Citing Zenger, he used truth as a defense and was acquitted.

The pre-revolutionary period in America was marked by the rise of printing establishments in every major city in the colonies, and new printers were frequently assisted on liberal terms by Benjamin Franklin, who not only owned a newspaper (the *Pennsylvania Gazette*) but also a paper mill, type foundry and ink factory. It was Franklin's assessment of Britain's unwillingness to change that tipped the scales among colonial printers; and the colonial press, in turn, paved the way for the revolution.

"The (American) revolution was effected before the war commenced," said the second US President, John Adams, writing to editor Hezekiah Niles in 1818. "The revolution was in the minds and hearts of the people, a change in their religious sentiments of their duties and obligations. . . . This radical change in the principles, opinions, sentiments, and affections of the people, was the real American Revolution."

The most powerful weapons in this struggle were the colonial newspapers, according to historian Mitchell Stephens. During the decade before the outbreak of revolution, newspapers "festooned themselves with polemical woodcuts: divided snakes, death's heads as mocking substitutes for tax stamps, and coffins designed by Paul Revere to represent the victims of the Boston Massacre" of 1774. Their rhetoric was heated, such as in this line from the *Massachusetts Spy* of 1773: "Shall the island Britain enslave this great continent of America, which is more than ninety nine times bigger, and is capable of supporting hundreds of millions of millions of people? Be astonished, all mankind, at her superlative folly" (Stephens, 2007).

Among the most famous agitators for American independence was Thomas Paine (1736–1809), an Englishman who emigrated to Boston in 1774. Paine's pamphlet *Common Sense* argued for a complete break with Britain and independence for the American colonies. In *The Crisis, 1776–1777*, Paine famously said:

Figure 1.10 "These are the times that try men's souls"—the words that turned the spark of rebellion into a campaign for American freedom emerged from the pen of Thomas Paine. After independence, Paine became involved in the French Revolution, then returned to the United States at the invitation of the then-president Thomas Jefferson. (Library of Congress)

These are the times that try men's souls. The summer soldier and the sunshine patriot will, in this crisis, shrink from the service of their country; but he that stands by it now, deserves the love and thanks of man and woman. Tyranny, like hell, is not easily conquered; yet we have this consolation with us, that the harder the conflict, the more glorious the triumph. What we obtain too cheap, we esteem too lightly: it is dearness only that gives every thing its value. Heaven knows how to put a proper price upon its goods; and it would be strange indeed if so celestial an article as FREEDOM should not be highly rated.

The success of the American revolution, and the role played by the press, meant that press freedom would be protected by the US Constitution in a way that was unique among nations. The First Amendment, Thomas Jefferson said, was "a great experiment . . . to demonstrate the falsehood of the pretext that freedom of the press is incompatible with orderly government."

France: the call for freedom and the descent into terror

In the decades before the French Revolution, official censors worked hard to contain the circulation of forbidden books, anti-monarchist booklets and the innumerable pamphlets (called "libeles") that floated around Paris and the provinces. Baron de Montesquieu had to work in secret on his *Spirit of the Laws*; Denis Diderot was hounded as he worked on his Encyclopédie; and *philosophes* François Voltaire and Jean-Jacques Rousseau had to flee the country at various times in their careers. The idea that these writers were being oppressed by small-minded censors seemed like "a flock of eagles submitted to the governance of turkeys" (Darnton 1989).

Not all official sympathies were against them. Diderot was once publicly accused of unpatriotic writing, and his apartments were searched by the same official who had previously arranged to hide Diderot's notes in his own apartment.

Like the American Revolution, the French Revolution was preceded by a shift in public sentiments expressed in the media. "What took place in 1789 could not have occurred as it did without a press or media revolution," said historian Jeremy Popkin (Popkin, 1995).

A new network of "assemblies and clubs, newspapers, pamphlets, broadsides, songs, and other media . . . closely and intensely tied to events" was in itself a central part of the "democratic culture" of the Revolution (Reichardt, 1988). In other words, the new form of the press was a symbol of the Revolution; the change in medium was part of the revolutionary message.

One of the most interesting moments of the revolution was when journalist Camille Desmoulins (1760–1794) was pushed to the front of an angry mob milling on a Paris street on July 12, 1789.

"I was carried upon a table rather than allowed to mount it. Hardly had I got up on my feet when I saw myself surrounded by an immense crowd. Here is my short speech, which I shall never forget: 'Citizens! There is not a moment to lose. . . . This evening all the Swiss and German battalions will sally forth from the Champs-de-Mars to cut our throats. We have only one recourse—to rush to arms.' I had tears in my eyes, and spoke with a feeling that I have ne'er been able to recapture, no less describe." (Snyder, 1962)

Two days later, Desmoulins helped organize the group that stormed the Bastille, an event commemorated every year as French independence day. Later that month his *La France Libre* was published, stating: "A popular and democratic government is the only constitution which suits France, and all those who are worthy of the name of men." His columns were widely circulated during the early years of the French Revolution, but his denunciation of the revolution's excesses led to his execution in 1794.

During the first decade after the French Revolution, about 350 newspapers were published in France (Schramm, 1988). Newspapers helped consolidate the gains of the revolution but also split into partisanship over the course of the revolution, with leading papers favoring the Girondists (liberal republicans) or the Jacobins (radical revolutionaries).

The press was needed in the early stages of the revolution, according to historian Robert Darnton, to circulate the Declaration of the Rights of Man, ideas for the new constitution, new currency, a new calendar, a new map and changes in the language itself. "At every stage in this process they use the same basic tool: the printing press," Darnton wrote.

Figure 1.11 "Citizens! Rush to arms!"—Camille Desmoulins, an impoverished French journalist and lawyer, is remembered for an impassioned speech that sparked the storming of the Bastille. One of the revolution's most insightful minds, Desmoulins opposed the radical Jacobin faction and was executed in 1794. (Library of Congress)

> Without the press, they can conquer the Bastille, but they cannot overthrow the old Regime. To seize power they must seize the word and spread it . . . When the revolutionaries grasped the bar of the press and forced the platen down on type locked in its form, they sent new energy streaming through the body politic. France came to life again, and humanity was amazed. (Darnton, 1989)

Jean Paul Marat, a Swiss physician who spent most of the pre-revolutionary years in London, arrived in France to help lead the Jacobins and wrote horrifying predictions about what would happen if the revolution failed. In a July, 1790 pamphlet entitled "C'enest fait de nous" ("We're done for!"), Marat wrote:

> . . . A false humanity has restrained your arms and stopped your blows. If you don't strike now, millions of your brothers will die, your enemies will triumph and your blood will flood the streets. They'll slit your throats without mercy and disembowel your wives. And their bloody hands will rip out your children's entrails to erase your love of liberty forever.

As history has so often shown, fanatical rhetoric in the media can lead to bloody deeds in reality. An estimated 40,000 people, including King Louis XVI and Queen Marie Antoinette, were executed by the radical Jacobins at the urging of Marat and others. The

Terror worsened when a Girondist (liberal) assassinated Marat at his home in 1793 while he wrote in the bathtub, but then ebbed with the establishment of the Directory in 1795. By 1798, Napoleon Bonaparte assumed power and many of the revolution's noble sentiments, including freedom of the press, lay in ruins. Napoleon was notoriously opposed to freedom of the press. A widespread system of censorship was put in place by 1808, and the number of newspapers in Paris dwindled to 13 and then finally to 4 by 1811. Censorship was lifted following Napoleon's defeat, then imposed and lifted again in cycles over the next century.

Figure 1.12 The little corporal, as Napoleon was called, is dwarfed by the printing press. Although he was a novelist and the publisher of several military newspapers early in his career, he also imposed draconian censorship during his reign as emperor of France.

The partisan press before the Industrial Revolution

News traveled slowly before the Industrial Revolution. A newspaper printed in New York might reach Boston in three days, Richmond, Virginia in five, and Cincinnati, Ohio in ten. It would take almost two months to cross the Atlantic to London or Paris until steamships became common in the 1830s, reducing the journey to about two weeks.

Yet newspapers flourished in the nineteenth century. In Europe, the number of daily and weekly newspapers grew from about 2,400 in 1820 to about 12,000 by 1900, even though publishers there were handicapped by censorship, higher taxes and higher postal rates.

In the United States, newspapers were supported by favorable postal rates as part of a strategy for democratic self government (Starr, 2004). In contrast to Europe, where postal rates held down newspaper circulation, the number of US daily and weekly publications grew from about 800 to nearly 16,000. With 50 newspaper and magazine subscriptions per 100 homes, twice as many publications were available by 1823 to Americans as the British, and the number grew to three times as many by 1900.

The US Postal Service was considered a public service, not a for-profit agency, operating with the idea of unifying a widely disbursed population. Printed information, rather than personal letters, made up 95 percent of the weight carried in the mail, but only 15 percent of the revenue (Starr, 2004).

Americans were enormously proud of their newspapers. In 1817, Niles Register claimed that New York state, with 96 newspapers, had "probably . . . a greater number than is published in the whole of Europe" (*Niles Register,* April 26, 1817, 12: 144). Although the figures are inaccurate, the assumption that Americans depended on newspapers more than other nations was essentially true.

"In America there is scarcely a hamlet that has not its newspaper," wrote French aristocrat Alexis de Tocqueville in his 1835 book Democracy in America (De Tocqueville, 1835). Because "there are no licenses to be granted to printers, no securities demanded from editors, as in France, and no stamp duty, as in France and England . . . nothing is easier than to set up a newspaper . . . Hence the number of periodical and semi-periodical publications in the United States is almost incredibly large."

Most newspapers in the United States or Europe were sold to a small circle of sub-scribers for at least five or six cents per copy, and the optimum economy of scale kept printing operations relatively small. Even national publications in the United States, like Baltimore's *Niles Weekly Register*, had circulations under 5,000.

Editors kept in touch with each other by sending their publications through the mails. If the newspaper was being sent to another editor in small town, it would be considered an "exchange," and other editors were free to print excerpts with attribu-tion. This was seen as so important in the United States that the Post Office did not charge to deliver an exchange.

But the system of low postal rates, editor exchanges and widespread competition would change rapidly, beginning in the mid-nineteenth century, as steam printing transformed local publishing and the telegraph changed the way national news was distributed.

Partisan papers in Great Britain

The Glorious Revolution of 1688 set the stage for reform in England, and in 1694 the Licensing Act expired. Parliament approved a resolution, drafted by John Locke, noting that prior restraint was impractical; it hindered scholars and hurt the print-ing trade. Dozens of newspapers emerged at this time supported by two major polit-ical factions who opposed each other in the press and every other every aspect of public life.

These two parties were:

- The Tory party, which supported the monarchy over Parliament and tended to resist social reform and support tradition. By the 1900s the Tories became the conservative party. (The name Tory derives from an insulting Irish term for robbers.)

- The Whig party, which supported Parliament over the monarchy, and supported free trade, religious toleration, abolition of slavery and expansion of voting rights. Whigs became known as liberals and as the labor party in the late 1800s. (The name Whig derives from a nickname for Scottish parliamentarians, Whiggamores, which meant cattle drivers.)

Early Tory newspapers included the *Post Boy* and the *Examiner*; Whig newspapers included the *London Times*, the *Flying Post* and the *Observator*. These newspapers existed in a world swirling with political controversy that also included Whig and Tory political organizations, Whig and Tory coffee houses, and even Whig and Tory fashions. "Party conflict covered almost every aspect of public, professional and even recreational life in post-revolutionary England" (Bucholz, 2009).

In 1701, a group of printers wrote to parliament in protest against a contemplated tax on newspapers. At the time, England had "five master printers" using about 20,000 reams of paper per year, or about 28,000 newspapers in circulation per day nationwide.

These sold for one halfpenny "to the poorer sort of people, who are purchasing it by reason of its cheapness, to divert themselves and also to allure . . . young children and entice them into reading." Hundreds of families, especially blind people, supported themselves by selling halfpenny papers on streets of London (*Encyclopedia Britannica*, 1911). The halfpenny press might have continued in England, but a stamp tax was imposed in 1724, and cheap newspapers vanished into an underground "pauper press" until 1855, when the tax was repealed. It was an extension of this same tax act to the American colonies in 1765 that aroused furor among American printers.

British authorities were finding the press very difficult to control, both at home and in the colonies, in the late 1700s. "For more than a century, newspapers and pamphlets had been strewn across the tables of clubs, inns, taverns and coffee houses and had fueled animated exchanges," wrote historian Jeffrey Smith. No one exemplified this problem better than the editor of the *North Briton*, John Wilkes. Wilkes had been a member of Parliament for six years when he criticized a speech by King George III. He was convicted of seditious libel in 1764 and fled into four years of exile in France. He returned in 1768 to a tumultuous reception. The crowds in the London streets made it clear that Wilkes was widely supported by public opinion (Smith, 1988). He asserted Parliamentary privilege, was released, and won re-election to Parliament in 1768.

His treatment by British authorities was watched carefully in the American colonies, and was considered one reason why American colonial printers believed that the social contract was being undermined by corrupt British leaders. Ironically, just as the revolution was breaking out in America, Wilkes became Lord Mayor of London and spent the rest of his life defending relatively conservative political views.

By the late 1700s, the news business was dominated by the *Times of London*, established by John Walter in 1785. In the beginning, the *Times* favored modest reforms and supported the "unalienable rights" of citizens, including freedom of speech and the right to petition the government (*Parliamentary Reform* 1785). Walter was not immune to the problems experienced by Wilkes, Cobbett and others, spending 16 months in Fleet Street jail on libel charges. Despite competition from the *Guardian* and other regional newspapers, the *London Times* remained the semi-official reform-oriented newspaper of the nation through the twentieth century.

What was the Fourth Estate?

The term "Fourth Estate" was a reference to the growing power of the press by Whig party leader Edmund Burke in a 1787 speech to Parliament. The speech was made when the visitor's gallery was opened to the press for the first time.

According to historian Thomas Carlyle, Burke said that there were three "estates" (walks of life) represented in Parliament: the nobility (House of Lords): the clergy; and the middle class (House of Commons). "But in the Reporters Gallery yonder, there sat a Fourth Estate, more important by far than they all."

This story is disputed. Editors of the *Oxford English Dictionary* say that they cannot confirm Carlyle's statement attributing the phrase "Forth Estate" to Burke. The earliest solid reference is in 1821 to William Cobbett, who was called "a kind of fourth estate in the politics of the country." Another reference is to a different speaker in the House of Commons in 1823 or 1824, and the idea was treated as original at the time.

The point of the historical debate is simply whether the political power of the press was widely recognized in the late 1700s or some 50 years later. Still, by the end of the nineteenth century, there was no doubt about the power of the press. As Oscar Wilde said around the time of his libel and "indecency" trial (for homosexuality) in 1895:

"In old days men had the rack. Now they have the press . . . Somebody . . . called journalism the Fourth Estate. That was true at the time no doubt. But at the present moment it is the only estate. It has eaten up the other three . . . We are dominated by journalism."

Trans-Atlantic connections

Journalists and their ideas traveled back and forth across the English Channel and the Atlantic Ocean as London became Europe's hothouse of political debate.

Benjamin Harris, a London publisher, moved to the Massachusetts, opened a coffee house and printed the first newspaper before moving back to London. Benjamin Franklin came to London after leaving his brother's newspaper in Boston, working to learn the trade and earn money to open the *Pennsylvania Gazette* in Philadelphia in 1731.

During the revolutionary period, journalists Thomas Paine and William Cobbett traveled between England, the United States and France. And during the later tabloid press period (late 1800s, early 1900s), publishers in England often adopted agendas and ideas from American counterparts. US publisher William Randolph Hearst and British publisher Alfred Harmsworth, for example, were friends who often traded ideas and techniques.

William Cobbett (1763–1835) was one influential journalist who was constantly in trouble with authorities. He originally wrote from a pro-British perspective in the United States in the 1790s, then returned to England in 1800 and established a Tory publication called the *Weekly Political Register* in 1802. His conservative views changed over the years as he observed cruelty, poverty and corruption of the age. In 1809, when he objected in print to a flogging and to the use of German troops to put down a mutiny, he spent two years in prison for seditious libel.

After his release from prison, Cobbett continued to edit the *Political Register*, supporting agrarian reform, Catholic emancipation and changes to the Poor Laws. But in 1817 Cobbett fled back to the US when the "Blasphemous and Seditious Libels Act" was passed. The act (one of the so-called "Six Acts") gave magistrates the power to seek and seize libellous materials. But the act was not especially effective, and juries were reluctant to convict editors, as Cobbett found when he returned to England. From 1819 to 1835, Cobbett fought off at least four serious libel charges.

Cobbett showed that the role of the British press in the social reform movements of the late 1700s and early 1800s could be daring, despite the frequent imposition of jail terms. The case for reform was largely accepted by British public opinion and reform governments by the mid-1800s.

Figure 1.13 Peter Porcupine—British journalist William Cobbett poured heated rhetoric into his US publications in the 1790s, warning in vitriolic terms of the excesses of the French Revolution and sympathizers like Thomas Paine. He celebrated his sharp personality with the pen name "Peter Porcupine." Returning to Britain in 1800, Cobbett attacked its "smothering system" that led to the Luddite Riots and vowed to expose Britain's "service and corrupt press" that had become an instrument in the "delusion, the debasement and the enslavement of a people."

Partisan papers in the United States

During the early years of the American republic, newspapers were usually financed and published by partisans of two major factions—John Adams' Federalist party and Thomas Jefferson's Democratic-Republican party.

Phillip Freneau's *National Gazette* sided with Thomas Jefferson and the Democratic-Republicans. The paper favored the French Revolution and opposed the Alien and Sedition Acts. Jefferson later said Freneau saved the country, "which was galloping fast into monarchy." After Freneau retired, Benjamin Franklin's nephew started a newspaper in Philadelphia called *The Aurora* that took up the defense of Democratic-Republican causes.

John Fenno's *Gazette of the United States* was the Federalist publication that sided with George Washington, John Adams and Alexander Hamilton on great questions of the day, such as the need for a strong federal government. The Federalists were alarmed by the French revolution.

In an attempt to head off an American version of the French Terror, Congress passed the Alien and Sedition Acts of 1798. Aimed at deporting French sympathizers and quelling criticism of President John Adams, the Sedition Act led to the imprisonment of about 100 people for speaking out against Adams and the government. Thomas Jefferson denounced the Sedition Act as a violation of the First Amendment of the US Constitution, which guaranteed freedom of speech and press. In the Virginia and Kentucky Resolutions, Jefferson and James Monroe argued that the states and not the federal government were ultimately sovereign, and therefore the federal government could not take away the rights of citizens. This argument, originally meant to support freedom of speech and press, was the basis on which the Confederate states justified secession from the Union in the American Civil War (1861–1865). Although the Alien and Sedition Acts expired in 1801, Jefferson's argument had unintended consequences.

Not all newspapers descended into political partisanship. *Niles Weekly Register*, published in Baltimore from 1811 to around 1844, was guided by what editor Hezekiah Niles called a principal of "magnanimous disputation" (Luxon, 1947). Niles was a forerunner of the more objective account of events, and his newspaper covered not only politics but economics, science, technology, art, literature and population growth. Niles is sometimes remembered today as the "Editor who tried to stop the Civil War" since he anticipated the conflict and attempted to outline economic policies like diversification and public works that might lead toward compromise and reconciliation. Remarkably similar policies would be advocated in the aftermath of the American Civil War by newspaper editors like Henry Grady of the *Atlanta Journal* (Kovarik, 1992).

The world of the printing "chapel" 1450s–1800s

Imagine, for a moment, a world where the scale and pace of life is smaller and slower, and yet to its inhabitants, just as rich with possibilities. It is a world that has barely changed since Gutenberg invented the printing press three and a half centuries ago.

It's a world where a printing company is still called a "chapel," partly because printing evolved from the scriptoria where monks once labored, and partly because, like a chapel, printing companies often have high ceilings and large windows to help printers see the details of their work.

If you were an apprentice in a printing chapel, you would find the work itself quite tedious. But the working environment would seem fascinating. Here, literacy and intelligence are rewarded, women often work with men, and the most interesting people in the city might show up at all hours.

As an apprentice, you would work under a system of rules much like other trades. You would start out at an early age, perhaps 10, and work your way up to journeyman by age 18 and then become a master printer in your 20s or 30s.

The language of craft printing: getting out of sorts, and by the same token, minding your ps and qs

Craft printing had its own culture and terminology, and there are remnants of this in everyday language. Many common terms and phrases—upper and lower case, out of sorts, by the same token, or minding your ps and qs—come from printing culture.

Figure 1.14 The printing chapel—a young Benjamin Franklin is depicted working in a British printing establishment during his apprenticeship. (Engraving by Charles E. Mills, Library of Congress)

The first step in making any kind of newspaper or book would be to set the type. Typesetting had to be done by hand, letter by letter, until the early twentieth century. Each typesetter would work in front of two cases with dozens of open compartments that held the individual metal letters. The capital letters were in the upper case and the small letters would go into the lower case. Both of these terms—upper case and lower case—are still in use today.

The cases had larger openings for commonly used letters, such as e, t, and a, and smaller openings for less commonly used letters. Samuel Morse, when thinking about how to design Morse code, consulted a printer on the frequency of letters used.

The type had to be set backward, since it would read forward once printed. You would pick the type up and place it into a long holder called a "stick." Let's say you wanted to set the type for the phrase *Life in a print shop*. You would start with the letter "p" in the lower case, then set o, h, s, quadrat (space), t, n, i, r, p, quadrat, a, quadrat, n, i, quadrat, e, f, i and then upper case L.

This can be confusing at first, and an apprentice typesetter might be told: "mind your ps and qs," because a "p" would look like a "q" when it went in backward.

The first job of an apprentice might involve breaking up the columns of type after they had been used to print a book or newspaper. You'd clean them off and sort type back into the type cases according to letter, font and size. Apprentices would have to be sure that each piece of type went back into the right slot and that the cases were ready for the typesetters.

If this took too long, the typesetters might be "out of sorts"—in other words, they would lack the sorted type of a particular font. Later, this came to mean that a person might be angry or upset.

Usually, typesetters would work from instructions written in longhand on a paper held to the top of the composing case by a spike. When an experienced editor was in a hurry, he or she might set type while they composed an essay. This was called composing "on the stick." Today being "on the stick" means that you are busy with a pressing task.

By the time you were a journeyman printer, you could probably set around 1,500 letters per hour, or about 20 words per minute. A column of type might take half the day—five or six hours—to set. Then you would spend another two hours redistributing the type after the book pages or day's newspaper had been printed.

Once type was set, the columns would be assembled in galleys on the composing stone and then held together inside a frame. The frame would be locked down with quoins and other "furniture." Then the type would be placed on a press.

One pressman (the "beater") would gently pound an even coat of ink into the type using two soft leather inking balls. Another pressman would place a damp page of blank paper into the frisket and gently fold it over the frame of inked type. The final stage was to roll the type down the carriageway underneath the platen. The pressman would pull on the long lever, and the paper would be pushed into the inked type. Then he would roll the type back, open up the frisket and hang the page up to dry.

A team of two pressmen and an apprentice would usually print a token each hour. A token was usually 258 sheets. The expression "by the same token" (still in use today) means turning the sheets over once the ink has dried in order to print on the other side of the paper.

Once the pages were printed, they had to be assembled carefully to make a book. This involved placing and trimming the pages in the right order and then sewing up the back of each "signature" set of pages, which would be from two pages to 16 or 24, depending on the size of the page and the kind of book being produced.

Playing quadrats and getting a washing
The work could be tedious and exacting. To make the day go by more quickly, one printer might be asked to read aloud from works of literature or the Bible.

Printers had strict social rules. They were not allowed to brag, or to whistle in the presence of a lady, or to leave candles burning when they were not present. Breaking any of those rules would result in a punishment, which they called a "solace," and this could be anything from having to perform a nasty chore to putting money into the "wayzgoose" fund. The wayzgoose was the printer's holiday that took place every August 24th.

But printers had some fun too. A typical pass-time was a game called "quadrats." Quadrats were square blank type pieces used for spaces between typeset words. Each has a nick, or indentation, on one of its four sides. The game was described in a 1683 book on printing customs:

> They take five or seven Quadrats . . . and holding their Hand below the Surface of the Correcting Stone, shake them in their Hand, and toss them upon the Stone, and then count how many Nicks upwards each man throws in three times, or any other number of times agreed on: And he that throws most Wins the Bett of all the rest, and stand out free, till the rest have try'd who throws fewest Nicks upward in so many throws; for all the rest are free: and he pays the Bet. (Moxon, 1683; Savage 1841)

But watch out ! If the sextant (manager) of the chapel caught you playing quadrats, he or she might have to decide on a solace (punishment). This could involve anything from paying into the chapel beer fund to having to sing an embarrassing song at the wayzgoose.

If you or a co-worker were in the habit of telling tall tales, sometimes other workers would express their disbelief by making loud banging noises on their

⇨

presses or type cases. When every person in the room did it, the drumming could be deafening (Savage, 1841). If, for some reason, a pressman resisted a solace, and the workers in the chapel were determined to enforce it, then the Spirit of the Chapel (sometimes called "Ralph") was said to be walking in the shop. Whatever mischief was done to the pressman, such as mixing up his pages or getting his type "pied" (mixed up) could then be blamed on the Spirit.

2

The commercial and industrial media revolution: from 1814 to 1900

The press is "the high priest of history, the vitalizer of society, the world's great informer, the medium of public thought and opinion, and the circulating life-blood of the whole human mind. It is the great enemy of tyrants and the right arm of liberty, and is destined, more than any other agency, to melt and mould the jarring and contending nations of the world into . . . one great brotherhood."—Samuel Bowles, 1851 (Brendon, 1983)

Steam-powered printing launches a new media era

It's six in the morning on November 29, 1814, and London's Fleet Street is beginning to fill with the cacophony of commerce. But the rows of hand-pulled presses at *The Times*, London, hardly changed since Gutenberg, have for once stopped their creaking and rumbling. The printers have been standing idle, and they are wondering how the newspaper will be produced today. They were told to wait for important foreign news to arrive. Then at dawn, John Walter II, owner of *The Times*—a thin man with a beak-like nose and a long black coat—bursts into the pressroom and calls for the printers to gather around. He is holding up this morning's issue of *The Times*—the same newspaper they had expected to be producing. Fearful glances are exchanged around the room.

"The Times is already printed—by steam" he announces grandly. He passes the newspaper out to the printers, who regard the boss with anger and suspicion as he explains. Today's *The Times* has been printed on a new kind of press designed by Friedrich Koenig, a mechanical engineer, he tells them. It was built in secret by Koenig's men in a guarded warehouse down the street.

It's a tense moment. Workers all over England have been losing their jobs to the steam engine. Three years before, in the industrial cities north of London, the

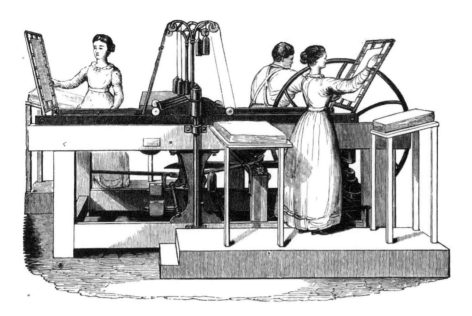

Figure 2.1 Steam powered printing—two Boston women help run an 1822 steam-powered Treadwell press, the first steam press in the United States. Women often had a role in printing and typesetting, especially in family-run printing shops. Benjamin Franklin and Horace Greeley fought the prevailing prejudice of the times and encouraged women to manage and write for newspapers, but they were not unique. (Engraving from Robert Hoe, *A Short History of the Printing Press*, 1902)

"Luddite" riots broke out when many thousands of textile workers were thrown out of work. Fifteen men were hung in York, and eight in Lancashire, for their roles in sabotaging the cotton mills.

Walter warns against any Luddite rebellions in his shop. But he also says that, unlike the textile industry, *The Times* will stand by its workers. There will be no layoffs. In fact, the faster press will mean more work for everyone.

The advantage of a steam press is not just speed, he emphasizes, but also less physical labor. This is an important point for the pressmen. Pulling that press lever hour after hour, day after day, leaves many men with one-sided muscle development. In fact, it's possible to tell an experienced pressman just from the loping way he walks.

Speed is also important for the business, Walter says. Where a crew of three men on a hand press might print 250 pages per hour, on one side, a crew of six men on the new steam press could produce 1,100 pages, on both sides, per hour—nearly four times the efficiency. (By 1828, it will be 4,000 pages per hour.)

And so, by investing in new technology, and treating its workers with respect, *The Times* scores a worldwide first.

The revolution from handcrafted printing to industrial printing production is momentous—costs of production come down, and due to mass circulation, the potential for advertising support goes up. The significance of the moment is difficult to overstate, but *The Times* calls it the "greatest improvement" since printing was invented:

> Our journal of this day presents to the public the practical result of the greatest improvement connected with printing, since the discovery of the art itself. The reader of this paragraph now holds in his hand one of the many thousand impressions of the Times newspaper which were taken off last night be a mechanical apparatus. (*The Times*, London, November 29, 1814, page 3)

Until this moment, books and news publications tended to be fairly expensive and oriented toward the elite. But the new steam powered press allowed the mass media to enter an industrial phase. With many more readers, advertisers found they could reach more customers, and the cost of printing a newspaper came down even more. The effect was to free the press from financial dependence on political parties and, with the rapid spread of information, to democratize politics.

The 'penny' press: a news media revolution

Before steam printing and the "penny press" revolution, most newspapers cost five to six cents each, and circulation was limited to the thousands. The primary effect of new printing technologies—introduced from 1814 to the 1850s—was to allow increases in newspaper circulation.

This, in turn, created secondary effects in the business model. Newspaper and magazine circulation in the tens or hundreds of thousands meant a better economy of scale by creating savings on the production side of the operation. It also allowed publishers to charge higher prices for advertising, creating greater profits. Rising circulation and advertising revenues meant that newspapers could afford to drop their street prices, often to as little as a penny per copy, to further increase circulation.

In other words, publishers could afford to sell papers for less than the cost of production because advertisers picked up the rest of the cost. And advertisers did that because advertising was more effective, since so many more people could now afford to read a newspaper.

Although steam printing was introduced at *The Times*, London in 1814, this new "penny press" business model took off first in the United States in the 1830s, where taxes did not hold back the development of competing newspapers. By the 1850s, the penny press revolution began to have impacts in Britain and the rest of Europe.

The use of advertising to support content development was also adopted by the broadcasting industry in the 1920s, and remained the primary mass media model until the early twenty-first century, when advertising income dropped rapidly, and the cycle began moving in reverse.

What history remembers best about the penny press revolution is another secondary effect: publishers could now serve broad public tastes rather than elite segments of a community.

It's important to recall that until this time, newspapers and books usually focused on great deeds, great ideas and the lives of great men. The daily lives and concerns of ordinary men and women "were not dignified by print," as historian Richard Kluger said. But in the 1830s, "a new spirit arose in the common man, who was encouraged to believe that his life, his voice, his vote were of some importance." New expectations were irrepressible once released, and a new literary form encompassing the humble as well as the great was now possible" (Kluger, 1986).

At a glance, the "new media" of the 1830s looked a lot like the old media. It was still a newspaper, printed on the cheapest possible paper, with long gray columns of type. But the editorial agenda had changing drastically, shifting from long political discussions to short descriptions of events, crimes and scandals; from summary essays about social trends to first-person accounts by paid "reporters"; from long-form descriptions to the "inverted pyramid" that placed key developments in the lead of the news articles.

The new publishers who catered to public taste also found that the public was fascinated by bizarre hoaxes, scathing editorials, shocking scandals and crime in the most lurid detail possible.

The US penny press

Four of New York's emerging daily newspapers in the 1830s are remembered as prototypes of the penny press revolution: The *Sun*, the *Herald*, the *Tribune* and *The New York Times*. Only *The Times* survives in its original form today, although the merged *Herald Tribune* has become an English-language newspaper based in Paris.

The rise and fall of the New York Sun

Benjamin Day's printing business had come to a standstill in the summer of 1833. Business was down because of a financial panic and a cholera epidemic that raged through the city. As Day cast about for new ways to earn money, the idea of starting yet another newspaper in the crowded New York market seemed quixotic to his friends. New York already had seven morning and four evening daily papers with circulations between 1,200 and 4,500.

These "elite" papers reported on politics, shipping and business to select clients. They sold for six cents a copy, over the counter or delivered to subscribers. Day wondered if it wouldn't be possible to print a penny paper and sell it on the streets. It had been tried before—Horace Greeley's *Morning Post*, sold for a penny, had failed the year before after only three weeks. Penny papers in Boston and Philadelphia had also failed.

But with little to lose, Day issued his first copy of *The Sun* on September 3, 1833, noting that the paper's purpose was to provide news of the day "at a price within the means of every one." The leading article was a humorous story about a dueling Irishman. Other items included charges of assault being heard in court; a suicide; three murders; an earthquake in Virginia; and an account of a boy who fell ill from whistling.

The paper was a modest success, and Day realized that New Yorkers were far more interested in a man who was arrested for beating his wife than they were in Andrew Jackson and the fight over the United States Bank. He hired a police court reporter and a small army of newsboys to hawk the paper on the streets. Within a month, circulation reached 1,200 and within a year it had reached 10,000 (O'Brien, 1918).

Other printers like Greeley did not think much of Day's efforts. While he tried to deal with the human condition in ways that the elite papers did not, the Sun had an unprofessional, smirking attitude, as this account shows:

SUDDEN DEATH—Ann McDonough, of Washington Street, attempted to drink a pint of rum on a wager, on Wednesday afternoon last. Before it was half swallowed Ann was a corpse. Served her right!

The reaction from the elite papers was predictable. Col. James Webb, editor of the *Courier* and *Enquirer*, bemoaned the success of "penny trash." Day shot back that the public had been "imposed upon by ten-dollar trash long enough."

But there were better penny papers on the way. James Gordon Bennett, formerly a political reporter for Webb's *Courier*, founded the *New York Herald* in May, 1835. A skilled reporter who knew how to find news, Bennett's crime reporting quickly began to eclipse *The Sun*.

In August of 1835, perhaps in an attempt to catch up to the *Herald*, *The Sun* published six stories about the fantastic discoveries of Sir William Hershel, a British astronomer who was known to be in South Africa at the time.

Figure 2.2 The moon hoax—the New York *Sun* was desperately trying to hang onto readers when it ran this pseudo-scientific news item in 1835: "We were thrilled with astonishment to perceive four successive flocks of large winged creatures, wholly unlike any kind of birds, descend with a slow even motion from the cliffs on the western side, and alight upon the plain . . . They averaged four feet in height, were covered, except on the face, with short and glossy copper-colored hair, and had wings composed of a thin membrane, without hair, lying snugly upon their backs, from the top of their shoulders to the calves of their legs. The face, which was of a yellowish flesh color, was a slight improvement upon that of the large orangoutang, being more open and intelligent in its expression, and having a much greater expansion of forehead . . . So far as we could judge, they spent their happy hours in collecting various fruits in the woods, in eating, flying, bathing, and loitering about on the summits of precipices."

To make the hoax more credible, *The Sun* invented the "Edinburgh Journal of Science," from which six long articles were purportedly extracted. The articles contained elaborate descriptions of new astronomical telescopes and detailed descriptions of lunar geography for three days before venturing into absolute fiction.

While *The Sun* never admitted that the moon hoax had been crafted by its editors, the absence of any confirming reports from England or Scotland soon led people to realize that they had been victims of a hoax.

The Sun took on a second life when it was purchased in 1868 by Charles Henry Dana, a Harvard graduate who had served uncomfortably as Horace Greeley's news editor. Dana's *Sun* emphasized the "human interest" story with brief articles about a wide range of activities, evolving into what has been called first "tabloid" newspaper. Lord Northcliffe (Albert Harmsworth) later said he modeled Britain's first tabloid, the *Daily Mail*, on Dana's editing of *The Sun*.

It was one of Dana's editors, John B. Bogart, who made what is perhaps the most frequently quoted definition of the news "When a dog bites a man, that is not news, because it happens so often. But if a man bites a dog, that is news."

The Sun is probably best remembered for its September 21, 1897 editorial by Francis P. Church, who wrote in answer to a young girl's inquiry: "Yes, Virginia, There Is a Santa Claus."

Figure 2.3 Is there a Santa Claus?—responding to a young girl's letter in 1897, New York *Sun* editor Francis P. Church said yes to the enduring spirit of childhood. The celebrated letter was part of a revival of the Christmas holiday led by many other writers and illustrator Thomas Nast. (Library of Congress)

Yes, Virginia, there is a Santa Claus. He exists as certainly as love and generosity and devotion exist, and you know that they abound and give to your life its highest beauty and joy. Alas! How dreary would be the world if there were no Santa Claus. It would be as dreary as if there were no VIRGINIAS. There would be no childlike faith then, no poetry, no romance to make tolerable this existence. We should have no enjoyment, except in sense and sight. The eternal light with which childhood fills the world would be extinguished . . .

There is a veil covering the unseen world which not the strongest man, nor even the united strength of all the strongest men that ever lived, could tear apart. Only faith, fancy, poetry, love, romance, can push aside that curtain and view and picture the supernal beauty and glory beyond. Is it all real? Ah, VIRGINIA, in all this world there is nothing else real and abiding.

No Santa Claus! Thank God! He lives, and he lives forever. A thousand years from now, Virginia, nay, ten times ten thousand years from now, he will continue to make glad the heart of childhood.

That same year of 1897, *The Sun* editor Dana died, and the newspaper began drifting out of its orbit. Financially struggling, *The Sun* entered into a series of mergers in 1916 and was gone by 1920.

The New York Sun was briefly revived as a conservative alternative to the *New York Times* from 2002 to 2008, but collapsed again with the economic recession of that year.

Bennett and the New York Herald

The most successful of the sensationalist penny newspapers was the *New York Herald*, founded in 1835 by James Gordon Bennett, a Scotsman who emigrated to America and worked for 15 years in the partisan and elite press before starting his own newspaper.

Bennett was exuberantly independent in style, full of energy, malevolent genius and shocking cruelty. He once horsewhipped the editor of a rival newspaper in the streets, and many victims of his pen felt they had been similarly treated.

He was widely disliked. Charles Dickens, for instance, saw the Herald as "foul mass of positive obscenity," and lampooned Bennett in a portrait of an American newspaper editor in his book *Martin Chuzzlewit* (Brendon, 1983). Benjamin Day wrote that the only chance Bennett had of dying an upright man "will be that of hanging perpendicularly from a rope."

To attract readers, the *Herald* served up a mix of robberies, rapes and murders almost daily. In 1836, the murder of a beautiful prostitute named Ellen Jewett became Bennett's obsession. He visited the scene of the crime, played detective and even described the corpse: "as white, as full, as polished as the purest Parian (Greek) marble . . . (with) the perfect figure, the exquisite limbs, the fine face, the full arms, the beautiful bust." Opponents in other newspapers compared him to a vampire or a vulture, but his investigations acquitted the man who had apparently been wrongfully accused of Jewett's murder.

Figure 2.4 A well-hated editor—James Gordon Bennett, founder of *The Herald*, brought professionalism and enterprise to the craft, but he also attracted enemies with astonishingly caustic editorial attacks.

The *Herald* redefined news in other ways, with reporting on Wall Street, sports events and society affairs. Bennett also set up bureaus in Washington, London and Paris.

Bennett's *Herald* carried regular church news, but its editorial page attacked the Catholic Church, as an institution reflecting the "darkness, folly and superstition of the tenth century." Ostensibly a Catholic, Bennett even attacked Americans who "kiss the toe of every debauchee whom the College of Cardinals may elevate to the triple crown (the papacy)." Shortly afterwards he was excommunicated.

During the US Civil War, the *Herald* was by far the leading newspaper, with a circulation of 400,000 daily. The *Herald* spent huge amounts of money on telegrams from the front lines. Editorially, Bennett was opposed to the war. He wrote of President Abraham Lincoln as the "great ghoul," although after his assassination, Bennett wrote that in 100 years, historians would still be astounded at his greatness. The "real origin" of the assassination, he said, was "the fiendish and malignant spirit developed and fostered by the rebel press, North and South" (Mitgang, 1989).

Bennett and his son, James Gordon Bennett Jr, insisted that the newspaper be first with news, rewarding or punishing reporters who scooped (or who failed to scoop) other papers. The *Herald* was the first to report the news of the defeat of Gen. George Custer against the Sioux at the Battle of Little Big Horn in 1876 and the first to report on the sinking of the Titanic in 1912.

Greeley and the New York Tribune

New York readers looking for something more than crude sensationalism were relieved when Horace Greeley established the *New York Tribune* in 1841 with the idea of publishing a more trustworthy and moral newspaper. Greeley was an eccentric man without much formal education, but his *Tribune* had a profound influence on American politics in the mid-nineteenth century. He had "sat at the feet" of Hezekiah Niles, editor of the Baltimore-based *Niles Weekly Register*. Greeley read every issue and absorbed many of Niles' ideas about abolition of slavery, national economic development and fairness in news reporting. Greeley continued the reform tradition by promoting social causes such as women's rights, labor unions and the end of monopolies.

Greeley was also fascinated with the American West, and was long remembered for the admonition: "Go west, young man, and grow up with the country." Greeley took that advice himself, traveling across the plains to California and recording the trip in "An Overland Journey from New York to San Francisco."

Greeley advocated preservation of redwood forests and supported the idea of national parks.

> I am sure they (the redwoods) will be more prized and treasured a thousand years hence than now, should they, by extreme care and caution, be preserved so long, and that thousands will then visit them, over smooth and spacious roads, for every one who now toils over the rugged bridle-path by which I reached them. (Greeley, 1860)

Greeley also expressed surprise at the way Mormons treated women:

> I have not observed a sign in the streets, an advertisement in the journals, of (Salt Lake City, Utah), whereby a woman proposes to do anything whatever. No

Mormon has ever cited to me his wife's or any woman's opinion on any subject; no Mormon woman has been introduced or has spoken to me; and, though I have been asked to visit Mormons in their houses, no one has spoken of his wife (or wives) desiring to see me, or his desiring me to make her (or their) acquaintance, or voluntarily indicated the existence of such a being or beings. . . . The spirit with regard to woman, of the entire Mormon, as of all other polygamic systems, is fairly displayed in this avowal. Let any such system become established and prevalent, and woman will soon be confined to the harem, and her appearance in the street with unveiled face will be accounted immodest. I joyfully trust that the genius of the nineteenth century tends to a solution of the problem of woman's sphere and destiny radically different from this. (Greeley, 1860)

Figure 2.5 The modern editor—Horace Greeley anticipated the desire for a higher moral tone in *The Tribune*, and was widely appreciated in his day, despite his partisanship in later life. He was remembered for writing: "Go west, young man, and grow up with the country."

Greeley was also concerned with events in Europe, and in 1851, hired Karl Marx as London correspondent. Marx wrote 487 articles for the *Tribune*, including this 1862 observation about the resistance by the British working class to the idea of entering the US Civil War on the side of the South:

The misery that the stoppage of factories and cutting of working time, brought on by the blockade (of Southern cotton from) the slave states is unbelievable and daily on the increase . . . English intervention in America has accordingly become a bread and butter issue for the working class . . . Under these circumstances, the obstinacy with which the working class keeps silent, only to break that silence to speak against intervention and for the United States is admirable. This is new, brilliant evidence of the independence of the English masses, of that excellence which is the secret of England's greatness . . . (Snyder and Morris, 1962)

Like other newspaper editors of the day, Greeley could also be mercurial. The *Tribune* advocated peace before the Civil War but proclaimed "On to Richmond" (the capitol of the Confederacy) when war broke out. Greeley disliked most politicians but promoted Abraham Lincoln's candidacy, then constantly hectored the president on the conduct of the war. He helped form the Republican Party in the 1850s but then ran for the presidency on the Democratic ticket in 1872, losing badly to one of Lincoln's generals, Ulysses S. Grant.

The *Tribune* merged with the *Herald* in 1924, and the combined *Herald Tribune* stopped US publication in 1967, although it continued in Paris as an English language newspaper for American expatriates.

The New York Times *as the national paper of record*

Shunning Bennett's sensationalism and Greeley's moral crusades, Henry Raymond founded *The New York Times* in 1851 as a frankly commercial and pragmatic newspaper of record. Like its namesake in London, *The New York Times* catered to elite readers. Greeley later said sourly that it gained circulation by pandering to the "ultra abuse" of abolitionists, spiritualists, women's rights advocates and reformers.

Raymond had a more neutral view of news in mind, somewhat akin to Benjamin Franklin's idea that printers need to be amenable to many points of view. And he foresaw a kind of neutrality that would later be called objectivity.

In the paper's first editorial on September 18, 1851, Raymond said:

Figure 2.6 Founding the paper of record—Henry Raymond founded *The New York Times* in 1851 to provide an alternative to Greeley's moralizing and Bennett's sensationalism. In the process, the *Times* became the country's leading newspaper of record, printing, as his successors would claim in the 1890s, "All the news that's fit to print."

> We shall be conservative in all cases where we think conservatism essential to the public good; and we shall be radical in everything which may seem to us to require radical treatment and radical reform . . . We do not mean to write as if we were in a passion . . . There are very few things in this world which it is worth while to get angry about; and they are just the things that anger will not improve.

One incident that did provoke Raymond's anger was the Edgardo Mortara affair of 1858, in which a 6-year-old Jewish boy was taken from his Jewish parents in Bologna, Italy and handed over by police to Vatican officials. This occurred because a servant in the Mortara household had secretly baptized the boy, and, under religious law in Italy at the time, Christians were not permitted to live with Jews. The boy was never allowed to return home. The affair was an "outrage," Raymond wrote in one of 20 articles carried in the *Times*, a "violation of one of the most sacred natural rights of man." Had the case occurred in another country, or had a Roman Catholic family been similarly treated in a Jewish or Protestant community, "the voice of civilization would have been just as loud in condemnation" (*The New York Times* December 4, 1858). (*The Times*, London, was just as strong in condemning the abduction and covered government and church protests to the Vatican.)

The New York Times continued its moderate but occasionally radical course after Raymond's death in 1869, strongly attacking the corruption of New York's political machine Tammany Hall in the early 1870s. *The Times*'s investigative work, along with Thomas Nast's cartoons in *Harper's Weekly*, mobilized public opinion against civic corruption and demonstrated the effectiveness of investigative reporting.

Adolph Ochs, a Southern publisher, bought *The Times* in 1896 and coined the paper's slogan "All the news that's fit to print." Once again, *The Times* was distancing itself from competitors such as Joseph Pulitzer's crusading *New York World* and William Randolph Hearst's sensationalistic *New York Journal*. As the leading newspaper in the nation's largest city, *The New York Times* became the newspaper of record in the United States by the turn of the century.

The penny press in Britain

The penny press did not emerge in England until the 1860s, even though England was more technologically advanced than the United States. Steam printing had been introduced in 1814, and other innovations quickly followed. Yet the political conditions were not right for establishing a penny newspaper. Stamp Act taxes alone amounted to 5 pence per newspaper, which meant that while the upper classes could afford newspapers, lower and middle classes had to be served by illegal unstamped newspapers called the "pauper press." Established papers, especially *The Times*, London, worked hard to keep taxes in place and competition at bay, noting the impacts of unfettered democracy and unstamped press in the United States meant that "the once hopeful Eden of liberty [would] remain a wilderness of weeds" (*The Times*, London, October 29, 1842).

Calls for reform in 1836 led to a reduction in the stamp tax but an increase in penalties for those who did not pay it. This, in effect, continued to protect the established press, especially *The Times*, against interlopers. Again, in 1854, there were calls for reform of the "tax on knowledge," and again they were opposed by prominent publishers and others in the publishing business. Charles Mitchell, an advertising agent with links to *The Times*, said: "Our experience convinces us that such a step (abolishing tax) would completely destroy the respectability of the newspaper press and reduce it from its present position, that of the highest in the world, to that of the American press" (Lee, 1937).

The story of the "Penny Magazine" shows how constraints on the alternative press worked at the time. Published by a social improvement society, it was sold at a cost of only a penny per issue. It offered "purer subjects of thought" than crime or politics, and in any given issue these might include poems, sermons, travel stories and short features on the improvement of everything from neighborhoods to the human race. The fact that it attained a circulation of 200,000 in 1832, with its appeal to purity, probably says more about the public demand for information than the quality of the publication itself.

The established British media saw America's penny press as "wretched and inferior, (given to) flippancy for wit, personality for principle, bombast for eloquence, malignity without satire and news without truth or reliability . . . " (Brendon, 1983). Such arguments were frequently used in favor of taxes on newspapers, but the House of Commons voted to lift the taxes between 1855 and 1861.

The Daily Telegraph

The end of newspaper taxes opened the door for the first of the British penny press newspapers, the *Daily Telegraph*, established in 1855 by Joseph M. Levy. The *Telegraph* immediately confirmed its opponents' worst fears about the penny press, featuring articles about crime, murder and curiosities modeled after the *New York Herald*, although somewhat muted to better suit British audiences.

In 1869, the *Telegraph* joined the *New York Herald* to back one of the best-remembered stunt reporting sensations of the age, the search for Dr David Livingstone, a Scottish missionary and explorer. Livingstone had been in Africa twice on

Figure 2.7 and Figure 2.7(a) Dr Livingstone I presume? The famed Scottish missionary and explorer had been searching for the source of the Nile River and working for an end to the slave trade when he disappeared in 1866. Three years later, reporter Henry Morton Stanley searched eight months on assignment for the *New York Herald* and the London *Daily Telegraph*. On November 10, 1871, Stanley located Livingstone in what is now Tanzania. The encounter took place with several hundred Africans observing. "I would have run to him, only I was a coward in the presence of such a mob—would have embraced him, but that I did not know how he would receive me; so I did what moral cowardice and false pride suggested was the best thing—walked deliberately to him, took off my hat, and said: 'Dr. Livingstone, I presume?' 'Yes,' he said, with a kind, cordial smile, lifting his cap slightly. I replaced my hat on my head, and he replaced his cap, and we both grasped hands. 'I thank God, doctor, I have been permitted to see you.' He answered, 'I feel thankful that I am here to welcome you.' " This stilted exchange became the stuff of newspaper legend.

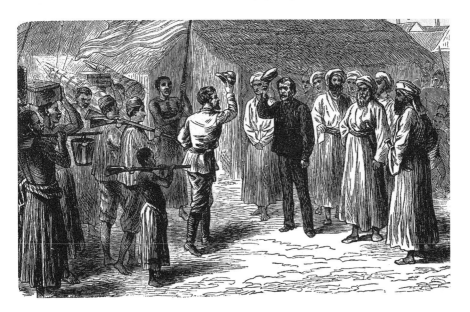

British-financed expeditions to chart a navigable river into the interior. He had not been heard from for over six years; apparently his many letters never made it back to London. British journalist Henry Morton Stanley, also working at the time for the *Herald*, proposed the search for Livingstone and, after two years, found him on the shores of Lake Tanganyika on October 27, 1871. He greeted him with the famous words "Dr. Livingstone, I presume?"

Ironically, after so much effort had been spent on finding Dr Livingstone, the missionary refused to return home with Stanley, insisting that there was more work to be done. He died in Africa in 1873, and most of his body was returned for burial in Westminster Abbey. His heart, however, was buried in Africa at the insistence of tribesmen. Stanley continued mounting expeditions into Africa, some of them ending disastrously, but he returned to London, and was later knighted and elected to Parliament.

William Stead and the Pall Mall Gazette

One of the most colorful characters of the emerging 'penny press' revolution in Britain was William Thomas Stead (1849–1912), editor of the *Pall Mall Gazette*, founded in 1869 as a gentleman's newspaper.

Stead turned the paper on its ear when he assumed deputy editorship in 1879 and then became editor in 1883. He promised "to secure the final overthrow of the Powers of Darkness in high places." An eccentric like Horace Greeley, Stead began what he called the "new journalism," but as historian Piers Brendon has noted, much of what Stead did was the same lurid treatment of news found elsewhere in the 'penny' press, with eye-catching headlines about crime mixed with crusades for reform of housing, expansion of the British empire and the abolition of prostitution (Brendon, 1983).

Figure 2.8 Idealist and crusader—William T. Stead may have been one of the most idealistic editors of the nineteenth century. His ideas about "government by journalism" never quite caught on, but he is remembered as a strong advocate for a European federation and a world court, both of which took a century to accomplish.

He personally investigated London's worst dens of iniquity—at one point buying a 13-year-old from her mother for five pounds—and he printed explicit details of what he called the "virtual slave trade" (prostitution). The series created a sensation, with crowds packing the street outside his office and presses running night and day. Denounced by many, praised by many others, Stead tried to employ the techniques of new journalism to support the old Puritanism in a thoroughly contradictory and modern manner.

One of Stead's more grandiose ideas was "government by journalism," in which the press would have its own leaders in Parliament with the power to inspect all government departments. Journalistic "major-generals" would be appointed to serve as public opinion pollsters and "interrogators of democracy." The idea never took off.

Meanwhile, Stead continued bombarding the public with divorce and scandal in high places, but he dissipated his energies in quack cures for cancer, miraculous fertilizers, spirit photography, a process for distilling gold from sea water, and other pursuits. Although considered one of the great editors of the day, Stead did not have the discipline to combine editorial flair with financial independence like James Gordon Bennett or Horace Greeley (Brendon, 1983).

Stead was the ultimate idealist. He advocated a "United States of Europe" and a "High Court of Justice among the nations"—two ideas that, in other forms, have come to pass. He reported the Hague Peace Conferences of 1899 and 1907 and is remembered with a bust (sculpture) at the Peace Palace in The Hague. He was en route to a peace conference in the United States aboard the Titanic in 1912 when the ship struck an iceberg. After helping women and children into the few lifeboats, Stead retired to the first class smoking room and was last seen in a leather chair reading a book (Lord, 1955).

The penny press in France

The French press played a pivotal role in the Enlightenment and French Revolution, but the on-again off-again censorship of the post-Napoleonic period held back its development.

Newspapers rose and fell as governments rose and fell, and as censorship rules were imposed or lifted. One newspaper from the 1830s still in existence today, *Le Figaro,* originally began as a satirical weekly.

Technology transformed the French press as quickly as it has the American press, and the penny paper of France was called the *presse à bon marché.* Two of these—Emile de Girardin's *La Presse* and Armand Dutacq's *Le Siècle* lowered subscription costs and attempted to make up the losses through advertising as did the *Sun, Herald* and *Tribune* in New York.

One French innovation was the serialized novel, called the roman-feuilleton. *La Presse* began by serializing Honore de Balzac's novel *La Vieille Fille.* While the concept attracted readers, many did not like Balzac's long descriptions and deep prose, and soon more versatile and journalistic novels appeared on the pages. One great success was the serialization of *The Three Musketeers* and *The Count of Monte Cristo* by Alexandre Dumas.

Serialization of novels had an enormous impact on the idea of the novel itself, according to Dean de la Motte. "There is no doubt that—because it forced the *hommes de lettres* to write as fast as journalists and because the product of their work had to attract and sustain the interest of as many consumers as possible—serialization had a great impact on narrative discourse and on the structure of the novel," he said (De la Motte, 1999).

Another French innovation of the period was the news agency, which later, with the aid of the telegraph, would become known as a "wire service." The world's first agency was founded by Charles Louis Havas in 1835 with the idea of exchanging and translating news among European nations. Havas used carrier pigeons to carry news of extremely important events to news clients. Havas also extended its reach to help found agencies in other countries, notably Britain, Germany and Spain.

By the 1850s, direct censorship was converted into a system of Ministerial *avertissements* (warnings) and suspensions, but French journalists considered the system just as deadly to social progress. "The press is the most powerful instrument of government in modern societies," said one French correspondent. Reforms in

England, brought about by the press, had calmed social tensions, he said, but repression had made things worse in France: "Frank and open liberty can alone calm the concentrated irritations which have survived our disorders" (*The Times*, London, November 12, 1858).

An 1880 law ending censorship put a stop to direct government punishment of news organizations, but libel prosecutions continued to be a problem.

The Dreyfus affair

On the morning of January 13, 1898, the daily newspaper *L'aurore* carried the famous headline in a banner across the front page: "J'Accuse . . . !" Emile Zola, one of the nation's leading writers, accused ministers at the highest levels of government of sending an innocent Army officer, Alfred Dreyfus, to the notorious prison on Devil's Island in order to cover up a miscarriage of justice. Dreyfus had been falsely convicted of treason and evidence of his connection to a real plot to spy for the German government was fabricated, Zola charged. The fact that Dreyfus was Jewish, and that anti-Semitism was rife in the Army, made him an ideal scapegoat.

The affair was deeply divisive, with the church and conservatives on one side and liberals on the other. Following the "J'Accuse" story, Zola was charged with criminal libel and convicted a month later. Rather than go to jail, Zola fled to England. He was pardoned a year later when the French president resigned in the wake of the affair. Dreyfus was brought back to France and completely exonerated in 1906.

The editor of *L'aurore* who wrote the "J'Accuse" headline was Georges Clemenceau, who had been in exile in New York during the 1880s for his role in the

Figures 2.9. and 2.10 "J'Accuse"—the headline roared from the pages of *L'aurore*, brought down the French government and echoed through media history as the classic example of investigative journalism overturning a wrongful and prejudiced criminal conviction.

revolutionary Paris Commune's newspaper. He continued editing newspapers and being involved in French politics until becoming Prime Minister of France during World War I.

Political and media revolutions in Germany

Political and media revolutions similar to those of England, the United States and France also took place in Germany in the nineteenth century, but over a shorter period of a few decades.

The various German states had a long history of press censorship, interrupted only by a brief period of liberalization during the Napoleonic period, when, for instance, Prussian authorities tolerated liberal nationalist newspapers like *Rheinischer Merkur* (1814–1816), if they opposed Napoleon. In 1819, the German states imposed formal censorship again, but over the years, the acceleration of publishing made censorship less and less effective. The number of books and newspapers doubled between the 1820s and the 1840s, and then doubled again during the revolutionary period. In reaction to the demands of the 1848 revolutionaries, censorship was dropped, but subsequent press laws set limits to the freedom of expression and put economic pressure on editors and publishers (Green, 2001).

Political revolutions of 1848

The revolutions of 1848 in Europe were mostly a series of urban uprisings on the European continent, from France to Poland and from Denmark to Italy. The revolutions led to tens of thousands of deaths, and were quickly put down. However, they had a long term impact, for instance, deposing monarchies, such as Louis Philippe, who abdicated in France in 1848, or in forcing monarchs to share power with national legislatures in Denmark and Hungary. In other cases, such as Italy, the 1848 revolution led into wars of unification.

Germany's "March revolution" of 1848 advocated freedom of the press as one of its most important demands, along with freedom of assembly and a national constitution (instead of the then-existing confederation of loosely allied German-speaking states). One result of the new press freedom was the founding of the Berlin *National-Zeitung* (newspaper) in 1848 by Bernhard Wolff, a former associate of Charles Louise Havas' news agency of Paris. The paper was a partisan (political party) opinion paper that merged with another paper in 1910.

Another newspaper, the *Bonner Zeitung*, was founded by revolutionary Carl Schurz (1829–1906). When the 1848 revolution collapsed, Schurz fled to the United States and founded a newspaper in St. Louis, Missouri. In 1867, Schurz hired a young Hungarian refugee named Joseph Pulitzer. Pulitzer would buy Schurz' newspaper and combine it with another to form the *St. Louis Post-Dispatch*. Schurz believed strongly in democracy and encouraged Pulitzer to get involved in politics. In 1869, Schurz was the first German-born American to be elected to the US Senate. He is famous for saying: "My country, right or wrong; if right, to be kept right; and if wrong, to be set right."

The journalist of the 1848 era who is best remembered by history is Karl Marx (1818–1893). Marx founded and edited a reformist newspaper, *Rheinische Zeitung*, in 1842 in Berlin. The publication was twice closed by the government, and in 1848, reopened as the *Neueu* (New) *Rheinische Zeitung*. Even then, with more liberal press laws, Marx was tried for incitement to rebellion. In a speech to the jury, Marx argued that the law must reflect social realities and, when those realities change, the law must also change. The jury acquitted him of incitement and even thanked him for expressing his views. Marx spent many years in exile in France and Belgium, where he wrote the Communist Manifesto in 1848.

By 1851 he was in London, working for Horace Greeley's *New York Tribune*, helping Americans understanding Europe after the 1848 revolutions and informing the influx of European immigrants to America about conditions back home (Chakravorti, 1993).

Marx was originally an advocate of a free press, and in 1842, said: "The free press is the omnipresent open eye of the spirit of the people, the embodied confidence of a people in itself, the articulate bond (between) the individual with the state and the world" (Marxist Internet Archive, 2010). Whether or not Marx turned against the idea of a free press in later years, as some have argued, his followers in Russia would later impose harsh censorship in the name of the revolution.

The mid-nineteenth-century German press that Schurz and Marx tried to build was essentially more elite in character than in other nations; most German editors at the time had university degrees and many had doctorates. Most newspapers did not cater to popular tastes and mass audiences, but rather, were opinion journals containing partisan analyses of political trends.

"A German daily is the slowest and saddest and dreariest of the inventions of man," Mark Twain said in his 1880 book, A Tramp Abroad. German newspapers had no personals, no sports reporting, no abuse of public officials and nothing of a local nature. "Our own (US) dailies infuriate the reader, pretty often; the German daily only stupefies him" (Twain, 1880).

This changed with the emergence of mass-circulation dailies in the 1870s, according to historian Corey Ross, since increasing reliance on advertising revenue and mass circulation meant increasing concern for public opinion. "What mattered was winning over new readers, and the best means for achieving this was by offering attractive entertainment at the lowest possible price," Ross said (Ross, 2008).

The *Berliner Tageblatt*, for example, was founded in 1871 by Rudolf Mosse, an advertising executive. By the mid-1870s, circulation rose to 50,000, but was challenged by entertainment entrepreneur August Scherl's *Berliner-Lokal-Anzeiger*. Hugo von Kupffer, the paper's editor, had been a reporter at the *New York Herald* and shared Scherl's view that German newspapers were too dry. Using the British and American formula of popular events and human interest stories, the daily soon rose to a circulation of 150,000 and remained the largest paper before World War I. Scherl's influence on the German press was so strong that tabloid journalism in Germany was called "Scherlism." Meanwhile, German editors from the elite press, like their contemporaries at *The Times*, London, worried that their profession was being undermined (Green, 2001).

The progressive era: crusading, yellow and tabloid journalism

Technological acceleration

The technology of the Industrial Revolution that made the 'penny press' possible in the United States, and then in other nations, continued to accelerate in the late nineteenth century. By the turn of the twentieth century, the once-solid columns of grey type had been transformed into a riot of eye-catching headlines, subheads, photographs and illustrations that would remain nearly the same for almost a century.

The effect of this ongoing technical revolution was to make possible the production of hundreds of thousands of copies of a newspaper daily, creating large-scale mass communication enterprises. Circulation of metropolitan newspapers grew from tens of thousands to hundreds of thousands. The secondary effects included greater profits for publishers and the expansion of chain ownership. It also meant expanded news coverage and new developments in newspaper and magazine journalism.

"The example of American journalism has greatly affected developments in England and other countries . . . (producing) very much the same effects, though at a slower rate," said *Herald* editor Whitelaw Reid around the turn of the century.

The press "barons" of the progressive age

Most of the prototypes of modern public affairs journalism emerged in the 1880–1920 period under a variety of labels—muckraking, yellow journalism, crusading journalism, objective journalism, literary journalism and others. They flourished under the direction of publishers who tended to put their personal stamp on far-flung news operations.

These publishers—sometimes called press "barons"—are a study in contrasts. Joseph Pulitzer, a high-minded crusader, was also mercilessly critical with his staff. William Randolph Hearst, with a reputation for "yellow journalism," also supported public service journalism—occasionally. E. W. Scripps, a pugnacious and uneducated publisher, also became the country's foremost promoter of science education, both in the press (with the Science Service) and in financing far-sighted research at Scripps Oceanographic Institute in California.

What they had in common were two overt objectives: to "promote the public good" (as Pulitzer said) and to attract readers and build up circulation. In many cases, the ideal of public service did not live up to the reality, and the press barons were routinely criticized for promoting private interests or personal preferences.

Crusading journalism and Joseph Pulitzer's *New York World*

Joseph Pulitzer (1847–1911) developed his famous crusading journalism style by studying the editorials of Horace Greeley, the sensational news style of James Gordon

Figures 2.11 and 2.12 Crusading editor—with a passion for his adopted country and a fiercely micro-managing style, Pulitzer was both adored and loathed. His editorial role was often one of a public scold, as in this Puck cartoon of 1900, where a resolutely isolationist Uncle Sam is refusing to intervene in the Boer War of South Africa, despite Pulitzer's nagging.

Bennett and the success of illustrated newspapers such as *Harper's* and the *Illustrated London News*. He used these elements in a novel way to increase his newspapers' appeal to working class readers, especially immigrants to America who needed to understand the politics and culture of the country in a positive light.

Pulitzer, too, was an immigrant. He'd left Hungary to join the Union cavalry in the Civil War, and then moved to St. Louis where he met Carl Schurz, a journalist who took part in the European revolution of 1848 and emigrated to the United States in the 1850s. He had become the first German-born American elected to the US Senate in 1869. Pulitzer began working for Schurz in the 1860s at the German-language daily, *Westliche Post*. In 1872, Pulitzer bought a controlling interest in the nearly bankrupt paper and made it a success.

Pulitzer was inspired by Schurz and the European revolutionaries of 1848, according to Hungarian historian András Csillag. "Joseph Pulitzer's atavistic love of freedom and the fighting spirit he imported from Hungary accompanied him throughout his lifetime," Csillag said. "For his entire life, he was a passionate devotee to the cause of liberty: the liberty of action, of opinion, of government" (Csillag, 2008).

The *Westliche Post* was a success, and following a series of shrewd business deals, Pulitzer bought the English-language *St. Louis Dispatch* in 1878. The combined *Post-Dispatch* crusaded against gambling and corruption in government. Five years later, building on that success, Pulitzer bought the failing *New York World* and began another set of crusades against corruption and slum housing in the nation's largest city. Pulitzer also enlisted readers in crusades, for example, printing the names of 120,000 people whose contributions helped build a pedestal for the Statue of Liberty in New York harbor in 1885 and 1886.

Pulitzer is often remembered for a bitter circulation fight with William Randolph Hearst's *New York Journal*. Together, Pulitzer and Hearst's newspapers pressured the US government into war against Spain in 1898. The affair was the low point of what

Figure 2.13 Yellow journalism—Pulitzer and Hearst, dressed in yellow baby gowns, fight over their war in this 1898 satirical cartoon. (Library of Congress)

came to be called "yellow journalism," named for the yellow ink used to color a comic character called the "Yellow Kid" created by Richard F. Outcault. The cartoon, usually a humorous take on working class life, was first printed in the *New York World* but later moved to Hearst's *Journal American* (Moritz, 1996).

Pulitzer regretted the role of the press in the Spanish–American war, and was proud that four years beforehand, in 1894, the *World* had helped keep America and Britain out of war. The two nations were on the verge of armed conflict over a territorial dispute in South America and the Monroe Doctrine. Pulitzer worked to avert the war and remind Americans of how much they had in common with Great Britain. One tactic was to publish essays by outstanding writers from both sides of the Atlantic expressing their admiration for the other nation, humanizing the public image of Britain and making them an unlikely enemy.

One of the *World*'s most controversial investigations involved charges that US President Theodore Roosevelt and the US government had been involved in a scheme to bribe foreign companies and manufacture a revolution to allow the construction of the Panama Canal. Roosevelt was furious and ordered the attorney general to bring a criminal libel indictment. Pulitzer responded: "The *World* cannot be muzzled," and told reporters he was preparing to go to jail. However, the courts refused to allow the case to go to trial, and the incident was seen as a victory for freedom of the press.

Pulitzer also crusaded against racism. In a 1909 editorial, the *World* railed against President William Howard Taft's decision not to appoint African Americans to federal positions in the South without the approval of Southern whites. "We cannot agree in drawing such a skin color or race line," he cabled the office (Brian, 2001).

Figure 2.14 Around the world in 72 Days—it was a daring bet for the young star reporter: Could a woman, alone, beat Jules Verne's fictional character who went "Around the World in 80 Days?" The trip turned into a sensation, as Pulitzer's *World* newspaper printed each telegraphic dispatch with extensive maps and descriptions of the countries she visited. She returned to a heroine's welcome, an exemplar of an age, as Brooke Kroeger said, when American women were vigorously asserting their right and need to shape history.

Nelly Bly, Investigative Reporter

One of the first assignments for Joseph Pulitzer's star reporter was to talk her way into a women's insane asylum. Nelly Bly (Elizabeth Cochrane, 1864–1922) was a fiery and fiercely independent reporter who worked for the Pittsburgh *Post-Dispatch* before moving to New York. She became famous overnight for her first-person account in the *New York World*, "Ten Days Inside a Madhouse" (Bly, 1890).

> Soon after my (arrival at the madhouse) a girl called Urena Little-Page was brought in. . . . The nurses . . . teased her until the simple creature began to yell and cry . . . She grew more hysterical every moment until they pounced upon her and slapped her face and knocked her head in a lively fashion. This made the poor creature cry the more, and so they choked her. Yes, actually choked her. Then they dragged her out to the closet, and I heard her terrified cries hush into smothered ones. After several hours' absence she returned to the sitting-room, and I plainly saw the marks of their fingers on her throat for the entire day. This punishment seemed to awaken their desire to administer more. They returned to the sitting-room and caught hold of an old gray-haired woman . . . She never spoke very loud, and at the time I speak of was sitting harmlessly chattering to herself. They grabbed her, and my heart ached as she cried: "For God sake, ladies, don't let them beat me."
>
> "Shut up, you hussy!" said (nurse) Grady as she caught the woman by her gray hair and dragged her shrieking and pleading from the room. She was also taken to the closet, and her cries grew lower and lower, and then ceased. The nurses returned to the room and Miss Grady remarked that she had "settled the old fool for awhile." I told some of the physicians of the occurrence, but they did not pay any attention to it."

Bly was also famous for one of the most interesting stunts in journalism history. The idea came to her out of frustration, as she had not been able to think about new stories to pitch to her editors and wished she was on the other side of the world. She left November 14, 1889, and after a quick visit to Jules Verne—whose book *Around the World in 80 Days* had inspired her—she was on the other side of the world. She returned to New York, to a tumultuous welcome, on January 25, 1890, having made the tour in 72 days.

Historian Brooke Kroeger said Bly was "an exemplar of an age when American women were vigorously asserting their right—indeed, their need—to shape history itself" (Kroeger, 1995).

In the end, Pulitzer's *World* "was a monument to the idealism and patriotism of the many men from Central Europe who went to the United States . . . turn(ing) their backs upon poverty, persecution and the autocracies of Europe," said Csillag. His legacy lives on in the Pulitzer Prizes and a journalism school at Columbia University in New York.

E. W. Scripps and the first newspaper chain

He called himself a "damned old crank," and more than almost any other newspaper editor, Edward Wyllis Scripps (1854–1926) exemplified the free spirited industrial age of the press. His enormous size matched an oversized personality and his wild lifestyle matched his lack of formal education. Yet later, scientists would compare him with Aristotle and Voltaire (McCabe, 1951).

In 1872, the 18-year-old Scripps helped his brother with a fledgling newspaper, the *Detroit Tribune and Advertiser*. He launched a second newspaper, the *Penny Press*, in Cleveland in 1878 and soon began launching a chain of regional "penny press" daily newspapers. By his death in 1926, Scripps owned 25 newspapers and a wire service—the United Press—set up in 1907 to compete with the Associated Press.

A famous incident early in his career involved accusations by a competing publisher that Scripps was harboring a mistress. Scripps called a press conference to answer the charges and produced—to everyone's astonishment—the mistress herself. Both made a full confession and then said, in effect, so what?

Scripps was also known for founding the Scripps Institution of Oceanography and the Science Service. Scripps came of age at a time of great opportunity in newspaper publishing, when the voice of the working man was not often reflected in small town newspapers. Using the formula also adopted by Pulitzer and Hearst, the Scripps would print sensational anti-corruption stories in the Progressive muckraking style. Unlike Pulitzer, who stuck with St. Louis and New York, Scripps aimed for small Midwestern cities and had fairly good business sense. His newspapers stayed profitable even through the depression years when Pulitzer's *New York World* newspaper folded and Hearst's empire began crumbling.

Figure 2.15 Scientific publisher—E. W. Scripps may have been barely educated, but he understood the significance of science to the public interest, and helped establish one of the world's foremost research labs—The Scripps Oceanographic Institution. He also founded the Science News Service. He said: "It's useless to think of making the world safe for democracy without thinking of making democracy safe for itself. And the only way of making democracy thus safe is to make it more intelligent. But since to be intelligent is utterly impossible without having much of the knowledge, method and the spirit of science, the only way to make democracy safe is to make it more scientific." (Library of Congress)

Bugville and the founding of the Science Service

It was an unlikely alliance. The famously cantankerous, barely educated newspaper publisher and the zoology professor with a Harvard PhD didn't appear to have much in common when they met in the summer of 1903. But the collaboration between E. W. Scripps and William Ritter changed the American view of science and created two modern mainstays of science: the Scripps Institution of Oceanography and the Science News Service.

For some reason, Scripps got on famously with William E. Ritter, a charming and articulate scientist who had been leading summer lab classes and gathering marine specimens on the California coast when friends brought Scripps by Ritter's lab for a visit in the summer of 1903.

What fueled this friendship was a powerful idea the two men shared—a joint vision of a way to improve American life through an understanding of science. By 1907, Scripps helped Ritter set up a permanent research station on 170 acres donated (at Scripps's urging) by city of San Diego. Permanent buildings were set up in 1910. By 1912 the institution was officially the University of California's Scripps Institute for Biological Research. Scripps, however, called it "bugville" (Pauly, 2000).

Nearly every day, Scripps dropped in on Ritter unannounced at the institute. Poking his head through a door, Scripps would remove his cigar and demand of Ritter: "What is this damned human animal anyway?" Ritter would drop everything and begin talking, sometimes for the rest of the day. Their conversation could encompass anything on earth or in the oceans. "Ritter started out as early as 1901 with the idea that the biological station should be involved in physical, chemical, hydrographic and biological research," said historian Oliver Knight, "but Scripps conceived a broader role for it."

> The ideal institution that I had in view was not a school of instruction but a school of research and compilation, and of generalization. . . . I am convinced that modern civilization is the outgrowth of philosophy, religion and of codes of ethics, of customs and institutions that were founded upon known data far inferior in quantity and in quality to what science can furnish today. This data is not only inferior in quantity and quality but much of it, perhaps the greater part, is false data. As a result of this condition of affairs, the lives of most human beings are unhappy. . . .
>
> I would have a school for the study of life—and perhaps life extends far and away beyond the borders of that field which the term biology is supposed to cover. I would have a school of life, the organization of which would be divided into three departments, the lowest, the elementary department of which would be engaged in what is called research. The second department would consist of one or more men who would record, correlate, assemble and segregate into groups the facts generated by the first department.
>
> The third department would consist of men who would generalize all the information gathered and recorded and there from make deductions which would b e passed out to the world as authoritative and as the last word so far uttered concerning what is actually known in order that the people might govern their conduct individually and as social organisms according to so much of nature's law as had been discerned.

This third stage would be no mere public relations department. The public mission of science was the raison d'être for the scientific research, the driving force behind the institution. Scripps wanted it all to be so original that it would not even have a library, and in 1906 he advised Ritter against buying a collection of books. "The library you should covet should be the one that is yet unwritten and un-cataloged." Some of the ideas were too much for the University of California, and around 1915 the academics insisted on a more conventional form of organization. Scripps blamed "a bunch of wooden-headed visionless university men" for tearing up his plans and accused them of having "burned down our temple to roast a little pig."

American science was emerging at this moment in history, but few publishers other than Scripps understood what that meant, and partly as a result, few in the public understood it either. If science was even mentioned in a newspaper, "it was in terms of magic or miracles, if not mere ridicule," said historian David J. Rhees. "It was standard practice to assign the staff humorist to cover local scientific conventions." The humorists would typically comment either on the length and luxuriousness of the beards worn by the assembled scientists or on the titles of papers which contained the longest and least familiar words, Rhees observed (Rhees, 1979).

Science news in New York at the turn of the century was characterized by sensationalism at both Joseph Pulitzer's *World* and William Randolph Hearst's *Journal*.

The *World* ran a column called "Wonders of Science" that focused on exciting and miraculous discoveries. Cures for cancer, especially if they involved radiation or colored lights, were particularly favored. The news about the 1910 return of Halley's Comet, as described by one editor, involved the following elements: a picture of a pretty girl, a "good nightmare idea like the inhabitants of Mars watching (the comet) pass," pictures of scientists and "a two-column boxed 'freak' containing a scientific opinion that nobody will understand, just to give it class" (Emery, 1988). Around the same time in New York, Hearst's editors were headlining lab tests showing that oysters, ice and milk sold throughout New York city were contaminated by dangerous bacteria. The hysteria would soon lead to the hunt for Typhoid Mary.

The sensationalistic media of the era reflected, in part, the sensibilities of the working class. Yet the more science influenced their world, and the visible world of politics, the more seriously journalists began to take it. Carr Van Anda rose to the top of *The New York Times* in 1901, in part because of his advocacy of serious science coverage. He became famous for his understanding of physics and math, even at one point correcting one of Einstein's formulas that had been badly transcribed. And by the 1920s, Walter Lippmann, the last editor of Pulitzer's *World*, would advocate a place for science at the heart of American life, alongside—or even instead of—religion.

Scripps, however, was the first publisher of this era to see the impact of science on America and was appalled by the news coverage which produced only a "vast quantity of misinformation." The real "adventures," he said, "dramatic as they are, seldom find their way into print."

Scripps began thinking about other ways to further the public mission of science. In 1918, he and Ritter planned with several national science academies to begin an institution "to translate and interpret science" for the American public. A nonprofit organization was endowed by Scripps and was called the Science News Service. It began distributing the Science News-Letter in 1922. (Both the Science Service and Science News continue in the twenty-first century.)

The newsletter was often dry and formal and not calculated to appeal to the public. Its editor, Edwin Slosson, was a chemist and a literary critic, not the popularizer Scripps wanted, although he came highly recommended from the scientific societies. Astronomy and archaeology were the most popular topics for the

Yellow journalism and William Randolph Hearst's *Journal*

Legend and truth are deeply mixed in the many accounts of press baron William
Randolph Hearst (1863–1951), the famed "yellow journalism" publisher whose career
spanned the late nineteenth to the mid-twentieth century. At its height in 1935,
Hearst's media empire included 28 newspapers read by 20 million people, as well as
13 magazines, eight radio stations and the International News Service.

For biographers, Hearst is a fascinating a study in contrasts. He was a populist
reformer who championed labor unions early in his career but fought bitterly against
them when they organized in his own newspapers. He used his inherited millions to
get started in publishing and then attacked monopolies under the motto of "truth,
justice and public service." He was huge man with a tiny voice, a war hawk in Cuba in
the 1890s but a pacifist in Europe in the 1930s (Nassaw, 2001).

Winston Churchill liked him when they met in 1929, thinking of Hearst as "a grave,
simple child . . . with a strong liberal and democratic outlook." Others disliked him
immensely. Sen. Sherman Minton (D-IN) said in 1936 that he was "the greatest men-
ace to freedom of the press that exists in this country" because he used his immense
media power for propaganda. "He would not know the Goddess of Liberty if she
came down off her pedestal in New York harbor and bowed to him," Minton said,
adding with sly reference to his personal life: "He would probably try to get her phone
number" (Brendon, 1983).

After being expelled from Harvard and spending a short time at the *World* newspaper, Hearst began his career as the young publisher of the *San Francisco Examiner*
in 1887. The *Examiner* was a small paper that had been purchased by his wealthy
father, George Hurst, who owned a string of western gold, silver and copper mines
and who had began serving a term in the US Senate that year.

Hearst loved running the *Examiner*. He used Bennett's formula of sensationalism,
illustrations and personality features to attract readers. He approached subjects with
energy, enterprise and originality, urging his staff to find illustrations "to attract the
eye and stimulate the imagination." Competing papers were mostly interested in politics, and Hearst was determined to create "a revolution in the sleepy journalism" of
San Francisco (Nassaw, 2001).

For Hearst, said a detractor, journalism was "an enchanted playground in which
giants and dragons were to be slain simply for the fun of the thing; a Never-Never

Land with pirates and Indians and fairies . . . " (Creelman, 1906). In 1895, Hearst purchased the *New York Journal*, a dying daily newspaper, and began a reckless circulation war with Pulitzer's *World*. For a penny, *Journal* readers could get the same lurid crime reports, scathing editorials and personality profiles that they would find in the two-cent *World*.

Unlike Pulitzer, Hearst had no professional boundaries. He could be dishonest in his approach to journalism, having reporters write fake news stories or plagiarizing the competition when it suited him. He also "raided" the staffs of the *World* and other competing papers, sometimes doubling their salaries. One who left Pulitzer for Hearst was the *World*'s comic strip artist Richard F. Outcault, whose cartoon about life in working class New York, "Hogan's Alley," featured the Yellow Kid. Yellow ink was something of a novelty at the time, and because it was so heavily used for the comics, it came to symbolize the era's style of tawdry journalism (Moritz, 1996).

Figure 2.16 Citizen Hearst—William Randolph Hearst was a notorious but gifted editor who knew how to appeal to the most lurid instincts in mass audiences. After a career studded with personal and professional scandals, he was an inviting target for the kind of caricature presented in Orson Welles' movie Citizen Kane.

In the fall of 1896, Hearst hired a reporter (Richard Harding Davis) and an artist (Frederick Remington) to cover an insurrection in Cuba against the colonial Spanish government. The insurrection was bitterly fought, with atrocities on both sides, and 200,000 Spanish troops moved tens of thousands of civilians into "re-concentration" camps where many died of disease. The drawings and stories shocked Americans when they ran in 1897, and Hearst, indignant at the brutality, kept up the pressure.

According to one of the Hearst legends, Remington wired Hearst to say there was nothing going on, and Hearst wired back "You furnish the pictures, Ill furnish the war." The exchange is one of the best remembered anecdotes of journalism and seems in character as a description of Hearst's arrogance. But Hearst later denied writing it, and historians who examined the issue say there is no evidence to support the legend and good reason to believe it was invented (Campbell, 2003). Biographer David Nassaw said if Hearst did write the telegram, it would have referred to the existing insurrection, not plans for a coming American invasion (Nassaw, 2001). But it was true, at least, that Hearst had already inserted his newspaper into a foreign intrigue in a way that no American newspaper publisher had ever before dared.

When the battleship USS *Maine* blew up in Havana, Cuba on February 15, 1898, the incident took over the front page of the newspaper for days, with headlines blaring "Spanish Treachery" and "Work of an Enemy." Hearst offered a $50,000 reward "for the detection of the perpetrator of the Maine outrage." Pulitzer also featured full front page coverage of the disaster, but emphasized the loss of life and noted that the explosion was "Caused by Bomb or Torpedo."

The Spanish–American war and the invasion of Cuba in the spring of 1898 were not caused by Hearst's newspaper coverage, but it was a factor. Hearst's enthusiasm for the war also drew him to Cuba during the war, where he faced gunfire and even personally captured a group of unarmed Spanish sailors—making headlines in the process.

Later, Hearst's involvement in politics included two terms in Congress (1903–1907) and then unsuccessful bids for mayor of New York, Senate and a US presidential nomination. He became known as William "also-ran-dolph" Hearst. He was a conservative Democrat, supporting and then breaking away from Franklin Delano Roosevelt, lashing out at income taxes and the imposition of labor regulations.

Hearst continued to be a sensationalist and sometime reformer as publisher, but his empire started losing money in the mid-1930s. The more his empire slipped away, the more he insisted on total control of each paper's content, even including the details of which politicians or film stars to feature and which to ignore.

He was widely despised toward the end of his life for a variety of reasons, especially a 1934 visit with Nazi leader Adolph Hitler which, he said, was an attempt to influence Hitler and to save Jews. Hitler used the visit to raise Nazi credibility.

In 1941 Hearst was caricatured by radio director Orson Welles in the RKO film *Citizen Kane*. Hearst and his media empire fought back in a classic confrontation (Cramer and Lennon, 2000). *Citizen Kane* has been consistently placed as the best film of the twentieth century, yet Hearst biographer David Nassaw notes that even without a battle over *Citizen Kane* that kept it out of theaters in the 1940s, *Kane*'s dark and difficult tone made it an unlikely commercial success. Ironically, it is Welles' caricature of Hearst, not the real person, that seems to live on in the public mind.

Tabloid journalism and Alfred Harmsworth's *Daily Mail*

Catching the imagination of the reading public is not easy, but it seemed like a snap for Alfred Harmsworth, one of Britain's most powerful tabloid publishers in the early twentieth century.

Can fish speak? Do dogs commit murder? How many people cross London Bridge each day? How much gold is in the Bank of England? If you mailed in the correct response to Harmsworth's magazine *Answers*, you could win a pound a week for life.

Such were the humble arts that brought an Irishman from a modest barrister's family to the heights of British journalism. He started in 1888 as the publisher of a group of small, youth-oriented humor magazines, but by 1894, Harmsworth had two million subscribers and had amassed enough of a fortune to buy a pair of moribund Edinburgh daily newspapers.

In 1896, after agonizing over the basic layout, Harmsworth started the London *Daily Mail*—and "struck a gold mine" with a circulation of 400,000 overnight. Londoners appreciated the same harmless but attention-getting tricks used in *Answers*. As historian Piers Brendon noted, the *Daily Mail* was amusing without being vulgar and its crime stories were exciting without being lurid.

Like Pulitzer and Hearst, Harmsworth backed a small war—the Boer War in South Africa (1899–1902)—and saw circulation numbers rise to one million. By 1903 he had also started the *Daily Mirror*, originally a newspaper for women. But he found far more success by turning it into an illustrated newspaper for men and women, and within a few years it became the nation's second largest newspaper. In 1908, Harmsworth also became owner of *The Times*, London, rescuing the venerable paper from decrepitude.

Figure 2.17 Can fish speak?—Lord Northcliffe, Alfred Harmsworth, began his meteoric publishing career asking that kind of question in print. With a knack for fascinating the British public, Harmsworth started the London *Daily Mail* and "struck a gold mine."

Meanwhile, the *Daily Mail* continued with stunts and promotions, especially in the new field of aviation, offering 1,000 pounds in 1907 for the first airplane that crossed the English channel, and 10,000 pounds for a flight to Manchester. The idea seemed so preposterous that the humor magazine, *Punch*, offered 10,000 pounds for a flight to Mars. Yet that year, an airplane flew to Manchester and a few years later, another crossed the channel.

Yet there was something tepid about the stunts, which substituted for the bare-knuckled investigative journalism favored by Pulitzer and the scandal-mongering of Hearst. The problem, as he discovered investigating the Lever soap "trusts," was that British libel laws favored the plaintiff far more than the publisher.

Harmsworth's support of British cause in World War I was so well received that he was elevated to the nobility and given the title Lord Northcliffe in 1918. He died in 1922, leaving his brother in charge of the operation. Editorial policy at the *Daily Mail* shifted toward fascism with editorials like "Youth Triumphant" in support of Adolf Hitler in 1933 and "Hurrah for the Blackshirts" in 1934. Its editorial stance remained conservative, but dropped all connections to fascism, in the late 1930s.

The *Daily Mail*, the *Daily Mirror* and other associated newspapers are still leaders in British publishing today.

Media transitions: four stages of the press

Absolute censorship, partisan media, the "commercial popular press," and "organized intelligence"

Figure 2.18 Walter Lippmann (1889–1974) was the last editorial page editor of Pulitzer's *New York World*, and after it collapsed in 1932, was a leading national author and columnist for the next four decades. He was a champion of liberal democracy, the scientific world view and the social responsibility of the press. It was Lippmann who coined the term "Great Society" that President Lyndon Johnson embraced in the 1960s.

Twentieth-century American journalist Walter Lippmann described what he saw as the three formative stages of the press—Authoritarian, Partisan and Commercial. Lippmann saw the commercial (or "penny") press as most beneficial to democracy, in that it freed the mass media from political party allegiances. But that form of press was too flawed to really fulfill its democratic role. Lippmann also foresaw a fourth stage of the press that he called "organized intelligence" (Lippmann, 1922).

Later, refining the idea, Lippmann saw a transition from the "romantic art" of the commercial penny press and yellow journalism era. "The new coming journalism is less temperamental. It deals with more solid realities. Journalism in the next epoch is inclined to become less Napoleonic at the top and less Bohemian at the bottom" ("Lippmann Sees end of Yellow Press," *New York Times*, January 13, 1931).

Another vision of the transition from authoritarian to commercial culture was offered by Jürgen Habermas, a twentieth-century philosopher. Habermas believed that authoritarian press was part of a "representational" culture that was akin to feudalism and designed to overwhelm the audience. The partisan press from the early 1700s onward (in England) and 1800s (in Europe) helped develop the "public sphere" of debate and dialogue, but the shift to commercial media diluted and corrupted the public sphere and undermined social progress. In an ideal speech situation, everyone would have equal access to media and an ability to contribute to social consensus, but commercialization undermined that idea (Habermas, 1991).

The visions of both Lippmann and Habermas would be realized, to some extent, in the late twentieth century as the World Wide Web enabled one-to-one and many-to-many communications. Computers became the most powerful tools for organizing intelligence that had ever been devised. And yet, the deterioration of consensus in the public sphere and the long slow decline of the news media would demonstrate that technological advances do not provide simple solutions to complex social problems.

3

Print media in the twentieth and twenty-first centuries

Th' newspaper does ivrything f'r us. It runs th' polis foorce an' th' banks, commands th' milishy, conthrols th' ligislachure, baptizes th' young, marries th' foolish, comforts th' afflicted, afflicts th' comfortable, buries th' dead an' roasts thim aftherward. They ain't annything it don't turn its hand to . . . They used to say a man's life was a closed book. So it is—but it's an open newspaper. (Finley Peter Dunne, 1902)

The printing revolution's last century

Publishers were at the top of their games at the beginning of the twentieth century. The technology was mature, profits were high and most cities were served by two or more locally owned daily newspapers.

By the 1970s, following a series of technology-driven mergers, most cities ended up with only one newspaper. Then, by the early twenty-first century, a familiar story played out: A profitable monopoly had underestimated the digital revolution and missed the curve in the road. US newspapers had lost one quarter of their readers, half of their advertising and 80 percent of their stock value. The free press as an institution, created in the Enlightenment to guide the democratic experiment, was in deep trouble.

If it were some other near-monopoly, the turmoil created by technological change might simply be inconvenient. But a nosedive in US newspaper publishing, along with declines in magazine and book publishing, had far more serious implications.

"The loss of newspapers translates to a loss of journalism," said a report by the University of Virginia's Miller Center in 2010. The capacity for public information was being lost, and a greater opportunity for government corruption was fostered when journalists could no longer serve as "watchdogs" of public institutions (Miller Center, 2010).

The UVA report echoed concerns from a half century earlier, expressed by the University of Chicago's Hutchins Commission, that the free press was being imperiled by accelerating technology and irresponsible publishers.

To understand what was at risk, this chapter considers some of the outstanding contributions of the twentieth-century press. During the "muckraking" period, the world wars, and the Civil Rights era, the press served as the eyes and ears of the pubic, the conscience of the nation, and occasionally even heroes to readers. The Vietnam–Watergate era tested that status. But in the twenty-first century, economic problems and declining readership meant increasing concern not only about the press but also the perils of uninformed partisanship.

The muckraking message 1900–1915

In first decade of the twentieth century, a young journalist named Will Irwin took off across the country in search of the American press. In a 14-part series published in *Collier's Magazine*, Irwin concluded that the press was "wonderfully able, wonderfully efficient, and wonderfully powerful (but) with real faults."

Yellow journalism, especially the tendency of publishers like William Randolph Hearst to trump up news for personal or partisan reasons, counted as one of the faults. But to Irwin, the biggest fault was that the press did not speak to his generation:

> It is the mouthpiece of an older stock. It lags behind the thought of its times. . . .
> To us of this younger generation, our daily press is speaking, for the most part,
> with a dead voice, because the supreme power resides in men of that older gen-
> eration. (Irwin, 1911)

Irwin put the blame on the Associated Press. No one could start a newspaper without telegraphic news services, and yet existing AP members were blackballing new start-up newspapers. "Until something happens to break the . . . AP monopoly, the way to journalism will be barred . . . for the young man of brains, enterprise and purpose." (See Chapter 7 for more about the AP/Western Union monopoly.)

Figure 3.1 Spirit of reform—Will Irwin's path-breaking 1910 magazine series on American newspapers found that they had many faults, especially since they spoke with the "dead voice" of an older generation. Irwin blamed the Associated Press.

In Irwin's view, the twentieth-century spirit of reform could be seen in magazines like *Cosmopolitan, Collier's Weekly, McClure's Magazine* and *Munsey's Magazine*. While there had been a few exposes in newspapers, nothing matched the magazine revelations about child labor, slum housing, tainted meat, political graft, insurance fraud, narcotic medicines and the corrupt Standard Oil monopoly.

The exposes were needed because the system had failed, S. S. McClure wrote in his magazine in January 1903. Lawyers, judges, churches and colleges— all were failing to uphold the law. The burden of reform had fallen to the people (Kochersberger, 1996; Tebbel and Zuckerman, 1991). But while they were determined to expose the evils of the system, the magazine reformers were not revolutionaries and had no intention of overthrowing the government. In fact, most of them saw then-president

Theodore Roosevelt as an ally. After all, as police commissioner in New York, he had walked slum alleys with photographer Jacob Riis, and as president, he had responded to the exposes by fighting for legislation that would reign in corporate abuses. He had even written for *McClure's* about social reform (Roosevelt, 1901).

Even so, by 1906, reform journalism had shaken the nation's business and political institutions to the core, and questions about social stability were being raised. Roosevelt hoped to ease some fears when he laid the cornerstone of the Cannon Congressional House Office Building on the morning of April 14, 1906. The speech is considered among the most important in American history. Writers who exposed social ills in magazines and newspapers, Roosevelt said, were useful, but they had to be careful not to go too far. They should not act as the "man with the muck rake" in *Pilgrim's Progress*, a well-known English moral allegory from 1678.

Roosevelt's "muckraker" speech instantly galvanized a national debate about the role of the press. Some warned that muckraking was being used to stir up agitators. Others said muckrakers were doing much-needed work, performing "an immense and beneficial revolution."

"The President was not particularly happy in his inspiration," *The New York Times* said in a critical tone, noting that he only seemed to approve of journalists when they did not go too far.

McClure's writer Lincoln Steffens, who specialized in exposing political corruption in Midwestern cities, said Roosevelt's speech was misunderstood by the bankers and the railroad men. "They rejoiced. Some of them laughed at me, saying the president had taken a fall out of me." And he told Roosevelt: "Well, you have put an end to all these journalistic investigations that have made (helped) you" (*The New York Times*, April 17, 1906).

William Allen White, a nationally famous editor from Emporia, Kansas, wrote humorously that Steffens had been through Kansas on a special train that carried his enormous muckrake. "It was a fierce looking instrument as it lay on its flat cars, teeth upward and menacing . . . Though dulled from recent use, [the teeth] still retain, on their blunted points, the hair and whiskers and fragmentary remains of a number of Congressmen," he joked (*Washington Post*, May 18, 1906).

White's humor approached a difficult subject, but David Graham Phillips, a writer for Hearst's *Cosmopolitan* magazine, was far more blunt. He said that Roosevelt's speech had been politically calculated to ease fears of Roosevelt's allies in Congress who had come under fire for corruption. The term muckraker was "an easy phrase of repeated attack upon what was in general a good journalistic movement." And a *New York Times* writer, Perry Belmont, noted that the "cue seems now to have been given to assume a tone of indignation at the turning of the searchlight of criticism upon all those holding public positions" (*The New York Times*, April 16, 1906).

By 1914, the era of American muckraking was over, ended in part by libel suits, magazine mergers, Roosevelt's criticism, public opinion fatigued by crusading reformers, and the onset of World War I (Miraldi, 1988). Historian Mark Feldstein has observed that investigative reporting tends to appear in times when social conditions create a demand for information and new media technologies and media competition create the means to transmit the information. Those conditions were met in the American Revolution and the muckraking era, and would not return until the 1970s with the Watergate investigations (Feldstein, 2006).

"The Man with the Muckrake," President Theodore Roosevelt, April 14, 1906

Figure 3.2 Theodore Roosevelt c. 1906. (Library of Congress)

In Bunyan's "Pilgrim's Progress" you may recall the description of the Man with the Muck Rake, the man who could look no way but downward, with the muck rake in his hand . . . The Man with the Muck Rake is set forth as the example of him whose vision is fixed on carnal instead of spiritual things. Yet he also typifies the man who in this life consistently refuses to see aught that is lofty, and fixes his eyes with solemn intentness only on that which is vile and debasing.

Now, it is very necessary that we should not flinch from seeing what is vile and debasing. There is filth on the floor, and it must be scraped up with the muck rake; and there are times and places where this service is the most needed of all the services that can be performed. But the man who never does anything else, who never thinks or speaks or writes, save of his feats with the muck rake, speedily becomes, not a help but one of the most potent forces for evil.

There are in the body politic, economic and social, many and grave evils, and there is urgent necessity for the sternest war upon them. There should be relentless exposure of and attack upon every evil man, whether politician or business man, every evil practice, whether in politics, business, or social life. I hail as a benefactor every writer or speaker, every man who, on the platform or in a book, magazine, or newspaper, with merciless severity makes such attack, provided always that he in his turn remembers that the attack is of use only if it is absolutely truthful.

At this moment we are passing through a period of great unrest-social, political, and industrial unrest. It is of the utmost importance for our future that this should prove to be not the unrest of mere rebelliousness against life, of mere dissatisfaction with the inevitable inequality of conditions, but the unrest of a resolute and eager ambition to secure the betterment of the individual and the nation.

So far as this movement of agitation throughout the country takes the form of a fierce discontent with evil, of a determination to punish the authors of evil, whether in industry or politics, the feeling is to be heartily welcomed as a sign of healthy life.

If, on the other hand, it turns into a mere crusade of appetite against appetite, of a contest between the brutal greed of the "have nots" and the brutal greed of the "haves," then it has no significance for good, but only for evil. If it seeks to establish a line of cleavage, not along the line which divides good men from bad, but along that other line, running at right angles thereto, which divides those who are well off from those who are less well off, then it will be fraught with immeasurable harm to the body politic.

The men of wealth who today are trying to prevent the regulation and control of their business in the interest of the public by the proper government authorities will not succeed, in my judgment, in checking the progress of the movement. But if they did succeed they would find that they had sown the wind and would surely reap the whirlwind, for they would ultimately provoke the violent excesses which accompany a reform coming by convulsion instead of by steady and natural growth.

On the other hand, the wild preachers of unrest and discontent, the wild agitators against the entire existing order, the men who act crookedly, whether because of sinister design or from mere puzzle headedness, the men who preach destruction without proposing any substitute for what they intend to destroy, or who propose a substitute which would be far worse than the existing evils—all these men are the most dangerous opponents of real reform. If they get their way they will lead the people into a deeper pit than any into which they could fall under the present system. If they fail to get their way they will still do incalculable harm by provoking the kind of reaction which in its revolt against the senseless evil of their teaching would enthrone more securely than ever the evils which their misguided followers believe they are attacking.

Who were the muckrakers?

Widely admired for their exposes of monopolies and corrupt public officials, the "muckrakers" were an eclectic group of writers, journalists and social reformers who led the Progressive reform movement of the early 1900s. They used investigative journalism (muckraking) to go beyond standard inquiries and uncover hidden problems.

Social reform was not a new idea for the press in the early 1900s. For example, *The New York Times* investigations in the 1870s helped curb the corruption centered around the city's Tammany Hall politics (Burrows and Wallace, 1999). In the 1880s, Henry Demerest Lloyd investigated grain and oil monopolies for the *Chicago Tribune*, and then worked with Jane Addams of the Hull House movement to fight child labor and poor working conditions (Lloyd, 1912).

Magazines and alternative media were often the only resort for investigative reporters since in many cases the news media was part of the problem. Ida Tarbell found that Standard Oil was paying newspapers in Ohio for continued favorable coverage, and Samuel Hopkins Adams found that patent medicine advertisers had contracts with many newspapers forbidding unfavorable publicity.

Figure 3.3 Ida B. Wells Baker-Barnett

Ida B. Wells Baker-Barnett (1862–1931)— An African American editor of *Free Speech* newspaper in Memphis, TN, Wells investigated the 1891 lynching of three innocent men at the hands of a white mob. Her newspaper was burned down and she had to flee to New York where she became one of the most influential leaders in the early civil rights movement.

Samuel Hopkins Adams (1871–1958)—In "The Great American Fraud," a series for *Collier's Magazine* in 1905, Adams exposed

Figure 3.4 Lincoln Steffens

Figure 3.5 Ida Tarbell

Figure 3.6 Upton Sinclair

dangerous narcotics and false advertising by the patent medicine industry, contributing (with Sinclair) to public opinion for establishing the Food and Drug Administration.

Lincoln Steffens (1866–1936)—"The Shame of the Cities" was the title of Steffens's 1904 series on municipal corruption for *McClure's Magazine*.

Cecil Chesterton (1879–1918)—As a reporter for London's *New Witness*, Chesterton exposed stock fraud and insider trading in the Marconi Scandal of 1912. French newspaper *Le Matin* also participated in the investigation.

Ida Tarbell (1857–1944)—Standard Oil company's rise to monopoly power through corrupt business practices was the theme of Tarbell's 1902 series in *McClure's Magazine*. Her findings were confirmed by Congressional investigations and as a result, antitrust laws were enforced to end the company's monopoly.

David Graham Phillips (1867–1911)—In "Treason of the Senate," a 1906 series in the Hearst-owned *Cosmopolitan* magazine, Phillips exposed senators who had taken direct bribes and campaign contributions by major corporations such as Standard Oil Co.

Upton Sinclair (1878–1968)—"The Jungle," a 1906 novel about grotesque conditions in the meat packing industry of Chicago, was based on investigations by Sinclair for the Socialist magazine *Appeal to Reason*. The resulting public uproar led to the establishment of the Food and Drug Administration.

World War I 1915–1920s

As they skirted French defenses to cross Belgium in August of 1914, German armies carried out carefully planned reprisals, executing thousands of civilians and burning entire towns to the ground. Although they intended to bully the Belgians into submission, the Germans, historian Barbara Tuchman said, "shocked the world of 1914, which had still believed in human progress" (Tuchman, 1962).

Among the witnesses to the atrocities were a remarkable group of American reporters, including Will Irwin and Richard Harding Davis. Because America was neutral, and had a large German population thought to be sympathetic to Germany, the reporters had been given permission to follow along. What they wrote, however, did anything but encourage sympathy. Davis' report on the atrocities in Louvain, a Belgian town of 42,000, is a classic of vivid reporting:

> Outside the station in the public square, the people of Louvain passed in an unending procession, women bareheaded, weeping, men carrying the children asleep on their shoulders, all hemmed in by the shadowy army of gray wolves . . . It was all like a scene upon the stage, unreal, inhuman. You felt it could not be true. You felt that the curtain of fire, purring and crackling and sending up hot sparks to meet the kind, calm stars, was only a painted backdrop; that the reports of rifles from the dark ruins came from blank cartridges, and that these trembling shopkeepers and peasants ringed in bayonets would not in a few minutes really die, but that they themselves and their homes would be restored to their wives and children. You felt it was only a nightmare, cruel and uncivilized. And then you remembered that the German Emperor has told us what it is. It is his Holy War. (*New York Tribune*, August 31, 1914)

The Berliner Tageblatt reported the situation in Belgium from a much different perspective:

> German refugees from Belgium are still coming to our office and reporting to us the terrible but true stories of Belgian fanaticism. A German butcher in the Rue Saint-Pierre in Brussels was literally cut to pieces by a wild mob. The crazed people shouted that they would give him a death in keeping with his trade. . . . (*Berliner Tageblatt*, August 12, 1914 in Snyder and Morris, 1962)

Questions about the veracity of these accounts led to inquiries by British and Belgian governments and interviews with over a thousand witnesses (Bryce, 1914). Their reports, along with eyewitness stories by journalists, had an important impact on public opinion in the United States and other neutral countries.

For the first time, governments issued blanket censorship regulations and put news correspondents into army uniforms. The Defense of the Realm Act in Britain and similar censorship laws in France literally left "large blank spaces" in newspapers (*The New York Times*, October 5, 1917). Censorship also meant that newspapers like *L'Homme Libre* could be suspended from publication by the French government for criticism of war readiness. That paper's editor, Georges Clemenceau, had spent the 1870s in political exile in New York and had returned to edit *L'Aurore* during the Dreyfus affair. Despite his struggle against government repression of the media, Clemenceau rode the French political roller coaster to become prime minister in 1917.

It seems ironic that Clemenceau, once an oppressed editor himself, would support censorship as a politician. Yet one wartime scandal—the 1917 Bolo Pasha attempt to insert German propaganda into the French press—explains some of his motivation.

The Bolo Pasha affair was a wartime German plot to finance the purchase of French newspapers using millions of dollars funneled through American banks. A German agent, Bolo Pasha, purchased a French newspaper, *Le Journal*, to deliberately advocate surrender to the Germans. The plot was discovered, in part by still-neutral American authorities, and the French executed Pasha for treason in 1917. When the war was over, someone asked Clemenceau if he would end censorship. "Do you think I'm a total idiot?" was his response.

Despite neutrality, most Americans sided with the British and French in the 1914–1917 period. One exception was newspaper chain publisher William Randolph Hearst, whose pacifism and pro-German stand infuriated the British. Long before the United States entered the war, correspondents for Hearst's International News Service (INS) were banned from France, and INS continued to cover it from behind German lines, sending dispatches back to the United States by way of the powerful radio transmitter in Nauheim, Germany. The Germans also supplied film for Hearst's newsreels, shown in theaters across the United States.

After the United States declared war in 1917, the attorney general's office investigated Hearst for his frequent meetings with Bolo Pasha, although no criminal charges were ever made. Hearst biographer David Nassaw said Hearst did not realize that Bolo Pasha was a German agent, or that his own correspondents and film distributors were on the German government payroll. When these facts were revealed, the impact on Hearst's reputation and his editorial staff was "devastating" (Nassaw, 2001).

The war era in the United States was marked by the arrest and persecution of thousands of dissidents under the Espionage Act of 1917 (Zinn, 1980). The Post Office banned German language and dissident newspapers from the mails, which usually meant bankruptcy. The German-language *New Yorker Staats-Zeitung* (one of hundreds of German language US newspapers at the time) noted constant attacks "upon everything that talks German or sounds German . . . Our America is to become an America that is strictly English from top to bottom. An America in which but one God, one language, one way of thinking and of living is to be allowed" (*The New York Times*, "Fears Racial Strife Here," August 23, 1917, p. 3).

The American media disliked World War I censorship and the morale-boosting, publication-censoring Committee on Public Information (also discussed in Chapter 6). "Why pay for comedy when we have a Creel Committee?" asked a *Washington Post* reporter, complaining about ham-fisted and illogical war censorship.

George Seldes, a reporter with the *Atlanta Constitution* and other newspapers, wrote of one important incident illustrating the counterproductive nature of front line censorship. On November 12, 1918, the day after Armistice, Seldes and three other reporters drove through German lines and found Field Marshall Paul von Hindenburg. "The American attack won the war," Hindenburg told the correspondents. The incident is important, Seldes said, because Hindenburg acknowledged that the war was won in the field, and did not make excuses or blame some kind of betrayal from the home front (Seldes, 1987).

When Seldes and the others filed their stories, US censors in Paris blocked them. Later, the Nazis would use the Dolchstoss, the "stab-in-the-back" myth by Jews in Germany, to explain away the German defeat in World War I. "If the Hindenburg confession had been passed (by US censors), it would have been headlined in every country . . . and become an important page in history," Seldes said later. Of course no one realized the full significance of the episode at the time, but in retrospect, Seldes

Figure 3.7 Censored Doughboys—American soldiers were not allowed to be seen drinking liquor. This 1918 photo was banned by US censors even though the beer steins were empty (Photo by US Army Signal Corps). Heavy handed censorship had more serious consequences as well, such as when censors blocked Field Marshall Paul Von Hindenburg's admission that the American attack won the war. Later, the Nazis explained the defeat as a stab in the back, a Dolchstoss, and this myth helped propel them to power.

said: "I believe it would have destroyed the main planks of the platform on which Hitler rose to power" (Seldes, 1987).

Journalist and novelist Ernest Hemingway also recalled the difficulty of describing the horror of war under censorship. "WWI was the most murderous, mismanaged butchery that has ever taken place on earth," Hemingway wrote. "Any writer who said otherwise lied. So the writers either wrote propaganda, shut up, or fought" (Hemingway, 1942).

The press in the Russian communist revolution

The first step in the Russian Revolution, according to Vladimir Ilyich Lenin, was to create a newspaper, and Lenin created a paper called *Iskra* (Spark). Not only would it carry the communist message, but the act of working for a newspaper in itself would transform the revolutionaries. In "Where to Begin," Lenin wrote in 1901:

The mere technical task of regularly supplying the newspaper with copy and of promoting regular distribution will necessitate a network of local agents of the united party . . . This work will train and bring into the foreground not only the most skillful propagandists, but the most capable organizers, the most talented party leaders, capable, at the right moment, of releasing the slogan for the decisive struggle and of taking the lead in that struggle. (Lenin, 1901)

The significance of the media in the Russian communist revolution did not mean that Lenin supported free speech. Quite the reverse, in fact. Leading Russian newspapers like *Pravda* ("Truth") and *Izvestia* ("News") became tightly run organs of the state bureaucracy, and no publication was permitted to print anything remotely critical about Russia or communism. Absolute censorship was enforced with prison sentences and summary execution during Russia's communist period (1917–1991). Lenin explained:

In capitalist usage, freedom of the press means freedom of the rich to bribe the press, freedom to use their wealth to shape and fabricate so-called public opinion . . . With the aid of plausible, fine-sounding, but thoroughly false phrases, [people are diverted] from the concrete historical task of liberating the press from capitalist enslavement. (Lenin, 1919)

Figure 3.8 Soviet revolutionary press—this impossible scene of a "mobile newsroom" belonging to the newspaper "Kolhoznik" (agricultural cooperative) near Kiev was staged around 1925. The banner behind the typesetters reads: "Let us secure the financial basis for Socialist way of life." The newspaper itself probably served to inform and to engage the workers, but the photo of journalists setting type on a truck in a wheat field is a classic example of Soviet communist propaganda. (FSA Collection, Library of Congress)

Some, like German communist revolutionary Rosa Luxemburg, argued that suppression of free speech in Russia was not only wrong but self-defeating. In 1916, Luxemburg said:

> Freedom only for the supporters of the government, only for the members of a party—however numerous they may be—is no freedom at all. Freedom is always the freedom of the dissenter. Not because of the fanaticism of "justice", but rather because all that is instructive, wholesome, and purifying in political freedom depends on this essential characteristic, and its effects cease to work when "freedom" becomes a privilege . . . Without general elections, without unrestricted freedom of press and assembly, without a free struggle of opinion, life dies out in every public institution, becomes a mere semblance of life, in which only the bureaucracy remains as the active element. (Anderson, 2004)

An American journalist who initially sympathized with the communist revolution was John Reed (1887–1920), who wrote a firsthand account of the Russian Revolution of 1917 that has become a classic of literary journalism. In *Ten Days That Shook the World*, Reed said he "tried to see events with the eye of a conscientious reporter, interested in setting down the truth."

Reed died in 1920 and is the only American to be buried in the Kremlin Wall. American diplomat George F. Kennan said later: "Reed's account . . . rises above every

Ten Days That Shook the World

"As we came out into the dark and gloomy day all around the grey horizon, factory whistles were blowing, a hoarse and nervous sound, full of foreboding. By tens of thousands, the working people poured out, men and women; by tens of thousands the humming slums belched out their dun and miserable hordes. Red Petrograd was in danger! Cossaks! South and south-west they poured through the shabby streets towards the Moskovsky Gate, men women and children, with rifles, picks, spades, rolls of barbed wire, cartridge-belts over their working clothes . . . They rolled along torrent-like, companies of soldiers borne with them, bungs, motor-trucks wagons—the revolutionary proletariat defending with its breath the capital of the Workers and Peasants Republic!" (Reed, 1919, p. 171)

Figure 3.9 *Ten Days That Shook the World*—John Reed's classic eyewitness account of the 1917 Russian Revolution won worldwide acclaim, and an introduction by Vladimir Lenin, but was banned by Soviet premier Joseph Stalin. Although Reed sympathized with the revolution, his aim was to tell the story as truthfully as possible.

other contemporary record for its literary power, its penetration, its command of detail. . . . (It is) a reflection of blazing honesty and a purity of idealism that did unintended credit to the American society that produced him, the merits of which he himself understood so poorly" (Kennan, 1989).

Repression of the media in Russia should be seen against the backdrop of a ruthless suppression of all political dissent known as the "Great Purge." During the dictatorship of Joseph Stalin, from the 1922 through 1953, no fewer than 15 million people died as a result of execution, or at prison camps, or due to forced famine (Conquest, 1990). Although the news media in the United States and Europe frequently reported on the repression, there were some, like *New York Times* correspondent Walter Duranty, who sympathized with Stalin and claimed the reports were exaggerated. A posthumous investigation of Duranty's 1932 Pulitzer Prize ended with the conclusion that he had been a willing tool of Stalinist propaganda and had produced "some of the worst reporting in this newspaper" (*The New York Times*, June 24, 1990).

Under subsequent Russian dictators from the 1950s through the early 1980s, repression was lighter but no less real, forcing writers underground, where they fell back on Medieval hand-copying of manuscripts to pass among small circles of readers. These manuscripts were called "samizdats" (same-as-that). In the late 1980s, Soviet Premier Michael Gorbachev began ending repressive policies and by 1991 the Soviet Union of Russia and 14 other nations was dissolved. Freedom of the press remains an elusive goal in many of these nations, as Reporters Without Borders, Article 19 and other international groups continue to document.

The press in India's nonviolent revolution

Like Vladimir Lenin, Mohandas (Mahatma) Gandhi also believed that one of the first steps in a revolution was to create a newspaper. In contrast to Lenin, however, Gandhi believed in democracy and nonviolence. He had a deep faith that good ideas would win converts, and that struggle for the liberation of India from British rule could take place with journalism helping to explain the struggle.

Born in India and trained in law in Britain, Gandhi began working as an attorney in South Africa and founded a newspaper called *Indian Opinion* in 1903. He thought it was critical to have the publication in order to explain Satyagraha, the principle behind nonviolent social revolution. Later, when he returned to India, Gandhi founded the weekly *Young India* to promote views on political reform, religious tolerance and economic self-sufficiency for India. The publication changed its name to *Harijan*, which meant "Children of God." It was published from 1919 through 1948. Gandhi also edited four other journals during his long career (Guha, 2003).

"Week after week I poured out my soul in columns expounding my principles and practices of Satyagraha," Gandhi said. "The journal became for me a training in self-restraint, and for friends a medium through which to keep in touch with my thoughts." In his autobiography, Gandhi said that "Satyagraha would probably have been impossible without *Indian Opinion*."

Figure 3.10 Power of truth—Mohandas (Mahatma) Gandhi, writing around 1946. Among many other accomplishments, Gandhi edited half a dozen newspapers during his long career as the leader for India's independence movement. (Library of Congress)

Journalism taught Gandhi the discipline of being fair and remaining cool even when he was attacked, said Shall Sinha, a Gandhi biographer. "It helped him clarify his own ideas and visions, to stay on track, to be consistent, to assume full accountability for his actions and words . . . The newspapers brought Gandhi in close communication with many deep thinkers and spiritual leaders. It kept broadening his horizon every-day. Gandhi pursued journalism not for its sake but also as an aid to what he had conceived to be his mission in life: to teach by example and precept" (Sinha, 2010).

Chicago Tribune correspondent William L. Shirer followed Gandhi for several years in India. "For those of us who glimpsed, however briefly, Gandhi's use of (Satyagraha); and who had the luck, for however short a time, to feel his greatness . . . it was an experience that enriched and deepened our lives as no other did" (Shirer, 1986). That experience, he said, helped him find the moral courage to describe the terror creeping over Germany in the 1930s when he worked for the Associated Press and CBS radio.

The German press and the Nazi revolution

It was a scene not witnessed since the Middle Ages: the flames engulfing tens of thousands of German books in May of 1933 seemed ominous harbingers of disaster to William L. Shirer, the Associated Press correspondent for Germany. The descent into barbarism began the moment that Nazi leaders decided that the arts, literature, the press, radio and films would exist only to serve the purpose of Nazi propaganda, he said.

Following the Reich Press Law of October, 1933, the country's 4,700 newspapers were either closed, confiscated or directly controlled by the Nazi party. Most notably, the Nazis closed *Vossische Zeitung*, a newspaper founded in 1704 and, at that moment in history, comparable to *The Times* of London or the *New York Times*. *Berliner Tageblatt*, one of Germany's original "penny press" papers, was another of many confiscated by Nazi party leaders. Editors who dared even the mildest criticism were sent to concentration camps (Shirer, 1960).

One notable dissent involved the printing and distribution of leaflets by German students in the White Rose movement. The pamphlets said "we will not be silent" in the face of "abominable crimes." Three students and a professor at the University of Munich were executed by order of a Nazi court in 1943 (Axelrod, 2001).

The Nazis also produced some of the most infamous newspapers in history, such as *Der Stürmer* which specialized in crude, vivid and vicious anti-Semitism. "Jewish murder plan against Gentile humanity" was one particularly virulent headline. The only solution, this newspaper often said, was "the extermination of the people whose father is the devil." The newspaper was published between 1922 and February, 1945, when editor Julius Streicher was sentenced to death for crimes against humanity. Streicher's final indictment at the Nuremberg War Crimes Tribunal in 1946 noted his incitement to murder and extermination, which "clearly constitutes persecution on political and racial grounds . . . a crime against humanity" (Bytwerk, 2001).

Nothing like *Der Stürmer* would be seen again on the world scene until the newspaper *Kangura*, published in Rwanda in the early 1990s, advocated genocide of Tutsi people. In 1994, an estimated 800,000 were killed by Hutus at the urging of *Kangura* and Radio Rwanda. *Kangura*'s editor, Hassan Ngeze, along with broadcast colleagues, was convicted of crimes against humanity by the International Criminal Tribunal for Rwanda and sentenced to life imprisonment, reaffirming the international legal principle that leaders of the mass media organizations can be held responsible for inciting genocide (Melvern, 2004).

The American press in World War II

The threat to freedom was never more clear than in the 1940s, and news correspondents willingly lent their talent to the allied war effort to stop fascism in Germany, Italy and Japan. Censorship was confined primarily to military security, although anything that depicted the enemy as human—for instance, the German army's routine compliance with truce agreements to recover wounded after battles—was subject to military censorship.

Censorship barely held down the cantankerous American press. A furious controversy raged on the home front over war preparedness and prewar conspiracies between American and German industries such as Standard Oil (Exxon) and I. G. Farben. Incidents from the front lines, such as Gen. George Patton slapping shell-shocked soldiers in hospitals, were picked up by muckraking columnists like Drew Pearson (Pearson, 1943).

Censorship was not as heavy handed in World War II as in other wars. One of most popular writers of World War II, Ernie Pyle (1900–1945), described this scene as the Allied armada sailed from North Africa to invade Sicily in 1943.

> The night before we sailed, the crew listened as usual to the German propaganda radio program which featured Midge, the American girl turned Nazi, who was trying to scare them, disillusion them and depress them. As usual they laughed with amusement and scorn at her childishly treasonable talk. In a vague and indirect way, I suppose, the privilege of listening to your enemy trying to undermine you— the very night before you go out to face him—expresses what we are fighting for. (Pyle, 1944)

Figure 3.11 Soldier's scribe—Ernie Pyle's columns for Scripps-Howard newspapers earned a Pulitzer Prize in 1944 and the devotion of US soldiers everywhere. He told stories about the regular guys slogging through the war rather than the great general and the grand strategies. (Courtesy of the University of Indiana)

Pyle had drawn from his experience as a correspondent roving across America in a station wagon with his wife in the 1930s, writing about conversations with all kinds of people (Pyle, 1935). During the war, Pyle used the same technique, focusing on the stories of ordinary soldiers rather than important generals and big strategies. In one often-quoted piece, "The God-Damned Infantry," Pyle wrote:

> There is an agony in your heart and you almost feel ashamed to look at them. They are just guys from Broadway and Main Street, but you wouldn't remember them. They are too far away now. They are too tired. Their world can never be known to you, but if you could see them just once, just for an instant, you would know that no matter how hard people work back home they are not keeping pace with these infantrymen. (Pyle, 2000)

Figure 3.12 War correspondent—only three years out of journalism school, Marguerite Higgins convinced editors at the *Herald Tribune* to send her to Europe in 1944. She also broke barriers for women reporters everywhere, convincing Gen. Douglas MacArthur to lift the ban on women correspondents in the Korean War in 1950.

Pyle died covering the troops in the fight on the Pacific island of le Shima in 1945. A memorial there reads: "At this spot the 77th Infantry Division lost a buddy, Ernie Pyle."

Women also covered the war, as historians Maurine H. Beasley and Sheila J. Gibbons pointed out in *Taking Their Place* (Beasley and Gibbons, 1993). Among the best known was Marguerite Higgins (1920–1966), a writer for the *New York Herald Tribune* who witnessed the liberation of the Dachau concentration camp in late April, 1945. "The liberation was a frenzied scene," she wrote. "Inmates of the camp hugged and embraced the American troops, kissed the ground before them and carried them shoulder high around the place." Higgens went on to win a Pulitzer Prize for coverage of the Korean War.

The African American press was initially divided over support for World War II. After all, in World War I, critical reporting on military race riots landed a black editor in jail under the Sedition Act. Simple concern for social reform led to investigations for disloyalty by the FBI (Washburn, 1986). The African American press settled on a dual strategy—the "Double V" campaign—which called for victory over the enemies of democracy both abroad and at home.

Reconstructing the German and Japanese press after the war was a special problem. A program to pay thousands of independent journalists and rebuild newspaper publishing operations cost the US government millions of dollars, according to historian Robert McChesney. At one point in the summer of 1945, then-general Dwight D. Eisenhower "called in German reporters and told them he wanted a free press. If he made decisions that they disagreed with, he wanted them to say so in print . . . " Gen. Douglas MacArthur took the same approach in Japan. "Eisenhower and MacArthur did not wait for the market to come up with fixes," McChesney said. "The work of establishing a free and independent press was too vital a task for that" (McChesney, 2010).

Press responsibility and the 1947 Hutchins Commission

During and after World War II, questions about press responsibility led to a commission financed by *Time Magazine* publisher Henry Luce. Leading the commission was Robert Maynard Hutchins, then chancellor at the University of Chicago, whose ideas about education had focused on communication as central to a lifetime of learning.

The Hutchins Commission found that freedom of expression had been imperiled by accelerating technology and by arrogant and irresponsible publishers. The commission urged publishers to "regard themselves as common carriers of information and discussion" and recommended five major points that it said society was entitled to demand of its press:

(1) a truthful, comprehensive, and intelligent account of the day's events in a context which gives them meaning;
(2) a forum for the exchange of comment and criticism;
(3) the projection of a representative picture of the constituent groups in the society;
(4) the presentation and clarification of the goals and values of the society; and
(5) full access to the day's intelligence.

"Where freedom of expression exists, the beginnings of a free society and a means for every extension of liberty are already present. Free expression is therefore unique among liberties: it promotes and protects all the rest," the commission said (Hutchins, 1947).

The commission's point about projecting a representative picture of constituent groups in society was especially troubling for the press in the 1950s and 60s as it grappled with new demands for equality from African Americans. The commission had said that it "holds to the faith that if people are exposed to the inner truth of the life of a particular group, they will gradually build up respect for and understanding of it." In effect, civil rights was the crucial test of what Thomas Jefferson had called the great experiment.

The press and civil rights

One of the finest moments in the history of the mainstream American press was its response to the civil rights movement that culminated in the 1950s and 60s. To understand that moment, however, it's important to understand that civil rights advocates had a long history of pleading their own cause in their own press for a century and a half before they were widely noticed.

Starting in 1827, with the founding of *Freedom's Journal* in New York, the African American press fought slavery and prejudice with low budgets and high expectations. "We wish to plead our own cause," said John Russworm, said the short-lived journal's editor. Several other small papers emerged in the pre-Civil War era, but none better known than the *North Star*, published from 1847 through the mid-1860s by former slave Frederick Douglass. A fiery orator and passionate writer, Douglass wrote:

> "The white man's happiness cannot be purchased by the black man's misery. Virtue cannot prevail among the white people, by its destruction among the black people, who form a part of the whole community. It is evident that the white and black must fall or flourish together." (Douglass, 1847)

Altogether some 2,700 African American newspapers came to life during the nineteenth and twentieth centuries, but most did not survive more than nine years on average. Despite its lack of financial power, the African American press became "the greatest single power in the Negro race" (Roberts and Klibanoff, 2007).

The two most influential newspapers in the African American media were the *Chicago Defender*, a weekly founded in 1905 by Robert A. Abbot, and the *Pittsburgh Courier*, founded by Edwin Harleston and Robert Lee Vann in 1907. Circulation of the two papers would eventually top 300,000, in part because both papers were circulated nationwide. They called on African Americans to move North, where there was more opportunity. Between 1910 and 1930, about 1.75 million left the South in what was called "the great migration"—with the *Courier* and *Defender* lighting the way.

As the nation's strongest voices for civil rights, the *Courier*, the *Defender* and the rest of the African American press provided a forum for African American community. They employed gifted writers like Langston Hughes and Ida B. Wells; they cam-

Figure 3.13 "The Double V"—*Chicago Defender* publisher John Sengstacke, seen here talking with an unidentified editor, was among leaders of the black press who worked for the "Double V" campaign in World War II—Victory in the war, and victory over racism at home. (FSA—Library of Congress)

paigned for integrated sports; they organized boycotts of racist films like "Birth of a Nation"; they covered race riots and investigated lynchings; they debated tactics and helped clarify the early goals of the civil rights movement.

Another important milestone for the African American press was the establishment of *Ebony* magazine in 1945 by John H. Johnson. Designed to look like other glossy magazines, Ebony emphasized entertainment and the success of African Americans, but also covered difficult issues of racism and segregation. The success of these and other publications gave a voice to millions of people who were not usually heard in the mainstream media.

At the time, the mainstream media paid little attention to civil rights. In 1944, Swedish journalist Gunnar Myrdal toured the American South and wrote that if the press ever did tell the story, the rest of the nation would be "shocked and shaken" and would demand sweeping changes. A decade later, Myrdal's prophecy turned out to be startlingly accurate.

The event that brought civil rights into the national spotlight was the May 17, 1954 *Brown v. Board of Education* decision by the US Supreme Court. The court unanimously decided that racially segregated schools were "inherently unequal" and that African American students had been "deprived of the equal protection of the laws guaranteed by the 14th Amendment."

Public opinion was strongly galvanized the next year with the 1955 murder of Emmett Till, a 14-year-old Chicago resident visiting relatives in Mississippi. Till was brutally beaten, shot and dumped in a river in apparent retaliation for supposedly whistling at a white woman.

His mother demanded that his body be sent home for burial in Chicago. When the coffin arrived, she had it opened "to show the world what they did to my baby." Photos of Till's horrifically beaten face were first printed on the front page of the *Chicago Defender*, and in *Ebony* and other magazines. "It gave a real picture to the brutality and terrorism against African Americans," said Roland Martin, editor of the *Chicago Defender*, in 2005 (Goodman, 2005). Reporters from around the world attended the trial of his accused white murderers. Despite considerable evidence of guilt, the accused white men were quickly acquitted. The slaying brought "strong criticism of (Mississippi's) white supremacy practices from other sections of the country," a *New York Times* reporter wrote (Roberts and Klibanoff, 2007).

As African Americans pressed for equality with bus boycotts, lawsuits, lunch counter sit-ins and other nonviolent tactics, the mainstream press wondered how to cover rapidly unfolding events.

At first the media settled into what seemed at first to be a gentlemanly debate over schools and desegregation. But by misreading the sentiments of the extremes in 1955, the *Times* "failed to see that the extremes would soon be in control," said Gene Patterson and Hank Klibanoff in *The Race Beat*, a 2006 history of civil rights news coverage.

In 1960, as part of a fund-raising effort, a group of Southern ministers ran a full page advertisement in the *New York Times* under the headline: "Heed their Rising Voices." The ad included a descriptions of events that had minor inaccuracies. Louis B. Sullivan, police commissioner of Birmingham, AL, sued the *Times* and won at the state court level. However, the US Supreme Court reversed the state court decision, and cleared the way for media coverage not only of the civil rights issue but of government in general.

"We consider this case against the background of a profound national commitment to the principle that debate on public issues should be uninhibited, robust, and wide-open, and that it may well include vehement, caustic, and sometimes unpleasantly sharp attacks on government and public officials," the Supreme Court said in its 1964 opinion in *New York Times v. Sullivan*.

The mainstream press, like the country, was divided on the civil rights movement. Editors James J. Kilpatrick of the Richmond, Virginia, *Times* and Thomas Waring of the Charleston, South Carolina, *Courier* advocated "massive resistance" to integration and encouraged Southerners to fight for states rights. On the other hand, more temperate Southerners advised gradual change. These included *Atlanta Journal* editor Ralph McGill, Greenville, Mississippi, editor Hodding Carter, and Little Rock editor Harry Ashmore.

Ralph McGill was especially known for crafting carefully balanced editorials to depict the civil rights movement as a sometimes uncomfortable but necessary and even inevitable process—a process that would help build a South that was too busy, and too generous, to hate. After an Atlanta bombing, McGill wrote in a 1959 Pulitzer-prize winning editorial: "This . . . is a harvest of defiance of the courts and the encouragement of citizens to defy law on the part of many Southern politicians."

McGill's protégé, Gene Patterson, made similar appeals. After Dr. Martin Luther King's assassination in 1968, Patterson wrote a front page editorial in the *Atlanta Journal* calling on white Americans to cease "the poisonous politics of hatred that turns sick minds to murder. Let the white man say, 'No more of this ever,' and put an end to it—if not for the Negro, for the sake of his own immortal soul."

In the end, the success of the nonviolent civil rights movement was closely connected with the media's ability to witness events. "If it hadn't been for the media—the print media and the television—the civil rights movement would have been like a bird without wings, a choir without a song," said John Lewis in 2005 (Roberts and Klibanoff, 2007). Eventually, even conservative editors like Kilpatrick admitted that they had been wrong about civil rights.

In witnessing the suffering of American civil rights demonstrators, the press came to be regarded with gratitude as an agent of national reconciliation.

Vietnam, Watergate and
the adversarial press

National reconciliation never really took place following the Vietnam War. Unlike the civil rights movement, the aims and conduct of the war in general—and the role of the press in particular—remained vexed political questions long after events had run their course.

The Vietnam War began as World War II ended and the French tried to re-establish colonialism. US assistance grew as the French lost control of the northern part of the country in the late 1950s. The United States supported a weak regime in the South through the 1960s and, after a series of military defeats, withdrew all forces in 1975. Two major points of controversy included the skepticism of the press corps and the impact of television images on public opinion.

The press corps was skeptical, but the reporters themselves saw it as part of their responsibility. One reporter in particular, World War II veteran reporter Homer Bigart, had never played the role of cheerleader for the home team, even in World War II. As colleague Malcolm Browne said:

> However critical his reporting of such military blunders as the Anzio beachhead (in World War II) could be, there was never any doubt which side had his sympathies. In Vietnam, by contrast, Homer could never wholeheartedly identify himself with an American team that often looked arrogant and wrongheaded and whose cause seemed questionable to him. (Browne, 1993)

Others, including Bigart's colleague and World War II *Herald-Tribune* veteran Marguerite Higgins, saw sensationalism and pessimism overwhelming the more optimistic assessments of the Vietnam War, which in turn provoked an escalation of the war in its early stages (Higgins, 1965).

The later generation of reporters had a different take. David Halberstam initially believed that a US victory was needed to discourage "so-called wars of liberation" (Halberstam, 1965), but eventually came to the conclusion that the war "was doomed," and that the United States was "on the wrong side of history" (Halberstam, 1965). Neil Sheehan, a UPI reporter, saw the war as being lost on the ground long before it was lost in American public opinion (Sheehan, 1988). And studies of US media coverage showed that public opinion against the war was significantly higher than the relatively neutral coverage of the war (Vaughn, 2008).

The role of television in bringing into American homes the horrors of war was also a point of contention long after the war. Although this view would later influence US military censorship policies, network concerns about the sensibilities of their audiences kept gory war footage off the air (Hallin, 1986). (Also see Chapter 9.)

For the military, the main lesson of Vietnam was that reporters would need to be managed. Press pools in conflicts ranging from the Falklands (1982), Grenada (1983), Panama (1989), the Iraq conflicts (1991, 2003) and Afghanistan (2000s) were kept away from war's gruesome scenes and troubling questions about civilian casualties.

The Pentagon Papers and Watergate

One of the major turning points in the public opinion about the Vietnam war was the publication in 1971 of the "Pentagon Papers," a secret history of the war drawn up by the US military and leaked to the *New York Times* by Pentagon consultant Daniel Ellsberg. The papers showed that three administrations had "systematically lied, not only to the public but also to Congress, about a subject of transcendent national interest and significance" (Apple, 1996).

Three days after the leak became public, President Richard Nixon asked the courts for an injunction to halt publication. A temporary injunction was granted, but after a week of examining the papers, and amid a dozen other leaks to other newspapers, the US Supreme Court lifted the injunctions, finding that the government had not met the heavy burden of proving that publication would cause "grave and irreparable" danger—proof that would be necessary to enforce censorship (*The New York Times*, 1971).

Concern about leaks to the press from inside the government led the Nixon administration to assemble a team of former CIA employees as "plumbers" who would fix the "leaks." One of their assignments was to break into the Democratic National Committee offices at the Watergate apartment and office building in Washington DC. When the burglars were arrested, two young reporters—Bob Woodward and Carl Bernstein—investigated ties between the burglars and the White House.

In the process, Woodward and Bernstein unraveled a web of illegal activities in the White House and the Justice Department, including extortion and bribery. This led to the resignation of President Nixon in 1974 and criminal convictions for seven high-level members of his administration.

Woodward and Bernstein were just starting their careers when they began investigating Watergate. Many senior reporters did not believe that a scandal of that magnitude could unravel, and were astonished at the success of their investigation. As we will see in future chapters, sometimes individuals who don't know enough to be discouraged can change the course of history. This was as true for telegraph inventor Samuel Morse and Apple computer inventor Steve Wozniak as it was for Woodward and Bernstein.

The combination of events surrounding Watergate and the Vietnam War led to a perception, especially among American conservatives, of an irrationally "adversarial press." But it also aroused a sense of admiration for the extent to which the press could fulfill its constitutional role as a check on government power. These views, although

Figure 3.14 Watergate—two young reporters, Bob Woodward (left) and Carl Bernstein, exposed the connection between president Richard Nixon and the burglars who broke into the Democratic National Committee offices during the 1972 election campaign. Nixon resigned two years later, unable to cover up the widening scandal. (*The Washington Post*, 1973)

not mutually exclusive, never reconciled in the coming decades with partisan political scandals of the Reagan, Clinton and Bush presidencies. Polls showed that trust in the press, at near 40 to 50 percent levels in the 1980s, declined to half those levels by 2010.

Literary and gonzo journalism

The civil rights movement, the Watergate scandals and the anti-war movement all played against a backdrop of a changing society where conventions of all kinds were being challenged.

One of the more important conventions of journalism was the idea of objectivity and the "inverted pyramid" form of writing. Magazine and newspaper writers took a different tact in the 1960s with the "literary journalism" movement. While still telling a nonfiction story, writers used novelistic devices like dialogue, omniscient narration and scene-by-scene construction to form a more interesting and personal narrative.

Sometimes "literary journalism" had the confusing label of "new journalism," but the narrative form wasn't so new after all. It had been used by Daniel Defoe, Charles Dickens, Stephen Crane, Ernest Hemingway, Richard Harding Davis, Ernie Pyle and many others. One significant example of literary journalism was John Hershey's August 1946 *New Yorker* article "Hiroshima" that was subsequently published as a book. Previous descriptions of the bomb's impact tended to be impersonal, but Hershey traced the experiences of six survivors hour by hour on August 6, 1945. He adopted a neutral style designed to let the personal stories of the survivors come through. As a result, Americans understood the horror of nuclear warfare in a way that had deep, long term impacts on public policy.

Advocates for the new literary journalism movement of the 1960s included Tom Wolfe, a newspaper feature writer who broke away from conventions and captivated readers with his rich, descriptive style in books like the *Electric Kool-Aid Acid Test* (about San Francisco in the 1960s) and *The Right Stuff* (about astronauts and the space race). In *The New Journalism*, Wolfe described what he saw as a reversal of the old hierarchy of literature. In the old days, he said, news and feature-writing journalists were at the bottom, columnists and essayists were in the middle and novelists were at the top. But the novel was dead, and the new literary journalism had now reached the apex of literature (Wolfe, 1975).

Wolfe's ideas set off a serious debate. Some journalists thought that Wolfe and company had lost their bearings in the fervid climates of 1960s counterculture. Especially controversial during this experimental era was what Rolling Stone writer Hunter S. Thompson called "gonzo" journalism. At best, the gonzo approach was a hilariously critical, first-person view of people twisted by political and social institutions. But at its worst, Thompson's drug-crazed writing churned grimly through a mélange of psychotic experiences.

Despite the criticism, literary journalism was a strong break from inverted-pyramid "telegraph-ese," and became a widely used writing style as the press struggled to keep up with, and serve, a rapidly changing society.

The story of the century: covering science and environment

Perhaps the most influential magazine article series of the twentieth century, after John Hershey's *Hiroshima*, was Rachel Carson's 1962 *New Yorker* series and subsequent book, *Silent Spring*. A biologist and accomplished science writer, Carson warned that overuse of pesticides such as DDT threatened bird populations and human health. The book set off a firestorm of controversy and re-ignited the conservation movement from earlier generations (Neuzil and Kovarik, 1997).

Silent Spring was published in an era when people were beginning to take science and environment seriously, but it was not always that way. In earlier generations, if science was even mentioned in the press, "it was in terms of magic or miracles, if not mere ridicule," said historian David J. Rhees (Rhees, 1979).

When scientific findings threatened the established order, the press reacted with churlishness. For instance, *The Times*, London, covered public health controversies from the 1840s through the 1880s, but noted: "We prefer to take our chance with cholera than be bullied into public health" (*The Times*, London, August 1, 1854).

The new appreciation for science dawned when the *New York Times* appointed Carr Van Anda editor in 1906. A gifted interpreter of science who was fluent in math, Van Anda was noted for spotting a poor transcription of one of Albert Einstein's equations (Fine, 1968). Another step forward was the Scripps Science Service, created in the 1920s (see Chapter 2). More improvements were seen in Pulitzer prizes for five science writers in 1937, along with a 1941 Pulitzer for the *St. Louis Post-Dispatch*'s crusade against air pollution ("smoke abatement") coverage in 1941.

A series of killer smogs and burning rivers in the 1950s and 60s, along with medical advances and the space race, led to increasing coverage of science and the environment. In 1969 *The New York Times* created a permanent environment beat, and other newspapers and magazines followed suit. The need to create a larger cadre of reporters to handle specialized beats was reinforced in the chaos of the Three Mile Island nuclear explosion in Harrisburg, PA, in April 1979. Despite the significance and popularity of the articles, *Times* news writers were constantly under assault by well-organized corporate lobbies for a supposed lack of objectivity. By the twenty-first century, most science and environment beats in the press had been scaled back. In 2008, Cable News Network even laid off its entire nine-person science unit.

The decline in reporting on complex but vital topics was decried by scientists and journalists alike. Carl Sagan, a noted astronomer and public scientist, said that we had approached a moment in history where "no one representing the public interest can even grasp the issues," due to a disdain for education and the "dumbing down" of the American media (Sagan, 1995).

By 2010, the press was so weakened that an industry public relations gambit to paint climate scientists as radicals had succeeded beyond all expectations. Almost half of the American public believed that climate change was some kind of hoax by politically motivated scientists, despite obvious and widely confirmed scientific evidence. "It is a challenge for legitimate news organizations to compete with that massive disinformation network," said climate scientist Michael Mann (*Globe and Mail*, February 20, 2010).

Five stages of printing technology

1455–1820s—print shops

If Johannes Gutenberg could somehow have come back to a printing shop in 1820, nearly four centuries after the first wave of the printing revolution, he would have been able to get right to work. Only a few decades later, by the 1830s and 40s, the Industrial Revolution changed printing along with the rest of the working world, and Gutenberg would probably have been astonished at the pace of innovation.

Figure 3.15 Composition at a printing shop

- **Typesetting**—Type is set by hand, letter by letter, from upper and lower cases, at a rate of about five words per minute.

- **Printing**—Paper is fed manually into hand-pulled wooden presses at about 250 impressions per hour (a "token"). Each impression is one-sided, which means that once the ink has dried, the "same token" has to get a second run.

- **Circulation**—Newspapers and magazines are sent to subscribers through the mail or sold in general merchandise stores. Favorable postal rates subsidize widespread publishing in the US.

1820s–1890s—penny press

Steam printing and stereotyping

THREE PAGE WIDE PRESS

Figure 3.16 Improved steam-powered press by R. Hoe & Co.

- **Typesetting**—Type is still set from large cases by hand. A large daily newspaper might employ 100 workers just to set type.

- **Stereotyping**—Hand-set type is too loose to use in higher speed presses. This problem is solved by casting metal copies of the beds of hand-set type in order to create "stereotype" printing plates. The plates are cast in cylindrical sleeves to allow rotary printing.

- **Presses**—The introduction of steam powered printing presses speeds up production to thousands of impressions per hour. This expands circulation of newspapers and magazines. The steam press, first used in 1814 at *The Times*, London, allows a new kind of low-cost "penny" papers by the 1830s.

- **Circulation**—Subscriptions by mail are common for magazines, but now children hawk papers on city streets.

1890s–1960s—hot type
Linotype, halftone and high speed printing

- **Typesetting**—German-American Ottmar Mergenthaler invents the first successful typesetting machine in 1886. Operators sit at a keyboard that releases blanks, then molten lead is poured over them to create a line of type. (Hence the name, Linotype.) At about 30 words per minute, Linotypes speed up the process by five or six times. Between 1893 and 1968, over 74,000 Linotype machines are sold. In the 1960s, a new Linotype might cost about $50,000 (Holtzberg-Call, 1992).

- **Halftone**—This process, invented in the 1880s, allows photographs to be etched into metal plates and then printed. Previously, only line drawings could be printed on a press.

- **Printing**—Automated presses use rolls (webs) of paper and can print, fold, cut and stack the newspaper or magazine. This allows tens of thousands of impressions per hour. Cheap paper is also a factor, with costs declining from 22 cents per pound in 1860 to about 1.5 cents per pound by 1900.

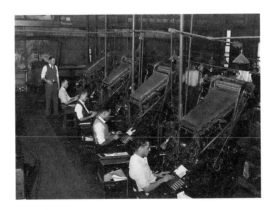

- **Circulation**—Subscriptions by mail are still common for magazines, but circulation wars break out between newspapers in big cities.

Figure 3.17 Linotype operators at the *Chicago Defender* around 1940.

1950s–1980s—cold type
Photo typesetting and offset printing

Figure 3.18 Photo typesetting ("cold" type) with early computers in the 1970s was five times cheaper and six times faster than "hot" typesetting.

- **Typesetting**—French-Americans Rene Higonnet and Louis Moyroud, with the help of Vannevar Bush and a publishers' cooperative invent a photo-mechanical process that sets type six times faster than Linotypes at a cost of about $10,000 for a small unit in the 1970s. Photo-composition is increasingly improved by the digital revolution in the 1970s, and by the 1980s, and word processing and type setting are now both handled by mainframe computers in most newsrooms.

- **Pre-Press**—Sheets of photo-sensitive paper containing separate blocks of type, headlines, and halftones are assembled (laid out and pasted up), then transferred to negatives and burned onto offset aluminum printing plates. Skilled pre-press workers are no longer needed, and the production work force is cut in half.

- **Printing**—Offset printing uses light aluminum plates instead of heavy cast-lead stereotypes. This allows smaller, cheaper, faster presses that can print color with accurate registration.

- **Circulation**—Newspaper delivery routes become common; postal service subsidies for publishers are reduced.

Figure 3.19 Desktop publishing and pagination were the "killer applications" for the 1984 Apple Mac

1980s–present—digital
Desktop publishing and pagination

- **Typesetting**—Personal computers like the Apple Mac (introduced in 1984) and laser printers allow "desktop" publishing, making it far easier and cheaper to prepare type and photos for the press. By the mid-1990s, a computer and printer might cost $2,000.

- **Pre-Press**—Improved computers allow digital layout (pagination), eliminating most pre-press layout and paste-up. Editors can now send pages straight back to the press, and nearly all the production work force is eliminated.

- **Printing**—Digital versions of pages are sent through the internet to large presses in centralized locations, bypassing small printing operations.
- **Circulation**—News of all kinds is now available to billions of people through digital networks like the World Wide Web.

Final decades of the printing revolution

Two waves of technological change affected US newspapers in the late twentieth and early twenty-first centuries. First, new technologies made papers more profitable—and more complacent. Then, as the digital revolution took hold, newspapers lost half of their advertising income, one quarter of their subscribers and 30 percent of their editorial capacity in the first decade of the twenty-first century, triggering hundreds of newspaper bankruptcies and tens of thousands of layoffs (Pew, 2010).

Analysts pointed out that the decline in newspaper advertising was far more pronounced in the United States, and that in many countries, newspaper circulation had been holding steady. (Editor & Publisher, 2010). This was especially true in countries where censorship was enforced before the fall of the Berlin Wall in 1989. Even so, the catastrophic collapse of US publishing indicated an abrupt change in business as usual, and possibly, the end of line for the centuries-old printing revolution.

"Now for the first time in modern American history, it is entirely plausible that we will not have even minimally sufficient resources dedicated to reporting and editing the news and distributing the information and informed analysis that citizens require," said John McChesney in *The Death and Life of American Journalism*. "Already much of government activity is conducted in the dark. Investigative journalism is on the endangered species list" (McChesney, 2010).

The beginning of the end

The complex chain of events that led to the collapse of the US publishing industry began with complacency about a near-monopoly that newspaper and magazine publishers enjoyed from the 1900s to the 1970s. Nearly all newspapers were small family owned operations, making five to ten percent annual profits. If they were members of the Associated Press, they were allowed to veto the entry of other start-up newspapers into AP membership. In effect, the business model allowed publishers to coast through the first half of the twentieth century.

Technological innovation in the 1950s and 60s triggered many of the changes in the publishing industry. Economic historian Elizabeth M. Neiva observed: "The forces that triggered the rapid transformation of the American newspaper industry were not self-serving publishing moguls . . . but the invention and popularization of a relatively simple new technology, photocomposition," she said (Neiva, 1995). Photo-composition (or "cold" type) replaced cumbersome and expensive Linotype ("hot" type) systems, allowing publishers to cut skilled work forces in half, greatly accelerating profits and enhancing the market value for newspapers.

One unexpected consequence of higher market value meant that the founders of family newspapers could no longer keep them in the family because the heirs could not afford the estate taxes. As a result, most newspapers were converted to public stock corporations and sold to chains like Gannett, Thompson or Knight-Ridder between the 1960s and the 1990s. These public stock corporations were no longer community-based organizations whose primary mission was to serve the public. Instead, Wall Street valued their consistent ability to post profits from 20 to 40 percent per year.

The shift in emphasis from public service to profit-making reflected two basic ideas about the modern corporation that were (and still are) contending. On the one hand, media experts like those on the Hutchins Commission insisted that publishers have a social responsibility (as we have seen earlier in this chapter). On the other hand, economists like Milton Friedman maintained that the only social responsibility that any corporation really had was to increase its profits (Friedman, 1962). Wall Street preferred Friedman's view and pushed the publishing industry to keep expanding.

Record-high profits for some newspapers were not matched by weaker competitors in many cities during the 1950s and 60s. Many began using "joint operating agreements" (JOAs) that consolidated printing and advertising operations while (theoretically) continuing competition between news operations. The JOAs were challenged in court and found to be contrary to antitrust laws, and in 1970, Congress passed the "Newspaper Preservation Act" allowing these JOAs between competing newspapers.

These operating agreements were originally promoted as a way to maintain diversity in the face of competition, but many who warned that they would lead to monopolies were proven right by the 1980s and 1990s as hundreds of weaker newspapers failed and went out of business.

Investors expected that dominant newspapers would continue to produce high profits whether their contents were first-class or third-class, industrialist and media investor Warren Buffet said in 1985. "That is not true of most businesses: inferior quality generally produces inferior economics," Buffet said. "But even a poor newspaper is a bargain to most citizens simply because of its 'bulletin board' value" (Shafer, 2009).

When the savings that came with cold type and offset printing had been exhausted, publishers turned to newsroom staff cuts. In *The Vanishing Newspaper*, Philip Meyer noted that Wall Street tended to support quality when newspapers had competition, but tended to demand cuts in editorial staff as competition declined. "There is no shortage of historical studies showing a correlation between quality journalism and business success . . . (even in) monopoly markets," Meyer said (Meyer, 2009). But the reverse was also true: declining quality also strongly correlated with declines in circulation (Lacy, 1998).

Economists have long observed that the general problem with monopolies is that the lack of efficiency makes the product over-priced, and cuts in quality lead to declines in consumer demand—a phenomena known as deadweight loss. As demand falls, prices stay high, and the downward spiral in quality leads to a search for alternatives.

"Newspaper publishers might believe that the abnormally high profit margins that they enjoyed relative to other businesses in the 20th century are their birthright, but they're not," Meyer said. "They were the result of a condition that no longer exists—their near monopoly control over retailers' access to their consumers" (Meyer, 2009).

Even before the digital revolution, publishing monopolies were being replaced by other forms of media that were aimed at demographics rather than geographic regions. The process was called media fragmentation or "de-massification," and it was well under way when, in the early twenty-first century, the Internet and the World Wide Web overtook newspapers as a source of information.

Publishers face the digital revolution

The best that can be said of the publishing industry's response to the digital revolution is that some organizations made a very modest attempt to meet the challenge. Although many saw it coming, only a few did anything to retool and adapt the industry, since that would mean cutting into profits.

In one early experiment, several newspapers including the *St. Louis Post-Dispatch* tried radio fax versions of the paper. In 1979, the Knight-Ridder newspaper chain began an experiment with online news called "Viewtron." The ill-fated experiment failed since consumer costs were high, graphics were far worse than television, and consumers could not participate in the market. The Viewtron project foundered in 1986, just as a similar project in France called Minitel caught on. The French experiment involved free terminals for phone users and far more open access to consumers who could place ads and get involved in discussion groups (Kovarik, 2001).

Newspapers also tried partnerships with online service providers, such as AOL and Compuserv. In May of 1994, the San Jose (CA) Mercury News was the first with an html-coded newspaper website. Early in the development of the World Wide Web, publishers saw that they could lose their monopoly over community bulletin boards and began a series of experiments. These included:

- New Century Networks (1995–1998)—A news aggregating site selling classified advertising was launched by major publishing chains including Knight-Ridder, Gannett, Hearst, the *Washington Post* and the *New York Times*. A total of about $75 million was spent over the network's short life, but few were convinced that a Google, Yahoo or eBay could ever replace classified advertising. "The feared competition never developed," said the *New York Times* (Peterson, 1998).

- Real Cities (1999–2008)—A network of local portals featuring news, email, search services, e-commerce and site-building tools was launched by Knight-Ridder in 1999, which spent $25 million per year, then sold off in stages between 2006 and 2008.

- Classified Ventures (1997–present)—This auto and real estate classified services includes Cars.com and Apartments.com and is owned by major publishing chains like Gannett, *Tribune* and the *Washington Post*. It charges only for premium services, but competition from other free services has kept the value of the site relatively low (Tate, 2010).

Another early innovation was Knight-Ridder's experiment with the "information tablet" in the 1990s at the Information Design Laboratory. The tablet idea was ahead of its time, and the lab was shut down in 1995. Newer technology allowed Apple Computers to create a version of the iPad tablet in 2010. Its main advantage is that it is more portable than a personal computer, but the iPad, like Knight-Ridder's tablet, was designed to be a top-down information utility (Rusbridger, 2010).

News and the Web

Experiments like Viewtron and Real Cities allowed users to read regular daily updates of news, but they did not enable creative uses of the technology. They were "top-down" technologies, not "generative" technologies.

"From the beginning, newspapers sought to invent the Web in their own image by repurposing the copy, values, and temperament found in their ink-and-paper editions," said media analyst Jack Shafer. "Despite being early arrivals, despite having spent millions on manpower and hardware . . . every newspaper web site (was) instantly identifiable as a newspaper web site. By succeeding, they failed to invent the Web" (Shafer, 2009).

The decline in classified advertising (the "bulletin board") was the earliest indicator that the value of a newspaper was diminishing, but it also began failing as a vehicle for international and regional news as Google and other search engines made it easy to access free news from national newspaper and magazine sites.

By 2008, more people were getting their news and information from the internet than from newspapers (Pew, 2008). And yet, journalists working for newspapers, wire services and television networks were the ones creating the internet-accessible news in the first place. A debate over whether to build "pay walls" or create a pay-per-view system was inconclusive, and news organizations struggled to find a sustaining revenue model (Pew, 2010).

There were some reasons to hope that the valuable contributions and traditions of the press would be transferred into the digital revolution. New business models such as non-profit news companies, consumer news co-ops, crowd-financed journalism and training for citizen journalists were among the approaches being tested. (See Chapter 12 for a discussion of these trends.) Also, journalism schools were taking on market experiments as part of an ethical responsibility, although they could not fill the rapidly expanding gap in news coverage.

Many lessons can be drawn from the collapse of publishing in the twenty-first century. Among them is the idea that a public service industry can lose its moral compass when subjected to overwhelming financial pressures. And yet, the continuing need for public service information probably means that new institutions will emerge to serve the need, as we will see in Chapter 12.

The old Scottish printer William Blackwood probably said it best in 1834: "The press, a machine than can no longer be broken, will continue to destroy the old world 'till it has formed a new one.'"

Section II
The Visual Revolution

Introduction to Section II

People have not only ceased to purchase those old-fashioned things called books, but even to read them! . . . The beauties of Shakespeare are imprinted on the minds of the rising generation in woodcuts; and the poetry of Byron (is) engraved in their hearts, by means of the graver . . . (In the future) Books, the small as well as the great, will have been voted a great evil. There will be no gentlemen of the press. The press itself will have ceased to exist. (William Blackwood, 1844)

Even before printed photos and movie theaters, people worried about the power of images. When a Scottish printer named William Blackwood worried that Shakespeare, Byron and the press itself would not survive the onslaught of images (above), the new media technology was already having an impact on the old media. *Punch* magazine and *The Illustrated London News* were both only a few years old and already immensely popular, and they would soon be followed by a host of other publications that featured engravings and cartoons. Louis Daguerre's process for capturing images was also new, although it wasn't yet possible to print photographs (that would come in the late 1880s).

The attraction to visual imagery was not new to nineteenth-century Britain. Anthropologists and psychologists believe that over the long span of human evolution, the human brain has become specialized in recognizing and remembering images. The Altamira Cave provides an interesting point of perspective.

Twelve-year-old María de Sautuola was the first to look up and notice the herd of bison, painted on the ceiling of the cave owned by her father near Altamira, Spain. She had been exploring the cave with her family by torchlight, and her father, Marcelino Sanz de Sautuola, also became fascinated by the artistry and power of the images. He realized that the paintings resembled bone carvings that he had seen in museums, and he hired a university archaeologist to help publish his findings in 1880. The idea that these were ancient paintings, however, proved controversial. Professional archaeologists, surprised at the artistic power and the well-preserved state of the paintings, accused Sautuola of fraud. Later, as similar paintings were found in other caves, Sautuola's scientific adversaries apologized, and archeologists began to take prehistoric images seriously.

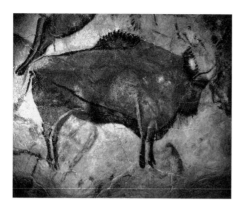

Figure II.1 Cave paintings—the discovery of the Altamira cave paintings in 1880 reflects the power and controversy that often surrounds visual communication. (Library of Congress)

Today, the Altamira cave is considered one of the great archaeological finds of the modern era, but the story illustrates the power and controversy that often surrounds visual communication. And the idea that a child was the first to notice the paintings says something about the significance of visual imagery in the human psyche.

Visual images are the keys to memory and the guideposts to the terrain of human psychology. The first experimental psychologists, Wilhelm Wundt and William James, observed in the 1890s that images—not words—were the building blocks of human psychology (Thomas, 2010). The insight was confirmed by twentieth century experiments on the "picture superiority effect" showing that concepts are much more likely to be remembered when they are presented as images rather than words (Nelson et al., 1976).

We now realize that visual communication predates writing by at least 32,000 years and that visually symbolic communication is found scattered across the ancient landscape. These symbols are sometimes expressed as stone circles, sometimes as paintings preserved in caves or tombs, and sometimes as small carvings whose microscopic markings show repeated use. The complexity of these symbols seems to increase over the epochs of time.

Among other things, a small carving might be used in a rite of passage ceremony, or as a token of privilege, or as a way to count natural cycles. The closer we come to modernity, the more complex these symbols seem to become, perhaps as a location for an increasing variety of symbolic uses (Marshack, 2003).

People have always had a knack for symbol making, according to psychologist Carl Jung. A person "unconsciously transforms objects or forms into symbols, thereby endowing them with great psychological importance, and expresses them in both his religion and his art" (Jung and Von Franz, 1964).

Before photography

Images from the Middle East and Asia

The earliest known printed images are from "cylinder seals" used in early Mesopotamian civilizations from around 3500 BCE. Made from hard stone, glass or ceramic materials, they were rolled across wet clay or textiles to create repeating patterns. These had decorative, authoritative or symbolic uses, or occasionally all three.

In China and Japan, wood block prints of Buddhist images were printed on silk earlier than 400 CE. Buddhist woodblocks combining text and images are known from about 627 CE onward. Woodblocks were often used for printing books on silk from 1000, and while moveable type was known, woodblocks of full pages were used because of the complexity of the Chinese character set, with thousands of pictographic images. The world's earliest woodblock printed book, the Diamond Sutra, is a Chinese scroll dating from 868. Woodblock printing is also found on textiles in the Arabic Mediterranean around 1000, and was transmitted to Europe before the 1300s. Color printmaking of nonreligious art emerged around 1700 with the Torii school and continued through the 1800s with the complex and Zen-like art of the Utagawa school.

Techniques for reproducing visual images were known in the ancient world of the Middle East, India, China and Japan. It is possible, some believe likely, that all kinds of printing techniques were transmitted between Europe and Asia even earlier, during the 1200–1300 CE era through the Mongol Empire (Christensen, 2006).

While some printing techniques, like woodcut, could have been adapted during this period by Europeans in the Renaissance, others, like metal plate engraving and lithography, were invented as part of the printing revolution.

European interest in Japanese and Chinese art styles resurged in the 1860s and influenced a broader discussion about art. Artists questioned the older formal styles of painting that merely reproduced landscapes or religious and historical events. Photography, they said, could accomplish that. But photographers would also try to show that their work was also a form of art.

Early visual communication in Europe

Printing techniques like wood block, engraving, etching and lithography were the first visual mass media. Unlike paintings or sculptures, printed images could be multiplied by the thousands. Maps and technical diagrams helped speed exploration, technology, medicine and science. Reproductions of paintings allowed mass access to art. Cartoons dramatized and democratized political debates. And savvy publishers, aware of the power of images, launched illustrated publications that succeeded in attracting large audiences.

European wood block printing of images began sometime in the mid-1300s. Religious images and playing cards were typical themes. Since wood blocks tend to lose resolution over time, printers turned to new techniques

Figure II.2 *Nuremberg Chronicles*—a crowning achievement in the earliest years of printing, the illustrated *Nuremberg Chronicles* (*Die Schedelsche Weltchronik*) provides a fascinating glimpse into the medieval mindset. (Library of Congress)

XXIX. GIN LANE. 1751. Engraving. 11½ × 14 in.

Figure II.3 London's Gin Lane—William Hogarth, an engraver from the early 1700s, illustrated allegorical stories intended to improve public morals. (Library of Congress)

like engraving in the 1440s, around the same time that Gutenberg was experimenting with moveable type.

in the mid-1500s. Artists first paint a metal plate with waxy varnish and then scratch an image into the varnish. When the plate is immersed in acid, the unprotected portions of the image are deeply etched and can hold ink through many thousands of impressions (Hind, 1908).

One of the most important early books using woodcuts was the 1493 *Nuremberg Chronicles* (in Germany: *Die Schedelsche Weltchronik* or *Schedel's World History*). As many as 2,500 copies may have been produced in Latin and German. The book offers a fascinating glimpse into the Medieval sense of history, following five Biblical ages from creation to the birth of Christ, then one age to the present and a seventh age leading to the Last Judgment. With over 1,800 woodcuts, the *Chronicles* was a crowning achievement in the earliest years of printing.

The publisher of the *Chronicles,* Anton Koberger, was one of the world's first media barons, owning 24 printing presses in cities from Lyon to Budapest. He was also the godfather of Albrech Durer (1471–1528), one of the finest painters and engravers of the Northern Renaissance. Durer is remembered for both religious and secular art, and for blending Italian classical composition with the practical style of northern Europe. A gifted artist from an early age, Durer's work was so skilled that he was imitated for centuries.

Artistic engraving and etching added immensely to the visual landscape of post-Renaissance Europe. Names of many famed artists are among those who used this printing technique to circulate their work more widely. They include Rembrandt (Harmenszoon) of the Netherlands, Hans Holbein of Germany, Francisco Goya of Spain, Honore Daumier of France, and William Blake and William Hogarth of England.

Hogarth (1697–1764) especially, is noteworthy as taking advantage of an age in which the visual environment was becoming increasingly complex. Artistic prints were widely circulated and shown on walls in homes, taverns, shops and public buildings, and Hogarth used printing and engraving to tell stories. "My picture was my stage," he once said. Hogarth's heavy-handed moral crusade used symbols to tell stories such as the Harlot's Progress, the Rake's Progress, Marriage, Industry and Idleness, Beer Street, Gin Lane, and the Four Stages of Cruelty.

Visual communication and the press

The use of mass produced images had enormous social effects. Maps and technical diagrams helped speed exploration, technology, medicine and science. Cartoons dramatized and democratized political debates. And savvy publishers, aware of the power of images, launched illustrated publications that succeeded in attracting large audiences.

One of the first newspaper illustrations in the United States was the "Join or Die" woodcut depicting a snake cut in pieces corresponding to the 13 colonies. The illustration, published by Benjamin Franklin in the *Pennsylvania Gazette* in 1754, encouraged greater unity among the colonies.

Figure II.4 Colonial Unity—the message in Ben Franklin's 1754 woodcut was that the colonies could not survive if separated. (Library of Congress)

The first regular publication to stress visual elements was the *Illustrated London News*, published between 1842 and 1971. It was founded by Herbert Ingram, an apprentice printer who was "seized with the belief" that it would be possible to publish a newspaper entirely devoted to illustrations. The paper did get a good reception at first, but when circulation started falling off, publisher Herbert Ingram sent free copies of the paper to every clergyman in England. Prominently illustrated in that issue was the installation of the head of the Anglican church, the Archbishop of Canterbury. Circulation reached 300,000 when the *News* ran engravings based on Roger Fenton's photos from the Crimean War in 1852.

Illustrated publications soon sprang up in other countries—*Harper's Weekly*, the *National Police Gazette* and *Leslie's Illustrated Newspaper* in America, *L'Illustration* in France, and *Über Land und Meer* in Germany. Pictorial newspapers followed with the development of halftone processes in the 1880s and 1890s, including the London *Daily Graphic*, the *Daily Mirror* and the *Daily Sketch*.

Lithography allows faster, cheaper reproduction of images

One important advance in the mass production of images was lithography, invented in 1796 in Germany as a way to publish music and posters at low cost. The process, a forerunner of offset printing invented a century later in England, takes advantage of the tendency of oil and water to separate. The image is first sketched onto a smooth limestone slab and then finished with a wax crayon, and the stone is treated to absorb water in the blank areas. An oily ink is applied, which sticks to the waxy surface and not to the water-soaked surface, allowing the image to transfer to paper.

The process became one of the cheapest and most popular ways of mass distribution of prints, posters and book illustrations.

Among of the most important lithography companies between 1834 and 1907 was Currier & Ives. The company produced over 7,000 titles, with millions of copies, depicting everyday life, battle scenes, famous people and usually conservative political commentary. Depictions of women and African Americans were often highly objectionable by modern standards, although at the time they were usually more clownish than hateful. The company's low prices and wide circulation meant that they outlasted many of their competitors, but the company closed when the photo halftone processes became widely adopted.

Figure II.5 Audubon Lithographs—John James Audubon's bird paintings were not initially popular in America. However, British art publishers and scientific circles received him enthusiastically, and his paintings were transferred to lithographs and published in London in 1827, with subsequent volumes over the years. Original copies of Birds of America are the second most valuable printed book in the world, after the Gutenberg Bible. (Library of Congress)

Another example of popular lithography was John James Audubon's Birds of America, printed in 1860. Based on Audubon's paintings made while traveling through the country, the 436 life-sized hand-colored prints resulted from Audubon's painstaking collaboration with a master lithographer.

Precursors of photography

Lithography was a better printing method than engraving or woodcut, but preparing the litho stones could be time-consuming work. French lithographer Joseph Niepce started looking for a way to speed things up. He began experimenting with light-sensitive chemicals in the 1820s and stumbled upon some of the key techniques needed in photography. Niepce's collaboration with Louis Daguerre led to first practical method of taking photographs, as we will see in the next chapter.

Another technology that set the stage for photography was the silhouette. Named for a French government official who liked to doodle, silhouettes caught on in France during the 1700s as a popular way to remember the exact likeness of a family member.

A silhouette could be done quickly by using a "camera obscura"—a dark room (called a "camera," similar to the English word "chamber") with a pinhole opening in the wall, allowing light through from the outside. The pinhole acts as a lens, and an image can be projected upside down on the far wall, making it easy to trace. The combination of a camera obscura with a light sensitive negative became the photographic camera by the 1840s.

Social impacts of the visual media revolution

As we will see in Chapter 4, Mathew Brady's exhibit of Civil War photos shocked New Yorkers in 1862. As the *Times* said: "If he has not actually brought bodies back and laid them on our dooryards and along the streets, he has done something very like it . . . There is a terrible fascination about it that draws one near these pictures . . . You will see the hushed, reverend groups standing around these weird copies of carnage . . . " (*The New York Times*, October 20, 1862).

Similarly, as we will see in Chapter 5, movies about the war in the trenches shocked and fascinated London audiences in 1916. "If women had sometimes to shut their eyes to escape for a moment from the tragedy of the toll of battle which the film presents, opinion seems to be general that it was wise that the people at home should have this glimpse of what our soldiers are doing and daring and suffering . . . " (War's Realities on the Cinema, August 22, 1916).

The question about the appropriate use of media is age-old.

"We have not sufficiently recognized the power of moving images," said Mitchell Stephens in his book *The Rise of the Image* (Stephens, 1998). In previous times, reading was one of the few ways of experiencing the wider world, but in the modern world, "the image is replacing the word as the predominant means of mental transport."

This is hardly a new issue. Publishers worried about the abundance of visual images emerging in popular culture as early as the 1840s, long before it became possible to print photographs. William Blackwood, a publisher in Edinburgh, Scotland, said in 1844, shortly after the success of the *Illustrated London News*, that the "new art of printing" threatened the old habit of reading:

> People have not only ceased to purchase those old-fashioned things called books, but even to read them! . . . Who has leisure to read? Who cares to sit down and spell out accounts of travels which he can make at less cost than the cost of the narrative? Who wants to peruse fictitious adventures, when rail-roads and steamboats woo him to adventures of his own . . . We are not told, but shown how the world is wagging. The magazines sketch us a lively article, the newspapers vignette us, step by step, a royal tour. The beauties of Shakespeare are imprinted on the minds of the rising generation, in woodcuts; and the poetry of Byron (is) engraved in their hearts, by means of the graver . . . Books, the small as well as the great, will have been voted a great evil. There will be no gentlemen of the press. The press itself will have ceased to exist. (Blackwood, 1844)

What's interesting about this rather crabby complaint from an old Scottish printer is that it sounds so familiar. Similar things have been said about film, about radio and television, and about the internet. Producers of older media rarely welcome competition from new media, especially when the new media seems, to them, shallow and yet more powerful than the old media.

Neil Postman summed it up neatly in a book called *Amusing Ourselves to Death*. The social problem for the media isn't simply that it can lead to tyranny envisioned by George Orwell in 1984, but also that it can lead to the "Brave New World" envisioned by Aldous Huxley. In Huxley's world, an abundance of superficial distractions degraded individual and social responsibility.

So it's not surprising that Thomas Edison and others who defended film in its early days used arguments about its educational and moral value to deflect criticism.

Stereotypes: injury and inspiration

Like any powerful tool, the power of images has been used in a variety of ways to elevate, to inspire and, all too frequently, to injure. Walter Lippmann, borrowing a

Figure II.6 Stereotyped image of women—this 1869 perspective on the right of women to vote is part of the Currier & Ives lithographic portfolio of 7,000 subjects and millions of copies. The firm went out of business after photo halftone printing was developed in the late 1800s. Many of its older ideas were also going out of fashion. Women finally overcame stereotypes like this one and secured the right to vote in 1920 in the United States, 1918 in Canada, and 1928 in Britain. (Library of Congress)

technical term from the printing industry, said that we all use "stereotypes" or "pictures in our heads" as mental shortcuts that allow us to make quick judgments. The power of the mass media to create these stereotypes and shape public opinion is well known.

From the wave of American race riots that followed the film *The Birth of a Nation* in 1915 to genocide in the Rwanda and Bosnia in the 1990s, the impact is clear. The path to genocide can be paved by a complicit media.

Should the media be held responsible? Or is hate speech a form of speech that should be free? Julius Streicher, publisher of *Der Stürmer*, attacked German Jews without mercy in the 1930s, as we have seen in Chapter 3. He was convicted of crimes against humanity after the Nazi defeat in World War II. But Leni Riefenstahl's film *Triumph of the Will* only helped glorify the Nazis and solidify Adolf Hitler's power grab in Germany. She endured a few years in prison, but escaped Streicher's fate. While she maintained throughout her life that she was merely naive and not political, she evaded the key ethical question: To what extent are individuals in the mass media responsible for the use of their artistic or literary gifts?

Aside from these extreme cases, stereotypes of gays, of African Americans and many other social groups have been known to injure in more subtle ways. "Media-promulgated stereotypes of various and diverse groups of people cause harm in both direct and indirect ways by presenting oversimplified, mostly negative, and often deceptive depictions," said Paul Martin Lester in his book, *Images that Injure* (Lester, 1996).

While images can injure, they can also inspire. For example, an image of the banishment of cholera was used to encourage slum cleanup in New York in the 1870s. Louis Hine and Jacob Riis used photography in campaigns for child labor laws and cleanup of slums. Also, the documentary photography of the Farm Security Administration from 1937 was an attempt to demonstrate the determination of the American people to come out of the Depression.

Figure II.7 Inspiring images of reform—The New York *Daily Graphic* uses a broom metaphor to inspire cleanup of slums and the banishment of disease. (Library of Congress)

Advertising and public relations as image-making

Advertising and public relations are functions that are as old as humanity, but the two industries emerged forcefully in the visual media revolution. Creating a positive image of a product or company can often spell the difference between success and failure, even for the most powerful companies.

As we will see in Chapter 6, advertising with images, especially powerful artistic images that evoked emotional responses, became common in the early 1900s. Even more than the physical artifact of an image, the idea of image-making also had a social impact, to the point where ideals were replaced by the all important personal and corporate image.

Similarly, politicians and others in public life have always relied on mental images and symbolism to make their point. In the mid-twentieth century, however, there seemed to be an increasing distinction between use of a symbol or stereotype to understand a position or event, and the use of imagery to create a bewildering set of impressions on the public debate.

Librarian of Congress Daniel J Boorstin is especially remembered for his concern about the rise of imagery in public relations:

> While (corporate logos) have become more important with each decade, a more abstract kind of image is the peculiar product of our age. Its tyranny is pervasive. An image in this sense is not simply a trademark, a design, a slogan or an easily remembered picture. It is a studiously crafted personality profile of an individual, institution, corporation, product or service. It is a value-carica-ture, shaped in three dimensions, of synthetic materials. Such images in every increasing numbers have been fabricated and re-enforced by the new tech-niques of the graphic revolution. (Boorstin, 1961)

Some have argued that advertising and public relations bears responsibility for undercutting the social meaning. French sociologist Jean Baudrillard has argued that the abundance of visual communication in the modern era has caused an effacement

Figure II.8 The Wild West—the exuberant image of the "wild West," and its appeal to newspaper readers back East, is reflected in this 1886 Police Gazette account of the jailbreak of real-life outlaw "Belle" Myra Maybelle Shirley Star. (Library of Congress)

of reality in which symbolic value ("sign value") becomes more important than exchange value. "Conspicuous consumption," once possible only among the leisure class, has been extended to everyone in the consumer culture. And so, in a world where everything is a commodity that is up for sale, psychological alienation is total (Kellner, 2009).

Yet advertising supports media financially in a way that government cannot, and public relations is, to a large extent, the voice of businesses competing in both financial markets and the marketplace of ideas. Questions of social impacts of media are profound, and the ability of a free society to curb corporate speech by law is a point of serious contention.

For additional reading, discussion questions, links to video and other suggestions, see www.revolutionsincommunications.com.

4 Photography: giving vision to history

"At first we did not dare look long on at the images he (Daguerre) produced. We were frightened by the clarity of these men, imagining that these small, indeed, tiny, faces, fixed on a plate, could turn back and look at us."—Charles Dauthendey, c.1850. (Johnson, 1991)

The arrival of photography

To the public of the mid-nineteenth century, it must have seemed that photography arrived overnight. Only weeks after Louis Daguerre donated his photographic patents to the greater good of humanity, dozens of entrepreneurs were setting up "daguerreotype" studios.

Like nearly all great inventions, photography grew out of many small advances that set the stage for the critical breakthrough. Thomas Wedgewood is sometimes called the "first" photographer because he experimented with light-sensitive chemicals and created the first unfixed photographic picture in 1792. British scientist Humphrey Davy wrote about experiments he shared with Wedgewood in 1802, noting that he was able to find chemicals so sensitive to light that even dim rays from a camera obscura would leave an imprint. However, he did not find a way to fix the images (Litchfield, 1903, p. 165).

Joseph Nicephore Niepce, a French lithographer, started experimenting with photography a decade later and, around 1826, found a partial solution to the problem. He coated a tin plate with asphalt, loaded it into a camera obscura and left it pointed out of the window for eight hours. Areas of asphalt that had not been hardened by sunlight washed off in oil. It is the first surviving photograph in history, but it was not a practical process, since the image was grainy and only buildings or fixed objects could be photographed.

Meanwhile, a Parisian artist named Louis Daguerre had almost given up painting elaborate theatrical scenes (called dioramas) that depicted history and fantasy with

Figure 4.1 First photograph—Joseph Niepce took this image over an 8-hour period in 1826. He gave the image to an English friend the following year, and it was lost until 1951.

painted backdrops, props and wax figures. Like Niepce, he was obsessed with finding a quicker way to accurately depict his subjects. In 1824, his wife went to see a famous French chemist to see if he could talk Daguerre out of spending all his time and money on foolish experiments. Instead, the chemist was so impressed that he offered to help Daguerre (*Photographic Times*, 1910).

Daguerre also heard about Niepce's experiments. Rather than becoming rivals, the two men began collaborating around 1829. Despite Niepce's death four years later, Daguerre persisted in trying to solve the problem of fixing the image permanently. Eventually he found sodium thiosulfate ("hypo") in 1837, and began taking and exhibiting pictures that he called "heliographs" (sun writing). But the pictures quickly became known as Daguerreotypes.

Figure 4.2 Inventor of photography—after years of experiments, Louis Daguerre found a practical way to take photographs in 1937.

"Daguerre's plates . . . aroused awe and fear of a radically new way of presenting the world in two dimensions," observed historian Paul Johnson (Johnson, 1991). But they were also widely hailed as a great scientific breakthrough.

Daguerre did not attempt to make a fortune with his process, nor did he attempt to control its use for profit or for a moral purpose, as later inventors would do with radio and movies. Instead, he disclosed the exact details of the process through the French Academy of Sciences and gave his invention as a gift "free to the world" on August 19, 1839.

Within a matter of weeks and months, photographic studios sprang up in cities around the world.

Samuel Morse, inventor of the Morse code for the telegraph, happened to be present in Paris when Daguerre's process was announced. At the time, Morse was still struggling to find funding for the telegraph. Thinking that photography would sustain him for a time, he ordered a camera and gathered materials to take back to New York. By September of 1839, he was teaching the art of photography. One of his students was Mathew Brady, the famed Civil War photographer.

"I was introduced to Morse (in 1839), who was then painting portraits at starvation prices in the university rookery on Washington square," Brady wrote. "He had just come home from Paris and had invented upon the ship his telegraphic alphabet of which his mind was so full that he could give but little attention to a remarkable discovery one Daguerre, a friend of his, had made in France" (Horan, 1955).

In 1844, Brady opened his portrait studio over a saloon on New York's busiest street—Broadway. Not only did he offer daguerreotypes at a reasonable price, but he also sought advice from the best chemists to help refine his techniques. His portraits soon began taking first place in competitions, and by the late 1840s he was a household name: "Brady of Broadway."

Brady also made a point of documenting the likenesses of the most famous people of the day for *The Gallery of Illustrious Americans*. His subjects were everyone still living who was important—Andrew Jackson, James Polk, and many other actors and politicians famous in their day.

In 1860, when an Illinois politician gave an important speech in New York's Cooper Union lecture hall, he also stopped into the Brady studio for a photo. It was reproduced by the thousands and became the best known image of the 1860 presidential campaign. "Brady and the Cooper Institute made me president of the United States," Abraham Lincoln said (Horan, 1955).

Figure 4.3 Presidential candidate—Abraham Lincoln, running for president in the 1860 election, stopped by Matthew Brady's studio in New York for a photo. The image was widely circulated and helped Lincoln win. (Library of Congress)

Brady is most often remembered as the man who photographed the US Civil War, but he was not the first war photographer. He was preceded by an unknown photographer who captured images from the Mexican–American war of 1848. More notably, Brady was preceded by Roger Fenton, a British photographer, who traveled to the Russian Crimean region with British troops in 1855. Some believe that Fenton's photographs were meant to offset anger from the British public over the disastrous Crimean War (Sontag, 2003, p. 126). Anti-war sentiment grew after London *Times* correspondent William Howard Russell reported on the Charge of the Light Brigade. A controversy over Fenton's photographic techniques emerged in later years. (See "Historical Detective Work" on page 120.)

Fenton avoided taking photos of the dead or wounded soldiers. A few years later, Brady did not hesitate to reveal the macabre aftermath of the battle to the public. When Brady exhibited photos of the Civil War dead in 1862 at his New York studio, the effect was sensational. *The New York Times* said that Mr. Brady "has rendered us a real service . . . by this work of his, undertaken so courageously and carried forth so resolutely" (*The New York Times,* September 26, 1862, p. 5). "If he has not actually brought bodies back and laid them on our dooryards and along the streets, he has done something very like it . . . There is a terrible fascination about it that draws one near these pictures . . . You will see the hushed, reverend groups standing around these weird copies of carnage . . . " (*The New York Times,* October 20, 1862, p. 5).

Brady, like Fenton, was not averse to staging photos for more artistic effect. But like Fenton and others before and since, Brady endured hardships and risked every-

Historical detective work

Roger Fenton's "Valley of the Shadow of Death"

On April 24, 1855, Roger Fenton, a British photographer, approaches a ridge over-looking the besieged town of Sevastopol, Ukraine. The artillery from the town has been so intense that he didn't peek over the ridge.

Figure 4.4 Roger Fenton—Valley of the Shadow of Death, the ON photo

Figure 4.5 Roger Fenton—Valley of the Shadow of Death, the OFF photo. (Library of Congress)

Instead he spent an hour taking two photos of a road in the "Valley of the Shadow of Death" leading to the ridge. Hundreds of cannonballs have landed in the valley. He took two photos and left, but later, historians will wonder which of the two photos came first—the one with the cannonballs ON the road, or the one where the cannonballs are OFF the road?

If the OFF photo came first, then the ON photo is decep-tive, possibly intended to dramatize the intense artillery. But the alternative explanation is that the cannonballs could have been cleared from the road, and the ON photo could be the first.

Errol Morris investigated the problem of the Fenton photos in "Which Came First, the Chicken or the Egg?" *The New York Times*, September 25, 2007 and, comparing the way the rocks fell down the hill in the ON photo, concluded that Fenton did, indeed, attempt to dramatize the shot.

thing for history. "No one will ever know what I went through," Brady said. "Some of these negatives nearly cost me my life." The negatives were nearly lost after the war, and Brady lost his studio and his fortune. Still, he had lived up to his ideals. "The camera is the eye of history," he said. "From the first, I regarded myself as under obligation to my country to preserve the faces of its historical men and women" (Horan, 1955).

Figure 4.6 Marcus Sparling, Fenton's assistant, wanted to have his picture taken just before going with Fenton to Valley of the Shadow of Death. Sparling " ... suggested as there were a possibility of a stop being put in that valley to the further travels of both vehicle and driver, it would be showing a proper consideration for both to take a likeness of them before starting," Fenton wrote. (Library of Congress)

Figure 4.7 Brady's war—two figures stand over a mass grave following the US Civil War battle of Antietam in September, 1862. This photo was taken by one of Brady's assistants and exhibited in the New York studios only a few days later. (Library of Congress)

Figure 4.8 Brady with the generals—Matthew Brady (second from left) with General Ambrose Burnside (reading newspaper) sometime in 1862. "The camera is the eye of history," he said.

A question of art and copyright

As photography became popular in the 1840s and 50s, the question of whether photography was art or simply some form of mechanical reproduction became important on an abstract cultural level and also for legal and economic reasons.

High culture of the mid-nineteenth century looked down on photographers. When, in 1859, a group of artists and photographers, including Eugène Delacroix, finally succeeded in getting photography included in the Paris Salon, patrons had to use a back entrance.

"Some painters, especially miniaturists, quickly began to feel threatened and intimidated by the new 'art' of photography," said historian David Haberstich (Haberstich, 1973). Honore Daumier, a noted artist of the day, depicted portrait photographers of Paris as lazy louts in his sarcastic print: "Patience is the virtue of fools."

Figure 4.9 Is photography art?—the question was not just an argument over aesthetics. This portrait of playwright Oscar Wilde, taken in 1884, was copied without permission by a New York lithography company. When the photographer sued, Burrow-Giles lithographers said that only the arts were covered by copyright law, and photography was not an art. But photographers argued that they brought a sense of art into the photographic process, and won the precedent-setting case.

By 1862, the legal question of whether photography was fine art or merely mechanical reproduction had to be settled, and a series of French and British cases were vehemently argued in the courts and salons. One of the most celebrated involved the re-sale of images of famous people originally taken by photographers working with Mayer and Pierson publishers in Paris. Another case involved a photographer who was originally commissioned to help a painter get an exact likeness for a portrait, but who then sold prints of the photograph.

Artists were furious, not only for what they thought was obvious theft, but also about the larger issue of "likening photography to art." In the Mayer and Pierson case, a lower court judge ruled that Daguerre's invention of photography was in the public domain, and so too were any products of the invention. When the case was appealed to the French high court, attorneys arguing for artists said "Photography lacks the qualities which are necessary to constitute a work of art: it is not a creation, does not have originality."

On the other hand, Mayer and Pierson's attorneys argued: "Photographic images, too, have their inspiration. This inspiration belongs entirely to the artist, and the sun is merely his compliant and splendid collaborator! Let us then give the mind its rights and limit the equipment to its proper role. It appears that there is a reliable *criterion* for judging this matter. The work of a machine may be identified by its uniformity. The work of man is identifiable by its variety, its diversity, its progress."

The French high court took a middle course, deciding that while photographs "*are not . . . creations of the mind or genius*" certain images could be considered artistic and therefore could have copyright protection (Bentley and Kretschmer, 2010; also Freund, 1980, pp. 81–4).

A similar controversy erupted in the United States in the 1884 when a photograph of playwright Oscar Wilde by the New York photographer Napoleon Sarony was widely reproduced. Sarony sued a lithographic company that reproduced this and other celebrity photos, and the case went to the US Supreme court.

In court, the company argued that the original wording of the US Constitution only allowed Congress to protect the "writings" of "authors," and so the Copyright Act of 1870, which included protection of photographs, was unconstitutional.

However, the court ruled in favor of the photographer, endorsing not only the power of Congress to regulate photography but also the concept that the law needed to be adaptable to challenges posed by new technologies (*Burrow-Giles Lithographic Co. v. Sarony 111 U.S. 53(1884)*).

Turning photography into art: pictorialism

The debate over the legitimacy of photography raged on long after the Mayer and Burrow-Giles cases were settled in France and the United States. A series of artistic movements and countermovements inspired new approaches by new generations of photographers and artists. "The pressures of industrialization pushing against the bedrock of agrarian and artisanal tradition were threatening to split apart the old orders, whether political, economic, or aesthetic," said one art historian (McCauley, 2008).

The snobbery of Parisian portrait painters over what was legitimately artistic spurred the "pictorialist" photographic movement. In defense of their art, pictorialists depicted subjects with soft visual effects and artistic poses. One part of the movement was the "The Brotherhood of the Linked Ring" founded in Britain in May, 1892. Similar clubs were formed in Vienna and Paris to promote the artistic side of photography.

American pictorialists included Alfred Stieglitz and Edward Steichen, who opened the 291 Gallery in New York. They were determined that photography would find its place "as a medium of individual expression," as Steiglitz said. The gallery was an enormous success, taking the forefront of the modern art movement in the pre-World War I period. Among the best known photos of the period is the Flat Iron Building, taken by Steichen.

Figure 4.10 Atmospherics: the flat iron building—taken on a damp winter afternoon in 1905, Edward Steichen's atmospheric photograph epitomized the pictorialist movement in photography. (Library of Congress)

The success of the 291 Gallery inspired another reaction in the Straight Photography movement.

Figure 4.11 Alienation: Wall Street—a perfect contrast with pictorialist atmospheric photos was Paul Strand's 1915 Wall Street photo, where people are dwarfed by the buildings and institutions of modern society. (Library of Congress)

Photographers like Paul Strand thought pictorialism was too apologetic, and did not take advantage of the new medium. Strand took photography into advertising and abstract work with the idea of "absolute unqualified objectivity" rather than artistically manipulated photos.

Strand was politically liberal, and like other photographers of the era used the camera to advance social causes as well as present artistic subjects. The overbearing architecture and isolation of people in his 1915 Wall Street photo is a social comment as much as an artistic expression. Like many American artists, Strand suffered from blacklisting during the post-World War II reaction to communism, and spent the last three decades of his life in Europe.

On the US west coast, a group of photographers who sided with Strand's Straight Photography movement formed the f/64 Group in the early 1930s. The name is a reaction to Stieglitz' 291 Gallery but is also a technical description of an approach to photography. F/64 is a lens aperture setting that requires long exposures and intense lighting, resulting in strong, clear images with extraordinary depth of field. The modernistic approach to photography is also seen in attention to underlying geometrical patterns. Ansel Adams' work is probably the best example. Other members of the group included Imogen Cunningham and Edward Weston.

Figure 4.12 Democratizing photography—before celluloid film, large cumbersome cameras were needed to hold glass plate negatives. George Eastman, founder of the Kodak Corporation, made photography accessible to everyone with a line of small easy-to-use cameras in the 1880s.

Photography made simple

While artistic photographers continued to use "large format" cameras with 8 by 10 inch negatives, this kind of equipment proved clumsy in the field and inaccessible to the general public.

The breakthrough occurred with the improvement of celluloid film in the 1880s. Rather than carting around boxes of fragile glass negatives, small cameras allowed everyone to be a photographer. Celluloid film also made motion pictures possible.

George Eastman, a photographer who founded the Kodak Corporation in 1884, was quick to see the possibilities. The company marketed a camera that was sold ready to take pictures and then returned to the company in Rochester. Another camera, loaded with 100 pictures, came back with the printed photos. "You push the button, we do the rest," was the Kodak slogan.

Early popular cameras had shutters with two settings—one for indoors, which could be held open for a longer time, and a snap shutter for outdoor light. But low-light conditions were difficult to photograph. The solution was a magnesium compound, invented in the 1880s, that would produce a flash of bright light to capture subjects in dark conditions.

Social change and photography

Among the first to use flash photography in the United States was photojournalist Jacob Riis (1849–1914), who used it to take photos of squalid conditions, dangerous alleys and suffering children. Riis was also able to take advantage of another new media technology—the "halftone" process that screened a photograph into small dots that could be printed on paper.

In his 1890 book, *How the Other Half Lives*, Riis published a mix of photos and drawings about what he found roaming the streets of New York with his friend Theodore Roosevelt, who was then commissioner of police. He wrote about crime, the lack of sanitation and the rising rate of disease. His photos magnified the effect of his scathing indictment of New York's indifference to its suffering population. The book set a standard for muckraking reporting and spurred investigations that changed the building codes and health rules for New York.

Another example of photography for social reform involved Lewis Hine (1874–1940), a photographer who joined the National Child Labor Committee in 1907. Hine's stunning portraits of children working with dangerous machinery proved to be more powerful arguments than anything that could be said or written. By 1916, child labor reform laws had been enacted.

Hine's work has been carried on by many photographers, in recent years notably by Sebastião Salgado, a photographer who works in the UN Global Movement for Children. "More than ever, I feel that the human race is one," Salgado said. "There are differences of color, language, culture and opportunities, but people's feelings and reactions are alike. People flee wars to escape death, they migrate to improve their fortunes, they build new lives in foreign lands, they adapt to extreme hardship. . . . "

The economic depression of the 1930s was another great social problem, involving a lack of confidence in the economic system and, for some people, the very concept of democracy. One response from Franklin Delano Roosevelt's New Deal administration involved the rural rehabilitation efforts of the Farm Security Administration. Among its other jobs, the FSA was supposed to boost national morale by sending photographers and writers out into the country to document the national spirit.

FSA photographers took over 200,000 photos documenting the condition of the country. The result was not always a morale boosting portrait, but rather, one of a people struggling to cope and not always managing. While the intent was to "introduce Americans to Americans," the underlying argument of the photos was for social reform.

Figure 4.13 Muckraking photography—Jacob Riis, a muckraking journalist, showed "How the Other Half Lives" in his 1890 book.

Figure 4.14 Breaker boys—the hopelessness on the faces of these children who were forced to work in the coal mines is what photographer and reformer Lewis Hine hoped to depict.

"The compassionate optimism of so many of the FSA photographs was not created solely by government decree," said historian Vicki Goldberg. "The belief was abroad in the land that with sufficient will, technology and the proper kind of government intervention, even the problems of the Depression could be licked" (Goldberg, 1991).

Photographic magazines

Henry Luce (1898–1967) founded a publishing empire in 1923 with the conviction that busy people needed a news magazine to help keep them informed. *Time* magazine, started in 1923, compressed the week's news into what one writer called a "capsulized abridgement of a condensation" (Swanberg, 1972). The magazine had an exuberant writing style that reminded readers of young men just out of college, which is a fair description of Luce and his colleagues. Unlike then-established magazines such as *Literary Digest*, *Time* magazine spoke to its generation. As it achieved success in the 1920s, Luce launched other ventures. *Fortune*, a magazine for the business community, was his first in 1930. But *Life* magazine, launched in 1936, became the star attraction, creating the platform for some of the most brilliant photography of the twentieth century.

The idea of a photographic magazine was not new. Probably the most direct influence on *Life* magazine was the *Berliner Illustrirte Zeitung* (*BIZ*), founded in Germany in 1891. The magazine was originally illustrated with engravings, but made the switch to photographs early in the twentieth century. Under Kurt Korff as editor-in-chief (1905–1933) the *BIZ* developed a new brand of magazine layout featuring photojournalism. Korff said the magazine's success came from a general shift toward a more visual culture and a "new relationship" with images themselves as conveyors of news

Figure 4.15 Modern child labor—documenting child labor in the twenty-first century, Sebastião Salgado carries on the work of reformers like Riis and Hine. This photo shows children carrying sacks of coal from a mine face to a train in India. (Photo courtesy Sebastião Salgado)

Figure 4.16 Power House—Hine also made "work portraits" that emphasized the human contribution to modern industry. This iconic photo was also an inspiration for Charlie Chaplin's 1936 comic film *Modern Times*. (Library of Congress)

(Ross, 2008). Korff fled Germany in 1933 when the Nazis took over, eventually working for Luce. Meanwhile, one of his most talented photographers—Robert Capa (Andre Friedmann) fled to Paris. He would later become famous as one of the world's great war photographers.

Life magazine editors also took cues from the *Illustrated London News*, which emphasized photos over text even more than *BIZ*, and from *Vu*, a French magazine, with modern typefaces and in-depth photo essays that told complex stories. The *Life* magazine manifesto, written in exchanges between Luce and Archibald Macleish, begins: "To see life, to see the world; to eyewitness great events; to watch the faces of the poor and the gestures of the proud; to see strange things—machines, armies, multitudes, shadows in the jungle and on the moon; to see man's work . . . to see and to take pleasure in seeing . . . " (Brinkley, 2010).

Life was an overnight success when it was first published in 1936, and its 50 weekly pages of photos spawned many imitators, such as *Look* and *Paris Match*. It lost momentum in the television age, struggled through the end of the twentieth century in various forms, and is now published primarily as an online archive.

The corner of her eye: Dorothea Lange

The most famous portrait of the era, or perhaps the twentieth century, was taken by Dorothea Lange, a photographer who visited migrant farm camps while working for the FSA in California. Her classically composed "Migrant Mother" photo, taken in March, 1936 in Nipomo, California, resulted from a combination of intuition and professional determination.

Figures 4.17, 4.18 and 4.19 Migrant Mother—One of the signature photos of the twentieth century was Dorothea Lange's 1936 portrait of a migrant farm worker and her children. The photos were taken while Lange (lower left) traveled on assignment for the Farm Security Administration. As she took the series of photos, Lange learned that the mother, Florence Owens Thompson, had just sold the tires from her car to buy food for the children. Lange passed the word to relief authorities who rushed food to the camp the next day. (FSA Collection, Library of Congress)

As Lange told the story, she had been on assignment for a month and was driving home when she said she noticed a "pea pickers camp" sign "out of the corner of my eye." She drove on in the rain for another 20 miles, convincing herself that she didn't need to go back to take one more set of photos. And then:

> Almost without realizing what I was doing, I made a U-turn on the empty high-way. I went back those 20 miles and turned off the highway at that sign, PEA-PICKERS CAMP. I was following instinct, not reason; I drove into that wet and soggy camp and parked my car like a homing pigeon. I saw and approached the hungry and desperate mother, as if drawn by a magnet. I do not remember how I explained my presence or my camera to her, but I do remember she asked me no questions. I made five exposures, working closer and closer from the same direction. I did not ask her name or her history. She told me her age, that she was thirty-two. She said that they had been living on frozen vegetables from the surrounding fields, and birds that the children killed. She had just sold the tires from her car to buy food. There she sat in that lean-to tent with her children

huddled around her, and seemed to know that my pictures might help her, and so she helped me. There was a sort of equality about it. (Lange, 1960)

The next day, Lange and her editors alerted federal relief authorities, and food was rushed to the camp. Lange also went on, with characteristic instinct and conscience, to photograph Japanese-descended Americans forced into relocation camps during World War II.

The subject of the Migrant Mother photo, Florence Owens Thompson, survived the Depression and raised her children in California. Thompson's daughters said she had avoided publicity until 1978 because she was ashamed at having been an icon of poverty. But FSA photos like the Migrant Mother gave no hint that the subjects had brought misery on themselves through any fault of their own. Instead, they portrayed good people as victims of a flawed system.

Parks and other
Life magazine photographers

Another FSA photographer, Gordon Parks, made a similarly iconic photo. Parks, a northern-born African American, was unaccustomed to the racism of the American South, so when he was hired in 1942 in Washington DC, his first assignment was to leave his camera behind and go to a lunch counter and the movies. He was turned away from both establishments, which was the reason he was given the assignment. Later that afternoon, as the somewhat angered Parks was settling into his new job, he noticed Ella Watson cleaning the building. He asked her to pose in front of a flag, broom in one hand and mop by her side, in the style of a famous Grant Wood painting "American Gothic." Parks' boss, FSA chief Roy Stryker, said he had the right idea but had overdone it, which could get them all fired. Parks went on to work for *Life* magazine for 20 years. He also became the first major African-American director in the United States with films like *The Learning Tree* (1969) and *Shaft* (1971).

Working for *Life* magazine was the way many great photographers stayed in the field. Along with Parks, the *Life* photography crew included some of the twentieth century's best photographers: Margaret Bourke-White, Dorothea Lange, Robert Capa, Alfred Eisenstadt, W. Eugene Smith, Edward Steichen, and many others.

Figure 4.20 American Gothic—Gordon Parks had just been hired by the Farm Security Administration when he took this photo of Ella Watson, who worked on the cleaning crew in the federal building. Parks was angry after having encountered racism in Washington DC. The photo shows a woman who has been victimized but who also has a deep personal resilience. (Library of Congress)

Twentieth-century war photography

While photography was tightly censored in World War I by the Creel Committee, World War II was a different kind of war, involving fully mobilized civilian populations. Propaganda was important and the image meant everything.

Among the most dynamic photographers of the war years was Robert Capa, a Hungarian-born refugee from Nazi Germany originally named Andrei Friedmann who found he could not get work as a photographer in Paris in 1933. With two friends, he advertised a new Paris photo agency being opened by the famous American photographer Robert Capa. At first, Friedmann was the non-existent Capa's assistant, but soon he was using the name as his own. "I invented that Bob Capa was a famous American photographer who came over to Europe," Capa admitted in 1947 (Kershaw, 2002, p. 29).

One of Capa's famous photos is that of the Spanish Civil War soldier at the exact moment of death in 1936. Although some have alleged that the photo was faked (Knightly, 2004), others insist that clues in the photo, along with corroborating evidence, demonstrate its veracity (Whelan, 2002).

Capa fled to the United States when the Germans invaded France in 1940, and worked on assignment for *Collier's* and *Life* magazines covering the war. He parachuted into Sicily with the Allied invasion and followed the grim Italian campaign of 1943–1944. He was reassigned to England and, after a round of parties with friends like Ernest Hemingway and John Steinbeck, Capa followed the invasion across

Figure 4.21 Falling soldier—taken at the very moment of death, this 1936 photo of a soldier in the Spanish Civil War made Robert Capa an international celebrity. (Photo by Robert Capa, Magnum Photos)

the English Channel. He was the only photographer on Omaha Beach on D-Day, and his photos were mishandled by darkroom assistants. Yet they were widely published and, in their hazy and overdeveloped way, seem to paint a moment of sharp contrasts and great confusion. Capa died in Vietnam in 1954 covering the unfolding war.

Another great American war photographer was Margaret Bourke-White. Her photos of the Depression era, especially the "dust bowl" of Oklahoma, had made her famous. Her pictures of the liberation of Buchenwald were so stark that then-US general Dwight Eisenhower soon arrived to confirm that the Nazi concentration camps were real. Of course, they were horrifyingly real, and Bourke-White later said that it helped to have a camera in between her and the pitiful victims of the camps. She also took a deceptively simple portrait of Mahatma Gandhi in 1946. Gandhi is shown with a spinning wheel in the foreground of the photo, which implied that a person can, with modesty, be a symbol of change and put the symbol forward, rather than themselves.

Joe Rosenthal was yet another great photographer of the war era, and his Associated Press shot of US Marines planting the flag on Iwo Jima is among the best known photos of the era. Like Lange when she shot Migrant Mother, Rosenthal had a feeling that he should keep going up Mount Suribachi even when he met other photographers and reporters coming down the mountain who said the flag had already gone up, but the views from the top were outstanding. As it turned out, Marines were preparing to raise a second, larger flag, and Rosenthal captured a well-remembered

Figure 4.22 Iwo Jima, 1945—Associated Press photographer Joe Rosenthal took this iconic photo of the US Marines raising the flag over Mount Suribachi during heavy combat on Iwo Jima. The photo became a symbol of the US Marine Corps. (Photo by Joe Rosenthal, The Associated Press)

photo that earned him a Pulitzer Prize. Asked about the photo later, Rosenthal would reply with typical modesty: "I took the picture. The Marines took Iwo Jima" (Leary, 2006). Rosenthal worked for the AP until his retirement in 1981.

Conservation and environmental photography

If photography has the power to change the way we look at ourselves, it also has the power to change the way we look at our environment. One of the most dramatic examples is "Earthrise," a photo of the earth from 240,000 miles out in space, taken Christmas Eve, 1968 by US astronaut William Anders aboard the Apollo 8 in orbit around the moon.

The photo was printed in thousands of newspapers, magazines and books, and was the cover for the Whole Earth Catalog. Wilderness photographer Galen Rowell called it "the most influential environmental photograph ever taken." Photos taken

Figure 4.23 Earthrise—on Christmas Eve, 1968, US astronaut William Anders snapped this shot of earth rising above the moon's horizon while aboard the Apollo 8 spacecraft. (US National Aeronautics and Space Administration)

from space remind us, said astronomer Carl Sagan, that we are all in this together: "In all this vastness, there is no hint that help will come from elsewhere to save us from ourselves."

Another NASA photo, taken from the TOMS satellite in 1984, showed clearly that the protective layer of ozone was decreasing in the atmosphere. The photo had a dramatic political impact. Within a few years, the United States signed the Montreal Protocol, an international treaty pledging to eliminate chlorofluorocarbon chemicals that were causing ozone depletion.

Photography inspired by the beauty of natural landscapes or remote corners of the world is a recurrent theme. Among the first to take advantage of the camera for this point of view were the Bisson brothers, who adored alpine hiking in the 1850s and took stunning shots of mountaineers on glaciers.

Carleton E. Watkins was known as an accomplished field photographer in the American West in the 1860s, hoping to give everyone "the best seat in the house."

Figure 4.24 Environmental photography—this photo of an expedition to a glacier was taken in the 1850s by the Bisson Brothers. (Library of Congress)

William Henry Jackson accompanied the Hayden Geological Survey of 1871. His photos helped persuade Congress to create Yellowstone National Park.

In contrast, Margaret Bourke-White's photos of the Oklahoma "dust bowl" brought back the misery of the experience in the 1930s. She wrote in *The Nation*:

> By coincidence I was in the same parts of the country where last year I photographed the drought. [Then] there was an attitude of false optimism. "Things will get better," the farmers would say. "We're not as hard hit as other states. The government will help out. This can't go on." But this year there is an atmosphere of utter hopelessness. Nothing to do. No use digging out your chicken coops and pigpens after the last "duster" because the next one will be coming along soon. No use trying to keep the house clean. No use fighting off that foreclosure any longer . . . (Bourke-White, 1935)

The increasing concern about environment and preservation of nature was a consistent theme of photography in the mid- to late-twentieth century. While Ansel Adams' photos of western landscapes spoke of the need for conservation, other photographers documented the increasing human cost of environmental degradation.

One of the most prominent photographer-filmmakers was Jacques Cousteau, who became known for his 1953 bestselling book *The Silent World* that described the beauty of underwater photography:

> The world . . . was twilight blue [and] flesh was a greenish putty color. The far-off sun gleamed on the chromed regulators, winked on the frames of the masks and ensilvered our exhaust bubbles. . . . The Athenian marbles were dark bluish shapes, blurred with blankets of marine life. We dug under with our hands, dog fashion, to pass cargo slings under them. As the stones ascended, color grew on the crust and, at the surface, they swung into the air ablaze with life. As they drained on deck, the Joseph's coat of flora and fauna faded into the earth shade of death.

Figure 4.25 Relocation Camp—this Ansel Adams photo from 1942 shows editor Roy Takeno reading a copy of the *Manzanar Free Press* in front of the newspaper office at the Manzanar War Relocation Camp in California, one of the ten major centers where 110,000 Americans of Japanese ancestry were held during World War II. Adams is well known for atmospheric photos, and the mountains in the background show his style; but like Dorothea Lange, Adams was also concerned about the injustice of the relocations. (Library of Congress)

Cousteau went on to win Academy Awards for his films; today his son and grandchildren are carrying on the struggle to save the world's oceans.

Another of the world's great photographers, W. Eugene Smith, must be mentioned. His photos of Pittsburgh, Pennsylvania, taken between 1955 and 1957, at the height of the smokestack era, reveal the grit and human costs of the steel industry. His portraits of the victims of mercury poisoning in Minimata, Japan, published in *Life* magazine June 2, 1972, shocked the world. The most famous of the photos shows Ryoko Eumura holding her severely deformed daughter, Tomoko, in a style similar to Michelangelo's sculpture, *La Pieta*. The photo was so good that Tomoko became an international symbol of the impacts of unregulated chemical industry, and the Eumura family asked Smith's heirs to withdraw the photo from circulation. Smith also suffered for daring to document a chemical factory's impact. He was seriously injured in an attack he believed was ordered by the chemical industry and never fully recovered before his death in 1978 (W. E. Smith and A. M. Smith, 1975).

Photographers are routinely targets of outrage, and nowhere more so than on the front lines of environmental conflict. Repeatedly arrested for covering environmental demonstrations in the Appalachians, photographer Antrim Casky said in 2009: "It's OK to pick sides. Photojournalists like Robert Capa were against Fascism. He supported the soldiers that he covered. In a sense, it's not much different here" (Roselle, 2010).

Nature photographers have also made important contributions to understanding the environment, and Eliot Porter is one of the leaders in that area. His bird photography and site-specific work on Glen Canyon, before it was flooded by Lake Powell, had a strong influence on the environmental movement. Porter worked with Ansel Adams to invent the "exhibit format" photo book which carried a message to conserve a particular place. Another photographer who worked to save Glen Canyon in the 1950s was Philip Hyde.

Two significant photographic journeys include Frans Lanting's *Journey Through Time*, for *Life* magazine in 2006, and Michael "Nick" Nichols' journey on foot across central Africa for *National Geographic* magazine in 1999.

Among many other great photographs in this category are Gary Braasch's portraits of climate change; Joel Sartori's glistening shots of endangered species; and Edward Burtynsky's vistas of frighteningly polluted landscapes. Other important conservation efforts include Jack Dykinga's desert landscapes; David Muench's photos of nature; David Doubilet's underwater photography; and C. C. Lockwood's portraits of bayou country.

Because conservation photography is so vital, an International League of Conservation Photographers was formed in 2003 (see www.ilcp.com). Another effort to inspire a new generation of photographers was the Environmental Protection Agency's "Documenting America" project, digitizing and posting photos on the Web.

Photography and ethics

Increasing concerns about the ethics of photography have also played a role in public appreciation for photography. For example, "spirit photographers" of the nineteenth century took advantage of gullible people by superimposing fake ghosts over the images of living people. Similarly, the New York *Daily Graphic* was able to use cut-and-paste techniques to alter news photos in the 1920s.

News photographers have always tried to strike a balance between public service on the one hand and sensationalism on the other. When AP photographer Nick Ut took a famous photo of children fleeing from a village in Vietnam in June of 1972, editors debated whether or not to use it, since it showed a young girl (Phan Thị Kim Phúc) whose clothes had been burned off by napalm. AP editors decided that the news value outweighed modesty. Ut took the girl to the hospital right after snapping the picture, and remained in touch with her over the years as she found a new life.

The new ability to digitally manipulate photos made fraud harder to detect in the late twentieth century but easier to suspect in old photos, such as those by Robert Fenton and Robert Capa, as we have seen.

One of the most controversial decisions to manipulate a photo was made by *Time* magazine editors following the arrest of O. J. Simpson on murder charges in 1994. *Time* and *Newsweek* magazines both ran the same police photo on the cover, but *Time* darkened the photo to make Simpson look more sinister. If the identical photo had not been on the same newsstands that same week, the controversy might not have broken out. *Time* later apologized to its readers.

Similar controversies broke out over digital manipulation of *L. A. Times* photos from the Iraq war in 2003 and over an *Economist* magazine manipulation of a shot depicting President Barack Obama standing near on the shore of the Gulf of Mexico in 2010.

The American Press Photographers Association code of ethics takes a strong position on digital manipulation of photos and advises photographers to "respect the integrity of the photographic moment."

Perhaps one of the darkest moments in the history of photography was the car chase that led to the death of Britain's Princess Diana in 1997. The paparazzi—freelance photographers who sensationalize celebrities—hounded Diana without mercy in the decade before her death. But a coroner's jury rejected claims that they murdered her, and put the blame primarily on reckless driving by the chauffer of her car.

One result of the Diana tragedy is that laws restraining invasions of privacy by photographers are becoming more common. Even so, the basic commitment to freedom of the press, along with the fact that celebrities are voluntary public figures, makes it difficult to draw the line.

Digital photography

Digital imaging technology was developed during the Cold War and the Space Race, like many other computer-related technologies. The first light-sensitive digital devices were developed by Bell Labs in 1960s and used for satellites and the moon program.

Consumers first started using digital imaging when one of the first online networks, CompuServe, developed a format for digital images called the Graphics Interchange Format (gif) in 1987. Meanwhile, a format that allowed higher compression and three color separation, called the jpeg, was developed by the International Standards Organization in Geneva, Switzerland.

By the late 1980s, jpeg formats were adopted for the Associated Press "Leafdesk" system in newsrooms throughout the world, creating an abrupt end to the century-old craft of halftone engraving. Similar tools would become available to consumers through Adobe and other companies in the mid-1990s.

Many of the companies that created the imaging revolution of the nineteenth and twentieth centuries found it difficult to transition into the digital revolution. Digital photos were far cheaper, of similar quality and, with a computer, far easier to process and print than the old film process.

Polaroid, the company that introduced "instant" photography in 1948, went bankrupt in 2001; and Agfa Photo, the German film company, declared bankruptcy in 2005.

Rapidly dropping sales for color films meant that Kodak stopped making Kodachrome film in 2009, but both Kodak and the Japanese film company Fujifilm managed to diversify operations and branch out into new areas.

Democratizing impact of digital photography

The replacement of film with digital photography shook up the industry, but it did not pose the kind of threat to democratic information systems as did the collapse of newspapers and magazines.

Instead, the fluidity and rapid transmission of digital images improved access and participation in the mass media. One development was the advent of photo sharing with companies like Flickr in 2004. White House photos are now freely available on the White House Flickr site.

A dramatic example of the impact of digital photography and networks took place following a massive 7.9 magnitude earthquake that killed 70,000 people in Sichuan Province of central China on May 12, 2008.

"The earthquake was reported as it was happening," said media analyst Clay Shirkey. "People were texting from their phones, they were taking photos from their phones, taking video from their phones . . . and uploading it to QQ, China's largest internet service." The BBC got the news from Twitter networks of friends connected to people in China.

"The last time China had a quake that size (in the 1970s), it took them three months to admit that it had happened." In contrast, photos of the 2008 earthquake were impossible to censor because they were produced by Chinese people inside China. Censors were relying on the Great Firewall of China, a surveillance and content control system set up in 2000. The system was designed to stop messages sent by foreigners into the country. It was not capable of filtering out the vast number of connected people and cell cameras inside China.

The future of photography

In 1889, a speaker at a New York photographers club said that within 50 years, the audience would marvel at stored solar energy lighting up buildings in the evenings; reporters attending meetings remotely; color photography; and push-button instant print cameras (*The New York Times*, March 6, 1889).

Each of these innovations took place, but almost in the reverse order. Edward Land patented the Polaroid instant camera in 1937; Kodak made color film available in 1935; reporters began attending meetings remotely via internet applications in the early twenty-first century; and solar energy, although practical, was not quite commercial in 2010.

A web search for the "future of photography" turns up many interesting ideas, including improvements to digital cameras, GPS signatures and other information embedded in photos, 3-dimensional and moving photos on reusable plasma screens and . . . the return of Polaroid-type instant prints.

5 Motion pictures: dream factories and popcorn palaces

"Whoever controls the motion picture industry controls the most powerful medium of influence over the people."—Thomas Edison. (The New York Times, *May 16, 1923)*

Other [media] have sprung up in a night, almost unheralded; these too have fallen first into the hands of men of vigorous imagination and ruthless temper [and] . . . aroused frenzies of fear and crusades of repression. The theater in the time of Shakespeare, the novel in the 18th century, the newspaper a century later, were also extravagantly hailed and extravagantly anathematized . . . (Thomas H. Dickinson, The New York Times, *July 6, 1923)*

Introduction

Cinema clobbers the senses, influencing the way people perceive each other and their environment like no other medium.

It's a "hot" medium, in the sense that a well-crafted succession of images leads people to "suspend disbelief" with little effort. Nothing else requires so little personal involvement or can deliver content so deeply into the human psyche.

Cinema is hotly controversial as well, and films generate heated debate for decades, while their great moments are so warmly remembered that they have become generation-spanning clichés. Although other media have the power to reflect, deflect and drive social change, none have achieved it with the artistic sweep and social force of cinema.

The story of cinema, from the Lumière brothers to the Cohn brothers, from Hollywood to Bollywood, from the Oscars to the Cannes Film Festival, is a story that parallels the social revolutions of the twentieth and twenty-first centuries.

When it first arrived, cinema was instantly seen as more powerful than any other media. The first glimpse of a "movie" in the early 1890s so frightened and astonished people that they would duck to avoid a head-on locomotive, or shout out warnings

Figure 5.1 and Figure 5.2 Moving images—
Eadweard Muybridge, a California photographer,
set up a series of cameras in 1877 to take
pictures of a galloping horse, winning a bet for
then governor Leland Stanford. The governor had
bet that all four feet leave the ground when a
horse is running. To celebrate the achievement,
Muybridge printed a century-old child's toy called
a "zoopraxiscope" to show his running horse.
(Library of Congress)

to images of endangered actors flickering across theater
screens.

Cinema drew from existing media, especially theater
and photography, also making use of the "persistence of
vision" phenomena well known in toys like flip books, the
Zoetrope (US) and the Daedalum (Britain).

An early glimpse of what cinema could become was
provided by Eadweard Muybridge, a San Francisco photographer, who used glass plate photos to sequence images.
California governor Leland Stanford hired Muybridge in
1877 to settle a bet about the way horses run. Stanford bet
that there is a moment when a horse, at a full gallop, is not
touching ground. Muybridge set up an experiment involving a series of cameras with shutters hooked to trip wires,
showed that a galloping horse does leave the ground, and
helped the governor win the bet.

Muybridge inspired other inventors, but glass plates
would not work for moving images. The introduction of

Figure 5.3 The system
designed in 1894 by the
Lumière Brothers was both
a film camera and projector.
(Wikimedia Commons)

flexible celluloid film in the mid-1880s led to a flurry of invention and two important
film systems.

Around 1894, Auguste and Louis Lumière patented the cinématographe system in
France and began showing films in theaters. And, somewhat earlier, Thomas Edison
patented a kinetoscope system and introduced it at the Chicago World's Fair
in 1893.

Figure 5.4 Fathers of film—George Eastman (left) and Thomas Edison pose behind a World War I-era movie camera. (Library of Congress)

Figure 5.5 First kiss on film—May Irwin and John C. Rice staged the first kiss ever seen on film for Thomas Edison in the film studio called the "Black Maria" in Menlo Park, New Jersey in 1896. Edison's short subjects were played on hand-cranked personal projectors in Nickelodeon halls. (Library of Congress)

It's not unusual for inventions to be simultaneous. Radio, television, computer chips and many other inventions emerged from dozens, or sometimes hundreds, of people competing to solve technical problems, as we will see in future chapters.

Edison as well as the Lumière brothers originally shot films of less than one minute on small enclosed stages. The very first films shot at Edison's Black Maria studio showed people doing rather ordinary things—sneezing, dancing, talking. These short films were shown in converted stores with individual "peep show" projectors, which would give a single person a minute's worth of film for a nickel (five US cents). "Nickelodeon" halls, as they came to be called, quickly spread in the United States, much like video game parlors in the 1980s. In 1907 there were 18 Nickelodeon halls in downtown Chicago. By 1910 there were over 500 in New York.

The experimental era took a different direction in France. The Lumière brothers were the first to take a film camera outside, shooting scenes of everyday life in Paris. They even sent camera crews around the world, and the films that came back thrilled audiences. Unlike Edison's "Black Maria" films, these travel films were carefully composed, organized narratives.

By 1900, theatrical-sized projectors had been introduced commercially in the United States, and theaters began showing films, often before or after live entertainers.

The new theater

Until the 1890s, theater had always been confined to actors on a stage or to slideshows of photographs using glass plate photos in a "magic lantern" projector.

Watching an early silent film was usually a lot like watching a theatrical performance. The camera may have provided the best view in the house, but it was usually fixed in one place. In George Méliès's 1903 *Trip to the Moon*, for instance, there are no closeups, no medium shots, and only a few transitions from one scene to the next.

This is typical of the early stages of a media revolution, in which the new media starts by following the form of the old media. As we have seen, the first printed books were designed to look like hand-lettered books, and the first photographs were often taken in the style of portraiture or landscape paintings. Similarly, radio followed the theatrical variety show format in the early years, and the first web pages resembled the prefabricated formats of internet service providers.

The earliest movies featured visualizations of then-familiar themes, including the life of religious figures, Jules Verne's science fiction and educational topics. But as the commercial prospects for film mushroomed, the topics became riskier—burglaries, train robberies, or stolen kiss in a shoe store—and these themes were threatening to the old cultural elites. The very fact that young people were congregating in dark, crowded theaters instead of churches or lecture halls was alarming to advocates of refined culture, especially in the older generation.

Some, like social reformer Jane Addams, worried that the "corrupt" art of movies was replacing true drama, which was needed to satisfy the craving for a higher conception of life. If young people "forecast their rose colored future only in a house of dreams," Addams said, society would founder on a "skepticism of life's value" (Czitrom, 1983, p. 52).

A more immediate cause for trouble was the carnival atmosphere and sexually suggestive songs and dances found in movie districts. The showdown came on Christmas Day, 1908, in New York. Reacting to testimony from religious groups that movies involved "profit from the corruption of the minds of children," the mayor revoked the licenses of 540 motion picture halls. Mayors in other cities quickly followed suit. In response, movie theater owners formed an association and sued the city. "This sort of treatment can go in Russia, but it can't go in this country," one of the theater owners said (*The New York Times*, December 29, 1908).

By January 7, 1909, the moralists lost the first round when the courts ruled that the mayor had no power to close all movie theaters, even though reasonable regulations over fire hazards and indecency could be imposed (*The New York Times*, January 7, 1909).

Another round in the early fight over film censorship involved the first African-American heavyweight boxing champion, Jack Johnson. In a well-publicized July 1910 match, Johnson won the title, beating James Jeffries, a white boxer who had been styled as the "great white hope." A film depicting Johnson's victory led to rioting in many US cities and at least eight deaths. Historian Robert Niemi called it an "exceedingly ugly episode in the appalling annals of American racial bigotry" (Niemi, 2006). The film's ideological significance alarmed racists in Congress who passed a federal ban on interstate sales of all boxing films in 1912 (S. T. Berry and V. T. Berry, 2007; Streible, 2008).

Another controversy blew up over films about prostitution a few years later. Film makers used the pretext of a 1912 report on vice in New York to show supposedly moralistic films depicting the evils of the "white slave trade." These "vice films" outraged moralists in the media. Films like *Damaged Goods*, *The House of Bondage* and *Guilty Man* "will pour oil upon the flames of vice," *The New York Times* said (*The New York Times*, November 4, 1913).

The contrast with newspapers is interesting. When newspaper publishers used the same sensationalistic tactics a generation before, they were rewarded. William T. Stead, who published London's *Pall Mall Gazette*, made an enormous profit exposing the "virtual slave trade" of London in 1883, treating the subject as a moral lesson but providing plenty of salacious detail. Pulitzer and Hearst also used the cloak of morality to expose shocking tales of vice and intrigue.

But film was new, and as a New York judge said in 1913, "tends to deprave the morals of those whose minds are open to such influences" (*The New York Times*, December 29, 1913). Although film makers said they were fighting for a principal, newspapers cast the issue in terms of films being "withdrawn" rather than "censored."

The Edison "Trust"

Around this time, Thomas Edison, a social conservative who owned many US patents for film cameras and projectors, attempted to control both the business and its cultural impacts by forming the Motion Picture Patents Company in 1908. Like other monopolies at the time, the MPPC was known as a "trust."

The MPPC "Edison Trust" included US filmmakers like Biograph and Vitagraph, and French filmmakers like Méliès and Pathé. But it did not include independent US film makers. The MPPC tried to stabilize a chaotic industry by setting standards and sharing patents, but as a monopoly, they were also able to keep independents from exhibiting in theaters or using their equipment. At the same time, the MPPC also formed a national censorship board to exclude anything that seemed immoral, leading the crusade for "moral purification" of movies.

The Edison Trust's attempt to control the business failed. The independents, especially the founders of Universal, Paramount and Twentieth Century Fox studios, moved away from the East coast to California, where mild weather and distance from the Edison company allowed feature film expansion. Then too, the dominance of European films from Méliès and Pathé ended abruptly with the outbreak of World War I in 1914. But more importantly, the emerging film industry once again went to the courts for protection.

In 1915, independent producers, contending that Edison's MPPC was an illegal monopoly, won a Supreme Court decision in *United States v. Motion Picture Patents Company*. That same year, the court also eased the fears of social conservatives in a related case, *Mutual Film v. Industrial Commission of Ohio*, ruling that films are not protected by the First Amendment. States were then free to set standards and film censorship boards of their own, and many did.

MPAA Code

Fearing a patchwork of censorship, and reacting to a series of Hollywood scandals fanned by Hearst newspapers, the film industry formed the Motion Pictures Production and Distributors Association in 1922 (which became the Motion Picture Association of America in 1945). Headed by Will H. Hayes, the MPAA fought both federal proposals for film censorship and critics within the movie industry who charged that it was a way to establish "complete monopoly" of major film producers over independent theater owners ("Theater Owners Open War on Hays," *New York Times*, May 12, 1925). This fight over control of theaters began an antitrust lawsuit that was finally settled in the *United States v. Paramount* case two decades later.

The MPAA code said: "No picture shall be produced that will lower the moral standards of those who see it." Under the code, criminals could never win, and partial nudity, steamy sex scenes and homosexuality were all strictly banned. The code survived numerous court challenges until the 1960s, then changed to a rating system (G, PG, PG-13, R and NC-17) that is still administered by the MPAA.

As a product of its times, the code did not prohibit narratives encouraging racism or anti-Semitism that came to be considered immoral in the later twentieth century. The code also made it more difficult for independent filmmakers to compete against the big studios; and it contributed to the Hollywood domination of international cinema well into the twenty-first century.

Modern critics contend that a secretive private ratings system, without an open appeals process, still amounts to a form of censorship and discrimination in favor of major studios against independent film makers. (For example, see the 2006 documentary *This Film Is Not Yet Rated*.)

The silent film era

Freed from the hobbles of Edison's monopoly, and with competition from European films now halted by World War I, US film makers embarked on an era of innovation and development.

Figure 5.6 and Figure 5.7 Racism on film—one of the least admired films of all time was the US-made *Birth of a Nation*, depicting post-Civil War southern women as victims of African Americans who needed to be rescued by secret terrorist societies like the Ku Klux Klan. A wave of violence against African Americans followed the release of the film in 1915. The National Association for the Advancement of Colored People (NAACP) mounted numerous and strenuous protests about the message the film conveyed. (Library of Congress)

The most innovative and controversial film of the silent era was D. W. Griffith's 1915 *Birth of a Nation*, a film that told the story of families torn apart in the aftermath of the Civil War. It depicted Reconstruction-era African Americans in the worst possible light, as drunkards, rapists and murderers, who were only thwarted when a heroic white vigilante group, the Ku Klux Klan, rode out to oppose them. Critics said it was "unfair and vicious" (*Outlook*, 1915). Riots broke out at theaters in major cities (*The Washington Post,* April 18, 1915). Performances were shut down in eight states, and many others were picketed by the emerging National Association for Colored People.

Some histories attribute an approving remark about "history written with lightning" to then-President Woodrow Wilson, who watched the film at a White House performance. However, the source for the remark is Thomas Dixon, college friend of Wilson and the author of *The Clansman*, the book on which *Birth of a Nation* was based. While Wilson did write approvingly of the Klan as an historian, before he was president, whether or not he actually approved of the movie is an ongoing controversy. Film critic Roger Ebert said: "My guess is that Wilson said something like it in private, and found it prudent to deny when progressive editorialists attacked the film" (Ebert).

The most famous icon of the silent era was Charlie Chaplin, whose "tramp" character delighted audiences worldwide. He created the character for film producer Mack Sennett when he was asked to put on a comic costume for a 1914 film.

Chaplin delighted fans worldwide with the tramp's down-at-the heels costume and his refined but bewildered demeanor. Two years later, he became one of the first great stars of the Silent Era, signing a contract with Mutual Films for over half a million dollars. At that point, Chaplin owned his own studios, producing classic silent films like *The Gold Rush* and *The Kid*. Chaplin would often begin filming with only the barest outlines of a concept and no written script. His film *The Immigrants*, for example, began as a comedy sketch about restaurant waiters, but ended as a film about a family's difficult journey across the Atlantic, through

Figure 5.8 The little tramp—Charlie Chaplin, young theater actor, made his way to Hollywood in 1914 and got a comic role in a Mack Sennett Movie. He said: "I had no idea what makeup to put on . . . However, on the way to the wardrobe I thought I would dress in baggy pants, big shoes, a cane and a derby hat. I wanted everything to be a contradiction . . . I had no idea of the character. But the moment I was dressed, the clothes and the makeup made me feel the person he was. I began to know him, and by the time I walked on stage, he was fully born" (Chaplin, 1964, p. 154).

US immigration and a reunion in the restaurant. At one point, Chaplin gives a US immigration official a sneaky kick in the pants and then whistles innocently as the official looks in vain for the culprit. The scene expressed Chaplin's own frustrations with the US government, but also endeared him to a generation of downtrodden workers.

Some of Chaplin's other work, such as *Modern Times*, showed frustration with the dehumanizing pace of modernization. His humane approach is also seen in the way he made fun of the stuffy and overwrought high culture in sketches like "Dance of the Cleaning Ladies."

Chaplin was also an innovator in business, founding United Artists in 1919 along with D. W. Griffith, Mary Pickford and Douglas Fairbanks. The distribution company

Charlie Chaplin, Super-Star

Figure 5.9 Celebrity—Chaplin drew a crowd wherever he went, such as this rally for Liberty Bonds in Washington D.C. in 1918. (National Archives)

Charlie Chaplin's celebrity reached such heights that he could set off near-riots by his mere presence.

Historian Corey Ross described a visit to Berlin in 1931 in which frenzied crowds surrounded the hotel and besieged the train station when he arrived. Left wing newspapers of the day celebrated the working class genius, conservative newspapers said it was inappropriate that he should be so highly celebrated, and Nazi papers said they were disgusted by the reception given to the "Jewish film clown."

The point is that the political parties were defining themselves in relation to the film star, not the other way around. "Chaplin's trip to Berlin . . . highlights not only the vital importance of the media to social and cultural life in the 1930s, but also their political impact, the challenge they posed to traditional values, their transcendence of social and national boundaries, and the complex relationship between cultural producers and their audiences" (Ross, 2008).

Figure 5.10 German Expressionism—*The Cabinet of Dr. Caligari*, a dark film about an insane doctor, was one of many post-World War I German films from the Expressionistic era. (Wikimedia Commons)

provided an important alternative to the studio system, through which a few executives at five big studios dominated the industry in its early years. By the late 1940s, United Artists pioneered the backing of independent films—a business model that eventually toppled the big studios (Balio, 1987).

Chaplin's competitors such as Buster Keaton are also remembered fondly. Keaton's specialty involved daring stunt techniques executed flawlessly but often at a great risk to his own life. Keaton's "Steamboat Bill" was so successful that it was parodied by Walt Disney in his first Mickey Mouse cartoon, "Steamboat Willy" in 1928.

By the 1920s cinema had begun to blossom as a serious art form. New techniques in storytelling emerged, for example in Russia, where Sergei Eisenstein created a film of John Reed's book *Ten Days That Shook the World*. But Eisenstein is best remembered for *Battleship Potemkin*. The film glorified an early episode in the Russian Revolution and was among the first to use montage, which is a compilation of shots, including extreme closeups and details, to convey a strong impression. Eisenstein and other directors found that film had its own language and logic, and that apparently unrelated film cuts could be related in many ways. For example, Eisenstein would continue the motion of different objects from one shot into the next, or punctuate the visual impression of a shot with music written specifically to accompany the montage.

In Germany, the expressionist movement in film embraced new and dramatically different styles of film production, as seen in *The Cabinet of Dr. Caligari*, a dream about an insane doctor; in *Nosferatu*, an unauthorized 1922 adaptation of the Dracula story; and in Fritz Lang's 1927 *Metropolis*. The Nazi rise to power put an end to this creative era, and many talented filmmakers fled to Hollywood.

End of the silent film era

Hollywood was already at the top of its game by the mid-1920s, and few saw any reason to change things. When Jack Warner agreed to spend $10,000 to build a sound stage in 1927, he changed his mind a few hours later—only to find the stage already under construction.

Warner Brothers used Vitaphone equipment, developed over the previous years by AT&T, and despite low box office expectations, *The Jazz Singer*, starring Al Jolson, turned out to be a major hit. Although Jolson's blackface act is offensive by modern standards, it was meant to be clownish and sentimental at the time, and had none of the virulent racism of *Birth of a Nation*.

The combination of sound and film changed everything, said film historian Scott Eyman. "It changed how movies were made, of course, but more importantly, it changed what movies were." Where silent film demanded participation in the experience, talking films were immersive but stylistically shallow. "Talkies were not an evolution, but a mutation, a different art form entirely; as a result, an art form was eliminated and hundreds of careers were extinguished" (Eyman, 1997). Early sound film technology limited camera movement and actors gestures, and often forced shooting into indoor studios. Some of the narrative sweep of silent films was lost for the time being.

Figure 5.11 The first "talkie"—*The Jazz Singer*, starring Al Jolson in a "blackface" getup, was an unexpected hit. Although Jolson's blackface act is offensive by modern standards, it was meant to be clownish and sentimental at the time, and had none of the virulent racism of *Birth of a Nation*. (Library of Congress)

Talking pictures produced new stars in the late 1920s. These included Walt Disney's Mickey Mouse, whose debut in the first fully-synchronized sound cartoon made Disney the nation's leading animator. And they led to fame for new directors like Alfred Hitchcock, whose first sound film, *Blackmail*, was also an enormous hit with audiences.

The last major silent film, *Modern Times* by Charlie Chaplin, was originally written as a "talkie," but Chaplin balked, fearing that his tramp character would hardly seem as romantic or wistful. Although *Modern Times* was a big hit in 1936, the motion picture audience had come to expect music and dialogue.

Golden Age of Hollywood

By the 1930s, Hollywood was one of the most visible businesses in America, and most people were attending films at least once a week. With better sound and film technology emerging, the industry was able to pursue new creative directions, entering a "Golden Age" of creativity and exploration. Although partly fettered by censorship, the film industry attracted audiences with strong narratives involving romantic characters struggling to overcome heavy odds.

Products of the Golden Age include a long list of what are today seen as classics— *The Wizard of Oz, Gone with the Wind, Stagecoach, Mr. Smith Goes to Washington, Casablanca, It's a Wonderful Life, It Happened One Night, King Kong, Citizen Kane, Some Like It Hot, All About Eve, Duck Soup, Singin' in the Rain, Roman Holiday*, and many more.

Hollywood operated like a factory, and the "studio system" churned out thousands of films, permanently employing tens of thousands of actors, extras and technicians. The studio system offered stable incomes and long term contracts, and as a result, studios like Paramount (formed in 1912), Columbia Pictures (1920), Warner Brothers (1923), Metro-Goldwyn-Mayer (1924), RKO Pictures (1928) and 20th-Century Fox (1935) were able to draw talent from all over the nation and the world.

The studio system had many faults as well. Actors and directors who did not comply with the demands of studio executives found that their stars could fall quickly. Theaters that were owned by individual studios did not serve audience interests by promoting their lower grade films along with the hits. Independent theaters were often forced to sign "block booking" contracts that guaranteed screens for unpopular films along with the popular ones. A lawsuit started in 1938 over block booking reached the US Supreme Court as *United States v. Paramount Pictures, Inc.* in 1948. The court's order to break up the link between theaters and film studios under antitrust law was the beginning of the end for the studio system.

Many of the same genres once explored in silent films were repeated and more fully explored in the Golden Age. Westerns, costume dramas, musicals, comedies, cartoons and horror films all found enthusiastic audiences. New genres, like "film noir," involving hard-bitten but soft-hearted detectives, such as Humphrey Bogart in *The Maltese Falcon*, found niche audiences before attaining cult-like status for later generations.

It's interesting that the most widely discussed film of the Golden Age was produced not only through the studio system, but also in spite of it. *Citizen Kane*, voted the most influential film of the twentieth century by the American Film Institute, was produced and directed for RKO Pictures in 1941 by Orson Welles, a brash and volatile radio and theater director famed for scaring American radio listeners with his "War of the Worlds" broadcast of 1938. Welles had never before produced or directed a film in his life, but he threw all of his genius into making the movie.

Citizen Kane is about the search for the identity of a newspaper tycoon who used his family wealth to build a powerful empire, promote his mistress and crush his

Figure 5.12 *Citizen Kane*—a parody of the life of William Randolph Hearst by Orson Welles, *Citizen Kane* used innovative techniques that were decades ahead of the times. Hearst hated the movie and forced RKO to retire it to the vaults, where it remained until rediscovered as a cult classic in the 1960s. In the American Film Institute's top 100 movies of all time, Kane is number one. (Wikimedia Commons)

Chaos on the set

What it was like when the Marx Brothers filmed "The Cocoanuts" in 1929

From *Harpo Speaks* by Harpo Marx with Rowland Barber, New York: Freeway Press, 1974. (Reprinted by permission of Hal Leonard Corporation)

Figure 5.13 Chico, Harpo, Groucho and Zeppo Marx

Our first picture *Cocoanuts* was shot in New York. . . . Shot was just the word for it. All they did was point the camera at us while we ran through our old stage version. . . . Still, it wasn't as simple as it might sound for the producer, Walter Wagner, or the directors, Joseph Stanley and Robert Florey. There were many long delays in the shooting, due mostly to the unexcused absences of Chico from the set. Since nobody had bought tickets to watch him, Chico figured there was nobody to squawk when he ducked out to consult with his bookie or play a few hands of pinochle. Trouble was, Chico would forget to come back if the action was good. Then Groucho, Zeppo and I would wander off looking for him. Sometimes Chico would return while we were gone, and he'd say the hell with it—if that's all we cared, he'd take the rest of the day off too.

When Stanley and Florey hit the jackpot and had four Marx brothers on the same set at the same time, and the camera got going, the shooting would be interrupted every time we started improvising. . . . The trouble was, Florey couldn't help breaking up. When he laughed, he laughed so hard he drowned out everything else on the sound track. Laughing left him very weak, so he would have to lie down to regain his strength before they could call a retake. This would give Chico a good chance to duck out to see how the action was going, which would soon send the rest of us out looking for Chico.

Wagner solved the problem by having the directors use hand signals, from inside a sound proof glass booth. We still played to Florey, however. When he flew into convulsions we knew we had done something good. It was the weirdest audience we had ever played to.

Then Wagner solved the Chico problem. He had the four cells used in the jail scene bolted to the studio floor. He had four signs made, one for each cell—CHICO, HARPO, GROUCHO and ZEPPO—and he had a telephone in the one labeled CHICO. Now Chico could call his bookie any time he felt like it, without bringing production to a standstill.

Between takes, we were locked behind bars and the directors were let out of the booth. When the shooting resumed, the directors were put back in their glass cage and the stars were let out of their jail cells. Too bad they didn't film the filming of *Cocoanuts*. It would have been a lot funnier than the movie was.

opponents. The film was intended to be a biting parody of the life of William Randolph Hearst, a powerful newspaper publisher who did in fact use his newspapers to promote his mistress and crush his opponents. Hearst saw the movie as a frontal assault on his reputation, and he did everything in his power to wreck the emerging career of Orson Welles. RKO "retired" the film after a few weeks, and both Welles and Hearst ended up losing, according to an excellent documentary, *The Battle Over Citizen Kane*.

Another Golden Age film worth a special mention is *The Grapes of Wrath*, starring Henry Fonda as a farmer who takes his family from the "dust bowl" of Oklahoma to the promised land of California. Based on the novel by John Steinbeck, the film used a style of cinematography based closely on the Depression era photography of Dorothea Lange, especially her "Migrant Mother" series. Even the few critics who scoffed at the Depression-era political message conceded that the film transcended social issues of the time with an enduring human story.

Animation and the cinema

Perhaps the earliest surviving stop-motion animation was a call to support British troops in the Boer War of 1899. Made by Arthur Melbourne Cooper, the animated short film showed matchsticks writing an appeal on a black wall. Cooper was a decade ahead of animation pioneers in the United States, where, for example, Windsor McCay's animated cartoon "Gertie the Dinosaur" debuted in 1914. McCay had to redraw every background scene in every frame of the five-minute cartoon—a tedious process that made the film look jittery.

Cel animation was a way to get around the jitters. Invented at the John Bray studios in 1914, celluloid ("cel") animation allowed backgrounds to remain stable while moving characters were inked on transparent sheets. Another innovation was the introduction of cartoon "stars" like Felix the Cat by Otto Mesmer and Mickey Mouse by Walt Disney.

The innovation that catapulted Disney to success was the marriage of sound with animation in 1928. Only a year after *The Jazz Singer* amazed audiences with synchronized dialogue and music, Disney produced a Mickey Mouse cartoon with tightly synchronized sound effects and orchestrated background music called "Steamboat Willie." The cartoon was a takeoff on Buster Keaton's silent classic, *Steamboat Bill*, released earlier that year.

Short animated films preceded a main feature movie at the time, but Disney achieved another first with the first feature-length animation, *Snow White and the Seven Dwarfs*, released in 1938. The cartoon used naturalistic figure drawing (as opposed to the unrealistic "rubber hose" approach used in other cartoons). It also was the first to use full color. Despite early doubters (even Disney's wife Lillian said no one would ever pay to see a dwarf picture) the film premiered to wildly enthusiastic audiences. *Snow White* was followed by animation classics like *Pinocchio* in 1940, *Dumbo* in 1941, *Bambi*, *Cinderella* and many others.

Disney was by far the most successful, in both artistic and commercial terms, of all animators, but the Disney studio's factory approach shows "the studio system's best and worst effects on the development of animation as an art form," said Michael Crandol in his *History of Animation*, since many talented animators were eclipsed by Walt Disney himself (Crandol, 2010).

Attempts to increase recognition and salary at the Disney studios were ignored and, in *Dumbo*, parodied by a parade of drunken clowns singing "we're gonna ask the big boss for a raise." Many of Disney's talented animators went on to create their own cartoons or found their own studios; Ub Iwerks left Disney during the 1930s to create Flip the Frog and Porky Pig; Hugh Harman and Rudy Ising who went on to create Loony Tunes for MGM in the 1930s; Don Bluth left the Disney studios in 1979 to create *The Secret of Nimh* (1982), *An American Tale* (1986) and *The Land Before Time* (1988).

Figure 5.14 Cartoon King—Walt Disney founded a studio that produced thousands of cartoon shorts and features, including the first full length animation, *Snow White and the Seven Dwarfs*, in 1938. (Library of Congress)

Hugh Harman's animated short, Peace on Earth, released in 1939 was a break from the Disney tradition in another way. The cartoon was a serious plea for peace on the eve of World War II. It depicted never-ending wars and the last people on earth killing each other, followed by animals rebuilding society using the helmets of the soldiers. The cartoon was nominated for an Academy Award—and the Nobel Peace Prize.

Other animators departed from Disney's naturalistic storytelling techniques to create physics-defying characters. Tex Avery, for instance, created Red Hot Riding Hood in 1943, in which a wolf's mouth is seen dropping down to its feet, while its eyes bulge out and its tongue unrolls. "That is the most wonderfully liberating spectacle," said Monty Python animator Terry Gilliam in a review of his ten favorite animations (Gilliam, 2001).

Another wave of animation began in the 1940s in Japan with the release of Osamu Tezuka's *Astro Boy*, the first anime cartoon. Japanese animators like Hayao Miyazaki, inspired by Tezuka and Disney, developed dozens of popular cartoons such as *My Neighbor Totoro* (1988) and *Princess Mononoke* (1997).

Propaganda films

The World War II era might be considered the "golden age" of propaganda films. While silent films (such as the 1915 US film *Birth of a Nation* and the 1925 Russian film *Battleship Potemkin*) could be effective in advancing reactionary or revolutionary agendas, sound-on-film could be more effectively used to play on emotions and deceive audiences.

A classic of the propaganda genre is Leni Riefenstahl's *Triumph of the Will*, made to glorify the Nazi Party in 1935 and celebrate Germany's return to power after its defeat in World War I. Using long tracking shots, triumphal music and masterful montage, the film depicted the 1934 Nazi party rally at Nuremberg. Given the

Figure 5.15 "Triumph of the what?"—a glowing 1935 depiction of the Nazi party celebrations in Nuremberg Germany, Leni Riefenstahl's *Triumph of the Will* is considered a classic in technique but a monster for glorifying the subject. Here Riefenstahl and camera crew are getting a ground-level shot for the film. (Library of Congress)

Nazi control of all German media at the time, *Triumph of the Will* was more or less the only image German people had of the Nazi party, and helped Hitler to consolidate power in the years before World War II.

Riefenstahl later claimed that she had no choice in making the film, and that she had no knowledge of Nazi concentration camps. She also claimed that artists should not be held responsible for the political problems their art causes. She spent several years in detention after the war but was never convicted of war crimes.

"Leni Riefenstahl is a monster," the *New Republic* said in reviewing a documentary about her life. We can admire her work, the magazine said, in the same way that we admire Soviet masterworks of film "for their art despite the heavy irony of their now blood-drenched enthusiasm."

Even more monstrous was the 1940 Nazi propaganda film *The Eternal Jew*, a violently anti-Semitic pseudo-documentary that provoked racial hatred in Germany with its comparisons of Jews to rats and other vermin. It was made by the Nazi propaganda ministry, but the extent of film director Fritz Hippler's involvement is in question. Hippler was a proponent of film as propaganda: "If one compares the directness and intensity of the effect that the various means of propaganda have on the great masses, film is without question the most powerful" (Hippler, 1937). But months before his death in 2002, he said: "If it were possible to annul everything (about the film) I would. Terrible things happened and I had many sleepless nights because of this."

By depicting Jewish people as sub-human, Nazi film artists like Hippler made the genocide of the Holocaust possible. Similar dehumanization paved the way for genocide in Serbia and Rwanda in the 1990s.

Fighting fascism with film

Counterpropaganda involved both comedy and serious documentary work in the US and Britain during the time around World War II.

In 1940, Charlie Chaplin's film "The Great Dictator" used biting sarcasm and hilarious slapstick to attack the cruelty of the Nazi regime. At one point, dictator Adenoid Hinkle of Tomania carelessly tosses a balloon globe into the air, only to have it pop at the end. Hinkle's look-alike, a Jewish barber, is mistaken as the dictator and gives a radio speech that reverses fascist ideology. "We are coming out of the darkness into the light," Chaplin's character says at the end of the film. "We are coming into a new world, a kindlier world, where men will rise above their hate, their greed and brutality."

Chaplin's moral courage in satirizing Hitler and defending Jewish people should not be underestimated. Few people in 1940 would have predicted the end of Nazi rule only five years later. Asked around that time whether he was Jewish himself, Chaplin said, "I do not have that honor" (Schickel, 2006). Film critics have seen *The Great Dictator* as Chaplin's way of symbolically reclaiming the Little Tramp's moustache from Hitler, but it was far more than that. It was a small but

Figure 5.16 *Great Dictator*—Chaplin's *Great Dictator* was a courageous film for its day, defending Jewish people and expressing the hope for a better world than the Nazis were offering. (Wikimedia Commons)

courageous voice standing up at a time when Hollywood was shackled by fear, isolationism and the Hays Code, which supposedly discouraged political messages in films and required that "people and history of other nations . . . be presented fairly" (Herschthal, 2008).

Other comedies were also heavy handed and perhaps equally courageous. The Three Stooges, for instance, released a film called *You Nazty Spy* lampooning events in "Moronia." The film was released nine months ahead of Chaplin's *Great Dictator*, in January of 1940. Two of the actors, Moe Howard and Larry Fine, said that *You Nazty Spy* was their favorite.

Disney also released a cartoon called *Der Fuehrer's Face* in 1943 that was circulated for a limited time during the war. Another set of cartoons, produced by Warner Brothers between 1943 and 1945, showed "Private Snafu" doing everything wrong—and helping educate soldiers and sailors about how to handle the challenges they faced.

The most significant American documentary was *Why We Fight*, first released in 1942 and directed by Frank Capra, who was chosen by the War Department because, they said, the director of *Mr. Smith Goes to Washington* and *You Can't Take It With You* understood American ideals. Capra said he was challenged by Leni Riefenstahl's propaganda films and worked to create a stylistic as well as ideological alternative. Rather than refute enemy claims, Capra worked with writers to craft a positive message.

The documentary was intended to substitute for morale-building lectures by Army officers, but it became emblematic of the beliefs of the nation. Although loaded with plodding patriotic music and gimmicky devices, the film lived up to Capra's ambition to combat Nazi propaganda and help win "a fight between a slave world and a free world." The film was thought so important that President Franklin Roosevelt ordered it released to the general public.

Figure 5.17 Giving a damn—Clark Gable, famed for his role as Rhett Butler in *Gone with the Wind*, became an officer in the Air Corps. After narrowly escaping death in combat, he made a documentary called *Combat America* that featured interviews with pilots and gunners. (National Archives)

Public relations efforts continued through the cold war. In *Big Picture*, a documentary on psychological warfare, an Army intelligence officer says: "Another very important phase of warfare . . . has as its target not the body, but the mind of the enemy. Its mission is to influence the thoughts of the enemy soldier and thereby weaken him and at the same time it brings to the no man's land of Communism . . . it carries on where the weapons have left off."

Films made for entertainment during World War II usually also had a moral about the war. *Mrs. Miniver*, produced in 1942, depicted an ordinary British family caught up in the Dunkirk evacuation and other war scenes. It concluded with a sermon in a bombed-out church emphasizing the novelty of a "people's war," that involved everyone. British Prime Minister Winston Churchill said the film was "more powerful to the war effort than the combined work of six military divisions" (Parish and Mark, 1981, p. 143).

Also significant as a war film was *Casablanca*, a 1942 film featuring Humphrey Bogart who encounters his lost love (Ingrid Bergman) fleeing the Nazi occupation of France to North Africa in the hope of finding passage to the United States. In one stirring scene, a group of Nazi officers try to sing Die Wacht am Rhein, a patriotic German song. In response, a French patriot asks the house band to play "La Marseillaise," the French national anthem. It's one reason—and there are many others—why film critic Roger Ebert called *Casablanca* the best loved film in cinema history (Ebert, 1996).

Postwar film industry

Despite fears that propaganda films like *Why We Fight* would make postwar Americans unwilling to be gracious in victory, the lineup of films of the late 1940s and early 1950s emphasized light entertainment. But there were also reconciliation stories about people caught up in the war years, such as *It's a Wonderful Life* by Frank Capra about a guy who stayed on the home front. Similar reconciliation films would be seen after Vietnam (*Forrest Gump*), the end of the Cold War (*K-19, The Hunt for Red October*) and the fall of the Berlin Wall (*Goodbye Lenin*).

One significant development in postwar cinema history was the new appreciation for Italian neo-realism. For instance, the 1946 *Open City* by Roberto Rossellini used low-budget location shots and nonprofessional actors to depict the everyday struggle for survival in Rome after the war. Another film of the genre was Vittorio DeSica's *Bicycle Thieves* (1948). Both won major film prizes and launched other Italian film directors, like Federico Fellini and Michelangelo Antonioni.

HUAC hearings into Hollywood communism

Back in the United States, concerns about the influence of Communists in Hollywood led to an investigation by the House Un-American Activities Committee beginning in 1947. As the hearings began, Walt Disney, Ronald Reagan and other prominent Hollywood actors and directors testified that the threat of communists in the film industry was serious. The committee also called a number of writers and actors and asked the question: "Are you now or have you ever been a member of the Communist party?"

Ten of these who tried to answer by framing the question as a breach of their Constitutional rights were convicted of contempt of Congress the following year and barred by the MPAA from employment in the film industry—a practice known as "blacklisting." As the investigation rolled on, no serious evidence concerning attempts by actual communists to influence Hollywood productions was uncovered. Yet by 1951, a booklet called "Red Channels," produced by the FBI, listed 151 names to be blacklisted. Most were forbidden from working in the US film industry, including Charlie Chaplin, Zero Mostel and writer Dalton Trumbo, who was jailed for 11 months.

Some actors courageously stood up to the HUAC investigations. These included Humphrey Bogart, Lauren Bacall, Danny Kaye and director John Huston who organized the Committee for the First Amendment to protest the hearings. Bogart had to back down, a little, in an article entitled "I'm No Communist" in the March, 1948 issue of *Photoplay*. But as Bogart reminded readers, "liberal-minded folks are pure Americans . . . devoted to our democracy" (Bogart, 1948).

It's important to remember that many of those blacklisted were simply liberals and young people of the 1930s who were not communists but saw the communist movement reflecting idealism. Russian communists were US and British allies during World War II, and were lionized in Hollywood productions like *Days of Glory*. The 1940s and 50s hunt for communists in Hollywood is seen today as an excuse to victimize innocent people in order to gain political power.

The highly publicized committee hearings dovetailed with witch hunts in other areas, and led to the "McCarthy era" in which US Senator Joseph McCarthy made wildly paranoid accusations about Communist influence in government. The real victim, in the end, was Hollywood. Despite the eagerness of Hollywood executives to root out supposed communists, many came under fire themselves,

Figure 5.18 Blackballed writer—Dalton Trumbo, a screenwriter who was briefly a member of the Communist Party, refused to implicate other Hollywood writers before the House Un-American Activities Committee and served an 11-month jail sentence. He was blackballed (not allowed to work) but brought back in the late 1950s to work on films like *Spartacus* and *Exodus*. (Library of Congress)

and box office receipts dropped quickly, even before competition from television. One studio owner, RKO's Floyd Odlum, simply sold his company. The chaos at RKO led to its early settlement of the Paramount antitrust case of 1948.

Movies bring empathy to the racial divide

One of the most important stories about Hollywood takes place not in a single film or production company, but over a span of decades in hundreds of films. It's the story of how African Americans came to be treated as equals on and off the screen, and how their contributions to cinema came to be respected. But the story is still one of a lack of serious influence in Hollywood or other mainstream media institutions in America, according to historians S. Torriano Berry and Venise T. Berry (S. T. Berry and V. T. Berry, 2007).

In the earliest days, films featuring white actors in "blackface" portrayed degrading and ridiculous themes, such as the *Watermelon Eating Contest* and *The Wooing and Wedding of a Coon*. The 1914 film *Uncle Tom's Cabin* should have been an exception, since the original book was an indictment of slavery and the original Uncle Tom was beaten to death for refusing to reveal the location of runaway slaves. However, in the film, the main character is transformed into a subservient stereotype.

Independent productions by black filmmakers included the 1912 *Railroad Porter* and others, and the new talking pictures led to studio productions in 1929 like *Hearts in Dixie*, the first all black musical. One star from *Hearts in Dixie* was Lincoln Perry, whose character Stepin Fetchit exaggerated the then-abundant stereotypes of ignorant, shiftless blacks.

Fighting these stereotypes, many black entertainers tried to perform with dignity and style. When Bill "Bojangles" Robinson tap-danced alongside white child-star Shirley Temple in the 1930s, the underlying message was that people could set aside their differences. The Nicholas Brothers' spectacular dancing abilities were also widely recognized as a serious contribution. Yet often these dance numbers would be cut out of films shown in the American South by movie owners who were all too aware that humane images of African Americans could speed reconciliation between races.

Strong images of African Americans were often stereotyped in the 1930s and 40s. Paul Robeson's *Emperor Jones*, in 1933, produced by United Artists, depicted an ex-convict who takes control of a remote Caribbean island and is caught up in voodoo and dishonest scams. Hattie McDaniel, who played the Oscar-winning role of Mammy in *Gone with the Wind*, is an example of a strong but still stereotyped image of black Americans.

In the World War II era, the expression of ideals in films like *Why We Fight* required that some of those same ideals be better honored at home. One film that featured the first fully glamorized African American woman was 20th Century Fox's movie, *Stormy Weather* with singer-actress Lena Horne. "They didn't make me into a maid, but they didn't make me anything else, either," Horne said later. "I became a butterfly pinned to a column, singing away in Movieland." Horne was an important figure "because she was able to bridge the gap between black and white in a way that others could not," said Eugene Robinson (Robinson, 2010).

Social issues were gingerly explored in the aftermath of the war, for example in the 1949 film *Pinky*, in which a black woman with light skin passes for white, but then realizes that she had almost lost her sense of humanity.

Fully realized human characters emerged slowly, but are evident in films like Daryl F. Zanuck's 1957 *Island in the Sun*, starring Harry Belafonte and Dorothy Dandridge. The film featured some limited interracial romance. A more direct approach is found in the 1967 *Guess Who's Coming to Dinner*, starring Sidney Poitier, Spencer Tracy and Katharine Hepburn. This film depicted an interracial couple's intent on obtaining their parents' permission to get married.

Sidney Poitier's performances advanced the cause of racial understanding, and his Oscar-winning 1963 film, *Lilies of the Field* is among many sterling performances. Like Horne, Poitier bridged the black–white gap in a way that attracted and educated audiences.

One of the most important aspects of cinema is its ability to humanize and evoke empathy for people in other walks of life, and nowhere did this occur with as much significance as in the evolution of images of African Americans. By providing these insights, Hollywood helped ease the way for the US civil rights movement.

The seductive, volcanic 1960s: antiheroes and social themes

Movies from the 1960s onward tended to both reflect and lead a major shift in world culture, away from patriotism and simple heroics, toward tolerance, introspection and personal growth.

The era is often described as post-classical cinema, characterized by the undermining of cultural hubris and devolution into artistic chaos. Heroes were seen as mere mortals and life was depicted in many shades of gray instead of black and white. While this helped keep audiences interested in movies, it was also an artistic reflection of volcanically turbulent social changes.

The shift is seen early in war movies that explored personal tragedy and human values more than heroics or the glory of combat. For example, where the 1941 film *Sergeant York* depicted an unvarnished backwoods hero of World War I, later movies explored more nuanced themes of betrayal, unwilling sacrifice and personal doubts. These include *From Here to Eternity* (1953), *The Bridge on the River Kwai* (1957), *The Guns of Navarone* (1961), *Dr. Strangelove* (1962) and *The Dirty Dozen* (1967).

Moral ambiguity is evident in this line from *The Guns of Navarone*, when Capt. Keith Mallory says: "The only way to win a war is to be just as nasty as the enemy. The one thing that worries me is we're liable to wake up one morning, and find we're even nastier than they are."

Western genre movies also emerged as morality plays that featured antiheroes. *The Magnificent Seven* (1960) was a direct takeoff from Akira Kurosawa's 1954 Japanese film, *The Seven Samurai*, in which a group of down-on-their-luck samurai defend a poor farming village from marauding bandits. *The Man Who Shot Liberty Valance* (1962), directed by John Ford, featured actors John Wayne and Jimmy Stewart. The film tells the story of a heroic legend who wasn't as much of a hero as his friend. Its classic line is: "When the legend becomes fact, print the legend."

A very different take on the Western genre was also seen in *Little Big Man* (1970). The movie starred Dustin Hoffman as he moves back and forth between white and Indian societies, finding both to be sympathetic in some respects and repulsive in others.

Science fiction and horror genre films also moved from cold-war proxy threats attacking from outside, as in the film *Invasion of the Body Snatchers* (1956), to the monsters lurking within apparently ordinary human beings, as in Alfred Hitchcock's *Psycho* (1960), featuring Anthony Perkins as a schizophrenic motel owner.

An early outstanding example of the science fiction genre is *The Day the Earth Stood Still* (1951), a story about an ambassador from outer space who tries to deliver a warning about self-destruction to the nations of earth. Despite the popularity of the science fiction genre, nothing equaled the quality of *The Day the Earth Stood Still* until the release of *2001: A Space Odyssey* (1969) and *Star Wars* (1977).

Many dramas reflected relatively new social themes, such as *To Kill a Mockingbird* (1962), about a town torn apart by racial injustice, *Rebel Without a Cause* (1955) about teenage rebellion, and *Easy Rider* (1969), about a drug-fueled motorcycle quest for personal freedom.

In some ways this edgier new approach was designed to attract movie audiences and give them something that could not be seen on television. However, the same cultural maturity and pessimism also began to be reflected in 1970s television programs like Star Trek, Archie Bunker and Monty Python.

Special effects animates blockbusters

With the demise of the Hollywood studio system, independent film makers had to innovate. Reaching for the "wow" moment in a film with special effects was one way to stand out and present audiences with something new and different.

Special effects have been around since the early days of film, when George Méliès sent a bullet-like spaceship crashing into the face of the moon in 1902. Considered to be the special effects master of his day, Méliès used in-camera effects, miniatures and matte painting to achieve results in over 500 other short films.

By the 1920s, improved matte painting techniques allowed well-proportioned backgrounds to be added to a film. Fritz Lang's 1927 *Metropolis* also featured effective miniatures and mattes.

Stop motion animation reached a new peak with Willis Obrien's work in the 1933 move *King Kong*. Ray Harryhausen extended the technique in adventure movies like *Jason and the Argonauts* (1963), with animated monsters and skeletons fighting live actors. Although influential, Harryhausen's films were box office disappointments. Ironically, most studios closed down their special-effects units by the mid-1970s (Zoglin and Dutka, 1986). This is another example of big companies missing the "curve in the road" that was such an important feature of the early digital revolution.

A new generation with interests in fantasy and science fiction made special effects a major element in developing the "blockbuster" film of the late twentieth and early twenty-first centuries. And independent film producers, with more independence and new special-effects technologies, were in a better position to create blockbusters than the old studios where they rented back lots.

Star Wars, which started as a back-lot experiment with new modeling and special effects techniques to bring viewers in closer to the action, grossed $4.3 billion in the 30 years since the first film was made in 1977. The relatively low-budget first film brought in special effects supervisor John Dykstra who had worked on *2001: A Space Odyssey*. Among other innovations, Dykstra developed a lightweight computer-controlled camera that could be precisely located for seamless matte compositing. The effects crew became Industrial Light and Magic Co., creating special effects for blockbusters such as *Harry Potter*, *Indiana Jones*, *Back to the Future*, *Terminator*, *Avatar* and many others.

An interesting issue that came up with *Avatar* in 2010, which won three Oscars for Art Direction, Cinematography and Visual Effects—but not even a nomination for the actors. The movie, made with "performance capture" technology, placed human actors into computer-animated scenes. Director James Cameron insisted that the actors deserved to be considered, arguing that the process was "actor-driven," and not simply made up in the computer as an effect (Abramowitz, 2010).

Digital issues

Digital technologies created special effects for the movie industry in the 1980s and 90s, but they also created new problems. The first controversy emerged around home use of videotape to copy whole programs or films. The MPAA said at the time that videotape would destroy the movie industry. In a 1984 case brought against electronics manufacturer Sony, the courts said that legal use of home video recorders for "time-shifting" was a "fair use" and not a violation of copyright. Video stores flourished and home video sales became a movie industry mainstay rather than an instrument of its demise.

More powerful home computers introduced in the 1990s presented a new sort of challenge, allowing high quality copying of music and video. Hollywood and the music industry moved quickly to protect their markets from copyright piracy, and Congress passed the Digital Millennium Copyright Act of 1998 (DMCA).

The act made music and video piracy a more serious offense, but it also contained a "safe harbor" clause that insulated internet service providers and search engine operators who allowed users to upload music and videos. The idea was that the users, but not the websites, would be responsible if the sites took down material when copyright owners objected. Websites that were primarily intended for copyright piracy could be taken down entirely.

The DMCA's legal doctrine was enforced following a suit by A&M Records against music-sharing website Napster in 2001. Other lawsuits stopped widespread sharing of copyrighted music through websites such as Kazaa and Pirate Bay in the following years.

As web user bandwidth increased in first decade of the twenty-first century, the music sharing controversy spread to video sharing sites, especially YouTube, purchased by Google in 2006. Viacom, owner of Comedy Central, MTV and other television and movie production companies, filed a suit arguing that Google had deliberately ignored copyright violations and profited from widespread video piracy. Google countered that it did not ignore the violations, pointing out that when Viacom presented a list of 100,000 violations in 2007, virtually all were removed within a day.

In June, 2010, a lower court found that YouTube was primarily intended to host user-generated content, and could not have known which videos were posted with permission and which were not. Since the DMCA put the burden of copyright enforcement on the music and movie industries, and since YouTube complied with take-down notices, the DMCA's "safe harbor" provisions shielded them from Viacom's lawsuit.

International cinema

With the advent of on-demand video, viewers by the second decade of the twenty-first century had increasingly broad choices of content. This meant that the once-dominant Hollywood system was now competing with, and sometimes promoting, films made in Asia and Europe. Films like *Crouching Tiger, Hidden Dragon*, a martial arts film made in China in 2000, proved enormously successful in US and European markets.

Other foreign-language films that have achieved hit status in English-speaking markets included the loveable, color-saturated *Amelie* (French); *Lagaan*, an Indian film about poverty in the time of British rule; *Spirited Away*, a Japanese anime that was the first to win an Oscar, and *Slumdog Millionaire*, an Indian film about modern poverty. It's interesting that a 2005 independent film by Quentin Tarantino, *Inglorious Bastards*, was created in German, French and English to appeal to the growing international audience.

European films have made a worldwide comeback by virtue of an artistic content that is often superior to formulaic Hollywood approaches. One interesting development in Europe is the Dogme 95 group, which has attempted to prove that high quality films can be made without huge Hollywood budgets. Directors using the Dogme 95 approach use hand-held shots and on-location sounds only, avoiding gimmicks and special effects.

India overtook the US and Europe as the world's largest film producer in the 1970s. The Indian film industry is centered in Mumbai, and is informally called "Bollywood." Like film industries everywhere, Bollywood caters primarily to mass audiences. Productions range from crime and action dramas to family-oriented comedies and musicals. However, an alternative to commercial Bollywood is the socially realistic Parallel Cinema movement.

An important influence on international cinema is the Cannes Film Festival, held every year since 1946 in the resort town of Cannes, France. Other film festivals, such as those of Venice, Berlin and Mumbai, also showcase the desire to produce higher quality cinema (Forbes and Street, 2001). The increasing participation of American and Asian films and stars shows a rising sense that a global cinema is emerging.

The end of the mass audience

Perhaps the most important trend in cinema is the decline of the mass audience. Movie-going became a weekly ritual during the 1920s, and even during the height of the Great Depression, 95 million Americans—nearly 75 percent of the population—went to see a movie once a week. This figure declined somewhat by 1948 to 90 million Americans—about 65 percent of the population—buying about 4.6 billion tickets per year.

Television cut deeply into movie ticket sales by the 1960s, with sales dipping below two billion per year, despite attempts by Hollywood studios to entice theater-goers with epic productions and special effects. By the 1980s, sales were half again, at about one billion US tickets per year, and have held more or less steady, with slight increases since then. Even so, movie-goers trended downward as part of the population. About 1.3 billion tickets were sold in 2010.

"What changed in the interval was that virtually every American family bought a TV set, and home entertainment largely replaced theater entertainment," said Edward Jay Epstein. In other words, theater-going as a habit virtually died by the twenty-first century. Entertainment became an individual or small group experience rather than a community experience (Epstein, 2005).

To make up for the decline in ticket sales, Hollywood advertised blockbusters—adding expense to its overhead—while counting on DVD sales to make up losses.

The strategy worked for most of the early years of the twenty-first century, but by 2010, DVDs could be ordered by web and delivered through the mail, or even through high-bandwidth internet connections, and companies like Netflix and RedBox were able to cut deeply into retail video rental companies like Hollywood Video and Blockbuster.

The result was that DVDs sold for less and the movie inventories of the big six—Sony, Disney, Fox, Universal, Paramount and Warner Brothers—were also declining in value. By 2010, most of the once-mighty studios were hovering on the verge of bankruptcy.

Nicholas Negroponte, former head of the MIT Media Lab, once noted a feeling of frustration, driving video tapes and DVDs back to the rental stores at night, since he was using massive amounts of steel, glass and petroleum just to move bits and bytes around. He predicted in 1996 that the first entertainment industry to be displaced by digital transmission technologies would be the video rental business. "And it will happen fast," he said. By 2010, video rental stores like Hollywood Video, Blockbuster, MovieStarz and others had filed for bankruptcy.

6

Advertising, public relations and the crafted image

"Historians and archaeologists will one day discover that the ads of our time are the richest and most faithful daily reflections any society ever made of its whole range of activities."—Marshall McLuhan. (Rothenberg, 1999)

Image and industry

When tennis champion Andre Agassi used the line "image is everything," in ads for Canon cameras in the 1990s, it was more than just a slogan. It was the credo of an era, reflecting an increasing preoccupation with both physical and mental images—a major theme in the history of advertising and public relations.

The rise of the image as the central focus of consumer and political culture was noted with concern in 1961 by historian Daniel Boorstin, who said the public landscape had been altered to the point where reproductions becoming more "real" than originals, and where pseudo-events were replacing real ones (Boorstin, 1961).

The power of images to promote products has been well known for millennia. Romans in the classical era used logos and symbols to promote everything from taverns to gladiatorial games. The Catholic Church first used woodcuts to promote piety in the early days of printing, then banned certain images that undermined church authority.

The industrial media that emerged in the mid-nineteenth century depended on advertising for most of its revenue, and advertisers increasingly discovered that it was the power of imagery that could attract consumers and build fortunes.

Dramatic photos of products, influenced by the pictorialist and straight photography movements, increasingly dominated advertising. Even radio ads asked listeners to visualize the product's benefits. As advertising became increasing image-oriented, the messages changed from product quality to product image. "Sell the sizzle, not the stake," became a byword of the business. Brand images, unique selling propositions and product positioning were among the core advertising strategies of the twentieth century.

Image as a persuasive tactic was an acquired taste of the twentieth century. Late-nineteenth-century soap advertisements, for instance, tended to focus on the cleanliness of a factory or the purity of the product. Fortunes were made when soap advertising shifted to a more appealing, image-building, consumer-centered message. A soap ad, for example, might feature an image of a beautiful woman endorsing the product, implying that you, too, can be beautiful if you use this soap.

Despite critics, advertising plays an important role in a free market as the financial lynchpin supporting independent media. Ads for cars, soap, toothpaste and the myriad of other products and services financed the independent news and entertainment media in a way that government could not.

Yet by the twenty-first century, the traditional model of mass media supported by broad-spectrum image advertising was breaking down. New approaches to advertising—such as internet metrics, social networking and "viral" web videos—became part of the new creative strategy.

Public relations, involving the creation and defense of metaphorical images for major industries, is another major theme in media history closely related to advertising. Railroads, petroleum, tobacco and other major industries turned to public relations experts to help sort out problems of adverse legislation and criticism from Progressive-era reformers in the early twentieth century.

Politicians, too, became more concerned with image in the early twentieth century, and "image politics" is often said to be a question of style over substance and personality over policy.

Polishing images—metaphorical and visual—is not a remedy for real problems. When international public health groups criticized Nestle Corporation for deceptive infant formula advertising in developing nations, Nestle found that despite public relations efforts, the company continued to face consumer boycotts and criticism well into the twenty-first century. BP's handling of the 2010 Gulf of Mexico oil well blowout is another example of an instance where public relations can't gloss over obvious mistakes.

Early advertising

Advertising is among the world's oldest professions. Street barkers loudly calling attention to products are typical in almost any market from antiquity to modern times. Advertisements painted on walls or wooden signs have been found by archaeologists in the ruins of ancient Egypt, Babylon, Greece and other lost civilizations.

One of the best-preserved glimpses into ancient advertising during the time is found in the ruins of Pompeii, a city of 20,000 that was suddenly inundated with volcanic ash in 79 CE and preserved for centuries near Naples, Italy. Pompeii's streets featured signs with logos and advertisements for wine, condiments, taverns, brothels, gladiatorial games and political candidates. These included "the quick surveyor," "Publius Cornelius Faventinus, barber," "Phoebus the perfume dealer," "Cresces the architect," and "Marcus Vecilius Verecundus, the tailor/clothes dealer" (Rokicki, 1987). Similar signs posted or painted on walls are still found in busy cities.

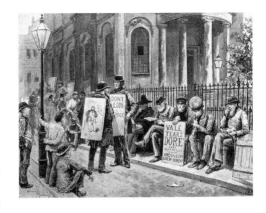

Figure 6.1 Sandwich men—the human billboards on the Strand in London take a break from their advertising duties in this sketch, c.1850.

Another ancient form of advertising is the town crier. In Medieval England, the town crier, or bellman, would ring a bell and shout "Oyez, oyez, oyez" (listen) to command attention and silence. After reading an official proclamation, the crier would post the notice on the door post of a local public house. The archaic phrase "oyez, oyez, oyez" is still used in some courts to begin official proceedings.

A variation on the town crier was the human billboard, described sarcastically by Charles Dickens as "a piece of human flesh between two slices of paste board." Before the advent of the popular industrial press in the mid-1800s, London streets were choked with people employed in this form of advertising.

Advertising through printed woodcuts is older than moveable type. From the 1400s on, churches distributed handbills to advertise religious fairs and to recruit soldiers to fight the Turks in the 1450s. Columbus used a woodcut image as the cover for his 1495 public relations pamphlet describing his voyages. The Protestant Reformation was successful, in large part, because of the power of printed text and images 70 years later.

The first printed text advertisement in English is often attributed to William Caxton who distributed a handbill promoting a newly printed book in the 1470s. Small announcements became one of the most common features of the emerging newspaper business from the early 1600s, and personal or "classified" advertising was also evident. The first newspaper ad may have been a notice about a stolen horse in *The Weekly Newes* in 1622.

Short notices of commercial or personal significance filled the back pages of newspapers until the early twenty-first century (Sampson, 1875). Some are particularly moving, such as this ad from London in the 1830s: "To A.M. Your brother implores that you will immediately return home . . . or write me and relieve the dreadful distress in which our parents are at your absence" (Knight, 1851).

Ads for brand name products are found as early as the 1600s. One ad appeared in a newspaper for Robert Turner's dentifrice in 1661. When the bubonic plague hit England, ads for all kinds of remedies ran in newspapers: Anti-Pestilential Pills, Incomparable Drink Against the Plague, The Only True Plague Water, Infallible Preventive Pills Against the Plague, and Sovereign Cordials Against the Corruption of the Air (Rothenberg, 1999).

With billboards, posters, newspapers, sandwich men and other advertising, London became so cluttered that Charles II proclaimed, "No signs shall be hung across the streets shutting out the air and the light of the heavens" (Rothenberg, 1999).

Some of the ingenious approaches to street advertising included the use of costumes, such as oversized tins of boot black. One feature of London in the early 1800s was a horse-drawn carriage built in the shape of a seven foot tall hat to advertise a hat maker. Historian Thomas Carlyle said the hat was not quite as large as the comic effect it produced, but it was tragic as well. "To me this all-deafening blast of puffery, of poor falsehood grown necessitous, sounds too surely like a Dooms-blast . . . God's blessing is not written on all this" (The Philosophy of Puffing, Circular, May 16, 1852, p. 1).

P. T. Barnum and the art of ballyhoo

One of the most celebrated showmen and public relations agents of the 1800s was P. T. (Phineas Taylor) Barnum. Founder of Barnum's American Museum in New York and a popular traveling circus, Barnum understood the public's taste for hokum and ballyhoo.

Barnum's enormous museum opened in 1842, covering half a block of lower Broadway. It was decorated with flags, banners, painted animals and murals. Inside, curious spectators who paid a small fee could find a zoo, wax museum, dioramas of famous events, scientific instruments, and all kinds of curiosities and hoaxes. One of Barnum's first hoaxes was a taxidermical concoction called the "Feejee Mermaid," sporting the tail of a fish and the head of monkey.

The museum burned down in a spectacular fire in 1865, along with tens of thousands of exhibits. *The New York Times* said that, despite the "innumerable sensations with which the intelligent public were disgusted and the innocent public deluded, and the ever patent humbuggery . . . the Museum still deserved an honorable place in the front rank of rare and curious collections of the world" (*The New York Times*, July 14, 1865).

Barnum did not coin the phrase often attributed to him: "There's a sucker born every minute." Instead, a rival hoaxer whose "Cardiff Giant" hoax had been called into question by Barnum coined that memorable phrase after Barnum promoted his own version of the Cardiff Giant in 1869. The "giant" was a 10-foot statue of a man created for the hoax and weathered with acid to seem ancient in order to show the "giants" described in Genesis.

Barnum opened the door to blatant hucksterism and ballyhoo in many areas of advertising and public relations.

An early example was the National Biscuit Co. (Nabisco) Uneeda biscuit campaign of 1898. Planned by N. W. Ayer advertising agency, the first packaged ready-to-eat food had a compelling name: Uneeda. The Uneeda biscuit marketing

Figure 6.2 Ballyhoo and Barnum— the king of boisterous advertising, called "ballyhoo" in the 1800s, was Phineas Taylor Barnum, owner of Barnum's Museum and a traveling circus. Barnum's philosophy was expressed by a rival: "There's a sucker born every minute." (Library of Congress)

campaign would come to a town with just one word on a billboard and in newspaper ads: "Uneeda." The next day, the ad would read "Uneeda biscuit." The following day it would read: "Do you know Uneeda biscuit?" And next: "Of Course Uneeda biscuit."

The Nabisco campaign was a smashing success, and was followed by Fig Newton, Animal Crackers, Lorna Doone and the Oreo. Interestingly, Oreo cookie was one of a trio of new products in 1913 and added as an afterthought. The other two new products—the Mother Goose Biscuit, depicting nursery rhyme characters, and the Veronese Biscuit, a sort of upscale Uneeda—were Nabisco's picks for success. But the Oreo caught on, eventually becoming the best selling cookie in the world (Burrough and Helyar, 1990). By 2005, 490 billion Oreo cookies had been sold (Toops, 2005).

British opinion of all this American ballyhoo was not high. British historian Henry Sampson wrote in 1875 that Britons "have not yet learned to sacrifice all that should be dear and honorable to humanity" as some of his American counterparts had. "The Americans are a truly great people," Sampson wrote, "but they have not yet settled into a regular system so far . . . as newspapers and advertisements are concerned" (Sampson, 1875).

And yet, the same ballyhoo techniques worked just as well in Britain. Thomas Lipton's approach to advertising his rapidly growing grocery chain in the late 1800s was to print fake currency that could be redeemed for low-cost produce, especially Irish ham. Lipton also hired a cartoonist who depicted an Irishman with a pig in a sack. "He's an orphan, so, out of pity, I'm taking him to Lipton's." Once the joke was known, pigs with ribbons tied in their tails would be paraded through the streets with signs showing that they were "Lipton's orphans" (Wood, 1958).

Figure 6.3 Biscuit campaign—The National Biscuit Company's "Uneeda Biscuit" ads were astonishingly successful for such a transparently hyped message. (Hartman Center, Duke University)

Figure 6.4 British ballyhoo— Thomas Lipton, a Scottish grocer, catapulted to world fame through shrewd marketing and strong advertising messages. (Library of Congress)

In 1881, Lipton announced that the company would import the world's largest cheese from New York to Glasgow for Christmas. The cheese would be sold in the Christmas custom with coins placed inside. "The streets were lined with spectators cheering the giant cheese on its way to Lipton's new store in High Street," according to a Glasgow city history. Police were called out to hold back the crowd. A few years later, Lipton staged a parade to announce his new line of packaged tea, for which the company is now known. An elephant led an army of 200 men dressed in Chinese garb, wearing sandwich boards with messages about the tea as they paraded through the streets of Glasgow (Waugh, 1950; Wood, 1958).

The Advent of Advertising Agencies

In its first four centuries, between the 1450s and the 1830s, newspaper, magazine and book publishers depended mostly on direct sales and subscriptions, also known as circulation revenues. Advertising was a service that editors could provide or, in some cases, might not, as they saw fit.

With the advent of industrial presses and greatly expanded circulation, penny press editors realized that they could sell their newspapers at one or two cents, actually losing money on circulation, but more than regaining it with advertising revenue. This shift in business models is one of the most important in media history.

Four models of advertising agencies developed in the nineteenth and twentieth centuries: (1) newspaper agency (taking orders for ads); (2) space jobbing (selling space to clients and then buying the ad space); (3) space wholesaling (buying large amounts of advertising space at a discount and then reselling the space to clients at regular rates); (4) advertising concession (contracting for advertising space and taking the risk of selling the space).

Before the penny press revolution, clients who needed to place ads in newspapers and magazines would simply go to the printing establishment and place their orders. But as commerce began to speed up, specialists who offered advertising services began to emerge.

The first advertising agency appeared in London in 1812, established by George Reynell, to handle legal advertising for lawyers and their clients. Ads for the Reynell agency itself begin to appear in *The Times* in 1832 (June 30, 1832, p. 2).

In the United States, Volney Palmer established the American Newspaper Advertising Agency in 1841 and quickly branched out with offices in New York, Boston and Philadelphia.

Others followed, and most early advertising agencies, like Palmer's, were buyers and brokers, either simply passing the orders along or placing ads into spaces they had already purchased.

In the 1870s, however, newer advertising agencies turned to a full service model, helping clients develop trademarks, package designs and marketing plans as well as advertising. Around the turn of the twentieth century, when big business was under fire from reformers and muckrakers, public relations was added to the full service suite.

As advertising specialists played an increasing role in commerce, advertising also began to draw critics. In 1850, Palmer decided to do something about it, and ran a contest for the best essay on the "Philosophy of Advertising." The winner was Horace Greeley, the well-known editor of the *New York Tribune*, whose business owed everything to advertising. Greeley said:

> Men of business are hardly aware of the immense change which a few years have wrought in the power of the public press . . . He who would build a business must

be like the times . . . To neglect (advertising) is like resolving never to travel by steam nor communicate by telegraph. It is to close one's eyes to the light and insist on living in perpetual darkness. . . . He who neglects the advantages of advertising not only robs himself of his fair advantages, but bestows the spoils on his wiser rivals. (Greeley, 1850)

Reaction to the essay was not uniformly positive. In "The Philosophy of Puffing," the *Circular* magazine was alarmed that every man could be his own trumpeter with the "vast amount" of newspaper advertising that had suddenly appeared: "Nature requires no man to make proclamation of his doings . . . There is not a man born into the world but feels that he is degrading himself if he speak of his excellencies and . . . supremacy in his craft."

Media critics of the era also noticed "a real evil . . . (in) the attempt to serve two masters: to sell space for the publisher and, at the same time, to act as an expert and impartial counselor for the advertiser" (Appel, 1939).

Full service agencies: J. Walter Thompson and N. W. Ayer

Publishers who need to find advertisers often sent sales agents into the streets. This was the origin of the J. Walter Thompson agency when, in 1864, William Carlton began canvassing for some of the New York City newspapers. Carlton hired Thompson, a Civil War veteran, in 1868, and ten years later, Thompson bought the company and renamed it for himself.

Thompson focused on the "full service" agency approach, helping clients craft and place ads. The agency specialized in ads with magazines like the *Century*, *Scribners*, *Godey's Lady's Book* and *Lady's Home Journal*. The company's portfolio include household and women's products like Ponds cold cream, Quaker Oats and Gerber baby food.

In 1899, Thompson's *Red Book on Advertising* echoed Greeley in its philosophy of advertising: "The merchant who does not believe in advertising does not believe in banks, insurance or other modern institutions. He is a relic of the lost ages . . . Advertisements cannot be too strong. You cannot catch the public eye too skillfully or too often." It also helped clients develop trademarks and package designs.

Figure 6.5 The Commodore—J. Walter Thompson created the first full service advertising agency in 1878. (Hartman Center, Duke University)

As the company grew, it pioneered testimonials, photography, psychological research, and broadcast advertising. The agency's name was changed to JWT in 2005.

Around the same time, another agency that established a full service approach to advertising was N. W. Ayer & Son. The name itself was a bit of a ruse, since

Telling the Story of Wool Soap

Wool Soap is absolutely pure. Clean, sweet tallow and specially imported vegetable oil used to make it so. No free alkali—nothing but pure soap. Cleanses. Good for washing the finest fabrics, laces, silks, linens, handkerchiefs—everything that you are particular about. Wool Soap produces a rich, soft lather, white and floats.

For fine laundry work, shave part of a cake of Wool Soap into lukewarm water. Work up suds. Dip the article into the suds. Wash, and rinse in clear water.

Swift & Company, U. S. A.

Figure 6.6 and Figure 6.7 The new face of advertising— throughout the 1800s, newspaper and magazine ads extolled the virtues of their products. It was only around the turn of the century when advertisers realized that simple "ballyhoo" was not enough, and that subjective approaches that appealed to user needs could be more effective. (Library of Congress)

the young Francis W. Ayer was not really in business with his father. As a 21-year-old starting off in Philadelphia in 1869, he just wanted it to appear as if the business was already established.

Ayer had purchased some of the remnants of Volney Palmer's old newspaper network, and also took a page from Greeley's "philosophy of advertising" when, in his own company promotional, "The Ayer Idea in Advertising," he wrote:

> Suppose you were to say "I do not believe in darkness; I do not want darkness." Will it not grow dark tonight quite the same? . . . You may not like the idea of the telephone or typewriter or adding machine . . . but these are established instruments . . . To refuse to use them stamps you as being behind the times, and competition with the man or business who does use them is no longer possible. (Ayer, 1912)

Behind this lofty rhetoric was Francis Ayer's determination to serve the client first. Ayer took an "open book" approach to clients, allowing them to see exactly how much money was being charged by the publication where the advertising was purchased. This assured clients that they came first, and not the need to sell advertising space that the agency had already contracted. "As Ayer saw it, he was working for the advertiser and the other agencies were working for the publisher," said Appel. Some of the company's early clients included seed companies, Montgomery Ward, John Wanamaker Department Stores and Singer Sewing Machines.

Even with his religious background, Ayer participated in some of the worst forms of advertising of the day. At one point, one quarter of the Ayer business was for "patent medicines." Ayer dropped the accounts in 1906, long after others had done so, when strong federal regulations were looming.

Advertising and patent medicine

Until about 1906, advertising in the United States resembled a lawless frontier. Especially troubling were ads for opium-based syrups designed to soothe children with toothaches.

"Poison for the poor" was how *Collier's Magazine* depicted the patent medicine business in a 1905 muckraking series of articles by Samuel Hopkins Adams.

"Gullible America will . . . swallow huge quantities of alcohol, an appalling amount of opiates and narcotics, and a wide assortment of varied drugs ranging from powerful and dangerous heart depressants to insidious liver stimulants," Adams said in the opening to "The Great American Fraud" (Adams, 1905).

The bottles of syrup and boxes of powders were called "patent" medicines because the brand names were often trademarked.

Cocaine and opium stop pain, but the narcotics are not the safest drugs to put into the hands of the ignorant, particularly when their presence is concealed in the "cough remedies," "soothing syrups," and "catarrhal powders" of which they are the basis.

It was a grave injustice, Hopkins said, that people could be hoodwinked into thinking that extract of witch hazel could cure meningitis, or that concoctions based on cocaine and opium could cure cancer, or that mildly acidic formulas could prevent yellow fever. Even worse were the "soothing syrups" made of opium, given to children to keep them tranquil.

Adams also charged that the American media was in league with the patent medicine advertisers. A "red clause" in the advertising contracts allowed the patent medicine makers to void the contract in case of adverse legislation. This meant that newspaper publishers had a strong financial interest in ensuring that no laws regulating patent medicine were passed at the state or federal levels.

Adams was not the first to point out that unregulated pharmaceutical and advertising industries had turned millions of ailing people into drug addicts. As early as 1892, the *Ladies Home Journal* had banned advertising for "patent" medicines. And Coca-Cola, a popular drug-store tonic, stopped including cocaine in the formula sometime around the turn of the century.

But Adams' articles came at a time when Americans were awakened to injustice and clamoring for reform. By 1906, Congress

Figure 6.8 Patent medicine—in 1905, a muckraking series of articles in *Collier's Magazine* exposed the fraud and abuse in the patent medicine business. Along with *The Jungle*, about the Chicago meatpacking industry, the Colliers article helped create the political momentum for reform. (Library of Congress)

Figure 6.9 Killem Quick Pharmacy—cocaine, opium and other dangerous drugs were openly available in 1900, when *Puck* magazine satirized the patent medicine industry with this cartoon. Here a bartender (left) watches the pharmacist with envy. "I can't begin to compete with this fellow," he says. It's notable that magazines led the charge for reform; newspapers depended so heavily on patent medicine advertising that many had agreed, by contract, never to say anything negative about the patent medicine business. The reform movement culminated in the establishment of the Food and Drug Administration in 1906 and the Federal Trade Commission in 1914. (Library of Congress)

passed the Pure Food and Drug Act requiring federal inspection of meat and labeling of the drug content of medicines. The act paved the way for the creation of the Food and Drug Administration (FDA), which monitors pharmaceutical advertising as well as food safety.

In another series of articles, Adams wrote about the deadly impacts of misleading advertising for Grape-Nuts, a popular cereal made of bran, molasses and salt. One advertisement read: "No Appendicitis For Those Who Use Grape-Nuts." Another said: "It is a practical certainty that when a man has approaching symptoms of appendicitis, the attack can be avoided by discontinuing all food except Grape Nuts."

"This is lying—Potentially deadly lying," Adams wrote in a *Collier's* editorial.

In response, Postum Company ran an ad in other publications saying that Adams and *Collier's* magazine were attacking them with "out and out falsehoods" in an attempt to win back their advertising contracts. In return, *Collier's* sued Postum for libel in 1907 and won, but the verdict was overturned on a technicality in 1912 (*The New York Times*, September 7, 1907 and February 17, 1916).

The upshot of the libel trial, said historian Clark Gavin, was that advertisers realized they didn't need to make extravagant claims for their products. "It was enough to show . . . a Hollywood star . . . using the product—copy was unnecessary" (Gavin, 1962). In other words, the power of the image was far more effective.

Public relations versus muckraking

The "muckraking" era of the American press involved exposes such as Adams' "Great American Fraud" along with Upton Sinclair's book, *The Jungle*. Both of these influenced Congress to pass the Food and Drug Act of 1906.

Other muckrakers also had major social impacts. Ida Tarbell's 1906 *History of Standard Oil* showed how John D. Rockefeller used bribery and underhanded tactics to absorb competitors into his oil monopoly. Others, like Charles Edward Russell, Ray Stannard Baker and Lincoln Steffans took on the railroad monopolies and corruption in politics.

At the time, reformers in government, led by President Theodore Roosevelt, had passed laws to break up monopolies and restore competitive markets. Public relations experts such as Ivy Ledbetter Lee emerged to help corporations craft a response.

Many business leaders did not see the necessity of public relations, and to some extent, Lee and other public relations experts fought a battle on two fronts. They worked for the corporations, but spent a lot time and energy convincing the corporations they were needed. The traditional nineteenth century corporate response to calls for government regulation and concern for public opinion had been openly defiant. "I owe the public nothing," banking tycoon J. P. Morgan said in this context. Similarly, William Vanderbilt became instantly infamous when, asked about public opinion of his railroad in 1882, he roared: "The public be damned" (Gordon, 1989).

Lee began in 1904 by forming the Parker and Lee company with experienced journalist George Parker. Lee's philosophy was that the companies and their public relations practitioners have a responsibility beyond obligations to the client. "Our plan is frankly, and openly, on behalf of business concerns and public institutions, to supply the press and public of the United States prompt and accurate information concerning subjects which it is of value and interest to the public to know about" (Tuney, 2010).

Lee's early work for the Pennsylvania Railroad turned the tables on the Vanderbilt approach, providing press releases and accurate information about a 1906 railroad accident before details reached the media from elsewhere. It was the first time that reporters had been given access to accident scenes and witnesses by a railroad (Princeton, 2010).

In 1914, a state militia killed 19 people, including two women and 11 children, during a coal miners' strike in Ludlow, Colorado. Ivy Lee was dispatched to the scene by the mine's owner, Standard Oil tycoon John D. Rockefeller. Lee quickly blamed the victims for carelessness in starting an accidental fire, and then circulated a bulletin, "How Colorado Editors View the Strike," quoting 11 editors who supported the coal

Figure 6.10 Ivy Lee and public relations—Ivy Ledbetter Lee was one of the first to set up public relations agencies to help industrialists deal with critics and political problems. Prompt and accurate information was the goal, but Lee did not always live up to his ideals. (Library of Congress)

industry. All 11 worked for newspapers owned by the coal industry—the rest of the state's 320 editors were not quoted (Olasky, 1987). Lee also had Rockefeller's son attend a social event in the mining camp and dance with the miners' wives to show he was a regular guy (Hiebert, 1966). Muckraking journalists, such as Upton Sinclair, said Lee tried to mislead them about the massacre. They labeled him "poison ivy" Lee.

Around this time, laws forcing the breakup of monopolies (such as the Sherman Antitrust Act of 1890) had passed Congress and were being enforced by the Supreme Court. Standard Oil Co., for instance, was broken up in 1911 following a civil trial showing that it had engaged in anticompetitive practices (*Standard Oil Co. of NJ v. United States, 1911*).

AT&T, the phone company founded by Alexander Graham Bell, was also under investigation by the Justice Department for buying up its competitors. Unlike oil, however, the telephone company argued that it was a "natural monopoly" and could provide service to every American.

As an AT&T president said in 1909: "The public does not know us . . . It has never seen us, never met us, does not know where we live, who we are, what our good qualities are." Ivy Lee worked with N. W. Ayer company to change all that. Ayer created a series of standardized ads that aimed at public familiarity and long-range corporate image building. It set the "right tone" of restrained but straightforward friendliness, not one of gaudy low appeal, like Prince Albert tobacco, but not high toned like Steinway pianos. The hope was to make people understand and love the company, "to hold real affection for it" (Marchand, 1998).

Figure 6.11 Promoting monopoly—the advertising campaign that helped American Telephone and Telegraph hold on to its regulated monopoly in the antitrust era was designed by Ivy Lee and N. W. Ayer. It emphasized reliability and universal service. (Hartman Center, Duke University)

The first of the AT&T ads, "Twenty Million Voices," began appearing in late June, 1908. "The usefulness of the telephone is in its universality as one system," the ad copy says. "Where there are two systems you must have two telephones—and confusion" (Griese, 1977). In the long list of great public relations campaigns, AT&T was called "the granddaddy of them all" (Marchand, 1998). The campaign paid off, and in 1913, AT&T and the Justice Dept. signed the "Kingsbury Commitment" which allowed the monopoly to continue under government regulation.

Lee continued to work for AT&T and the railroads, insisting that external public relations was also good for employee morale. He also served as the publicity director of the American Red Cross during World War I. But Lee's true allegiance was with Standard Oil Co., and he helped it through numerous crises in the 1920s.

One of Standard Oil's biggest public relations problems was its agreement with I. G. Farben, the German dye and chemicals trust to protect each other's patents and interests in the years leading up to World War II (Borkin, 1978). Lee traveled, at Standard Oil's request, to Germany in January of 1934. He met with Adolf Hitler and advised

German propaganda ministry officials to take an "equality of armaments" line with regard to breaking their rearmament treaties.

When he returned to the United States in July, 1934, a Congressional "Un-American Activities" committee called Lee to testify. Lee insisted that he told the Nazis that Americans would never be reconciled to their treatment of Jewish people. But he had a difficult time explaining why this advice would be worth over $25,000 (*The New York Times*, July 12, 1934). Lee died later in 1934 from a brain tumor before the contradiction could be cleared up.

Tobacco advertising

When R. J. Reynolds, the famed tobacco baron from Winston-Salem, NC, decided to market a brand of pipe tobacco nationwide, he called the N. W. Ayer creative team in 1907. Together Ayer's and Reynolds' American Tobacco Co. came up with Prince Albert, the name of the popular son of Queen Victoria who had just become King Edward VII. They found a photo of the prince with Mark Twain, copied it, and put it on a tin can filled with tobacco. The ad caught on, and American Tobacco sales went from one-quarter million to 14 million pounds in four years.

In 1913, American Tobacco took the financially risky approach of marketing pre-packaged cigarettes, which at the time were not popular. Reynolds used local and Turkish tobaccos, and, playing up the mysterious eastern connotation, called the cigarettes Camels. Again, the Ayer company led the account and, like its Uneeda biscuit campaign, the cigarette would be introduced into each market with teaser ads. First: "Camels" and then "The Camels are coming" and then "Tomorrow there'll be more camels in this town than in all Asia and Africa combined!" and finally "Camel Cigarettes are here."

"It was breathless and brazen, and by modern standards, hokey," said historian Bryan Burrough. "But it made the first national cigarette a major event." At 20 cents a pack, Camels undercut other brands, and within a year, 425 million packs were sold (Burrough, 1990).

After World War I, tobacco companies began to look for new markets and began thinking about women as an overlooked market. At the time, social conservatives considered the idea of women smoking as a sign of low morals. Early ads featuring women smoking took an indirect approach. In 1926, for example, Liggett & Myers, owners of the Chesterfield brand, ran an ad with a young woman, who was not smoking, saying to a young man: "Blow some my way."

American Tobacco, hoping to get in on "a new gold mine right in our front yard" hired Lord & Thomas advertising firm, which specialized in delicate issues (such as feminine hygiene products). They also hired another public relations expert, Edward Bernays.

Figure 6.12 Breathless and brazen—Camel cigarettes were the first to be mass marketed through advertising. (Hartman Center, Duke University)

Somewhere West of Laramie

SOMEWHERE west of Laramie there's a broncho-busting, steer-roping girl who knows what I'm talking about.

She can tell what a sassy pony, that's a cross between greased lightning and the place where it hits, can do with eleven hundred pounds of steel and action when he's going high, wide and handsome.

The truth is—the Playboy was built for her.

Built for the lass whose face is brown with the sun when the day is done of revel and romp and race.

She loves the cross of the wild and the tame.

There's a savor of links about that car—of laughter and lilt and light—a hint of old loves—and saddle and quirt. It's a brawny thing—yet a graceful thing for the sweep o' the Avenue.

Step into the Playboy when the hour grows dull with things gone dead and stale.

Then start for the land of real living with the spirit of the lass who rides, lean and rangy, into the red horizon of a Wyoming twilight.

JORDAN

JORDAN MOTOR CAR COMPANY, Inc. Cleveland, Ohio

Figure 6.13 Appealing to women—cigarette makers weren't the only ones appealing to women. One of the most colorful pieces of copywriting ever written, the Jordan car ad of 1923 lived on long after the actual company vanished. "Somewhere west of Laramie, there's a broncho-bustin' steer-roping girl who knows what I'm talking about . . . " (Library of Congress)

Figure 6.14 Scientific PR—Edward Bernays pioneered a more scientific approach to public relations, using polling and focus groups to help companies understand public opinion before being committed to a position. (Library of Congress)

Bernays was called the "father of scientific public relations," in the sense that he would use social science research techniques to inform his campaigns. In his book *Crystallizing Public Opinion*, Bernays equated "manipulation of the public mind" with the "social purpose" of speeding change and preventing chaos (Olasky, 1987).

He found that, even after winning the right to vote in 1919, women were concerned with freedom and independence. His idea was to promote cigarettes as symbols of freedom. Bernays organized demonstrations of women smoking Lucky Strike cigarettes in public, culminating in the 1929 NY Easter Parade. They carried placards identifying their cigarettes as "torches of liberty." Photos and articles were distributed to small town newspapers across the nation (Schudson, 1978).

The Lucky Strike campaign grew to $19 million a year by 1931, and included themes of sex appeal as well as freedom. Ads featuring slim women were headlined: "Reach for a Lucky instead of a sweet."

A Congressional committee expressed its outrage over women smoking. "Not since the days when the vendor of harmful nostrums was swept from our streets has this country witnessed such an orgy of buncombe, quackery and downright falsehood and fraud as now marks the current campaign promoted by certain cigarette manufacturers to create a vast woman and child market," one senator said (Schudson, 1978).

Around this same time, Bernays helped another company deal with a crisis. U.S. Radium Corp. had been severely criticized for legal tactics and delays in a case involving the "radium girls" watch dial painters who had radiation poisoning. In 1928, the *New York World* newspaper criticized U.S. Radium and the courts for barring the doors of justice to the dying women. While the company was negotiating an out-of-court settlement, Bernays worked to ensure that medical uses of radium were kept in the public eye (Neuzil and Kovarik, 1997).

"The implications of Bernay's public relations paradigm ... alarmed some political, academic and religious observers during the 1930s, as concern about the political effects of mass manipulation . . . became more widespread," said historian Marvin Olasky. "For instance, in a 1934 letter to President Franklin Roosevelt, Supreme Court Justice Felix Frankfurter referred to Bernays and Ivy Lee as 'professional poisoners of the public mind,' exploiters of foolishness, fanaticism and self interest."

Madison Ave goes to war

In April of 1917, a few days after the United States formally entered World War I, President Woodrow Wilson created the Committee on Public Information, also known as Creel Committee for its leader, George Creel. The committee also included Edward Bernays, who later remarked that "the essence of democratic society" was the "engineering of consent."

The committee used all available media to spread its message, and historians estimate that 6,000 government ads and news releases found their way into the press (Mott, 1966). Some of these even advised Americans to beware of people speaking German, creating a climate of fear in German-American communities in the upper Midwest.

The committee also served a role that would later be filled by radio and television when it recruited about 75,000 "four minute men" (Ward, 1996, p. 449). These were volunteers who would stand up at the beginning of movies, church services, and other public events to speak for four minutes about subjects ranging from the draft to rationing, war bond drives, victory gardens and the reasons America had entered the war. By 1918, the four minute men made more than 7.5 million speeches to 314 million people in 5,200 communities.

Creel later wrote in his memoir, *How We Advertised America*: "In no degree was the Committee an agency of censorship . . . Our effort was educational and informative throughout, for we had such confidence in our case as to feel that no other argument was needed than the simple, straightforward presentation of the facts." Yet many journalists at the time saw the work as ham-fisted and illogical.

Commercial advertising did not dry up during World War I, even though consumer goods were in short supply. Business owners were able to buy ads that also stressed the role of their business in helping the war effort and promote sales of government war bonds. The successful campaigns led the advertising trade journal *Printers' Ink* to recall that "it is possible to sway the minds of whole populations, change their habits of life, create belief, practically universal, in any policy or idea."

During World War I, as the US government assumed unprecedented power, large corporations that had been under fire in the muckraking age could now gain legitimacy through war advertising. Many felt it helped break down "imaginary, artificial barriers" between the corporations and the national cause. Advertising professionals

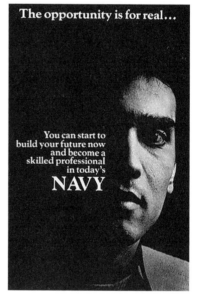

Figures 6.15(a) to 6.15(d) Recruiting posters—four recruiting posters for the Navy show the evolution of style over the nineteenth and twentieth centuries. The first is designed to recruit volunteers for the Confederate Navy in 1863. The second was a highly successful "I want you" direct appeal that was widely copied in World War I. The third, from World War II, shows a heroic figure in action. The fourth, from the Vietnam era, emphasizes training and opportunity with low-key graphics. (National Archives)

Figure 6.16 Who needs comedy?—George Creel's committee on public information was not universally popular, as this *Washington Post* cartoon from 1917 shows. Despite censorship in World War I, it's notable that open criticism of the censors could still slip by. (*Washington Post*, October 7, 1917)

also believed that their efforts in the war helped them gain new prestige as professionals (Marchand, 1998).

World War II

By the 1940s, when World War II broke out, public relations and advertising were ready once again to support the war effort and show the role corporations were playing. This time they started with a serious handicap.

In years after World War I, American oil and automotive industries had grown close to their German counterparts in terms of technology, politics and long-term business strategy. General Motors and other major companies helped rebuild Germany's defense industries in the 1930s. IBM helped the Nazis with a census that tracked Jewish populations (as noted in Chapter 10). Texaco, an American oil company, helped fascists win the 1930s civil war in Spain and provided a New York haven for German spies and diplomats in the months before the US entered World War II (Sampson, 1975). Standard Oil (Exxon) had allied with German chemical giant I. G. Farben and helped undermine production of key war materials such as synthetic rubber (Borkin, 1978).

Some of this information came out before the war, but as the US entered World War II, the British security agencies provided the evidence to expose the compa-

They've got more important places to go than you!...

Save Rubber
CHECK YOUR TIRES NOW

Figure 6.17 War Advertising Council—the campaign to save rubber was one of the War Advertising Council's big projects and one way that civilians were engaged in the early years of World War II. Natural rubber supplies from Southeast Asia had been blocked and synthetic rubber production from petroleum was taking too long. (Library of Congress)

nies in the US press and in Congressional investigations (Stevenson, 1978). The resulting public anger was a serious problem for companies who were suddenly anxious to prove their patriotism.

"Once problems and scandals are revealed, corporations are often faced with negative public reactions and perceptions," said historian Deborah Petersen-Perlman. "It is common for these corporations to engage in public relations campaigns which highlight these corporations' good deeds" (Petersen-Perlman, 1994).

Texaco began sponsoring the Metropolitan Opera Broadcasts in 1940 "as atonement for past sins," Petersen said. Standard Oil hired Roy Stryker, the famous former head of the Farm Security Agency photography effort, to document the role that petroleum was playing in the war (Plattner, 1983).

The War Advertising Council was organized in 1942 to help prepare voluntary advertising campaigns for wartime efforts. *Advertising Age* saw a connection between the fervent patriotism exhibited by the advertising industry and investigations by then-Senator Harry Truman.

"The industry launched a frontal campaign to protect itself, promoting its importance to the war effort and construing itself as 'the information industry'" (Rothenberg, 1999). Overall, the council garnered $350 million in free public service messages. After the war it was renamed the Advertising Council.

Broadcast advertising

The idea of putting advertising on the radio in order to pay for programs is usually attributed to David Sarnoff and his radio memo to the American Marconi Corporation in 1916. But it's worth noting that the concept was already being tested by several amateur groups in the upper Midwest.

Radio advertising seemed like a perilous venture at first, said historian Roland Marchand, because it would intrude into family home life. But when RCA and other radio manufacturers found they could not finance radio programming simply through sales of radio equipment, and when the US decided not to follow Britain's 1922 lead when it subsidized the British Broadcasting Corporation, then advertising was the only route forward.

Early broadcasters soon adopted the print media model of advertising support for programs. Sometimes a single advertiser would support a program: Orson Welles'

Mercury Theater radio program was supported by Campbell's Soup in the 1930s; and the GE Theater television program was supported by General Electric in the 1950s. Most programs were supported by a variety of advertisers who would package their messages in 15 to 30 second commercials that were priced according to the size of the audience they could reach.

Radio may have been limited to sound, but it opened the doors to imagination as well. Often radio advertisers took advantage of this "theater of the mind" concept. Comedian Stan Freberg demonstrated the effect on his radio show in 1957, using sound effects to dramatize the towing of a 10-ton cherry onto a 700-ft. mountain of whipped cream floating in hot-chocolate filled Lake Michigan, with 25,000 extras cheering. The bit was later used by the Radio Advertising Bureau to promote radio advertising.

Both radio and television were regulated by the Federal Communications Commission, and worked under additional ethical codes as well. The National Association of Broadcasters code prohibited the use of profanity, any negative portrayal of family life, irreverence, alcoholism, cruelty, detailed techniques of crime, and negative portrayal of law enforcement officials, or use of subliminal messages in advertising, among other things.

This did not, however, prevent broadcasters from promoting tobacco, even to children. Lucky Strike cigarettes sponsored many radio and television comedies, for instance, including the Jack Benny Show, the Kollege of Musical Knowledge, and the Lucky Strike Hit Parade, which featured teenage singers like Frank Sinatra. Tobacco companies also sponsored TV shows such as I've Got a Secret and the Flintstones cartoon series. At one point, cigarettes were the dominant factor in television advertising sponsorships. In 1963, teenagers were exposed to 1,300 cigarette commercials per year (Elders, 1994).

The most significant ad icon of the twentieth century, according to *Advertising Age*, was the Marlboro Man cigarette campaign. First conceived by the Leo Burnett agency in 1954, the Marlboro man image involves cowboys, often riding horses in a Western setting. Originally the ad campaign was seen as a way to increase the popularity of filter cigarettes, since unfiltered cigarettes were considered more masculine. Sales went up 300 percent in two years.

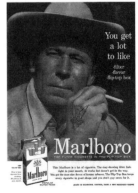

That same year, tobacco companies released "A Frank Statement," the first in a campaign to counter reports that smoking cigarettes could cause lung cancer. But within a decade, a Surgeon General's report concluded that lung cancer and other serious health effects were, indeed, caused by smoking. Tobacco advertising was banned from broadcasting by Congress starting January 2, 1971. All printed advertising must now display a health warning from the US Surgeon General.

Figure 6.18 Marlboro Man—developed in 1954 to embody the rugged American spirit, the Marlboro Man was considered the top advertising campaign of the twentieth century. (Hartman Center, Duke University)

Public relations and crisis communications

After World War II, Ivy Lee's one-way press agent concept expanded into a two-way concept of public relations advocated by Edward Bernays. Corporations should listen to public opinion and tailor some activities with the public in mind, Bernays said. Still, the symmetry of the communication varied considerably.

For some companies, public relations was nothing more than a defensive tactic to be used when under fire from public opinion and potential regulators. Others with longer range vision used ethical principles and accepted corporate responsibility, which in turn made their public relations efforts far more successful.

Several controversies from the era showed how varied the approaches could be. In the 1970s, public health officials in developing countries noticed a disturbing trend. Infant mortality rates were rising as mothers switched from natural breast feeding to infant formula. A major factor in the switch included advertising techniques designed to convince mothers from Aruba to Zimbabwe that infant formula was cleaner and safer. In Europe and the United States, these tactics might not have been entirely honest, but they were at least not damaging. In the developing world, switching to infant formula was like "signing the death certificate of a child," according to a United Nations health committee. That was because mothers in poorer regions lacked clean water to mix with formula powder, and often couldn't afford to keep buying baby formula (*Time*, 1976).

In 1974, one of the leading infant formula manufacturers sued the publishers of *The Baby Killer* for libel in Switzerland. After a two-year trial, Nestle won a settlement of 300 Swiss Francs—a verdict that upheld Nestle's view that it hadn't directly broken Swiss law, but that it had, in the eyes of the court, acted unethically. An international boycott of Nestle products was launched in response. At one point the Episcopal church contacted the parent of a Nestle executive to encourage a change in behavior—without success. In 1984, Nestle agreed to abide by an international health code, but the boycott was reinstated in 1988 after an investigation showed continued patterns of violations. In 1999, Nestle insisted in a public relations campaign that it was acting ethically and responsibly, but a British Advertising Standards Authority found that the contention was not supported (Ferriman, 1999). As this book went to press the boycott was still in effect.

In contrast, a 1982 crisis involving Tylenol poisoning showed how a major business ought to handle a disaster. The crisis began when seven people died after taking Tylenol pain reliever due to malicious tampering with Tylenol packages. Although the company was not at fault, Tylenol maker Johnson & Johnson issued an immediate recall for all of its products, refunded all consumers, staffed phone banks and developed tamper-proof packaging (Rehak, 2002).

Often a company's reaction would do more harm to its reputation than original incident. The 1979 partial meltdown of the Three Mile Island nuclear reactor was one such event. During the ongoing disaster, neither the utility nor the Nuclear Regulatory Commission (NRC) had a way to get information from people who had it (in the control room and at the site) to the public and the press, with enormous confusion resulting (President's Commission, 1979). The public was not informed about the accident itself until hours after it took place, nor was it informed of gas or water releases containing high levels of radiation (*Washington Post*, 1999).

Similarly inaccurate information and attempts to control media access fueled public outrage about the explosion on a BP oil drilling rig in the Gulf of Mexico in 2010. The outrage was even more widespread due to the new ability of the Web to spread many-to-many communication, and also as something of a backlash to the attempts to create a business personality. While these efforts worked for AT&T in the early twentieth century, they seemed to have backfired on BP in the late twentieth century. "The more successful they are in creating such a personality, the more there is to love—and hate," said a *Financial Times* analyst (Kelloway, 2010).

Public relations expert James Grunig, who developed the idea of the "two-way symmetrical flow" of communication, contends that ethical public relations helps a company avoid problems in the first place by altering management to seriousness of a problem and encouraging responsible reactions (Grunig, 1989). "By working to implement a symmetrical system of internal communication, public relations professionals can, in turn, affect organizational culture" (Sriramesh et al., 1996).

Ongoing controversies tarnished the public images of Nike, Nestle, BP, the nuclear industry and many other businesses, and continue to demonstrate that public relations alone cannot obscure irresponsible corporate behavior. Personalizing a corporate image may help in good times, but when things go wrong, the personality becomes a target of consumer outrage.

Ad agencies in the late twentieth century

As consumer culture caught on in the years after World War II, advertising agencies began developing psychologically based marketing theories that would give them an edge over their competition and frame their efforts to reach audiences. It was a time of personality, creativity and opportunity (Cappo, 2005). Among the creative personalities were the following:

Leo Burnett (1892–1971) believed in personalizing and sentimentalizing products, creating icons like the Jolly Green Giant, the Pillsbury Doughboy, Charlie the Tuna, Tony the Tiger, and most famously, the Marlboro Man.

Norman B. Norman (1914–1991), one of New York's original ad men, tied advertising to theories of empathy for clients including Colgate-Palmolive, Revlon, Ronson, Chanel and Liggett & Myers.

Helen Lansdowne Resor (1886–1964), worked for J. Walter Thompson to help market products to women. Woodbury Soap's ad, "The skin you love to touch," was typical of her use of personal appeals to attract interest.

David Ogilvy (1911–1999) believed that "brand personality" drew consumers to products. At the height of his career in 1962, *Time* magazine called him "the most sought-after wizard in today's advertising industry." He was known for a career of expanding the bounds of both creativity and morality in advertising. Ogilvy's campaigns included "The man in the Hathaway shirt" (featuring a model with an aristocratic eye patch) and "The man from Schweppes is here." In 1989 The Ogilvy Group was bought by WPP Group, a British parent company which, by 2010, was the largest ad agency in the world.

Rosser Reeves (1910–1984) was a pioneer of broadcast advertising who saw repetition of a "Unique Selling Proposition" (USP) as the key theory. These were often translated into slogans (such as M&M's candy that "melts in your mouth, not in your hand") or dramatic demonstrations. Reeves was famous for annoying pain reliever commercials with cartoons that would depict anvils inside people's heads being hit with hammers. In one commercial, a nerve-wracked daughter shouts "Mother Please! I'd rather do it myself." Reeves was the model for the protagonist in a television series about advertising called Mad Men.

William Bernbach (1911—1982) rejected the "USP" idea and developed off-beat, attention getting campaigns that made him a leader in the "creative revolution" of the 1960s and 70s. His "think small" campaign for Volkswagen was the top campaign of the twentieth century according to *Advertising Age* (Klein and Donation, 1999). Emphasizing that creativity was the path to audience interest, Bernach warned against thinking of advertising as some kind of science.

Maurice and Charles Saatchi (1946–) and (1943–) were among the first to take a global approach to advertising when they founded Saatchi & Saatchi in 1970. Through a series of mergers and acquisitions in the 1980s, the company became the world's largest advertising super-agency by 1988. The Saatchi brothers split off from the main agency, now owned by Publicis Groupe, to run a smaller creative agency M&C Saatchi.

Lee Clow (1942–) took Bernbach's creative revolution of the 1970s into the next generation, crafting television ads like the famous Apple "1984" commercial. He is also known for the Energizer Bunny, Taco Bell chihuahua, and California Cooler campaigns.

Advertising regulation: Europe and the United States

Advertising regulation in Europe has traditionally been more paternalistic, yet advertising graphics tend to be far more explicit than in the United States. For example, ads for tobacco and alcohol are tightly regulated in Europe, and yet ads with nudity or suggestive themes are not considered as offensive to European tastes.

UK advertising regulation was assumed by the Advertising Standards Authority, which consolidated advertising regulatory authority from television, radio and print commissions. The code is described as a mixture of self-regulation for non-broadcast advertising and co-regulation for broadcast advertising. Like US advertising laws, ads cannot be misleading or cause "physical, mental, moral or social harm to persons under the age of 18."

Controversies about advertising in France often revolve around attempts to maintain French traditions amid an increasing internationalization of both advertising and the English language. French advertising laws discriminated against non-French products until around 1980, when Scotch whiskey manufacturers sued France in the European Court of Justice. By 1991, French laws prohibited all tobacco advertising and alcohol advertising on TV or in cinemas. Some relaxation of restrictions on wine advertising took place around 2008.

The view of advertising as a free speech right has changed dramatically in the United States. Before 1976, US courts drew a sharp distinction between the right to political speech and the right to advertise. While local and state governments could not prohibit strictly political dissent without running afoul of the First Amendment, they could control the content of commercial messages.

This meant, for example, that when laws were passed to curb the abuses of patent medicine advertising, there was no basis to complain that the First Amendment rights were being violated. But it also meant that in 1928, when the United Mine Workers of America wanted to place ads in local newspapers during a coal strike, state courts could grant a coal industry injunction to stop them (*Washington Post*, Feb. 28, 1928).

The idea that advertising could be regulated as states and localities saw fit was reinforced by the courts in a case called *Valentine v. Christensen*. The dispute started in 1940, when a surplus World War I submarine was being exhibited for profit, and the city of New York stopped the owner from passing out advertising on city streets. The US Supreme Court heard the submarine case in 1942 and ruled that the city was free to regulate advertising because commercial speech did not have First Amendment protection (*Valentine v. Christensen, 316 US 52, 1942*).

A much more difficult case was presented in 1964, when a lawsuit over a Civil Rights ad became the focus of a major national decision on the right to criticize public officials. (See Sidebar "A landmark advertising and libel case," page 188.)

The Sullivan case involved an advertisement that was clearly political, and the US courts tried to maintain a sharp distinction between commercial and political speech. However, ten years later, several advertising cases came up that presented both political and commercial dimensions.

In one case, a Virginia law prohibited advertising for what had become legal abortion services (*Bigelow v. Virginia, 421 US 809, 1975*). In another case, a citizens' consumer council asked the court to overturn a Virginia state ban on advertising for generic drugs. Although the case was primarily commercial, the citizens group argued that this was a case of discrimination against the elderly, who needed price information to make better choices, and therefore the advertisements had a political dimension (*Virginia State Board of Pharmacy v. Virginia Citizens Consumer Council, 425 US 748, 1976*).

At this point, the Supreme Court began ruling that while state or federal agencies could prohibit false or deceptive advertising, they could not prohibit truthful advertising about lawful products in most cases. (Tobacco advertising was one important exception). A state or federal agency could only regulate the time, place and manner of advertising, but the regulations had to be content neutral and narrowly tailored to meet a compelling government interest.

Subsequent cases confirmed the link between the First Amendment and the right to advertise, while still upholding the ability of governments to regulate false advertising.

A difficult case involved shoe manufacturer Nike Inc. in 1997. Investigators alleged that people making Nike shoes in Vietnam and other Asian nations were subject to dangerous and abusive working conditions. When Nike responded with a public relations campaign that denied such abuses existed, an activist named Marc Kasky sued Nike under California laws prohibiting false advertising. The state supreme court agreed, saying, "when a business enterprise, to promote and defend its sales and profits, makes factual representations about its own products or its own operations, it must speak truthfully." The case was sent to, and then sent back from, the US Supreme Court, without resolution. Eventually the case was settled out of court, and while both sides were not entirely satisfied, the validity of regulating untruthful advertising in a commercial area was upheld.

A landmark advertising and libel case

The New York Times.

Heed Their Rising Voices

Your Help Is Urgently Needed . . . NOW !!

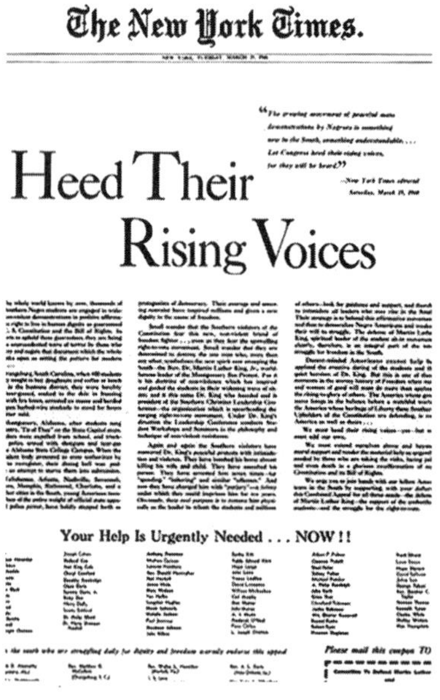

Figure 6.19 Free speech and advertising—one of the most significant free speech cases of the twentieth century involved the reaction to this March, 1960 advertisement in *The New York Times*. Alabama state officials who opposed the Civil Rights movement sued for libel, but the Supreme Court said that political advertising was protected by the First Amendment and that everyone had a right, and even a duty, to participate in open public debate.

As the Civil Rights movement began gaining ground in the United States, arrests of leaders became more frequent. In March, 1960, a group of ministers hoping to raise money for the defense of Martin Luther King placed an ad in *The New York Times* asking for donations and urging Americans to "Heed Their Rising Voices." The ad described repression faced by the movement in a critical tone, noting that many demonstrators had been expelled from their schools and that police had taken hostile action against them. In some cases, the descriptions of events had minor inaccuracies, and these provided the basis for Montgomery, AL, police commissioner L. B. Sullivan to sue

⇨

for libel. Sullivan was successful in Alabama state courts, as was expected since the power structure of the Old South was unsympathetic to the Civil Rights movement and to what was often seen as outside criticism.

However, when the U.S. Supreme Court heard the case, there was unanimous agreement that *The New York Times* had not libeled the police commissioner. On the contrary, the criticism in the ad was considered to be valuable political speech in the tradition of a "profound national commitment to the principle that debate on public issues should be uninhibited, robust, and wide-open."

The Sullivan standard did three things: It put the burden of proof on the plaintiff in a libel case, not the defendant; it said citizens had not only a right but a duty to criticize public officials; and it said the plaintiff had to prove "actual malice" (defined as when a defendant knowingly published or broadcast a falsehood or acted in reckless disregard for the truth).

The case cleared the way for "sharp, even caustic" debate in the United States, permitting nonviolent reform movements the maximum amount of latitude to make their arguments. It also had a profound impact on law in other nations, such as the United Kingdom, Australia, New Zealand and many European nations, where libel laws were reformed in subsequent years. Only Canada seems to have maintained an older, more paternalistic view of libel and resisted the Sullivan standard in the first decade of the twenty-first century.

Corporate consolidation

The creative revolution of the 1960s and 70s gave way, in the 1980s, to a deeply depressed business climate for advertising agencies.

Before the 1980s, agencies would take care of all creative work and also handle media buying, getting a 15 percent commission in return. If a client bought $100 million in advertising, the agency would collect the $100 million but only be charged $85 million by the publication or broadcast network where the ad was placed. "It was a sweet deal," remembers advertising historian Joe Cappo.

European agencies led the way in the 1980s toward a split in the creative and buying functions. A client could now purchase advertising directly through media brokers who only charged from two to five percent, and hire ad agencies to do the creative work. The idea of the agencies as a full service marketing partner vanished.

As a result of the contraction in business, major corporate advertising mergers began to take place. The economies of scale that appealed to publishers and broadcasting companies also made sense in an advertising business that was rapidly contracting. Out of 20 major ad agencies in the 1980s, only one was still independent by 2005, according to Cappo. Four major agencies dominated 80 percent of the market in the United States and 50 percent of the market worldwide.

New advertising models
in the digital age

The collapse of the newspaper and magazine publishing industries in the first decade of the twenty-first century was not a complete surprise. Advertising executives had been worried that digital information systems would undermine traditional forms of classified and display advertising for at least a decade. The surprising part was how rapidly the change began taking hold.

Between 1950 and 2010, the newspapers and magazines lost more than half their shares of US advertising revenues, with the steepest decline coming in the 2005–2010 period (Varian, 2010). Newspaper ad revenues dropped from a peak of $47 billion in 2005 to less than half of that by 2010 (NAA, 2010).

Radio and television advertising also dropped in the face of market fragmentation and a wider variety of alternative news and entertainment sources. On a typical night in 1976, about 92 percent of all viewers were watching the three networks, but by 2010, four networks could attract only 46 percent of TV viewers (Auletta, 2010). Broadcasting also experienced declines in advertising, although not as severe as the print media (Wikinvest, 2010)

Clearly, the same forces that undermined the print media business model are at work for broadcast media as well. Advertisers in both media counted on a "bundled" package of information that would appeal to mass audiences. A person might buy a newspaper to read garden advice or the comics, but mass advertising also supported news and public affairs programming. Publishers and broadcasters never had to keep track of whether enough people were tuning in to reports on Parliamentary elections, fashion news or Brazilian business.

Internet search engines effectively "unbundled" the content, allowing those with interests in politics, fashion or business to find exactly the stories they wanted without having to buy information they didn't ask for.

As a result, the business model of an independent media with a variety of information types, supported by mass advertising, faded rapidly in the twenty-first century. Nearly two centuries after the penny press business model was adopted for print, and almost a century after it was adopted for broadcasting, the old business model could no longer support the traditional news and information system.

In contrast, internet advertising rose rapidly from its beginnings. After Congress permitted commercial use of the internet, the first banner ad campaigns appeared on the Web in October, 1994. From these modest beginnings, internet advertising rose to about $22 billion in 2010 (Internet Advertising Bureau, 2010). Spending on internet ads outpaced radio in 2008, magazines in 2010 and was on track to exceed newspaper advertising revenues early in the next decade.

What's new about internet advertising is that it is not aimed at mass markets, but rather at individuals and small groups of consumers. The Nike plus campaign is an example. Using a small sensor in a Nike running shoe connected to an iPod, runners can keep track of their progress and connect with other runners in their area. As a result, customers are coming to the company, rather than the other way around, and Nike is spending less money with traditional media.

"We're not in the business of keeping the media companies alive," Edwards said (Story, 2007).

The vast majority of the new internet advertising revenue comes to one company—Google, which began as a search engine for the internet in 1996 and expanded into a marketing and data mining giant by 2010. Google's AdWords system offers pay-per-click (PPC) advertising, in which a client is charged when users click through to the client's site. The fact that advertisers are charged only when consumers take action is revolutionary.

John Wanamaker's quip was once a standing gag in the advertising business. The department store founder once said: "I know I waste half the money I spend on advertising. The problem is, I don't know which half" (Rothenberg, 1999). With Google, not only does a company know which half is being wasted, it also knows all kinds of other details about its consumers, from demographics to purchasing history to web surfing behavior. As a result, precisely targeted advertising can be used in a way that is far more effective than mass market advertising.

Google's approach to advertising is being mimicked by others in various ways. Organizations like Demand Media and Associated Content produce thousands of "pieces of content" that are created in response to web searches and other measurements of topic popularity. "We can predict the return on investment on each of these pieces of content," says Demand CEO Richard Rosenblatt (SXSW, 2010). Writers who make less than minimum wage in some of these start-ups are not so sanguine (Carr, 2010).

Google is also working on ways to streamline demand management for information by monetizing high-value ad space and auctioning lower-value. From a one-way advertising model, the company expects to develop far more user-centered advertising and information servicers that create new opportunities for quality information. The concept will take a decade to fully develop, as the traditional media copes with increasing chaos (Fallows, 2010).

The new models seem to fit some of the old media theories. As Marshall McLuhan said: "If the audience can become involved in the actual process of making the ad, then it's happy—Sort of like quiz shows. They were great TV because they gave the audience a role, something to do" (Hirshberg, 2007).

McLuhan's optimism about audience interaction was increasingly questioned as new forms of individually targeted advertising emerged in the second decade of the twenty-first century. Coupons, once clipped from newspapers and magazines to allow consumer discounts, could now be downloaded onto mobile phones, along with personal information about the consumer. The convenience of an instant discount is offset, consumer advocates said, by increasing concerns about invasions of privacy through "behavioral targeting." Groups like the Center for Digital Democracy have asked the Federal Trade Commission to regulate the flow of personal information to marketers (Cha, 2010).

It's interesting that a 2002 science fiction film, *Minority Report*, depicted highly invasive advertising techniques of the year 2054. In the story, a police captain walks through a shopping mall and is bombarded by holographic ads calling him by name. It is a mark of the rapid acceleration of communications technology that ideas about a distant future would be within reach only a few years later.

Advertising spending

An analysis of trends in advertising shows the rapid decline in newspaper advertising and a rapid increase in internet advertising in the first decade of the twentieth century. Other media—Radio and television—have remained relatively flat.

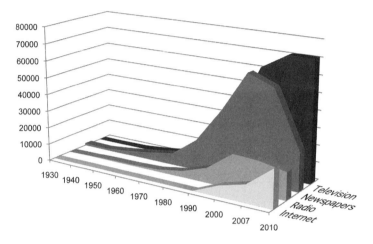

Figure 6.20 Traditional media revenue drops.

Notes: 2010 figures are estimates
Millions of constant 2008 dollars / adjusted for inflation

Sources: Internet Advertising Bureau, National Newspaper Association, TV Bureau of Advertising

Section III

Electronic Revolution: From 'National Neighborhoods' to the Global Village

Introduction to Section III

*It would not be long before the whole surface of this country would be chan-
neled for . . . a knowledge of all that is occurring throughout the land, making,
in fact, one neighborhood of the whole country. (Samuel Morse, February 15,
1838)*

The significance of the electronic revolution

Rapid communication over long distances has often been associated with divine forces, for example, in Greek and Roman mythology, with Nike, Hermes and Mercury carrying messages for the gods.

For ordinary mortals, however, communication has historically been very difficult, as it was confined to the speed of a running horse or fast ship. History and literature are full of references to the role of messengers bringing the long-delayed news of victory or defeat. The runner from Marathon, the messenger in Shakespeare's *Henry IV*, the signal flags of Trafalgar are among many examples of the place communications held in pre-industrial history and culture.

Perhaps the classic example of news failing to arrive in time involves the needless loss of life at the Battle of New Orleans. When the United States and Britain fought the battle on January 8, 1815, the armies in the field could not have known that a peace treaty had been signed before Christmas of 1814. It took seven weeks for the fastest sailboat to carry the message from London to Louisiana.

Yet in about 50 years, the same message might have taken less than an hour to be relayed by electronic telegraph using Morse code. The unique combination of hardware (electric wires) and software (a simple arrangement of dots and dashes) changed the world, brought down the barriers of time and distance, and opened the door to the electronic and digital mass media revolutions. No other development since printing had so many impacts in so many different walks of life.

The telegraph and telephone as mass media

Historians usually see one-to-one personal media (telegrams, telephones,) as entirely separate from mass media (newspapers, radio, TV) until the late twentieth century, when the two basic types of media were brought together by digital networks (giving us cell phone video, for instance).

Yet media can't be so easily separated. For instance, even though letters sent through the post office are one-to-one communications, the US Postal Service served as the infrastructure for printed mass media. The service carried newspapers and magazines at very low postal rates that were specifically meant to subsidize the US publishing industry. In contrast, higher postal rates in Europe held back the development of printed media, as we saw in Chapter 2.

Similarly, the telegraph carried private, one-to-one communications in the form of telegrams, but it also carried political and economic news across the world through the mass media. Between the 1850s and the 1980s, the telegraph was the essential infrastructure of a two-stage mass communications system. News generated in one location flowed up the chain and was then distributed to local newspapers by wire services like Reuters, Havas and The Associated Press.

The telephone system, used mostly for private one-to-one communications, also served as the infrastructure of the national radio networks when they emerged in the 1920s. News, drama, comedy and other programs originating in one place would usually be carried to the rest of the country by static-free telephone lines and then broadcast by regional radio stations. Like the telegraph, the telephone was indispensible to the two-stage mass communications system until satellites arrived in the 1980s.

The business models for the telegraph and telephone also had an impact on the overall shape and diversity of the mass media. In the United States, a joint Western Union–Associated Press monopoly shaped the economics of publishing, creating barriers to entry and making it difficult for newspapers to compete. The very device that expanded the spatial and temporal reach of communication seemed to weaken its depth and flexibility. Younger journalists complained that the newspapers spoke in the voice of an older generation, as we have seen in Chapter 3. Meanwhile in Europe, the competitive economics of publishing took different forms since government-owned telegraph and telephone systems did not favor any one particular group of members, and this contributed to a greater diversity of expression.

While the electronic revolution began with the telegraph and telephone, neither of these prototype electronic technologies can be historically isolated from radio, television and satellite broadcasting. Their scientific origins and business models were intertwined. Industrial print and early radio and television grew up in an interdependent network, around the telegraph and telephone, from the beginning. To a large degree, the concept of media "convergence" is not just an artifact of the computer age, but rather, a constant condition in mass media history.

Cycles of open and closed technologies

Innovation in communication technology often follows a cycle that can be described in three stages: open, closed and alternative. The first stage of the cycle involves open experimentation, competition and development of a new media. It may be followed by a second stage in which stakeholders close the technologies around profit-generating activities protected by patents. If the stakeholders are successful, they may be able to dominate the market. In a third stage, successful monopolies become stagnant, charging more and more money for fewer and fewer services. The downward spiral often encourages the search for technological alternatives to circumvent the old monopoly. Once a promising new avenue is found, the open competition starts again.

Although the cycle of open-closed-alternative technologies is a useful generalization, it doesn't fit every media technology exactly. As we've seen in Section II, photography was born as an open source technology, with its exact secrets revealed from the outset. In contrast, the earliest cinema companies attempted to control the industry through patents and industry associations. Although direct industry control failed, indirect content control through the Motion Picture Production Code become the norm.

As we will see in Chapter 7, telegraphy also went through a period of open experimentation, and Samuel Morse, at least, wanted it to stay that way. Like Daguerre, he also hoped that the government would own the hardware. But in the US, as over 500 telegraph companies emerged, fought, and then merged by 1866, telegraphy became a national monopoly under the Western Union company. Operating without regulation, Western Union and its sole partner in the Associated Press exerted an enormous amount of control over which ideas and people would compete in the information system of the nineteenth century.

One response was a US campaign for legislation to transfer the telegraph to the Post Office, which was already taking place in Britain. When that failed, the same campaigners who fought the telegraphic monopoly helped create the telephone system in the 1870s. Through its control of patents and market manipulation, the Bell telephone system also became a monopoly around the turn of the twentieth century. Anxious to avoid problems that had surfaced with Western Union, the US Justice Department forced AT&T to take a neutral "common carrier" position with respect to content and charges for services.

As we will see in Chapters 8 and 9, broadcasting also began with a cycle of open innovation among scientists like Heinrich Hertz and James Clerk Maxwell.

Entrepreneur Guglielmo Marconi attempted to control the emerging radio telegraph system, and was initially successful, but the US and UK governments curbed the monopolies in the pre-World War I period. American Marconi eventually became the Radio Corporation of America, which in turn created the National Broadcasting Company. Meanwhile, inventors like Lee Deforest and Reginald Fessenden turned to radio telephony, and some of their key patents were purchased by AT&T. By the 1920s, radio technology had more or less closed, and television technology was opening. By the 1950s, television technology was closed, and the search for circumventing technologies would lead to satellite and cable systems by the 1980s.

Social responsibility

With the power of amplified sound and moving images, radio and television created new opportunities to both abuse people and to elevate the human condition, and history provides examples of both. The tragedies of the Holocaust, the Rwandan and Bosnian genocides, and countless others, would not have been possible without a mass media to incite hatred.

Like the printing press, however, the new electronic media also provided many opportunities for expanding tolerance, diversity and freedom. Radio rallied the public and was a key ingredient in elevating nationalistic sentiment in the 1930s and 40s. Televised news helped crystallize public opinion around civil rights issues in the 1950s and the Vietnam war in the 1960s.

To a society accustomed to a slower pace of life, it seemed, suddenly, as if the world were laid out at the viewer's feet, that every activity could be known, that every culture could be understood. But the distortions of the mass media proved difficult to counteract, as the imbalance in media power from developed to developing nations in the 1970s created what was termed "Hollywood hegemony." The apparent threat of Western modernity to traditional cultures created a violent reactions at the end of the twentieth century and the beginning of the twenty-first.

Today, with instant, global, full spectrum communication possible through dozens of media, we are indeed a global village, but we are not a peaceful one. We are not yet reconciled to each other's differences, aware of each others strengths, or tolerant of each other's weaknesses.

As Henry David Thoreau once observed, communication technology can be nothing more than an improved means to an unimproved end. And yet, many people had a larger and more positive vision for the role of mass media technology—a role that has yet to be fully cast for a vision that is still being articulated.

For additional reading, discussion questions, links to video and other suggestions, see www.revolutionsincommunication.com.

7

The first electronic revolution: telegraph and telephone

"It is obvious, at the slightest glance, that this mode of instantaneous communication must inevitably become an instrument of immense power, to be wielded for good or for evil . . . "—Samuel Morse, 1838. (Morse, 1914)

"There are only two forces that can carry light to all corners of the globe—the sun in the heavens and the Associated Press down here. I may seem to be flattering the sun, but I do not mean to do so . . . "—Mark Twain, 1906. (Twain, 1920)

The telegraph as the first electronic network

The telegraph arrived in the mid-1840s as part of "a widespread revolution in communications" that included mass production of newspapers, magazines and books, along with improvements in transportation such as canals, steamships and railroads (Howe, 2007).

The invention of the telegraph marks the beginning of the electronic revolution, which led to telephones, radios and televisions. It was also one source of the digital revolution, since Morse code, based on a dot-or-dash signal, is a binary system.

Socially, the telegraph was the first electronic network, or as historian Tom Standage said, the "Victorian Internet." Telegrams were delivered within hours and responses could be sent right away (Standage, 1998).

The Western Union telegraph system, in tandem with the Associated Press, became the first monopoly in America. In Europe, governments took over the telegraph companies to avoid the abuses of a monopoly system. Meanwhile, inventors worked on a way to circumvent the monopoly through a system called the telephone.

Signals over distance

The problem of signaling over a distance is an ancient one, and some of the most complex systems have been used in military campaigns. Greek historian Thucydides described naval flag systems in the Peloponnesian War that may have been similar to those still in use today. The Roman army used a complex "box cipher," according to historian Polybius. The cipher used a system of two torches whose positions could be used to indicate 25 letters, with 1-1 representing A; 1-5 representing E; and 5-5 representing Z (Kahn, 1967).

Figure 7.1 First telegraph—this "optical" telegraph was developed by Claude Chappe in France 40 years before Samuel Morse began thinking about using electricity for signals over distance. The optical telegraph was too expensive for routine use and was limited by visibility problems in bad weather.

The term "telegraph" was first coined for a 1792 French invention, also called the Napoleonic semaphore, by Claude Chappe. This original mechanical telegraph was a system of pivoting shutters placed atop signal towers to send coded messages. The system was used extensively by the French and British military during the Napoleonic era to carry signals from Paris and London to the fleets at naval bases along the coast.

Telegraph towers were used only by the government, but they were widely known, and the word "telegraph" quickly entered the popular lexicon. When Admiral Horatio Nelson sent a message using traditional naval signal flags just before the battle of Trafalgar in 1805, newspapers at the time said he "addressed his fleet by telegraphic communication" with the message: "England expects that every man will do his duty" (*The Times*, London, December 2, 1805).

Businesses were not able to use military systems, so when events were pressing and a few hours advantage could mean large profits, news would be sent by carrier pigeon. In 1815, a group of London stock speculators learned of Napoleon's defeat at Waterloo by carrier pigeon, allowing them to buy stocks in advance of the rapid rise in value when the news became official. Carrier pigeons remained a useful tool for news agencies like Havas in Paris until the advent of the telegraph in the 1840s.

For most people, couriers or the regular mail were the only ways to send messages, and important information could easily be delayed.

Samuel Morse and his code: the software of telegraphy

It's often said that Samuel F. B. Morse invented the telegraph. But as we have seen, there were many kinds of "telegraph" in use during the early 1800s. What Morse really invented was the software—the Morse code—that made it easy to use telegraphic devices. It was a key insight, similar to Gutenberg's invention of moveable type (not the printing press), and Tim Berners-Lee's idea for a World Wide Web (and not the network itself). In these and many other cases, a rising technical capacity seems dormant until inventors arrive at the key insights.

What obsessed Samuel Morse about long distance communication was not military power or the stock exchange, like other telegraphic inventors. Instead, he was motivated by his wife's sad death in 1825 following childbirth. He was in New York, painting a portrait of the revolutionary war hero Marquis de Lafayette, and she was only a day's ride away, in Connecticut. But the letter calling him to her sick bed took so long to arrive that he was too late to attend her funeral (Morse, 1914).

After his wife's death, Morse spent years studying art in Europe. On a ship homeward bound in October 1832, he began talking with other passengers who were interested in electromagnetic experiments. Pacing the deck after dinner one night, he came up with the idea of sending signals through wires and sketched out his ideas in a notebook.

The idea of an artist like Morse becoming an inventor may seem far-fetched, but Morse was a Yale University chemistry graduate and came from a university tradition that saw "arts and sciences" as parallel and interrelated pursuits.

Morse's technical insight was not to overcome the mechanical problems of transmitting bursts of electricity; that had already been accomplished by many others. Steven Gray first sent electric current 700 feet through a line in London in 1727. Benjamin Franklin in the United States was famous for his experiments with electricity. And in England, William Fothergill Cooke and Charles Wheatstone, unknown to Morse, were working on a complex telegraph sending and receiving system that was patented on June 12, 1837. The Cooke and Wheatstone system used five wires and a pattern of letters that could be selected with indicator needles on either end (Munro, 1891).

Fortunately, Morse was not well informed about other inventors at the time, and persisted despite many obstacles. He developed a working mechanical system that was an improvement over other electrical telegraphs. And like Cooke, Morse originally tried a system of numbers for individual words and used electric signals to mark a paper tape. Morse patented his device on October 3, 1837.

Working with a collaborator, Alfred Vail, he continued to develop the simplified set of dots and dashes known as Morse code.

To create the code, Vail and Morse puzzled over the problem of the relative frequency of letters in English. They wanted to match the simplest signals with the most frequent letters. A visit to a nearby printing firm helped solve the problem. In a typical type font, printers stocked 12,000 letter Es and 9,000 Ts, and these were assigned the simplest signal: E was one dot and T was one dash. Morse and Vail also found that the letters Q and Z were rarely used, with

Figure 7.2 Franklin's kite—in June of 1752, American printer and scientist Benjamin Franklin raised a kite to test his theory that lightning was similar to the charge that could be generated with chemical batteries. This extremely dangerous experiment was one of many being conducted at the time into the nature of electricity. (Library of Congress)

Figure 7.3 Daguerreotype of Morse—Samuel F. B. Morse, inventor of an electromagnetic telegraph, is seen here in a Daguerreotype taken in 1845. The hardware for telegraphy was well known, but Morse's simplified code made it easy to use the telegraph, in effect, solving a hardware problem with a software solution. Within a decade the Morse code had been adopted for international use. (Library of Congress)

400 and 200 letters in the type case, and so Morse gave them the most complex symbols: Q --.- and Z --..

Morse's unique contribution, then, was an extremely simple way to transmit information using bursts of electricity. In effect, it was an elegant software solution to a hardware problem that others like Cooke and Wheatstone had not solved.

Morse had a difficult time finding investors, but he clearly understood the significance of his invention. In a remarkably prophetic letter to Congressman Francis Smith in 1838, Morse wrote:

> It is obvious, at the slightest glance, that this mode of instantaneous communication must inevitably become an instrument of immense power, to be wielded for good or for evil, as it shall be properly or improperly directed. In the hands of a company of speculators, who should monopolize it for themselves, it might be the means of enriching the corporation at the expense of the bankruptcy of thousands; and even in the hands of government alone it might become the means of working vast mischief to the Republic.

Morse suggested that the government buy the patent and license it to private companies, creating "a systems of checks and preventatives of abuse . . . to permit only the good and neutralize the evil" (Morse, 1914).

Between 1838 and 1842, Morse approached hundreds of potential investors in the United States and Europe, in the hope of financing more experiments on telegraphy. He also attended an 1839 lecture in Paris by Louis Daguerre, and returned with the equipment and know-how to teach photography in New York.

Inventors thought the idea of an electric telegraph to be more like a conjuring trick than a useful invention, let alone a profitable one. But in 1842, Congress surprised Morse when it agreed to fund an experimental line from Washington, D.C. to Baltimore, MD. On May 1, 1844, news from a Whig Party convention reached Morse's headquarters in the capitol building an hour ahead of the train, and crowds waiting for news were jubilant, praising Morse for his invention. In a formal demonstration later that month, Morse sent the famous message: "What Hath God Wrought" (*The New York Times*, May 1, 1894).

Meanwhile in England, Cooke and Wheatstone had finally managed to set up an ongoing public demonstration along a section of railway track between London and Windsor. It was a curiosity at first, but the speed with which royal announcements could be made, and the coordination of police forces in catching criminals fleeing by train, eventually convinced conservative Brits that the Cooke–Wheatstone telegraph was useful. The view was reinforced when the Royal Navy contracted a telegraph along the same route between the admiralty in London and its main port in Portsmouth—a route once noted for Britain's original mechanical telegraph.

By the fall of 1845, Morse formed the Magnetic Telegraph Co. in Washington, D.C., while Cooke and Wheatstone had formed the Electric Telegraph Co. in London. With regular service, public enthusiasm soon replaced skepticism, and telegraph lines began doubling yearly. By 1850, in the United States, 12,000 miles of line were run by 20 different companies. At the height of the speculative fever, some 500 telegraph companies were competing.

The telegraph also took off quickly in other countries. By 1852, Britain had over 2,000 miles of line, and Germany had 1,500 miles radiating out from Berlin. France lagged because their early lead in mechanical telegraphy meant that they were less willing to adopt a new system (Standage, 1998). (It's interesting that France enjoyed a similar early lead in computer networks with the Minitel system in the 1980s, and had a similar and short period of reluctance to adopt new computer networks developed outside France in the 1990s).

Telegraphic companies in continental Europe had to cross many borders, and this led to two major differences between US and European systems: First, the telegraph was owned and operated by the postal service in nearly all nations; and secondly, international cooperation started as early as 1849, culminating in the 1865 formation of the International Telegraph Union. The organization adopted a version of the US system that became known as International Morse Code.

By 1870, the United States had built over 120,000 miles of telegraph line, and by that time, nearly all were owned by one telegraph company—Western Union. Also in 1870, Britain abandoned private ownership of the telegraph, beginning a 26-year process of absorbing all existing companies into its post office.

Telegraph ushers in a new era of communication

The advent of the electric telegraph promised "universal interests and the world-wide victory of Christianity," enthusiasts said. "The public mind will be stimulated to greater activity with the rapid circulation of news. . . . The whole nation will be impressed with the same idea at the moment. One feeling and one impulse are thus created from the center of the land to the utmost extremity" (Czitrom, 1983).

Naturalist and writer Henry David Thoreau, on the other hand, considered the telegraph little more than an "improved means to an unimproved end." He said: "We are in great haste to construct a magnetic telegraph from Maine to Texas; but Maine and Texas, it may be, have nothing important to communicate" (Thoreau, 1854).

Figure 7.4 Not impressed—naturalist and author Henry David Thoreau was not impressed when telegraph lines stretched across the New England landscape, considering them to be an "improved means to an unimproved end."

As it turned out, Maine and Texas, on the verge of Civil War, had plenty to discuss. So did North America and Europe, and the first attempt to cross Atlantic with telegraph cable failed when it was laid across the Atlantic in 1858. The next successful attempt came in 1866, when the Civil War was over.

The telegraph did more than ease the spread of information. Like any communications revolution, it made new *functions* of communication possible

"Telegraphy gave rise to both the modern conception of news and methods of news gathering," Daniel Czitrom said. Before the telegraph, colonial newspapers printed news as it arrived in the mail, or by word of mouth, seldom seeking out news. Timeliness was secondary to record keeping. For instance, the pre-telegraphic *Niles Weekly Register*'s motto was: "The present and the past, for the future."

After the telegraph, the emphasis tended to be on standardization and information rather that storytelling, especially for news transmitted via telegraph by wire services like The Associated Press. The AP dispatches were "more free from editorial comment than most reporting for single newspapers" (Schudson, 1976).

The model of AP reporting was, according to AP's Kent Cooper, "the finest moral concept ever developed in America and given the world . . . that news must be truthful and unbiased" (Siebert, 1963). But the ideal of unbiased news took root slowly among the newspapers that depended on the AP, according to historian Michael Schudson (Schudson, 1979).

Telegraph changes writing styles

The telegraph certainly changed basic styles of news writing as the costs of telegrams forced journalists to condense their facts and fit the most important information into the very first few words of the dispatch, in case it was cut off by accident or censorship. The change illustrates McLuhan's idea that the medium IS (or at least has a major influence on) the message.

For instance, compare these two news reports: The first is from William Howard Russell's famous 1854 dispatch about the Charge of the Light Brigade, a unit of the British army, written from the Crimean Peninsula of Russia before telegraph lines were available. The second is the lead of a wire dispatch from Washington to New York only seven years later:

Before the telegraph:
If the exhibition of the most brilliant valor, of the excess of courage, and of a daring which would have reflected luster on the best days of chivalry can afford full consolation for the disaster of today, we can have no reason to regret the

melancholy loss which we sustained in a contest with a savage and barbarian enemy. (William Howard Russell, *The Times*, London, November 13, 1854)

News sent by telegraph:
Our troops, after taking three batteries and gaining a great victory at Bull Run, were eventually repulsed, and commenced a retreat on Washington. (Henry Villard, *New York Herald*, July 22, 1861)

While Russell exemplified the finest moments of early English journalism in his letters to *The Times* from the Crimean War, the effect of the telegraph was to reduce the value of the individual war correspondent and their lengthy dispatches sent from the front.

The wire service's condensed style became a journalistic gold standard, emphasizing facts over opinion. But it did not always obscure opinion, as seen, for instance, in the "our troops" comment by Villard. The short, punchy style of writing was lionized by writers such as Ernest Hemingway, for example, who called it "telegraphese" (Baker, 1972).

Nor did the new medium guarantee that the news would be truthful and unbiased, as AP often claimed. In fact, the AP's hand-in-hand monopoly with Western Union proved controversial for nearly a century.

Figure 7.5 Before the telegraph—dispatches written by *The Times* London correspondent William Howard Russell (above) from the front lines of the Crimean War in 1854 were not limited by the pressing demands of telegraphic systems. Howard's report on the famous Charge of the Light Brigade, delivered by letter, was long, flowery and patriotic. In contrast, dispatches from the front lines of the American Civil War tended to be factual and terse. (Library of Congress)

Telegraph changes news business

Before the advent of the telegraph, newspapers could compete with each other by catering to select audiences, and every city could have several newspapers. But the telegraph forced newspapers into a new business model.

The change began in 1846; when the Mexican–American war began, telegraph lines from New York and Boston only stretched as far south as Richmond, VA. Because communication from the front lines of the war was so difficult, five New York newspapers, including *The Times* and the *Herald*, agreed to share an express service to quickly bring home war news.

This agreement was the beginning of a permanent newsgathering cooperative that also included cooperation through an 1848 Harbor News Association in New York, leading to the formation of the New York Associated Press in 1851 (Pyle, 2005). By then, the few hundred miles of wire had turned into a telegraph network of over ten thousand miles (Howe, 2007).

A second "Associated Press" formed around Chicago and St. Louis in 1862. This western Associated Press cooperated with the New York group and eventually merged with it in 1900.

By the mid-1860s, Western Union and the two AP groups agreed on low rates, exclusive use of AP and Western Union services by all members, and a mandatory refusal to pass along "hostile" information about AP or Western Union. One of the most objectionable features of the monopoly was that existing members could veto the entry of new members. Attempts to start newspapers in San Francisco, Chicago and other cities failed when AP membership was not granted.

The situation generated a continuous storm of controversy. In the post-Civil War era, the US Congress considered 96 bills and resolutions along with 48 committee reports about the telegraph and AP monopoly.

"The issue of telegraph regulation was very prominent in the public sphere," said legal historian Menahem Blondheim. "It was debated extensively in the press and even constituted a favorite topic for college exercises in rhetoric and debating" (Blondheim, 2004).

AP argued that it could not be regulated, since the First Amendment guaranteed freedom of the press. Although Western Union had no such standing, its relationship with the press meant that public opinion was constantly tilted in its favor.

Some reformers saw this as a dangerous situation. Gardiner G. Hubbard, the leading lobbyist for a postal telegraph service and father-in-law of Alexander Graham Bell, said the AP-Western Union monopoly was "a power greater than any ever wielded by the French Directory, because, in an era when public opinion is omnipotent, it can give, withhold, or color the information which shapes that opinion. It may impart an irresistible power to the caprice of an individual" (Blondheim, citing S. Rep. No. 48-577, 1884).

The complex controversy was never resolved at the Congressional level, although an enormous amount of testimony accumulated about the AP-Western Union monopoly's underhanded business practices, such as theft of secret information for stock trading and exclusion of competitors from key newspaper markets (Parsons, 1899; US House, HR 3010, 1912).

Among many instances of underhanded business practices was the AP role in forming its supposed competitor, the United Press, in 1882, with a secret agreement funneling profits back to AP. When the agreement was exposed in 1891, AP withdrew its support and began enforcing its non-competition clause, forcing newspapers to choose between AP membership and UP service. In some cases, the courts forced AP to back down and permit newspapers to subscribe to more than one wire service. But UP went bankrupt in 1897, in part because at that point, AP had an exclusive deal for European news with Reuters.

Opposition to the monopoly eventually grew to the breaking point. The state of Texas, for example, passed an anti-trust law in 1899 specifically "aimed at the Associated Press" with stiff daily penalties for any organization that refused to sell news to competitors (*The New York Times*, May 28, 1899).

The AP also lost a 1900 antitrust case brought by the Inter-Ocean News when it was refused membership in the AP. In ruling against AP, the Illinois courts said:

> No paper could be regarded as a newspaper of the day unless it had access to and published the reports from such an association as (the AP). . . . For news gathered from all parts of the country, the various newspapers are almost solely dependent

Poisoned at the Source

Figure 7.6 Poisoned—this cartoon from *The Masses* depicts The Associated Press pouring lies into "The News." The issue was coal mining in Appalachia and the way the AP passed along reports from newspapers owned by the coal industry, with suppressed facts, slander and inaccurate reports about labor organizations. The Associated Press was outraged and filed a suit for libel. (Library of Congress)

> on such an association, and if they are prohibited from publishing it or its use is refused to them, their character as newspapers is destroyed and they would soon become practically worthless . . . (*Illinois/Inter-Ocean Publishing Co. v. Associated Press, 184 Ill. 438, 1900*).

The response from the Associated Press was to move from Illinois to New York State, where business laws were more lenient. AP continued to be remarkably thin-skinned. For instance, it went so far as to sue for libel when *The Masses*, a socialist magazine, published a cartoon showing an AP executive dripping poison into a reservoir of "The News" with the label "poisoned at the source." The cause for concern involved one-sided stories coming out of the labor struggles in Appalachian coal mines. AP later dropped the suit in the face of public criticism.

New competition for the AP: United Press and International News

Meanwhile, the response from independent publishers was a second wave of attempts to create separate news agencies. E. W. Scripps, publisher of the first US newspaper chain, created a competing news service called United Press Association in June, 1907. (UPA was unrelated to the United Press that had been driven into bankruptcy ten years earlier.) Two years later, William Randolph Hearst created the International News Service for his newspaper chain.

"One result of these successive changes was to encourage new papers by making it easy for them to secure a comprehensive news service," said Whitelaw Reid in an

Encyclopedia Britannica article in 1911. "The almost official authority with which the public formerly attributed to an Associated Press dispatch declined."

Congressional hearings in 1912 established that a long history of attempts to regulate telegraphy had failed, and that prices in Europe were less than half of the same prices for telegraphic messages in the United States. But this was only one of many Congressional investigations into monopolies at the time, and represented a changing legal climate. After 1913, both UP and INS wire services were able to use the telegraph at the same cost as AP.

Newspaper publisher E. W. Scripps later said: "I regard my life's greatest service to the people of this country to be the creation of the United Press." Lucian Carr, a beat-generation writer who served as a UPI editor in the 1950s, once said: "UP's great virtue was that we were the little guy [that] could screw the AP."

The AP-Western Union news monopoly was a product of the times, but as one of the first major monopolies, it also set the pace for others to follow. Virtually every other industry was consolidating in the late 1800s. Oil, railroads, distilleries, sugar, grain and other commodities all developed a "trust" in which stock was held by a monopoly combination to control trade. In some cases, the increased efficiency lowered prices for consumers and helped widespread adoption of new technologies. But the trusts also ignored customer needs, drove competitors out of business, and raised or lowered prices as they pleased. Antitrust laws, passed first by states and then by the US Congress in 1890, began to force breakups in the commodity trusts.

Critics of the AP monopoly pointed out that news was far more important than a simple commodity. Americans had a longstanding commitment to a "robust sharing of ideas," long before the telegraph, as seen for example in low postal rates for newspapers and magazines (Starr, 2004).

Despite its well known devotion to high quality journalism, AP's resistance to competition would not end until 1945, when it lost an antitrust suit brought by the Justice Dept. AP argued that it was protected by the First Amendment, but the Supreme Court responded: "Freedom to publish means freedom for all and not for some. Freedom to publish is guaranteed by the Constitution, but freedom to combine to keep others from publishing is not" (*Associated Press v. United States, 326 U.S. 1, 1945*).

United Press and International Press, meanwhile, merged in 1958 to become United Press International. The organization fell on hard times by the 1990s, and in 1999 its news service contracts were sold to the AP. The company then went through a series of owners, including a cult church, and vanished as a news organization.

Figure 7.7 Wire service—this teletype machine, used by The Associated Press for most of the twentieth century, allowed member news organizations to send and receive dispatches. While AP had a strong commitment to quality journalism, the organization's structure helped members hold down competition until an anti-trust suit in 1945. (Photo by Bill Kovarik)

The US telegraph system, in the end, did not develop as a widely distributed system of small independent providers, as Morse envisioned, nor as a government monopoly, following the European business model. Instead, the telegraph was a commercial monopoly information system operating in tandem with the Associated Press.

Later, Guglielmo Marconi and Thomas Edison attempted to take the same route using patent rights to monopolize radio and film. They were thwarted by regulations that were, in part, a reaction to the AP-Western Union monopoly.

Figure 7.8 Learning Morse code—this Western Union telegraph delivery boy was photographed in 1910 by Lewis Hine learning Morse code between assignments. Hine criticized Western Union for child labor practices. (Library of Congress)

European Wire Services

In Europe, three major wire services grew out of a French translating and courier agency founded before the telegraph. Agence Havas of Paris began in 1835 when Charles-Louis Havas started supplying news about France to foreign customers, often by courier pigeon.

Bernard Wolff and Paul Reuter were Havas employees who, in the 1840s, founded two other major telegraphic news agencies. Wolffs Telegraphisches Bureau served Germany from 1849 to the 1930s. Reuters News Agency, founded in Britain in 1851, continues as the major British news service. Like AP, the big three European wire services were able to dominate the competition. Unlike AP, they were not able to develop monopolistic agreements with the postal services that ran the telegraph system.

A May, 1865 convention decided to adopt Morse code as the international telegraph alphabet and to protect the right of everyone to use international telegraphy. The group continued to meet regularly, and eventually became the International Telecommunications Union (ITU), the oldest organization incorporated into the United Nations system in the mid-twentieth century (ITU, 2010).

Havas was also influential in a fourth agency set up in Spain by Nilo María Fabra in 1870. Fabra merged with two other agencies in 1939 to form EFE, the largest Spanish language wire service.

The European wire services were often seen as semi-official agencies of their respective governments. Wolff's had little choice in 1933 when the Nazis merged the agency with smaller competitors, and the agency was dissolved during World War II. Today, the Deutsche Presse-Agentur (DPA) is Germany's largest agency. The French Havas was also replaced after World War II by Agence France Press (AFP).

Today the AP, Reuters, AFP, EFE and DPA wire services compete for twenty-first century global news markets.

The telephone

The invention of the telephone in 1876 was a direct reaction to the monopoly power of Western Union.

Angered at the control over financial and political information, Boston lawyer Gardiner Hubbard—called the "national nemesis" of Western Union—first tried to have the telegraph system nationalized as part of the Post Office through an act of Congress. When that attempt failed, he financed a set of promising experiments by Alexander Graham Bell, who was working on systems to amplify sound for people with hearing loss. When Bell secured patent rights to the new telephone in 1876, it was Hubbard who organized the financing to create the Bell Telephone company. Bell married Hubbard's daughter Mabel, who had been one of his hearing-impaired students, in 1877.

The telephone would have been invented without Bell and Hubbard—Elishia Grey of Chicago filed a similar patent only a few hours later on the same day as Bell at the US patent office, and controversy still remains concerning details of their patent applications. But courts decided that Bell had the best claim.

As Hubbard organized the company, Bell launched a series of lectures to popularize the new invention, starting with a description of the telephone and then pointing out a telegraph line that he had leased. A few miles away, Thomas A. Watson, Bell's assistant, would be waiting.

"I had at my end one of our loudest telephones specially adapted for the purpose," Watson said in his autobiography. On Bell's signal, he would have to tell a brass band to start playing. But that was just the warm-up, because the audience really wanted to know whether the telephone could talk.

> I shouted such sentences such as "How do you do?" and "What do you think of the telephone?" which the audience could hear . . . (Also) I had to do something of importance for Bell's audiences, called by courtesy, singing . . . I sang Yankee Doodle and Auld Lang Syne . . . My singing was always a hit . . . (and) I was usually encored to the limit of my repertory. (Watson, 1926)

At one point in 1876, Hubbard and Bell may have attempted to sell the Bell patents to Western Union. Skeptical Western Union businessmen were aghast:

> Hubbard and Bell want to install one of their "telephone devices" in every city. The idea is idiotic on the face of it. . . . Why would any person want to use this ungainly and impractical device when he can send a messenger to the telegraph

Figure 7.9 Inventor and his family— Alexander Graham Bell, Mabel Hubbard Bell and two daughters around 1885. Bell's father-in-law was one of the country's chief opponents of the Western Union telegraph monopoly and financed Bell's experiments with the telephone. (Library of Congress)

office and have a clear written message sent to any large city in the United States? (Pershing, 2010)

With Western Union having rejected the phone proposal, Hubbard focused on the organization and Bell focused on showmanship. The work paid off, and the Bell telephone system began stringing wires in 1877.

Within ten years, 150,000 people owned telephones. While Bell continued working on improvements, such as Thomas Edison's carbon microphone, some of his patents expired in the mid-1890s, and 6,000 phone companies created their own phone systems. Research into telegraph and telephone electronics paved the way for other developments to the point where some historians have seen the telephone as the "father of broadcasting" (White, 2010).

While the telephone was intended for one-to-one conversations, home entertainment was an option before radio. In 1893 a Hungarian system called *Telefon Hirmondó*, began operation in Budapest. A similar system, the United States Telephone Herald Company, was a failure (White, 2010).

American Telephone and Telegraph, created by the Bell company in 1885 to build long distance lines, became Bell's parent company in 1899. At that point, only about half of the nation's telephones were part of the Bell system (Starr, 2004). In order to control the market, AT&T waged a ruthless campaign to undercut competition. AT&T denied access to long distance lines and undermining competitors credit (Marchand, 1998). In 1907, a trade newspaper called *Telephony* warned independent companies that the Bell system secretly bought a company that built switching equipment and used components claimed under Bell system patents. Once the "infringing" equipment was purchased, Bell would seize it and force the independents out of business (*Telephony*, 1907, p. 136).

The tactics led to an antitrust investigation by the US Justice Dept., and the possibility emerged that AT&T could be broken up or that the United States would follow the European model and nationalize telephone and telegraph services under the Postal Service. In response, AT&T launched one of the strongest public relations campaigns in history, placing thousands of newspaper and magazine ads with the slogan "One System, One Policy, Universal Service." The claim was that telephony was a "natural" monopoly that would work better than a patchwork system to provide service to everyone. As noted in Chapter 6, the campaign succeeded, and in 1913, the Justice Department negotiated a deal with AT&T called the Kingsbury Commitment that allowed AT&T to continue as a regulated monopoly. The deal, named for AT&T vice president Nathan Kingsbury, also forced Western Union to carry competing wire services such as United Press and International Press at the same rate, allowing them to compete with the Associated Press.

The Kingsbury Commitment also meant that AT&T had to stop the trade war and guarantee system access for all independent phone companies. However, the government allowed AT&T to keep buying up independent companies and manufacturing telephone equipment through Western Electric, which had been Western Union's manufacturing arm. In effect, the regulations slowed but did not stop AT&T's quest for monopoly. By the mid-twentieth century, Bell owned 80 percent of the US phone market.

Figure 7.10 New media—
Alexander Graham Bell is
wearing headphones in order
to listen to the radio, which
at the time was the latest
development in new media.
The photo was probably taken
in 1922, the year Bell died.
(Library of Congress)

In 1974, the Justice Department sued AT&T under anti-trust laws, and in 1982, courts ordered the company to break up into regional carriers, opening the door to more competition and lower long distance rates for individual consumers. However, the breakup of AT&T did not stop radio and television broadcast networks from switching to cheaper, higher quality satellite service—a circumventing technology they used to replace AT&T's costly long-distance lines.

The AT&T breakup also led to the decline of Bell Labs, once a leading international research center, with seven Nobel Prizes and vital work on radar during World War II to its credit. Perhaps the most significant of the Bell Labs inventions was the transistor, which changed radio from a complex household item using radio tubes to a far more portable device. The transistor was also a milestone in the digital age, changing the computer from an expensive military system to an affordable information processing system for banks, insurance companies and telecommunications systems.

Bell Labs also developed communications satellites, the Unix computer operating system, digital switching and cell phones. But there were also commercial flops, such as the 1964 picture phone that debuted at the Seattle World's Fair.

Despite its achievements and the public relations campaigns, not everyone was fond of "Ma Bell" during the heyday of its monopoly. Phone "freaks" developed ways to avoid paying for expensive long distance phone calls, and it was the challenge of beating the system that helped draw Steve Wozniak, a co-founder of Apple computers, into electronics. In 1975, just as a prank, Wozniak and friends used the circumventing technology to make a free call to Rome, Italy. Wozniak called the Vatican and, with a thick German accent, claimed to be then-secretary of state Henry Kissinger. The Vatican asked him to call back, and an hour later, refused to connect him with the pope. "So I guess they checked up on my story," Wozniak told a documentary filmmaker (Cambeau, 2006).

Conclusion

The peak year for the telegraph was 1930, when 211 million telegrams were exchanged in the United States. The very last telegram was sent in 2009, and by then, Western Union changed its business model to become an international financial service.

With the introduction of cell phones in the 1990s, and the addition of text, photos and video on demand, the telephone also changed from a one-to-one medium to a mass medium virtually overnight. Old-fashioned landline phones went from a necessity, with 97 percent market penetration in 2001, to something of a luxury, with 74 percent market share in 2010 that was in rapid decline.

Controversy over the roles of AT&T's spin-off companies, such as Verizon Corp., and the uniformity and neutrality of access to telecommunications services, remain permanent fixtures of the regulatory environment, as we will see in Section IV.

The Western Union-Associated Press monopoly was the first controversial and highly contested monopoly, but it was also the first to begin linking the world together. Along with AT&T, the communications technologies of the nineteenth and twentieth centuries served important social purposes, albeit imperfectly.

"We need a good network to pull together the community of humans," said Robert Miller, Director of Communication Technology Research at AT&T. "I think in the end, it (communication) will probably keep us from blowing ourselves up" (Cambeau, 2006).

8

Radio:
the electronic hearth

"It's of no use whatsoever." (Heinrich Hertz, 1888, in response to questions by students about the practical value of his experiments)

"Oh, the Humanity." (Herbert Morrison, radio reporter at the scene of the Hindenburg disaster, 1937)

"This . . . is London." (Edward R. Murrow, 1940, reporting the blitz for CBS)

Auroras and equations

The mysterious forces surrounding electric currents fascinated scientists of the eighteenth and nineteenth centuries—from Luigi Galvani and Alessandro Volta in Italy to Benjamin Franklin in America and Michael Faraday in Britain. When telegraph lines began stretching across continents, the mystery deepened as scientists tried to explain occasional fluctuations in electrical current that seemed to be associated with the Aurora Borealis and solar flares.

Particularly mysterious were the events of September 2, 1859, when the sky filled with auroras of writhing purple and red colors unlike anything ever seen before.

"Around the world, telegraph systems crashed, machines burst into flames, and electric shocks rendered operators unconscious," said Stuart Clark in a book about the auroras of 1859. "Compasses and other sensitive instruments reeled as if struck by a massive magnetic fist" (Clark, 2007).

"I have cut my battery off and connected the line with the earth," tapped out a Boston operator on the morning of September 2. "We are working with current from the Aurora Borealis alone. How do you receive my writing?" The other operator, who had also cut off his batteries, responded "Much better than with batteries on" (*The New York Times*, September 6, 1859).

In New York, a telegraph operator having trouble on the evening of September 3 happened to look out the window and saw "broad rays of light extending from the zenith toward the horizon in almost every direction."

We now know that the worldwide auroras of 1859 were the same as the "northern lights" usually seen in polar regions; the auroras expanded for a few days due to a giant solar flare. We also know that electromagnetic fields travel invisibly through the atmosphere.

At the time, however, scientists wondered how electricity was related to magnetism and how the auroras of 1859 could create electricity in telegraph wires.

One piece of the puzzle was solved a few years later, when James Clerk Maxwell, a British mathematician, published a paper describing how electric and magnetic forces could be carried through space without wires. Maxwell called it displacement current. Another part of the puzzle involved Thomas Edison's observations about the behavior of one electrical circuit when it was near a similar circuit. The phenomenon, when one circuit mimics another without actually touching it, was called the "Edison effect." Some historians think Edison's labs could have created radio, had he not focused on a sound-recording device (the phonograph, patented in 1878) and the electric light (patented in 1879).

In the 1880s, Heinrich Hertz, a German scientist, found a way to test Maxwell's theory by generating electromagnetic waves, detecting them, and measuring their velocity. When he published his findings in 1888, Hertz thought he had simply verified an interesting scientific speculation (Aitken, 1992). "This is just an experiment that proves Maestro (teacher) Maxwell was right," he said. "We just have these mysterious electromagnetic waves that we cannot see with the naked eye. But they are there."

Asked about the value of the experiment, Hertz told students: "It's of no use whatsoever."

Like discovering a new continent

If Hertz saw no practical value in radio telegraphy, others were racing to lay claim to what seemed like a new continent that was just being discovered. In the United States, Nikoa Tesla began giving demonstrations of short range wireless telegraphy in 1891. In Britain, Oliver Lodge transmitted radio signals at a meeting of a British scientific society at Oxford University. Similar experiments were being conducted in Germany, Italy, India, Russia, Brazil, and by the US Navy in New York around the same time, and all faced the same problem: usually the signals would not travel more than a few dozen meters.

An unlikely inventor is often credited with making radio telegraphy practical. Guglielmo Marconi, a 20-year-old from a wealthy Irish-Italian family with little formal education, had become fascinated with electronic waves while attending a friend's scientific lectures at the University of Bologna.

In 1894, Marconi was able to duplicate Hertz' experiments in his home laboratory, but he faced the familiar problem: he was not able to receive a signal over any great distance. At the time, most research was focused on the higher frequency part of the radio spectrum, and physicists hoped to understand the relationship between radio waves and light waves. Marconi moved down the spectrum, using lower

Figure 8.1 Radio entrepreneur—using trial and error techniques, Guglielmo Marconi found a way to transmit radio over long distances. With influential backing, Marconi patented early radio technology and commercialized radio telegraphy (Library of Congress).

frequency waves. He also used high powered transmitters and larger, grounded antennas.

Marconi was not the first to think of using what we now call a "ground," but he was the first to use it specifically for radio signaling, and he was also the first to fully describe the commercial potential of long-distance signaling. He arrived at just the right time with the right financial and political backing connected with his family's Jamison Irish whiskey fortune.

In 1896, Marconi was introduced to officials in the British Postal Service who, just that year, were finalizing the purchase of the last remaining commercial British telegraph company. This was being done to avoid the information bottlenecks created by monopoly systems like Western Union in the United States. Having nationalized the telegraph system by merging it with the post office, postal officials now saw a duty to fully investigate an entirely new communications system.

In 1897, on a windy day on the Salisbury plains near the ancient Stonehenge monument, Marconi showed government officials a practical radio telegraph system that could send a signal for 6 kilometers (3.7 miles). Over the next few years, the range of Marconi wireless systems expanded with higher power amplifiers, and their value became obvious when radio helped rescue ships crews in distress off the English coast.

Figure 8.2 Wireless telegraph—this replica of a ship's radio telegraph shows the telegraph key and transmitter coils. Common on ships between 1900 and 1915, radio telegraphy often saved lives but tragically slowed the *Titanic* rescue efforts. (Photo by Linda Burton)

As radio began saving lives and money, insurance companies like Lloyds of London ordered ships to install the new devices. By 1900, the Marconi radio telegraph could be found on most large ocean-going vessels. In several cases, Marconi operators saved the lives of many passengers. For example, in 1910, an operator named Jack Binns became famous for using radio to save passengers on the HMS *Republic*—a sister ship of the ill-fated *Titanic*.

Radio and the *Titanic*

Radio problems played a major role in the *Titanic* disaster of April 14, 1912, when the British passenger liner sank after hitting an iceberg in the mid-Atlantic.

The *Titanic* was on its first voyage from Britain to the United States, and had just crossed the point where messages from ships at sea could be exchanged from the easternmost North American wireless station in Newfoundland. After sending personal messages from the *Titanic*, the operators were taking down news and stock reports for the passengers to read the next morning.

Just minutes before the *Titanic* hit the iceberg, a wireless operator on a ship eight miles away, the *Californian*, attempted to contact the *Titanic* to tell them they were surrounded by dangerous icebergs. The *Californian* had even stopped in the water. But the *Titanic*'s operators were busy. They rudely told the operator on the *Californian* to "keep off" (the air) so that *Titanic* operators could hear the weaker signals from Newfoundland.

The *Californian*'s Marconi operator took off his headphones and climbed into his bunk, only to be awakened about four hours later by officers on his ship who wondering whether the *Titanic* might be in trouble. By that time, it was too late to help.

Commissions of inquiry were incredulous. "Do I understand rightly then that a Marconi operator . . . can only clearly hear one thing at a time?" a British commissioner asked. Unfortunately, it was true, and as *The New York Times* said a few weeks later: "Sixteen hundred lives were lost that might have been saved if the wireless communication had been what it should have been" (*The New York Times*, May 2, 1912).

The official cause of the disaster was the negligence of the *Titanic*'s captain in ignoring iceberg reports. However, the delayed rescue effort was also a crucial issue, a US Senate committee found. "Had the wireless operator of the *Californian* remained a few minutes longer at his post . . . that ship might have had the proud distinction of rescuing the lives of the passengers and crew of the *Titanic*" (*The New York Times*, May 29, 1912).

One immediate impact of the *Titanic* disaster was the Radio Act of 1912, which required that ships at sea monitor the radio for distress signals 24 hours a day. Another requirement was that no one radio system would be permitted to exclude other radio systems from communication—a problem that had not slowed the disaster relief effort but which had created similarly dangerous problems. In effect, that the airwaves were free to be used by all, and no one company would be allowed to monopolize them.

The *Titanic* disaster also illustrates key issues about broadcasting and the effect of monopolies in the early twentieth century.

The *Titanic* used wireless technology that was rapidly becoming obsolete. Marconi was not a scientist, and when he found an effective system based on previous scientific work and his own trial-and-error results, he used the patent system to freeze the technology into place and buttress his commercial monopoly. While research on better systems was taking place in smaller companies, such as Reginald Fessenden's National Electric Signaling Company, none of these had the commercial power of the Marconi company.

Technically, the problem with the radio telegraph systems on the *Titanic* was that Marconi's "spark" system soaked up large segments of the bandwidth and created interference even when there were only a few ships on the vast ocean. As many engineers were realizing at the time, it was better to use continuous wave radio transmitters (where signals were carried inside the wave) rather than intermittent spark transmissions (where interruptions in the wave *were* the signal). A continuous wave could be "tuned" to allow a variety of frequencies. And it could use shorter wavelength radio transmissions, which carried over long distances by bouncing off the electrically charged outer layer of the atmosphere called the ionosphere—the region where auroras form. This more modern approach uses the ionosphere as a resource, rather than as an obstacle to be overcome, as was the case with Marconi's out-of-date, high-powered low frequency approach.

With large profits from international radio sales, Marconi could have investigated a variety of technical paths to improve radio. Instead, the company focused on a narrow technical path—low frequency, spark transmission, high power transmitters—that was initially successful but not flexible enough in the long run. In effect, said historian Hugh Aitken, the personal stubbornness that made Marconi a commercial success prevented him from envisioning a wider variety of engineering solutions to obvious problems. (Aitken, 1992)

"Now I have realized my mistake," he told an audience of radio engineers in a 1927 speech in New York city. "Everyone followed me in building stations hundreds of times more powerful than would nave been necessary had short waves been used" (Aitken, 1992). After the speech, Marconi laid a wreath at a small Battery Park memorial for Jack Phillips, the wireless operator who had gone down with the *Titanic*, still sending out distress calls to the last. (*The New York Times*, October 18, 1927).

Early radio technology

Technical development of radio kept expanding with new abilities to tune frequencies, to broadcast voice and music, and to deliver far more powerful signals.

One of the most startling was the 1906 Christmas Eve broadcasts by radio engineer Reginald Fessenden.

Around the same time, the problem of tuning the radio and broadcasting voice and music was solved with the invention of the "audion" (triode) tube by Lee DeForest, but the device would undergo many improvements before it became part of commercial radio broadcasting in the 1920s.

The electronics engineer who contributed the most to the development of radio was Edwin H. Armstrong, who devised and patented a new kind of radio tuning circuit in 1914. Bypassing DeForest's audion patents, Armstrong developed as system that took part of the current and fed it back to the grid, strengthening incoming signals. As a young man testing this concept in his house in Yonkers, NY, Armstrong began receiving distant stations so loudly that they could be heard

The Christmas Broadcast of 1906

Figures 8.3 and 8.4 Christmas broadcast of 1906—on Christmas Eve, 1906, operators in the "radio shacks" of ships around Cape Cod were sending and receiving routine messages in Morse code over the airwaves. Suddenly their headphones picked up a strange sound . . . Through the static, they heard a violin, playing O Holy Night. Even more astonishing . . . the voice of Reginald Fessenden reading a passage from the Bible. The Canadian radio inventor and entrepreneur had developed a continuous wave system to broadcast voice and music after years of experimentation in universities and with the US Weather Service. With the help of investors, he built a high-power continuous wave transmitting station in

Brant Rock, MA, designed to compete with Marconi's spark transmitting system. Fessenden's financial backers hoped to sell the telephonic radio system to AT&T, but the company was not interested. Marconi, then dominant in radio telegraphy, stayed with spark technology until the *Titanic* disaster of 1912.

Figure 8.5 Exuberant inventor—Edwin H. Armstrong, inventor of FM radio and many other improvements to radio, was fond of climbing radio towers. He is seen here atop the 115-foot tall RCA radio tower in New York on May 15, 1923, opening day of RCA's Radio Broadcast Central.

without headphones, which were necessary until then. The story is that he was so excited he woke up his sister Cricket, shouting "I've done it! I've done it!"

Armstrong later found that when the feedback was pushed to a high level, the tube produced rapid oscillations acting as a transmitter, and putting out electromagnetic waves. He also developed FM (frequency modulation) radio, which had far less static than AM (amplitude modulation) radio.

Although Armstrong developed the electronic key to continuous-wave transmitters that are still at the heart of all radio and television operations, a bitter patent fight with RCA broke out. The fight was one reason that AM radio technology dominated commercial broadcasting until the 1960s.

But commercial radio was still a dream when, in 1914, amateur radio operators across the country formed the American Radio Relay League (ARRL). Soon afterwards, legend has it, a young Marconi employee, David Sarnoff, wrote a "radio music box memo" about the possibility of commercial broadcasting to Marconi:

I have in mind a plan of development which would make radio a "household utility" in the same sense as the piano or phonograph. The idea is to bring music into the house by wireless. While this has been tried in the past by wires, it has been a failure because wires do not lend themselves to this scheme. With radio, however, it would seem to be entirely feasible.

The new system would be supported with advertising, rather than by subscription or government subsidy, Sarnoff said. While there is some historical controversy about the memo, there is evidence that Sarnoff pushed for commercial radio at the time.

Ideas about commercial radio had to be put on hold, however, with the outbreak of World War I, and all radio operations were suspended. Armstrong donated all his patents and know-how to the government to help fight the war, and served as a captain in the US Army Signal Corps.

The 'radio craze' of the 1920s

They called it the "radio craze," and after World War I, young people put on headphones and tuned into the weak signals from half a dozen major radio stations. The sets were so popular that Radio Corporation of America—the new US company created from American Marconi at the end of World War I—pushed its radio tube manufacturing from an average of 5,000 tubes per month in 1921 to over 200,000 by June of 1922. (By 1930, the number would rise to 125 million per month.)

Radio listeners originally heard a haphazard and eclectic schedule of literary readings, church sermons, foreign news and musical recitals put together at the whim and convenience of local radio stations. Only four station schedules were listed in *The New York Times* "radio section" when it was included in the newspaper in May, 1921, and of these, only one was near New York. The others were in Pittsburgh, Chicago and Springfield MA.

Consumer demand surprised everyone, especially the electronics industry, which was preoccupied with a complicated set of patent lawsuits between Edwin H. Armstrong and RCA, Westinghouse and AT&T. Their original plan was to freely broadcast educational music and high-toned programming, making money by marketing home radio receivers. But since demand for the receivers was already so high, the focus turned to a business model for radio broadcasting.

Some 732 radio stations were on the air in 1927, among them, the two stations owned by RCA in New York and Washington D.C. Other affiliates would form the two networks for RCA's National Broadcasting Company division. The affiliates were either in the Red network, offering commercial entertainment; or the Blue Network, originally to have news and cultural programs without sponsors. Also in 1927, a small group of radio stations formed the Columbia Broadcasting System headed by the young heir of a cigar company, William S. Paley.

Before radio could be a commercial success, the chaos in the airwaves had to be straightened out. After a failed attempt at voluntary regulation, Congress created the Federal Radio Commission (FRC) in 1927 with the idea that radio should serve the public interest, convenience and necessity. But the commission found "public interest" to be an elusive concept, and on August 20, 1928, the FRC issued General Order 40, a set of regulations that split radio licenses up into three classes.

Third class amateur radio operators were not permitted to broadcast news, weather, sports, information or entertainment. The FRC also confined them to an undesirable part of the AM spectrum. Second class medium-sized radio stations were assigned low broadcasting power and limited hours. Many of these were educational stations owned by unions, universities and churches. But they were labeled "propaganda" stations by the FRC.

Twenty-five "clear channel" first class radio stations were given strong frequencies, and of these, 23 were affiliated with NBC. They were not permitted to play recorded music, which meant that all music had to be live on the air. Only a very large company could afford its own in-house orchestra. In this way, radio became a centrally controlled national medium rather than a widely distributed locally controlled medium (McChesney, 1994).

Publicly, FRC commissioners said the educational stations differed greatly in their technical qualities. But privately, they hoped to do away with these "small and unimportant stations" by requiring four license renewals per year and by assigning them poor low-power frequencies. Within a year of the 1927 regulations, 100 radio stations had folded up, and by 1930 only a handful of the original educational stations remained.

Figure 8.6 Radio legend—David Sarnoff was a pivotal figure in twentieth-century broadcasting. According to one legend, now proven false, Sarnoff stayed by his telegraph key for days relaying news of the *Titanic*. Another legend, possibly true, was that Sarnoff envisioned the future of commercial broadcasting in 1915. However, there's no question that, as a longtime executive with RCA and NBC, Sarnoff put his personal stamp on the way radio and television broadcasting developed. (Library of Congress)

WNYC, a station owned by the city of New York, was among those assigned a part-time, low-power channel. The city appealed to the FRC and lost. Other stations, such as a handful of Brooklyn-based Jewish community stations, also lost in the rush to create a large central network.

The US process failed to make the best possible use of the medium, noted legal analyst Philip J. Weiser. In contrast, Britain, Australia and Canada created hybrid systems where both commercial and nonprofit educational stations coexisted and were funded by taxes on radio.

Fear of the power of the new media was one of the reasons that the US government excluded small nonprofit stations, but censorship was already taking place on many levels. Complaints about the treatment of controversial speakers were typical in the early days. Congressman Emanuel Celler of New York noted that speakers had been cut off in mid-sentence, plays had been censored and even political speeches had been edited before air time (*The New York Times*, May 29, 1927). Norman Thomas, a leading US democratic-socialist, warned that radio had lost the capacity for genuine discussion of great ideas in the rush to commercialism (*The New York Times*, March 30, 1934).

In idealizing radio policy, US president Calvin Coolidge, insisted that control remain in the hands of the government:

> "In its broad aspects, radio is a new agency brought by science to our people which may, if properly safeguarded, become one of our greatest blessings. No monopoly should be allowed to arise, and to prevent it, the control of the channel through the ether should remain in the hands of the government, and therefore of the people, as the control of navigation upon our waters; that while we retain the fundamental rights in the hands of the people to the control of these channels we should maintain the widest degree of freedom in their use. Liberty is not license in this new instrument of science. There is a great responsibility on the part of those who transmit material over the radio." (*The New York Times*, November 20, 1938)

But the reality was far from the ideal. The government promoted a monopoly radio network and shoved the small independent educational stations off into a corner, where most just gave up or joined NBC or CBS.

Radio licensing and censorship in the 1930s

It is not surprising that a system favoring tight content control would be the original framework for the new medium. Film, also relatively new at the time, was regulated for similar reasons. No one was sure what the social effects of the medium would be.

Some of the new programs and stations posed serious challenges to the emerging radio system. Licenses for two radio stations were revoked in the early 1930s by the FRC, which said that the stations were "sensational rather than instructive" in nature. John R. Brinkley, a Kansas City surgeon, used his radio station KFKB to advocate medically fraudulent implants of supposedly rejuvenating animal organs. When his medical license was revoked in 1930, the FRC also revoked the radio station's license. He moved the operation to Mexico, where his station was one of the most powerful in North America.

Two years later, the FRC also revoked the license of KGEF, a radio station owned by Rev. Robert P. Shuler and the Trinity Methodist Church. Shuler was a shrill muckraker who mounted extreme anti-Semitic attacks on corrupt politicians in Los Angeles. In denying the church's legal appeal, a federal court said radio was only an "instrumentality of commerce." The First Amendment did not apply to broadcasting, the court said, and the license revocation was simply an "application of the regulatory power of Congress."

This broadcast licensing case stands in sharp contrast with the 1933 newspaper censorship case, *Near v. Minnesota,* in which a state tried to shut down *The Saturday Press* of Minneapolis. The Supreme Court said that printed media, no matter how offensive, could not be censored outright, even though radio could be censored. Even so, as the 1930s progressed, other means of radio censorship would be employed.

The golden age of radio

Radio became the first "electronic hearth," helping bring families—and nations—together to face the crises of the 1930s and 40s. Media theorist Marshall McLuhan saw radio having a "re-tribalizing" effect, creating an electronic return to oral culture and representing a departure from literacy. Radio was also an extension of, and new twist on vaudeville and theater, and during its golden age in the 1930s and 40s, radio attracted the best entertainers in the world.

Originally, the NBC network, led by David Sarnoff, took a high-minded approach to public service. An advisory group of 17 prominent citizens helped shape the programming schedule with lessons in music appreciation, productions of Shakespeare, political debates and symphonies. By 1928, the network made its first profits (Smith, 1990).

Sarnoff "had a vision of what radio and television could become in terms of being informational, educational, cultural, relevant," said his great-nephew, Richard Sarnoff, in 2008. "He said 'OK, we've got radio, let's put Tchaikovsky on!' . . . The reason the

Figure 8.7 Radio clowns—actors Freeman Gosden and Charles Correll created the first big radio hit, *Amos 'n' Andy*, depicting comic slices of life in an African-American taxi company. Although offensive by modern standards, the show also provided occasional glimpses into the real-world dilemmas of American minorities. (Library of Congress)

broadcast media didn't end up being this public trust type of programming . . . is that radio and television is just so good at delivering audiences to advertisers. Business being what it is, whatever you're good at, you concentrate on, you maximize, and that ends up delivering value to your shareholders" (Auletta, 2010).

While "high-brow" symphonic and theatrical productions drew audiences, people were far more interested in popular entertainment. Vaudeville, the variety entertainment genre of theater, became the model for many local and national radio programs, provided a platform for comedians, musical variety and short dramas. Children's and family-oriented programs were also especially popular, and these included Western dramas and comic-book heroes.

The most popular show on radio at the end of the 1920s and all through the 1930 was *Amos 'n' Andy*. The show shamelessly stereotyped two African American taxi cab owners, but the roles were also complex and human. At first in 1926, white actors Freeman Gosden and Charles Correll syndicated the show by distributing recorded episodes. The show proved to be an unexpected hit, within a few years attracting 40 million listeners per episode—far more than any other program at the time. NBC contracted with Gosden and Correll in 1929.

"*Amos 'n' Andy* profoundly influenced the development of dramatic radio," broadcast historian Elizabeth McLeod said.

> Working alone in a small studio . . . (the performers) created an intimate, understated acting style that differed sharply from the broad manner of stage actors . . . . The performers pioneered the technique of varying both the distance and the angle of their approach to the microphone to create the illusion of a group of characters. Listeners could easily imagine that that they were actually in the taxi-cab office, listening in on the conversation of close friends. The result was a uniquely absorbing experience for listeners who, in radio's short history, had never heard anything quite like *Amos 'n' Andy*.

The show was not only offensive by modern standards—it was also offensive to some people by the standards of the 1920s. Bishop W. J. Walls of the African Methodist Zion Church said it was "crude, repetitious, and moronic." A petition drive was taken up to have the show taken off the air. But *Amos 'n' Andy* was only mildly controversial in the African American community, since the show's two white actors were favorite guests at Bud Billekin picnics and parades in Chicago. Nor is there any mention of controversy in several references to the show in *Chicago Defender* (Ellett, 2010).

This may have been because the show provided occasional glimpses into the real world of African Americans. For instance, at one point, the show depicted an innocent Amos undergoing brutal interrogation by police—an event not at all uncommon at the time. The National Association of Chiefs of Police took *Amos 'n' Andy* so seriously that they protested to the network, and the story had to be rewritten to show that it was nothing more than a dream.

Following the success of *Amos 'n' Andy*, high-brow symphonies and educational programs were pushed off the air, and radio comedies and dramas began to dominate. The public, anxious to escape the grim realities of the Depression, bought radios by the millions. NBC and CBS worked hard to keep up with the demand for programming.

One of the favorite and best-remembered radio dramas of the 1930s was *The Shadow*, a melodrama concerning a crime-fighter with psychic powers. Its opening line, delivered with manic and sinister laughter, was: "What evil lurks in the hearts of men? Who knows? The Shadow knows."

Apparently the FCC knew as well. The FCC objected when a Minneapolis, MN radio station allowed "certain words" (damn and hell) to go on the air when they broadcast Eugene O'Neill's play "Beyond the Horizon." And the FCC was "outraged" (even as audiences were "electrified") when, on December 12, 1937, NBC's

Figure 8.8 "Give me trouble"— Mae West got more trouble than she anticipated with a 1937 NBC comedy sketch about the Garden of Eden. (Library of Congress)

Eve: You don't know a thing about women.

Adam: You apparently forget you were one of my own ribs.

Eve: Yeah, I'm ribbed once, now I'm beefin'.

Adam: Me? I know everything about women.

Eve: That's covering a lot of territory. Listen long, lazy and lukewarm. You think I want to stay in this place all my life?

Adam: I do, and I tell you, you're one of my ribs.

Eve: Yeah, but one of your floatin' ribs. A couple of months of peace and security and a woman is bored all the way down to the bottom of her marriage certificate.

Adam: What do you want, trouble?

Eve: Listen, if trouble means something that makes you catch your breath, if trouble means something that makes your blood run through you veins like seltzer water, mmmm, Adam, my man, give me trouble.

Chase & Sanborn Hour carried a skit featuring Mae West and Don Ameche in the Garden of Eden. The skit depicts Eve as adventurous and hoping to "develop her personality." She was seen as bored with life in the Garden and encouraged Adam to "break the lease." At one point Adam asked what's wrong with life in the Garden, and West says, "give me trouble."

These provocative words led the FCC to issue a "stern reprimand" for violating the ethics of decency. The agency began considering how to deal more effectively with content on the radio networks—not just allowing or taking away station licenses, but reaching more into the core of the program development process.

Radio and the news

As radio became more popular, radio broadcasters were able to bring fascinating new sounds to the American public. From the volcanoes of Hawaii to the acoustics of a submarine, the microphone could go everywhere and try everything. Its power was particularly noticed during a prison riot on April 21, 1930, in Columbus, Ohio. A line to the radio station, which had already been installed months before to pick up the prison band, now carried the sound of a prison riot and fire. One prisoner, identified only by number, described the fighting and confusion that killed 317 men. "The microphone was at the heart of the grim tragedy, at times no more than 30 feet away from the crackling flames," said a *New York Times* account (*New York Times*, January 24, 1932).

Radio gained audience and advertising power during the Depression, increasing ad revenues 40 to 50 percent per year as newspaper advertising dropped. American newspaper publishers began to fear radio, fanning the "smoldering fires of opposition" to the new medium, as NBC radio president M. H. Aylesworth warned in 1930. Yet he argued that radio and newspapers are natural allies. "Gutenberg's conception of printing, coupled with Marconi's perfection of the radio, has armed society with its greatest weapon against darkness" (*The New York Times*, April 25, 1931).

NBC's olive branch did not win the friends the network NBC needed, and in 1933, the three wire services (Associated Press, United Press and International Press) agreed with the publishers association to boycott radio news. AP began with lawsuits against radios broadcasting their news without permission the next year.

CBS radio, at that time a far smaller organization than NBC, responded by creating its own news service. William Paley, president of CBS, found a sponsor for a news program and CBS had gathered 600 part-time reporters in major cities across the world. But in December of 1933, CBS and NBC succumbed to pressure from publishers and wire services to scrap individual broadcast news divisions and form a "Press-Radio" bureau. Under what was called the "Biltmore Agreement," the bureau would air two 5-minute broadcasts per day, except when issues of "transcendent" importance came up. The broadcasts would not be in prime time and they would refer listeners to their newspapers for more details.

Local radio stations more or less ignored the Biltmore Agreement, even though they now had no wire service access to national and international news. But the

Figure 8.9 Radio news—Edward R. Murrow and William L. Shirer fought with the CBS bureaucracy to create a news program from European capitols. With Murrow in London and Shirer in Berlin, Americans by 1938 began hearing some of the disturbing developments first-hand. (Library of Congress)

networks held back on news coverage until the 1936 elections. Tensions began running high between the networks and the publishers. For instance, when CBS gave *all* presidential candidates air time—including an unlikely candidate from the Communist Party—the Hearst *Journal-American* ran an editorial cartoon of CBS president Paley on a soap box waving a red flag.

One incident proving the value of radio news involved the May 6, 1927, Hindenburg disaster. Herbert Morrison was narrating the airship's landing, which was being recorded to be broadcast the next day on Chicago's WLS radio station. Morrison talked as the airship, arriving from Frankfurt, Germany, burst into flames as it attempted to land at the Lakehurst, NJ airfield. His exclamation "Oh the humanity" as he helplessly watched passengers die shows the deeply emotional nature of radio. The phrase has become an idiomatic cliché of the twentieth century.

Demand for radio news grew with the rise of tensions in Europe, and one of the talented young CBS news producers, Edward R. Murrow, was tapped in 1937 for the job of heading the network's European offices. Murrow was initially frustrated that his plans for wider coverage of Europe were not supported, but events on the ground were moving quickly. The Nazi takeover of Austria on March 11, 1938 was the first time that Murrow and other correspondents, such as William Shirer, were able to broadcast a full report from the field. NBC also broadcast the event, doing a better job than the CBS team. CBS president Paley, at this point, began to come around to Murrow's point of view, and then claimed to have invented the "World News Roundup" himself. Murrow and Shirer were hardly in a position to argue when they finally got the OK for their project.

As radio proved its worth, cooperation between radio news organizations and the wire services grew. By the 1938, as major events began overtaking minor disputes, AP stopped worrying about whether radio was carrying their news. Now all news organizations started focusing on the increasingly irrational demands of Nazi leader Adolf Hitler. In September, 1938, war was temporarily averted when Britain and French leaders met with Hitler in Munich, Germany and agreed not to intercede if the Nazis invaded part of the Czech Republic. Radio reports were now coming in daily, and audiences were becoming attuned to urgent news announcements for the first time. Yet they were not accustomed to taking a critical view of the media.

Martian invasion panics millions

The whole thing began as something of a Halloween prank by a young theater director named Orson Welles. He had been hired by CBS to present noncommercial dramas such as adaptations of Treasure Island, Dracula, the Count of Monte Cristo, and Huckleberry Finn. CBS management hoped the productions, which had no sponsorship and no advertising, would help ward off FCC concerns about over-commercialization.

Welles and the under-funded Mercury Theater were always under tremendous pressure to present these Sunday night programs, and when the idea for an adaptation of H. G. Wells' *War of the Worlds* came up, Welles and others worried that it would be their least successful program to date. They decided to frame the narrative inside a series of newscasts to make it seem a little more realistic.

The show aired on October 31, 1938. Over the course of an hour, the Martian invaders traveled from their home planet, landed in New Jersey, released clouds of lethal gas and then took over New York. In the end, of course, the Martians were defeated by the humblest of earth's creatures, the bacteria. All within an hour.

Listeners panicked as they heard what seemed to be a news broadcast about an invasion. Without interruptions for commercial sponsors, station identification or even any warning that it was all just in fun, hundreds of thousands of listeners took to the streets, especially in New Jersey, as they attempted to flee the approaching Martians.

John Housman later recalled that the script writers for the *War of the Worlds* did not believe the script was quite up to standard. They studied Herbert Morrison's Hindenburg disaster reporting as they rewrote it so that they could achieve the live news effect. "We all felt its only chance of coming off lay in emphasizing its newscast style—its simultaneous, eyewitness quality," Houseman said (Houseman, 1948).

Although no deaths or major incidents were reported, reaction to the prank was fairly strong. Within a month, some 12,500 newspaper articles were written about the broadcast (Hand, 2006). Houseman attributed the press reaction to its disdain for radio itself. "Having had to bow to radio as a news source during the Munich crisis, the press was now only too eager to expose the perilous irresponsibilities of the new medium."

A similar Spanish language radio drama based on the original Orson Welles script was broadcast in 1949 in

Figure 8.10 Martian invasion—radio and theater producer Orson Welles panicked millions of Americans with an hour-long program that used news bulletins to depict an invasion from Mars. Welles went on to produce and direct the movie "Citizen Kane." (Library of Congress)

Quito, Ecuador with a much more serious effect, according to historian John Gosling. The broadcast was interrupted when a full-blown panic emerged in the city streets. Thousands mobbed cathedrals for last rites. When the infuriated listeners realized they were victims of a prank, a mob set the radio station on fire, killing as many as 20 people (Gosling, 2009).

Censoring hate speech on the radio

If radio could convince people of a Martian landing, how much more damage could it do? As Hitler said, "By clever, constant propaganda, a people can be convinced that heaven is hell or that a miserable life is paradise" (Brown, 1939).

One American who attempted to prove Hitler right was Father Charles Coughlin, a Catholic priest with a syndicated radio talk show and 16 million listeners. Coughlin started out as a democrat, a union supporter and a champion of the oppressed working class. But by the middle of the 1930s, he had become so disgusted with Depression-era capitalism that he embraced fascism and anti-Semitic rhetoric, for example, calling FDR's "New Deal" the "Jew Deal." He also repeated German Nazi propaganda nearly word-for-word in his newspaper columns and secretly took money from Nazi front groups (Warren, 1996).

In the summer of 1938, Coughlin threw his arm out in a Nazi salute and told a rally of supporters: "When we get through with the Jews in America, they'll think the treatment they received in Germany was nothing" (Manchester, 1974). The treatment in Germany took a turn for the worse in November 1938, as Nazi party members destroyed synagogues and killed Jewish people across Germany in a pogrom called "Kristallnacht." Coughlin tried to defend it, saying that persecution was only natural since Jews had been "numerous among radical leaders" on the left, and that many Christians had been persecuted by communists in Russia.

It was a moment of truth for many Americans, who reacted with horror. It was a turning point for Coughlin as well, since NBC and CBS networks refused to pass along "errors of fact" and demanded Coughlin's advance radio scripts from that point forward. Coughlin refused, and continued his broadcasts through independent radio stations for another year. The Nazis trumpeted the censorship, saying Coughlin was not being allowed to broadcast the truth, even though censorship in Nazi Germany had risen to totalitarian levels.

While the FCC wondered how to approach content regulation, the National Association of Broadcasters changed the code of ethics to bar the sale of airtime for the presentation of controversial issues except in political races. The effect was to take Coughlin and others like him off the air permanently in 1939. "This new rule closed the one loophole that remained in the networks' and stations' ability to censor controversial opinion: the dollar loophole," said historian Michelle Hilmes. "The ability to pay was no longer [enough] . . . In fact, now broadcasters had an obligation to restrict all those outside the broad mainstream of political views" (Hilmes, 2006).

A few months later, in January of 1940, the FBI raided the secret New York hideout of 17 armed Nazi saboteurs who had been associated with Coughlin's group. Although

Figure 8.11 Fascism on the air—Charles Coughlin, a Catholic priest, ran a syndicated talk show that drew 16 million listeners in the mid-1930s. He began as a pro-labor reformer, but when he openly backed the Nazi party and its treatment of Jews, radio networks pulled the plug. (Library of Congress)

he tried to defend their ideas, it was clear that Coughlin had totally misunderstood American public opinion. He was forced by the church to retire from public life.

Coughlin also inspired counterpropaganda efforts. Rachel DuBois, a New Jersey high school teacher, started an influential radio program on diversity because she was infuriated with Coughlin when he yelled things like "This is a country for White Christians!" She proposed a series, financed by the Dept. of Education, entitled "Americans All, Immigrants all" that described the variety of ethnic streams that made for a diverse and stronger country (Hilmes, 2006).

Coughlin was one of several popular fascist Americans whose views were marginalized and undermined by network regulation during the years before World War II. The process was disconcerting to many who felt, at the very least, that Americans needed to understand what they would soon be fighting. But the security threat was real. German attempts to keep America neutral had been exposed in the Bolo Pasha-Hearst affair in 1917 (see Chapter 3) and similarly well-financed attempts to influence the American public were also taking place in the 1930s (Shannon, 1995).

"To permit radio to become a medium for selfish propaganda of any character would be shamefully and wrongfully to abuse a great agent of public service," said US President Franklin D. Roosevelt. "Radio broadcasting should be maintained on an equality of freedom which has been and is the keynote of the American press." (*The New York Times*, November 20, 1938).

Developing a governing philosophy of broadcasting

By the late 1930s, the power of radio was being seen as far greater than anyone originally imagined. To give First Amendment freedoms to the enemies of the First Amendment took faith in the American public.

On the one hand, many argued for freedom of speech and trust in the public. "The American people are not boobs," as one pundit picturesquely said (Saerchinger, 1940). On the other hand, the FCC had become increasingly concerned about controlling the content of the media. The Coughlin problem, the Mae West episode, the War of the Worlds panic and dozens of other issues provoked calls for outright censorship.

In FCC hearings in 1938, regulators talked about "the right of free speech and liberty of thought." The FCC chairman said censorship was "impracticable and definitely

Figure 8.12 Fireside chats—US President Franklin D. Roosevelt's "fireside chats" were an innovative use of media at the time. Roosevelt used them to reassure Americans during the Great Depression and rally the country during World War II. (Library of Congress)

objectionable," and then called for self-regulation of radio as the only traditional American way to avoid a plague of innumerable and unimaginable evils (*The New York Times*, November 20, 1938). The National Association of Broadcasters responded with changes in its voluntary code of conduct in 1939, effectively taking Father Coughlin off the air and advanced the idea of greater scrutiny of radio programming. While controversial ideas would still be heard on the air, they would be part of news programs or balanced panel discussions.

A formal FCC policy on fairness and objectivity, known as the Mayflower Decision, came in January 1941. The context was a contended radio station license in Boston, MA. Mayflower Broadcasting Corp. challenged the existing license holders because they endorsed political candidates. While not siding with Mayflower, the FCC agreed that the station (WAAB) had made a mistake when "no pretense was made at objective, impartial reporting."

"Radio can serve as an instrument of democracy only when devoted to the communication of information and the exchange of ideas fairly and objectively presented," the FCC said. "A truly free radio cannot be used to advocate the causes of the licensee [owner]. It cannot be used to support the candidacies of his friends. It cannot be devoted to the support of principles he happens to regard most favorably. In brief, the broadcaster cannot be an advocate. The public interest—not the private—is paramount" (*The New York Times*, January 18, 1941).

This policy was the precursor of the 1947 Fairness Doctrine, which applied to both radio and television, as we will see in Chapter 9. Since it was based in part on the idea of the scarcity of radio frequencies, courts upheld the Fairness Doctrine until 1984, when competition from other media made it clear that regulation of the marketplace of ideas was not necessary.

Radio in World War II

The long-expected shooting war arrived in Europe on September 1, 1939, when Nazi Germany's armies invaded Poland, although America would remain neutral for another two years. Radio became the way that Americans best understood what was at stake for the British as they faced the Blitz.

Edward R. Murrow is particularly associated with giving a human and dramatic flavor to news from London during the bombings of the early 1940s. His signature opening, "Hello America: This is London calling," was heard by millions around the world. Murrow would often report from rooftops with the sound of bombs and antiaircraft fire in the background, describing the gritty determination of Londoners and the hardships of the war.

Among the best remembered speeches in history is Winston Churchill's June 4, 1940 address carried on the radio: "We shall defend our island, whatever the cost may be. We shall fight on the beaches, we shall fight on the landing grounds, we shall fight in the fields and in the streets, we shall fight in the hills; we shall never surrender."

Americans gathered around the radio when, on September 7, 1941, the Japanese bombed the US Naval base at Pearl Harbor, Hawaii. The next day, 81 percent of American homes listened to the radio as Roosevelt asked Congress for a declaration of war. Roosevelt's December 9, 1941 informal radio address the next day—one of a series of his fireside chats— is remembered for its eloquence: "We are now in this war. We are all in it—all the way. Every single man, woman and child is a partner in the most tremendous undertaking of our American history."

The war hardly meant unanimity of opinion in all things. Debates about the best way to go about defeating the Nazis, and how best to mobilize the American public, took place at many levels of society. As Hilmes notes, a group of prominent writers in the Office of War Information resigned in 1943 after objecting to advertising-agency and publicity style tactics that were aimed at manipulating rather than informing the public. They also objected to the way that home-front controversy was censored from news sent to the soldiers through radio and newspapers (Hilmes, 2006).

On the front lines, radio news reporters carried each twist and turn of the war to the home front. Radio news reporters were a brave and storied lot, climbing into bombers and broadcasting from the front lines of the war. Among them were Edward R. Murrow; Walter Cronkite, later to become the famed news anchor for CBS television; Chet Huntley, who became the NBC television news anchor; and William L. Shirer, whose 1960 history, *The Rise and Fall of the Third Reich*, would become a classic.

Cronkite's February 26, 1943 CBS broadcast gives a feel for the air war. Parts of the broadcast were obscured by static, so a full transcript was never made:

> In what should be the peaceful [unintelligible], up where the blue skies begin fading into only a haze, I witnessed a man-made hell of bursting anti-aircraft shells, of burning tracers, of crippled Fortresses, and exploding Nazi fighters, of men parachuting to a [unintelligible] plunge in the North Sea, and of other men not so lucky, plunging to death in fiery planes . . . those who made the supreme sacrifice for their country. For two hours I watched a vicious gun duel, so excited I had no time to be scared. That came later. I have seen what it's like to [unintelligible] in the dark, what it is like to fight German airmen and dodge German flak. We put our bombs just where they were supposed to go, but we paid a price. As you know, seven of our bombers did not come home. I guess we were lucky. Other formations felt the brunt of German fighter blows, and we watched Fortresses and Liberators plucked from formations around us as if an invisible hand had reached out and pulled them to the ground.

Cronkite wrote about the experience for United Press the following day, but the newspaper dispatch had only some of the immediacy and personal drama of the radio report (Walter Cronkite, "Hell 26,000 feet up," *The New York Times*, February 27, 1943).

In an outstanding broadcast at the war's end, Murrow described the notorious Buchenwald concentration camp:

> There surged around me an evil-smelling stink, men and boys reached out to touch me. They were in rags and the remnants of uniforms. Death already had marked many of them . . . As we walked out into the courtyard, a man fell dead. Two others, they must have been over 60, were crawling toward the latrine. I saw it, but will not describe it . . .
>
> I pray you to believe what I have said about Buchenwald. I reported what I saw and heard, but only part of it. For most of it, I have no words . . . If I have offended you by this rather mild account of Buchenwald, I'm not in the least sorry . . .

Figure 8.13 Women in radio—the contribution of women in World War II was as courageous as its depiction in this US Navy poster. (Library of Congress)

Murrow and colleagues had proven the value of radio news in ways that could have hardly been imagined a decade before. Colleagues in the print media did not allow Murrow to join the London Correspondents Club in 1937. By war's end, he had been elected the club's president (Sperber, 1998).

But radio news had its own particular problems that would extend into television. A single company would sponsor a news or entertainment show and expect the show's stars to attend the company's business functions, cut ribbons at factory openings and even invite company executives to their summer homes. Murrow had this relationship with the Campbell Soup Company, and the company followed his work very closely.

In a postwar "Hear it Now" show, Murrow described people in the town of Anzio, Italy, now recovering from heavy combat a few years beforehand. In the course of the report, Murrow mentioned that the mayor happened to be both Catholic and communist. The soup company started getting complaints from American listeners and even threats to boycott company products. A company advertising executive wrote to warn Murrow to be more pro-American in his reporting. "There are comments . . . that you are pink," the man warned, asking him to give "careful thought as to what to do about it." ("Pink" here meant slightly "red," which is to say, sympathetic to communism.)

The postwar Blue Book controversy

The structure of the news media has always been a contentious issue. During the 1920s, under a Republican administration, the FRC helped NBC and CBS networks establish dominance over the airwaves. But under the democratic administration of

Franklin D. Roosevelt, concentration of media power was considered to be a problem by the new Federal Communications Commission. In 1939, following a lengthy controversy, NBC was ordered to sell the Blue Network. It became the American Broadcasting Company (ABC), and the Supreme Court backed the FCC order up in 1943.

Attention turned once again to the structure and performance of radio at the end of the war. Since only a limited number of radio stations could use the publicly owned broadcast spectrum, the question became how well they were serving the public interest.

On March 7, 1946, the FCC issued "Public Service Responsibility for Broadcast Licensees," also known as the "Blue Book" report. The report expressed disappointment in the overcommercialization of radio, high wartime profits, a lack of public service programming, and generally lax quality standards in the industry. The report also insisted that broadcasters had an obligation to serve the "public interest, convenience, and necessity," and that obligation could be enforced by revoking station licenses (*The New York Times*, September 18, 1947).

"Shabby commercialism" and a "listeners be damned" attitude is how *Kiplinger* magazine depicted the issue in 1947. (Kiplinger, 1947) "Wayward" radio executives will not be punished by forcing them to listen to their own programs, said Charles R. Denny, FCC chairman, because that would be cruel and unusual punishment (*The New York Times*, October 24, 1946).

Meanwhile, a report by Robert Hutchins' Commission on Freedom of the Press devoted a chapter to radio (although it had primarily been concerned with newspapers and magazines, as we have seen in Chapter 3). The commission joined the FCC in its concern about commercialism in radio, saying that the networks and electronics companies had a responsibility to do more. "Unless broadcasters themselves deal with over-commercialism, the government may be forced to act. So far this challenge has produced little from the National Association of Broadcasters except outraged cries about Freedom of Speech and suggestions for a new code, which, of course, would not go to the heart of the problem." (Hutchins, 1947).

Broadcasters "howled" about free speech and encroaching communism, and said that a peril to press freedom could emerge when new technologies, such as newspaper-by-fax, allowed newspapers to be delivered via broadcasting (*Washington Post*, June 19, 1947). But newspaper publishers sided with the FCC, saying that broadcasters had to get their own house in order.

The controversy died down when the broadcasters issued a new code and Denny resigned in 1947 to take a job with NBC. But the complex question remained over how much pressure the FCC could put on broadcasters to improve their public service when station licenses were only rarely suspended or terminated.

Another regulatory issue emerged around the same time. Newspapers were refusing to accept advertising from businesses that also advertised on radio. The US Justice Department brought a case against the *Loraine Ohio Journal*, questioning its "refusal to deal" as a violation of antitrust laws. The Supreme Court agreed in the case *Loraine Journal v. United States* (1951), and the principle that advertising had to be accepted in competitive situations was established. Both cases would come up in subsequent media antitrust actions, such as the when the US Justice Dept. sued

Microsoft in 1999 over its alleged refusal to deal with competing web browsers (see Chapter 11).

New competition for markets

Radio was at the center of news and entertainment during the war years, but afterwards, the rise of television meant that radio's original role as the "electronic hearth" and prime source of news and entertainment was becoming obsolete.

At this point, radio reverted to more local content as networks focused their efforts on television. Sometimes the local content focused on news and sports, but increasingly, radio turned to music that could be heard while driving or doing other things. It was inexpensive to program and, station owners found, it was increasingly appreciated by the post-World War II baby boom generation.

With universal technical standards for what was called high-fidelity music in the 1950s, a market for record sales began driving the content of a new kind of locally produced radio. The radio format was called Top-40, and its theme was a kind of competition between music artists to see whose record could become the best-selling top of the charts hit.

Typically, radio DJs (disk jockeys) would "count down" from the top 40, inserting commercials, announcements and wise-cracking commentary between three-minute songs. Some DJs became celebrities on their own right; probably the most famous in the 1960s was New York DJ, Murray the K (Murray Kaufman).

As the recording industry income grew, the pressures to promote records to teenagers grew as well. Underpaid DJs began taking various kinds of bribes to promote records, especially when a particular band would be coming to their city. Investigations in the 1950s and 60s led to criminal prosecutions for what was nicknamed "Payola" (Hilmes, 2006).

Congressional hearings looking into radio and television programming practices also found that television quiz shows had been rigged. Stronger regulations against bribery for music promotion or programming followed.

The recording industry, boosted by radio, doubled in size between 1960 and 1970 from $600 million to $1.2 billion in the United States and more than doubled again by 1980. Similar acceleration was seen in Britain, France, Germany and Japan (Gronow, 1983).

But as the radio audience grew, in part because of the postwar baby boom, content fragmented into a multitude of formats.

By the 1970s a fair-sized city might have a dozen separately owned radio stations, each with a distinct approach to music and culture, including Top 40, heavy metal, classic rock, golden oldies, middle of the road and classical symphonic music and "talk radio" programming.

This broad variety of programming was expensive to maintain locally, and in the 1980s and 90s, station owners turned to syndicated radio shows. Starting around 1981, radio stations could buy music program packages delivered by satellite at costs geared to market sizes. While this produced profits in the short term, over the long term, radio again drifted into national syndication and began losing its local following and advertisers.

Ownership rules for broadcasting changed during the 1980s and 90s as well. Under the original FCC rules, ownership of radio and TV stations was limited to the "rule of sevens"—seven AM, seven FM and seven TV stations. The idea was to keep ownership local and thus encourage local broadcasting.

Then, in the 1996 Telecommunications Act, ownership regulations were lifted almost entirely as part of a sweeping reform of telephone, satellite, cable and broadcast industries. In theory, the act was supposed to allow a better efficiency of scale for radio. Dozens of aggressive radio companies would own several hundred stations each, and that would create more competition. But "merger mania" took over, and within five years, two major companies—Clear Channel and Viacom/CBS's Infinity Broadcasting—bought up several thousand radio stations and controlled all of the major radio markets. In some cities the entire radio spectrum was owned by only two companies (Boehlert, 2001).

The stations did not always play it safe—Infinity got into repeated trouble with the FCC due to indecency from "shock jocks" like Howard Stern—but the commercial and non-local orientation did not help make their media offerings more appealing.

And as it turned out, the Telecommunications Act of 1996 consolidated radio ownership and changed the landscape of community oriented broadcasting. There was hope at one point that low-power FM stations would be able to serve individual communities, but regulatory barriers remained throughout the first decade of the twenty-first century, according to the Prometheus Radio Project, one of the top advocates for low-power community FM.

Emergence of talk radio

One of the most important developments in radio during the late twentieth century involved the distribution of "talk radio" shows to older AM radio stations and mainstream FM stations. With 400 radio stations around 1990, talk radio grew to nearly 3,000 stations by 2010 (Pew, 2010).

A typical talk radio show would last from one to three hours daily and focus on political issues, often with telephone call-ins from listeners. Research by the Pew Center in 2004 showed that 17 percent of the public were regular talk radio listeners and tended to be male, middle-aged and conservative.

The talk radio format had partisan precursors in Father Charles Coughlin's Sunday talks, but also in the more balanced panel programs such as "America's Town Meeting of the Air," put on by NBC from 1935 to 1956. The end of the "Fairness Doctrine" in 1987 gave a green light to partisan political radio shows that became popular in the 1990s, when passionate conservative viewpoints connected with a popular market.

One of the first of the conservative talk radio success stories was Rush Limbaugh, whose show was carried on 600 Clear Channel network radio stations. Other conservative talk show hosts included Bill O'Reilly, Michael Savage and Glenn Beck.

Liberal talk radio is relatively rare in comparison, with hosts such as Ed Schultz, Stephanie Miller, Randi Rhodes and Bill Press. A network designed to carry liberal talk shows, Air America, started in 2004 but went bankrupt by 2010, partly because overall radio revenue fell by 20 percent or more per year in the economic recession. But Air America itself had problems. It was based on a broader and more expensive concept of audience service, business observers said. Another liberal talk radio program, Ring of Fire, relies mostly on a podcast subscription service to circumvent radio networks. Conservative talk radio programs are sold to individual radio stations and have their own individual following. Progressive radio "remains a solid business proposition" said Bill Press, but it takes business and radio experience first, and not ideology (Press, 2010).

Satellite radio

The idea for direct satellite radio service for consumers dates back to the 1980s, when new telecommunications satellite link-ups allowed programs produced in Los Angeles or New York to be broadcast through local radio stations. Bypassing the "middle man"—the small local radio station—seemed like an attractive business strategy.

Broadcasting directly to the consumer was technically feasible by the early 1990s, and the idea attracted great hopes. "A new technology will eventually compete with local stations," said media writer Edmund L. Andrews (*The New York Times*, January 13, 1995). But it was not until 1997, over the strong opposition of the National Association of Broadcasters, that the FCC finally approved satellite radio, with the condition that the two major entrants in the field—XM Radio and Sirius—never merge.

Within a decade, competition from other digital media was so strong that both satellite radio companies were on the brink of bankruptcy, and the FCC allowed the two companies to merge into one monopoly service that would compete against traditional radio. Despite a wide variety of programming, with hundreds of channels ranging from shock jocks to sports to all kinds of music genres, consumer barriers included the need for a specific satellite radio receiver in the car or at home, and the monthly subscription costs were relatively high.

Meanwhile, in the rest of the world, satellite radio became significant for its ability to promote development and international interconnections. Radio is the only accessible medium in many rural and developing areas, and several low-earth orbit satellites carry development and peacekeeping information programs from the United Nations to rural Africa, Asia and Latin America. Peacekeeping missions involve a mix of terrestrial and satellite transmissions for the Congo, Kosovo, Liberia, Haiti, Timor-Leste and other conflict regions.

Internet audio and radio streaming

Digital audio file exchanges were possible early in the history of the internet (see Chapter 11), but they were slow. In the early 1990s improvements in network connection speeds and file compression formats made audio exchanges possible.

For example, before the new compression format, a Mac or Microsoft audio file three minutes long might be 50 megabytes in size. Using networks common in the early 1990s, such a file might take two hours to transfer.

After new compression formats were introduced, the same file could be compressed to the size of about 5 MB with no apparent loss of quality. This new software format standard was set by the International Standards Organization's Motion Picture Experts Group (MPEG) (a similar group set the JPEG standard, as we saw in Chapter 4). The MPEG compression technologies were effective because they first removed the data in audio ranges that were not audible to the human ear.

The speed and ease of audio file exchanges, especially music downloads, became appreciated in the late 1990s when digital versions of popular music were exchanged through services like Napster (see Chapter 11). This free exchange of copyrighted music was opposed by the Recording Industry Association of America, and Napster was out of business in 2001.

Around the same time, Apple computers offered digital audio files that could be played on a small player called the iPod. They also introduced a network that allowed the sale of copyrighted music at reasonable prices. The iPod freed audiences from passive roles and allowed them to create their own playlists and even send their own podcasts back into the system. It was an instant hit.

As people began using iPods and other MP3 players more and more, radio audiences started shrinking, cutting revenue for both traditional radio stations and satellite broadcasters. In the US between 2008 and 2009, the percentage of people who spend less time with radio because of their iPods has increased from 37 percent to 42 percent and will probably keep rising.

Since nearly two-thirds of radio audiences are listening in their cars on any given day, the introduction of iPods or other programmable digital audio technology as standard in cars is having a major impact on radio audience size.

Other mobile devices, such as cell phones, are also allowing consumers to receive both live "streaming" and stored audio files in their cars and cell phones, wherever they go. These developments probably spell the end of the traditional radio broadcasting station. The people formerly known as the "audience" will now have the technology to easily pick and choose their own music playlists and talk programs without the intervening broadcast medium. Once again, a circumventing technology was used to undermine a monopoly.

The future of radio

From its earliest days, predictions about the future of radio involved many ideas that today seem impractical or even absurd. Some predicted that radio would help speed up crops growing in fields with a kind of fertilizing effect. Others predicted that radio microwaves could be used to send electric power over long distances without wires, an idea that is possible in theory but extremely dangerous in practice.

Over a century after the birth of radio, it turns out that its enduring value is its ability to accompany people as they do other things, such as walking, driving and working, in situations where video would be too distracting.

To the extent that music and talk programs are now available through new wireless technologies, the connection between telephones, cars and home computers will allow people to program a wide variety of music, news or educational experiences before or during these activities.

And so, one frequently made prediction for radio is coming true. The future of radio, Guglielmo Marconi said in 1928, involved its ability to avoid the expense of cable wiring. "The value of the cables has been very great," said the man who helped create wireless, "but I would hesitate to express an opinion about their future" (*The New York Times*, February 25, 1928).

9 Television: a new window on the world

> *If there are any historians about 50 or 100 years from now . . . they will find recorded in black and white, or color, evidence of decadence, escapism and insulation from the realities of the world in which we live . . . This instrument can teach, it can illuminate; yes, and it can even inspire. But it can do so only to the extent that humans are determined to use it to those ends. Otherwise it is merely wires and lights in a box. There is a great and perhaps decisive battle to be fought against ignorance, intolerance and indifference. This weapon of television could be useful. (Edward R. Murrow, 1958)*

Television embodied the dream

As the central source of information and entertainment since the 1950s, television has reflected and shaped the hopes and fears of the age.

From its crude beginnings in the 1920s, television electronics rapidly improved with color, high definition, cable and satellite delivery systems in the late twentieth century. Through this electronic cornucopia came stories of conflict and reconciliation, reports of war and peace, parades of comically low-brow stuff, and, occasionally, works of genius.

Television embodied the dream of universal international communication more than its electronic predecessors. And yet when these dreams did come true, it exposed and compounded the clash of cultures as much as it contributed to peace and understanding.

In 1954, the United States had only three television channels (NBC, CBS and ABC) and Britain had two (BBC and commercial ITV). The range of programming and possibilities for television seemed limited. Nevertheless, the American radio industry threw everything it had into television, from talent to engineering, while the British held back, and retained radio as a medium for news and entertainment well into the twenty-first century.

But as the television medium crossed the millennia mark, longstanding trends undermined its once central position in the political world, while new digital technologies fragmented its channels, empowering its audiences—and its critics.

Early concepts of television

Advances in telegraphic and radio technology in the late nineteenth century led visionaries to imagine that, like electricity, light itself would soon be sent through wires. The "telephonograph" was just around the corner, and French artist Albert Robida, among others, imagined flat screen televisions that would soon be entertaining Parisians in their living rooms.

In 1898, British science fiction writer H. G. Wells wrote about a man waking up 200 years in the future and being introduced to new technology. "There is an optical contrivance we shall use . . . It may be novel to you. You stand in a very bright light, and they see not you but a magnified image of you thrown on a screen—so that even the furtherest man in the remotest gallery can, if he chooses, count your eyelashes" (Wells, 1898).

Even in 1925, with television on the threshold of feasibility, futurists were trying to imagine life with television. A British college professor A. M. Low drew this scenario in *The New York Times*: "At breakfast, which may come up by tube from a communal kitchen, a loud speaker will take the place of a morning paper, giving him all the news, while a 'television' machine will replace the daily pictorial newspapers . . . "

Science fiction was not that far ahead of reality, as it turned out. Building on work involving the light-sensitive properties of the element selenium, German inventor Arthur Korn developed a way to scan photographs and send the signal through wires—an early fax machine. A series of demonstrations around Europe in 1907 convinced police departments to use the device to exchange photographs of wanted criminals. "We can now send a not-too-complicated photograph over very long distances in six or seven minutes," Korn said. "The problem of television is not yet solved . . . the great difficulty is the speed required" (*The New York Times*, November 24, 1907).

"Now that the photo-telegraph invented by Prof. Korn is on the eve of being introduced into general practice," said *Scientific American*, "we are informed of some similar inventions in the same field, all of which tend to achieve some step toward the solution of the problem of television" (*Scientific American*, June 15, 1907).

The principles Korn developed would be tried in a dozen different ways before a gifted Idaho high school student named Philo Farnsworth conceived of a television system using an electronic scanning principle that lit up phosphorous on the back of a glass screen. Farnsworth demonstrated the television in 1928, but found he was in competition with Westinghouse engineer Vladimir Zworykin. A patent fight between RCA, Westinghouse and Farnsworth was eventually decided in Farnsworth's favor, but he is sometimes seen as

Figure 9.1 Future television—Albert Robida, a French artist, imagined the future of television in the 1880s with this sketch of Parisians watching a battle in the desert.

Figure 9.2 Inventor of TV—Philo T. Farnsworth (right) is seen directing a television production around 1928. (Photo courtesy University of Utah)

the last of the lone inventors in the mold of Thomas Edison. Invention now was becoming a group effort and a company product, especially in electronics.

Originally, Zworykin estimated that it would cost $100,000 over a year and a half to develop commercial television. Ten years later, after an engineering team spent $50 million, Sarnoff announced the "birth of television" at the World's Fair in New York on April 20, 1939:

> Now we add radio sight to sound . . . [Television is] a new art so important in its implications that it is bound to affect all society. It is an art which shines like a torch of hope in a troubled world. It is a creative force which we must learn to utilize for the benefit of all mankind. (Sarnoff, 1968)

Zworykin's RCA team developed four models that were first put on sale at the fair. Westinghouse, General Electric and other manufacturers also had competing versions, but prices were high—about the equivalent of a new car. Few of these television sets sold, and marketing plans had to be put on hold with the outbreak of World War II. Newspapers, radio and newsreels would inform the public during the war, but television audiences had to wait for the duration.

The transition from radio to television was not an easy one. The earliest programs simply radioed a view of an announcer or live theatrical productions staged for the camera. News was particularly difficult. "The notion that a picture was worth a thousand words meant, in practice, that footage of Atlantic City beauty winners, shot at some expense, was consid-

Figure 9.3 Torch of hope—David Sarnoff announces the birth of television at the World's Fair in New York, April 20, 1939, calling it a "torch of hope in a troubled world." (Library of Congress, LC-USZ62–91145)

ered more valuable than a thousand words . . . on the mounting tensions in Southeast Asia," said historian Eric Barnouw (Barnouw, 1970). Television news broadcasters also had to cope with network expectations of high profits to cover the costs of developing television technology.

FCC and the structure of post-World War II television

At war's end, the question of how to deal with controversial issues in the content of broadcasting was revived. The FCC's Mayflower decision of 1941 banned radio broadcasters from taking sides in controversies (see Chapter 8). Radio was seen as a neutral forum for the views of others, not a vehicle for the owners' political viewpoints. This changed somewhat as the war ended. One influence was the 1947 report from the privately funded Hutchins Commission. The report said that the underlying theory of media regulation should involve the duty of social responsibility in general. Especially important was the broadest possible access to information with fair representations of minorities. (Also see Chapter 3.)

Following this reasoning, the FCC reversed the Mayflower decision in 1949, allowing TV and radio broadcasters to take sides on issues so long as they also gave audiences a balanced presentation from all sides. This "Fairness Doctrine" became, until the mid-1980s, the guiding philosophy for rationing the publicly owned broadcast frequencies. The Fairness Doctrine was upheld by the courts through the years, for example in the 1969 *Red Lion Broadcasting v. FCC* case, but fairness proved difficult to enforce in the 1970s as contentious new issues emerged. Particularly difficult were demands by environmentalists to secure equal access to the airwaves and counter advertising claims of the oil and automotive companies.

The FCC also disagreed with the Hutchins commission recommendations in another area—how to deal with the scarcity of broadcast frequencies for television. The Hutchins commission recommended that more stations be licensed to prevent

Figure 9.4 First Lady's first show—former First Lady Eleanor Roosevelt hosted a weekly forum in the early years of television. Shown here on February 11, 1950, discussing "what to do with the hydrogen bomb" were, left to right: Senator Brien McMahon, Hans A. Bethe, Mrs. Roosevelt, David E. Lilienthal and J. Robert Oppenheimer. (Photograph by Leonard McCombe, Library of Congress)

the concentration of ownership. Instead, the FCC took the opposite approach in the 1940s and 50s, continuing a policy from the 1920s that constrained the number of broadcasters with the idea of producing higher quality content. Critics countered that the strategy had not worked with radio and probably would not work with television (Hilmes, 2006).

As prosperity increased in the postwar years, television programming and home television set sales boomed. By 1948, the United States had 108 television stations under construction or on the air, and most were affiliated with the big three networks or a few independent startups like the DuMont network. At this time, the FCC froze television station licensing in order to reexamine the technology. Yet at the same time, manufacturers kept churning out television sets that were not compatible with possible new higher quality technologies.

By 1952, one-third of all homes, or about 15 million, had television sets. Color television technology could have come online at this point, but the problem of "backward compatibility" meant that existing television sets would have to be considered. The technical problem, although somewhat arcane today, meant that the FCC had to choose between two rival systems—one advanced by NBC and the other advanced by CBS. The NBC system, with lower quality but high-powered lobbying, eventually gained the upper hand.

Confrontation on television: Murrow and McCarthy

The most important global political development of the post-World War II era was the start of the "cold war" between Western democracies and communist China and Russia. While communist leaders embraced a totalitarian ideology that suppressed freedom of speech, the Western democracies, including the United States, France, Britain and the Commonwealth nations, were determined to preserve individual human rights and free market economies.

Communism had an appeal to liberal-minded reformers in the 1920s and 30s, before its dark side was appreciated, but it was not particularly popular in the United States. Even so, the reaction to the communist military threat grew into a media-fueled national witch-hunt in the postwar years. One of the first of episodes was the 1947 investigation of communist influence in Hollywood movies by the House Un-American Activities Committee, as we have seen in Chapter 5. While no actual communist conspiracy was found, the political atmosphere had become highly charged with partisanship.

Amid growing tension, a relatively unknown US Senator named Joseph McCarthy (R-WI) catapulted to national fame in February 1950 when he claimed to have a list of communist spies operating in the US State Department. The reckless accusations were widely repeated in the media, but a Senate investigation led by Democrats that year labeled McCarthy's charges a "fraud and a hoax." The committee said that McCarthy's charges did nothing but "confuse and divide the American people [...] to a degree far beyond the hopes of the communists themselves." Republicans backed McCarthy and responded to the committee report with accusations of treason.

Radio and print media exposure fueled McCarthy's continued accusations during the early 1950s. Specific accusations were usually made from the safety of the Senate floor. But two major instances of television exposure dramatically changed public opinion about the corpulent, beetle-browed senator, in part because few had ever seen McCarthy up close or heard his arguments for more than a few minutes at time.

Figure 9.5 Seeing it now—Wisconsin Senator Joseph McCarthy speaks in front of a CBS camera in 1953. (Library of Congress)

McCarthy's first major television exposure involved 32 days of Senate hearings concerning charges that McCarthy had used his influence to obtain favors for friends in the Army. During April 1954, ABC television carried the hearings live from the US Senate, and many previous charges by McCarthy about spies in the Pentagon were exposed as fabrications that damaged innocent individuals. The high point of the hearings was the moment when the legal counsel for the US Army responded to a McCarthy charge by saying: "You've done enough. Have you no sense of decency, sir, at long last? Have you left no sense of decency?"

The second instance of extended television exposure was a classic confrontation between a journalist and a politician. CBS news broadcaster Edward R. Murrow, famed for his radio reports from London during World War II, had made the transition to television with a program called "See it Now." In one episode of "See it Now," Murrow told the story of a young Air Force officer named Milo Radulovich who had been classified as a security risk simply because his sister and father read a Serbian-language newspaper. In another, Murrow focused on McCarthy himself and the lack of substance behind most of his allegations.

Murrow concluded:

> We must not confuse dissent with disloyalty. We must remember always that accusation is not proof and that conviction depends upon evidence and due process of law. We will not walk in fear, one of another. We will not be driven by fear into an age of unreason, if we dig deep in our history and our doctrine, and remember that we are not descended from fearful men.

McCarthy demanded equal time, and Murrow was happy to oblige, turning over the entire half-hour program. McCarthy directly attacked Murrow for friendships with left-of-center figures and supposed ties to communist groups. With no evidence and astonishing bluster, McCarthy succeeded only in exposing himself as a political bully. Conservatives with genuine concerns about communism began to see him as a liability,

Figure 9.6 Murrow responds—CBS News editor Edward R. Murrow responded to Sen. Joseph McCarthy's reckless charges by urging Americans not be driven into an age of unreason. (Library of Congress)

and in December, 1954, the US Senate passed a motion to censure Sen. McCarthy. He died in 1957, abandoned by his party and his supporters.

Murrow, hailed as a champion of free speech, also came to be regarded as a liability by CBS network executives. News stories about cigarettes and lung cancer, about segregation and schools, about apartheid in South Africa were controversial. Some entertainment-oriented higher-ups thought Murrow was trying to "save the world every week" (Friendly, 1967).

In 1956, "See it Now" lost its sole sponsor (Alcoa Aluminum) and was transformed into an irregularly scheduled documentary series. By 1958 the program had been taken off the air. Simple controversy was one problem, but another factor was the profitability of easily produced quiz and game shows on other networks in adjacent time slots. "It was as though an highly successful amusement park had gone up across the street from a school, said CBS producer Fred Friendly. "Suddenly the property values had changed" (Friendly, 1967).

Murrow went on to work in the Kennedy administration as head of the US Information Agency. When he died in 1965, a colleague said "We shall live in his afterglow a very long time . . . we shall not see his like again" (Emery 1997).

Sputnik builds bridges among world "archipelagos"

The news on October 6, 1957 that Russia (the former Soviet Union) had launched a satellite around the world came as a shock to the United States and Western

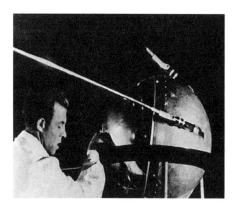

Figure 9.7 Sputnik crisis—a Russian technician prepares the Sputnik satellite for launch in 1957. The launch was a wake-up call for US science. It led to the space race, promoted international telecommunications and inspired the defense computer networks that formed the technical foundation of the internet. (National Aeronautics and Space Administration photo)

Europe, long accustomed to seeing themselves in the vanguard of science. The feat was hailed as a triumph of the communist system but denounced in the Western press as "political rather than scientific" (*Washington Post*, October 10, 1957).

The "Sputnik crisis," as it was called, revealed cutbacks in scientific research programs and gaping deficiencies in American scientific education. The reaction to the crisis in the late 1950s and 60s led to a chain of events and initiatives that had a profound international impact. Among the best known initiative was President John F. Kennedy's goal of sending astronauts to the moon by 1970. Others included the creation of the National Aeronautics and Space Agency (NASA) in 1958, new federal funding for science education, and new investments in computer hardware, software and networks that would, in time, form the basis of the internet (see Chapter 11).

The most visible side of the US space program was the competition with the Russians to put astronauts in orbit around the earth (the Russians were first with the spaceflight of Yuri Gagarin on April 12, 1961) and to land on the moon (which the United States accomplished in July, 1969). Also fairly visible were non-defense satellite projects such as the 1958 SCORE satellite and the Telstar communications satellite, launched in 1962 as a cooperative venture between the United States, Britain and France.

The first geostationary satellite was launched in 1964 and was used to send television broadcasts to the United States from the Summer Olympics held that year in Japan. The advantage of geostationary satellites, as first conceived by British science fiction writer and mathematician Arthur C. Clark in 1945, was that they were ideal telecommunications relays. Rather than pushing a signal through thousands of miles of wire, a broadcast signal could be sent through a dozen miles of atmosphere, and then through space without interference.

An important milestone was the 1964 formation of the International Telecommunications Satellite Consortium (INTELSAT), an international satellite organization with 143 member countries.

By the 1970s, satellites were being routinely launched to help broadcast unions and networks around the world uplink and downlink programs to affiliates. These allowed consumer television offerings to expand in the United States with Cable News Network, the Weather Channel and Home Box Office, and also allowed regional broadcasters to exchange programs at far lower cost than ever before.

These satellites allowed the exchange of broadcast information from all over the world for the first time. They also had an important secondary effect in that they required international cooperation in all kinds of standard formats for information interchange through United Nations groups (such as the International Telecommunications Union and the International Standards Organization). Some of these standards, such as those for photos and motion pictures, had an important influence on computer networks that are well known today. These included picture files called JPEGs (from the Joint Photographic Experts Group) and audio and video files called MPEGs (from the Motion Picture Experts Group).

"Young people today find it difficult to imagine how far we were . . . from the global view that now seems so familiar," said Raymond Frontard of the International Standards Organization in Geneva, Switzerland. "The earth did not yet shake at the slightest tremor in its most remote region. It was, instead, an archipelago of distinct worlds" (Frontard, 1997).

Television culture: golden age or vast wasteland?

The popular myth is that television of the 1950s and early 1960s reflected a golden age of a prosperous and contented time in American life. Yet the same complaints once vented about radio were heard once again, with more force, about television.

These included the lack of quality, overcommercialization of the public airwaves, under-representation of minorities and the unwillingness of the networks to sacrifice any profits for public interest programming in return for their use of a public resource.

An early platform for television critics involved hearings by Sen. Estes Kefauver (D-TN) on juvenile delinquency, starting around 1955. A host of witnesses testified about the many negative social influences on young people, including comic books, movies and violence on television. Network executives defended themselves by pointing to the National Association of Broadcasters Code of Conduct, most of which had to do with avoiding controversy over moral issues. The code also limited commercials to 6 to 10 minutes per hour at night and 10 to 14 minutes per day, but these limits were not always observed, especially among segments of the television industry that were less profitable.

Controversy continued over the effects of having single sponsors for television programs, one prime example being the impact on CBS News when Alcoa dropped its sponsorship of "See It Now." Eventually, the networks stopped the decades-old practice of having one sponsor per program and sold advertising by the time slot rather than on a single program basis.

Quiz show scandals

The most serious crisis for network television in the 1950s came with the quiz show scandals. In a 1959 Congressional investigation, witnesses testified that the shows had been fully scripted and that contestants had been coached to give right or wrong answers. Americans were shocked. Even President Dwight Eisenhower said it was "a terrible thing to do to the American public."

One of the contestants, Charles Van Doren, confessed to the Congressional committee: "I was involved, deeply involved, in deception . . . I realize that I was really giving a wrong impression of education. True education does not mean the knowledge of facts exclusively. I wrote articles trying to express this feeling but few were interested. Instead, I was referred to as a 'quiz-whiz, a human book of knowledge, a walking encyclopedia'" (*The New York Times*, November 3, 1959).

Figure 9.8 Quiz scandal—quiz show "21" host Jack Barry turns toward contestant Charles Van Doren in 1957 as fellow contestant Vivienne Nearine looks on. Two years later, Van Doren would confess to a Congressional Committee that he was "deeply involved in deception." (Photo by Orlando Fernandez, Library of Congress)

No federal laws had been broken by the deception, although that soon changed as the FCC wrote new regulations to enforce a more honest approach in such shows. But it was also the abundance of cheap, easy to produce, yet highly profitable quiz and game shows that bothered media critics.

Vast wasteland

Most of what television presented to the public over the first few decades of its life was not memorable or even significant for its time. An endless parade of trivial entertainment was enough to capture eyeballs and boost network profits. But there were notable exceptions.

Perhaps the most popular entertainment program of the age was *I Love Lucy*, a situation comedy that concerned Hispanic band leader Desi Arnaz and his ditzy but loveable wife Lucille Ball. The show's themes often verged into controversial areas, such as alcohol content in medicine (which made Lucy drunk when she filmed a commercial) or sweatshop labor (in a scene where she couldn't keep up with the conveyor belt, much like a similar scene in Charlie Chaplin's *Modern Times*). Other comedies of the time, such as *Gilligan's Island* and *Donna Reed*, reflected white American values but not much in the way of substance.

Westerns were popular venues for social commentary, and shows like *Bonanza* and *Gunsmoke* (which evolved from a radio series) frequently involved themes of justice and the treatment of minorities and women. Still, violence was the usual solution for problems and minorities were badly stereotyped. While mild controversy was tolerated and sometimes even celebrated, real social issues and serious change were rarely considered until the 1970s, when programs like Archie Bunker and MASH went on the air.

The idea of television as a "vast wasteland" came up in a speech by a newly appointed FCC commissioner Newton Minow as he addressed an audience of the National Association of Broadcasters on May 9, 1961. The phrase became a cliché for television critics who advocated more public interest programming. Minow said:

> "When television is good, nothing—not the theater, not the magazines or newspapers—nothing is better. But when television is bad, nothing is worse. I invite each of you to sit down in front of your own television set when your station goes on the air and stay there, for a day . . . until the station signs off. I can assure you that what you will observe is a vast wasteland. You will see a procession of game shows, formula comedies about totally unbelievable families, blood and thunder, mayhem, violence, sadism, murder, western bad men, western good men, private eyes, gangsters, more violence, and cartoons. And endlessly commercials—many screaming, cajoling, and offending. And most of all, boredom."

Television executives worried about the speech, saying that while there was always room for improvement, having the chair of the FCC as their chief critic was uncomfortably close to government censorship. "At what point does criticism become coercion?" asked NBC president Robert Sarnoff in 1961. "Where does freedom leave off and interference begin?" (*The New York Times*, December 8, 1961, p. 1). Despite the protests, broadcast journalism as a public service expanded greatly by 1962, with over 400 documentaries produced that year by the three networks (Hilmes, 2006). By 1963, the 15-minute evening news programs had expanded to half an hour.

Minow was happy but not entirely satisfied with the scope of the improvements in public service programming. However, the only tools the FCC had were license revocations (extremely rare) and the ability to encouraging competition. One way to boost competition was to expand the available channels to UHF, and under Minow, the FCC passed a regulation that new television sets would have to be capable of picking up the higher-frequency channels. Many of these independent television stations would, by the 1970s, be linked together in satellite and cable television systems that Minow also championed.

Another form of competition was the introduction of a public education channel. The Corporation for Public Broadcasting was first authorized in 1967, and PBS went on the air in 1970.

Television and the US presidency

Television was not taken too seriously in its early days, and advertising for the 1952 Eisenhower presidential campaign featured a cartoon of Uncle Sam and an elephant leading a brass band in a parade with a catchy musical jingle. His opponent, Adlai Stevenson, took a dim view of campaign ads on television. "The idea that you can merchandise candidates for high office like breakfast cereal is the ultimate indignity to the democratic process," he said. He had the same idea in 1956, when he ran, and lost, again.

Television became a serious factor in the 1952 campaign when vice-presidential candidate Richard Nixon was accused of taking $16,000 in bribes for campaign expenses. Eisenhower was just on the verge of replacing Nixon, six weeks before the election, when, on the advice of aides, Nixon bought a half hour of prime time TV.

From the well-lit set of a Los Angeles theater, Nixon explained that the fund was legal and intended for campaign expenses. He also spent time explaining his personal finances and work-ethic background and praising Eisenhower. The speech was remembered because, to clinch public support, Nixon said that he had only taken one gift—a cocker spaniel dog named Checkers that had been sent to his children. Most Americans were impressed by the sentiment of the speech. Public opinion over-whelmingly shifted to Nixon, but the huge wave of support was, to Walter Lippmann, "disturbing . . . with all the magnification of modern electronics, simply mob law" (Morris, 1990).

After a few years in office, Eisenhower opened the doors to television cameras at press conferences. The print and radio media were not happy, because the presence of television tended to formalize meetings that had been relatively informal until then. The new realities of television also meant that important political announcements had to be made by 2.00 p.m. eastern standard time in order to be reported on the evening news. "After Eisenhower, television was no longer a novelty, but a central premise in all political logic," said Roderick P. Hart (Hart and Triece, 2010).

Although he was one of the first politicians to effectively use television with his "Checkers speech," Nixon performed poorly during television debates with John F. Kennedy during the presidential campaign of 1960. It was the first time that candidates of the two major parties faced each other on TV, and the contrast between Kennedy's calm demeanor and Nixon's apparent unease on camera was apparent. The series of four nationally televised debates moderated by members of the press would

Figure 9.9 Confrontation in Moscow—then US Vice President Richard Nixon (right) pokes a finger at Russian Soviet Premier Nikita S. Khrushchev in 1959 at a US exhibit in Moscow, Russia depicting the average American home with a stove, washing machine, radio and other appliances. With television cameras rolling, Khrushchev said he didn't think the average American could afford such a home. Nixon responded: "Diversity, the right to choose, the fact that we have 1,000 builders building 1,000 different homes is the most important thing." (Photo by Thomas J. O'Halloran, Library of Congress)

Figure 9.10 Presidential debate—the first presidential debates on television took place in 1960 between Richard Nixon and John F. Kennedy. The debates were crucial in the election, and most people believed that Nixon did not come across well on television. Nixon avoided debates in the 1968 and 1972 presidential campaigns. (Library of Congress)

not be repeated until 1976, but the presidential debate has become a fixture of presidential races ever since.

The significance of television as the central medium of the post-World War II era came into sharp focus with the assassination of President John F. Kennedy on November 22, 1963. CBS news anchor Walter Cronkite was eating lunch at his desk when a wire editor burst in with the news that Kennedy had been shot in Dallas. Someone must have asked him what he would write, because he yelled: "The hell with writing, just give me the air." When Kennedy's death was confirmed an hour later, Cronkite choked up on the announcement and paused to wipe away tears, quietly expressing the profound sense of grief and shock shared by the nation and the world. People gathered around television sets, finding not only news but also a sense of social cohesion and resilience in the face of catastrophe. "Before that, TV had been a theater and a sports stadium," said CBS producer Don Hewitt. "All of the sudden it became a sort of chapel where Americans went to hold hands with Cronkite. He was everyone's anchor, and everyone's clergyman" (Garvin, 2009). Similar scenes, where people gathered for days around their television sets, would be repeated world-wide in subsequent disasters, such as the September 11, 2001 attacks that destroyed the World Trade Center.

If television could be a chapel, it could also be a political wrestling arena, as President Lyndon Johnson proved with one of the first negative campaign ads aired briefly during the 1964 presidential campaign. It only aired once, but the publicity surrounding the ad brought it to everyone's attention, and it was a factor in President Lyndon Johnson's victory over Barry Goldwater. The ad was targeted at Goldwater's idea of using nuclear weapons in Vietnam. It begins by depicting a young girl picking the petals off a daisy and counting. But when she reaches nine, she looks up in the sky as an ominous male voice counts down to a nuclear explosion. Johnson's voice says: "These are the stakes! To make a world in which all of God's children can live, or to go into the dark. We must either love each other, or we must die." Another voice then says: "Vote for President Johnson on November 3. The stakes are too high for you to stay home."

A similar ad attacking Democratic candidate Hubert Humphrey in 1968 had positive images and bandwagon music dissolving into headache-inducing reverb effects and photos of riots and the Vietnam War. Attack ads in other campaigns included the infamous "Willie Horton" ad of the 1988 campaign, in which Democratic candidate Michael Dukakis was attacked for being the governor in a state where a convicted murderer got out on parole; and the "swift boat" ads that attacked the military record of presidential candidate John Kerry in the 2004 campaign.

Overall spending on political campaign TV advertising reached an estimated $2.5 billion in 2008, up significantly from $1.6 billion in 2004 and about $800 million in 2000. Television advertising consumes about 80 percent of overall campaign resources and has become the dominant factor in political campaigns.

Vietnam—the first living room war

The impact of television on public opinion during the Vietnam War remained a contentious issue well into the twenty-first century. The traditional myth was that the "living room war" proved too horrible for sensitive Americans and had a morale-sapping effect. Then-president Richard Nixon said: "Our worst enemy seems to be the press" (Hammond, 2007). "Public support for U.S. involvement in Vietnam declined drastically once the television networks began suggesting that the war was a stalemate" said media critic Stephen J. Farnsworth (Farnsworth and Lichter, 2007).

The idea that the press "lost the war" through its negative coverage has an eerie similarity to the Dolchstoss "stab-in-the-back" myth that Germans used to explain their defeat in World War I. "The entire vernacular of American politics has been altered" by the use of the Dolchstoss myth about Vietnam, observed Kevin Baker in 2006 (Baker, 2006; Lembcke, 1998).

Closer studies of television and public opinion in the Vietnam era show a far more complex picture, and the steady drop in public support for the war seems unrelated to any one set of events or images, but rather, to highly public national debates about its overall purposes and conduct which were carried in the media as a matter of course.

One controversial incident involved a 1965 report about the burning of the small village of Cam Ne. CBS news correspondent Morley Safer watched as American soldiers burned thatched-roof huts while elderly Vietnamese stood by helplessly. "This is what the war in Vietnam is all about," Safer said to the camera, as a soldier set an old man's roof on fire in the background. "The marines are burning this old couple's home because [gun] fire was coming from here. The day's operation burned down 150 houses, wounded three women, killed one baby, and netted four prisoners." The incident sparked immediate public controversy and an outraged phone call to CBS president Frank Stanton from then-President Lyndon Johnson, indicating the important role that television images had taken on in the national debate over the war.

Other dramatic television and photographic images from the war included a napalm attack on a village that resulted in injuries to children and the street execution of a suspected Viet Cong insurgent. Television news tended not to broadcast more serious images of the US massacres, such as My Lai, and tended to support the US position on the extent of Viet Cong atrocities such as the Hue massacres of 1968.

Historians Daniel Hallin and William Hammond reviewed years of television coverage of the war and found that most television news was upbeat in the early years. The occasional negative report, although inevitable in war coverage, was greatly outweighed by the sympathetic light in which American soldiers were invariably seen (Hallin, 1986).

Hammond, a military historian, challenged assertions that the media lost the war by swaying public opinion. In an encyclopedic set of books, Hammond said the media tended to follow rather than lead public opinion. While government and the press shared a common vision of containing communism in the early years of the war, upbeat government press releases were challenged by journalists' experiences in the field. As public sentiment shifted, Presidents Lyndon Johnson and Richard Nixon each tried unsuccessfully to manage the news media to project an image of success even though the military and strategic picture was discouraging.

One turning point in the war was the 1968 in-depth report from experienced World War II correspondent Walter Cronkite, then anchor of CBS news. While nuanced and respectful, Cronkite concluded that the military was not winning or losing the war, but rather the "bloody experience of Vietnam is to end in a stalemate." Johnson took Cronkite's disaffection with the war so seriously that he told advisor Bill Moyers that if he'd lost Cronkite, he'd lost middle America (Halberstam, 1979; Murray, 1999). Was this a factor in Johnson's decision not to run in the 1968 election?

Figure 9.11 Bowing out—President Lyndon Johnson makes a surprise announcement that he will not run again for president in 1968. The impact of the televised Vietnam War was a factor. (Courtesy Lyndon B. Johnson Presidential Library)

Some historians say the influence of television was exaggerated, and Johnson had other things on his mind (Campbell, 2010).

Civil rights and television

Television was the medium that the civil rights movement needed to get its message to the American people. Although gruesome photographs of Southern brutality had been widely circulated, nothing caught the conscience of the world like the televised images of snarling police dogs turned on demonstrating children in Birmingham, AL, or the cruel clubbing of civil rights demonstrators amid clouds of tear gas at the foot of the Edmund Pettus bridge in Montgomery, AL on March 7, 1965. Meanwhile, churches, homes and shops with ties to the civil rights movement were being bombed, and television carried the stories.

At a time when American soldiers were fighting communism in Vietnam, the images of embattled civil rights demonstrators were deeply embarrassing for the administration of President Lyndon Johnson. A renewed commitment to civil rights, and national legislation stiffening laws against voter intimidation, were among the direct results of the new awareness brought about by television.

"The ascendancy of television as the new arbiter of public opinion became increasingly apparent at this time to civil rights leaders and television news directors alike," according to the Museum of Broadcast Communications. Yet the television audiences in the South closest to events of the civil rights era were often kept in the dark. Many southern TV stations routinely cut national network feeds of civil rights coverage, often pretending that they were having technical difficulties. Newspapers were also neutral or quite often hostile to civil rights in the 1950s and 60s, and usually omitted wire service coverage of civil rights issues unless there was a white "backlash" angle. (Important exceptions included the *Atlanta Constitution* or the Greenville, MS, *Delta Democrat-Times*).

While newspaper publishers were free to do as they pleased under the First Amendment, broadcasters had an obligation to fairness under Fairness Doctrine, and their station licenses were controlled by the federal government. Broadcasting offered more opportunity to force change than the print media.

The WLBT–United Church of Christ case

Beginning in 1954, a group of civil rights activists began studying the pattern of racially biased news and public affairs programming on television in the South. The Jackson, Mississippi chapter of the NAACP filed repeated complaints with the FCC about one particularly racist television station, WLBT in Jackson. Requests for a public hearing when the station license came up over the years were consistently turned down by the FCC.

In May, 1963, the pressure led WLBT to make one small concession. The station allowed a charismatic civil rights leader, Medgar Evers, on the air to speak about the need to end segregation. Three weeks later he was assassinated at his home in Jackson.

Around this same time, the United Church of Christ, a liberal national church from the Congregational tradition, met with Martin Luther King, Andrew Young and others to work on methods for challenging the southern broadcast media. Dr Everett Parker, a professor at Yale Divinity School, became involved because he had developed a method of content analysis that would hold up under the FCC review process.

"I really looked at stations throughout the (region), from New Orleans to the East Coast, and found that it was a very bad situation," he said in a 2008 interview. "When Thurgood Marshall won Brown v. Board of Education and was on NBC, [WLBT] put up a sign—'Sorry, cable trouble'—and blamed it on the telephone company. But anyway, I hit on WLBT, simply because of the terrible things that it was doing" (Goodman, 2008). WLBT also blacked out an award-winning three-hour NBC documentary on civil rights, "The American Revolution 1963."

When WLBT applied for what it thought would be a routine renewal of its broadcasting license in 1964, the church and a coalition of Civil Rights leaders formally challenged the license. They charged that the station blacked out nationally produced civil rights news about nearby events; had promoted race-hating points of view without balance or regard for the Fairness Doctrine; and refused to feature African American speakers in any context, even on Sunday morning church service broadcasts.

The WLBT response was typical for stations whose licenses were challenged: It ginned up a list of all its public service activities from its log books, including service to the African American community. Usually complaints would stop at this point, and in effect be buried in red tape. But the coalition had an ace up its sleeve—it responded that the

Figure 9.12 Television and civil rights—the impact of television on the civil rights movement was profound, not only from the standpoint of live coverage of the 1963 "I have a dream" speech by Rev. Martin Luther King at this March on Washington, but also in terms of conveying the suffering and brutality of white Southern resistance. The civil rights movement also changed television, at least to the extent that reformers who challenged television licenses could finally get a hearing before the Federal Communications Commission. (National Archives)

station's log books were highly inaccurate, and presented evidence from Parker's content analysis, which had been kept secret up until that point.

The back story behind the content analysis group is that white faculty members at nearby Millsaps College kept detailed logs and recordings of WLBT's programs. The group met in secret and kept their names confidential; even Parker could not reveal their identities if he were to be captured by the white power structure of Mississippi. "Don't forget, this was almost immediately after the murder of Medgar Evers," Parker once told an interviewer.

In a formal hearing, the FCC denied the United Church of Christ "standing" in the case, meaning that they had no formal right to come into the agency's legal process and argue their case. Without remarking on the facts of the case, the FCC renewed the WLBT license for one year. Usually, the bureaucratic procedure at this point would be for the station to show evidence that it was mending its ways, but the WLBT management had a deep ideological commitment to segregation and remained defiant (Horwitz, 1997).

The church appealed the decision to a federal court. The UCC attorneys did not really expect to win both the case and the much larger battle over FCC's regulatory procedure. Yet in 1966, the appeals court ruled that the FCC would conduct public hearings on the license and that the citizens would have standing before the FCC. The court decision, written by Judge Warren Burger (who would later become the Chief Justice of the US Supreme Court) eloquently restated the longstanding tradition of broadcast regulation:

> "A broadcaster is not a public utility . . . but neither is it a purely private enterprise like a newspaper or an automobile agency. A broadcaster has much in common with a newspaper publisher, but he is not in the same category in terms of public obligations imposed by law. A broadcaster seeks and is granted the free and exclusive use of a limited and valuable part of the public domain; when he accepts that franchise it is burdened by enforceable public obligations. A newspaper can be operated at the whim or caprice of its owners; a broadcast station cannot. After nearly five decades of operation the broadcast industry does not seem to have grasped the simple fact that a broadcast license is a public trust subject to termination for breach of duty . . .
>
> Under our system, the interests of the public are dominant. The commercial needs of licensed broadcasters and advertisers must be integrated into those of the public. Hence, individual citizens and the communities they compose owe a duty to themselves and their peers to take an active interest in the scope and quality of the television service which stations and networks provide and which, undoubtedly, has a vast impact on their lives and the lives of their children . . . The 1964 renewal application (for WLBT) might well have been routinely granted except for the determined and sustained efforts of Appellants (the civil rights church coalition) at no small expense to themselves. Such beneficial contribution as these Appellants, or some of them, can make must not be left to the grace of the (Federal Communications) Commission." (*United Church of Christ v. FCC*, 1966)

The public hearing ordered by the court took place in May, 1967, in a small room in the Jackson, Mississippi Post Office, because state officials refused access to other public buildings. The room was overflowing with WLBT supporters waving Confederate flags, and the FCC hearing examiner treated the church coalition with obvious contempt.

In the face of this official prejudice, Charles Evers testified that WLBT had created the atmosphere that led to the assassination of his brother Medgar four years beforehand (Horwitz, 1997). After considering the evidence from the hearing, the FCC commissioners renewed WLBT's license in a bitterly split 1968 decision. But the decision made the Court of Appeals furious, and in a 1969 ruling, the higher court said the FCC's conduct was "beyond repair."

In an unprecedented move, the Court of Appeals ordered the FCC to vacate WLBT's license and hold hearings to consider new applicants. The coalition organized an integrated group, Communications Improvement Inc., and proposed a unique arrangement, splitting station profits between public broadcasting in Mississippi and Tougaloo College in order to teach communications to African American students. Communications Improvement Inc. got the license, although the continuing legal battles would not be resolved until 1983.

The success of this one case in which a license was revoked for public interest reasons did not lead to long-lived reform, said communications scholar Robert B. Horwitz. "The really sobering thought is that the old broadcast reform coalition has clearly collapsed, and a new . . . conservative movement . . . seeks to limit standing, curtail the ability of citizens to bring legal actions and diminish public intervention in general." It has become increasingly difficult to approach reform with a non-market theory of public interest, he said (Horwitz, 1997).

Although television's powerful images of the civil rights struggle helped Americans understand its human dimensions, TV coverage of rioting following the assassination of Martin Luther King in 1968, and of other riots in Watts, Detroit and Washington, D.C. in the 1960s "provoked a reaction by the end of the decade, marked by the presidential campaign slogans calling for law and order," said the Museum of Broadcast Communications. "Consequently, many of the very images that supported the movement simultaneously helped to fuel the national backlash against it" (MBC, 2010).

Television stars join activists

In the wake of the Medgar Evers assassination and the controversy over racism at television station WLBT, students at Tougaloo College began a letter writing campaign to ask performers visiting Jackson, Mississippi to cancel their appearances in protest of segregated music halls and fairgrounds. Many did, including Original Hootenanny USA, trumpet player Al Hirt, and piano player Gary Graffman.

The cast of *Bonanza*—Lorne Greene (Ben Cartwright), Michael Landon (Little Joe) and Dan Blocker (Hoss)—also agreed with the students and canceled a contracted appearance at the county fair in January, 1964. Blocker even sent a telegram to the Jackson *Daily News* explaining that he was disgusted with residents of the town. In response, Jackson's two daily newspapers started a "black out Bonanza" campaign, but local ratings remained unchanged. "Most white viewers, when pressed to choose between enjoying a favorite television show or upholding the claims of racial segregation, chose the former," said historian Michelle Hilmes (Hilmes, 2006).

Only a few months later, in April, 1964, a *Bonanza* episode featured the story of an opera singer who had been invited to come to Virginia City. When the singer arrives, people realize for the first time that he's an African American, and a variety of prejudiced reactions result. He's also jailed on a mistaken warrant as an escaped slave, and the Cartwrights have to help straighten out the problem.

"The importance of appealing to the uncommitted middle in achieving a solution to the racial problem was related in the final scene, when the singer forgets his humiliation and gives his concert," a *New York Times* reviewer said. The show "added to the stature of popular TV entertainment." General Motors, the sponsor of *Bonanza*, was concerned about potential controversy, but NBC executives for once stood firm against the sponsors (*The New York Times*, April 27, 1964).

Many television and film stars joined the civil rights movement in the 1960s, including Harry Belafonte, Tony Bennett, Frankie Laine, Peter, Paul and Mary, Sammy Davis, Jr and Nina Simone. However, few of these had the impact on white southern opinion like the stars of *Bonanza*.

Social responsibility and media reform

Public broadcasting

Forty years after the Federal Radio Commission shoved educational and public broadcasters out of the way to create the RCA/NBC network, an act of Congress created a framework for the Public Broadcasting Service and other educational efforts. It took 40 years for the "broadcast reform movement," as it was called, to finally find a national home on the airwaves.

One major focus for the reform movement was the National Association of Educational Broadcasters (NAEB), which began as an alternative to the NAB in the 1934. Their studies and lobbying led the FCC to reserve radio frequency space for educational channels in the 1940s. Because it was so expensive to lease telephone lines, a "bicycle network" of taped educational radio programs allowed stations to share programs.

When the FCC thawed out the frozen television frequency allocation system in 1952, one innovation was the reservation of 242 channels nationwide for noncommercial education use. New ideas about educational programming also began emerging at various universities at this time, aided by new momentum from the "sputnik crisis" of 1957. The next year, Congress passed the National Defense Education Act to aid direct school-to-home and other instructional TV projects. The act got unexpected support from Southern congressmen who were opposed to school integration and were looking for a way to maintain education outside the public school system.

By the 1960s, networks of regional educational stations were springing up and new federal funding was helped them expand. Innovative programs like Julia Child's *The French Chef* series and Fred Rogers' *Mister Rogers' Neighborhood* made the networks increasingly popular. Also significant was the creation of the Children's Television Workshop in 1968, which produced *Sesame Street* for PBS that first aired in 1970 and other children's programs like *The Electric Company*.

Educational programs from British Broadcasting Corporation (BBC) also padded out the broadcast schedule for public television in the United States. The BBC's educational programs had a dual purpose of both improving broadcasting quality in Britain and strengthening the "open universities," which were the equivalent of American community colleges. Costume dramas that depicted nineteenth-century literary classics, along with television lecture series like Jacob Bronowski's *The Ascent of Man* and James Burke's *Connections* series were funded as supplements to university education.

The major milestone in educational broadcasting, and the culmination of 40 years of the broadcast reform movement, was the 1967 Public Broadcasting Act authorizing federal operating aid to educational stations. But the act was flawed in that it depended on year-to-year funding rather than other more permanent funding mechanisms. (An alternative, suggested by the Ford Foundation, would have been the use of profits from satellite communications to finance educational television.)

Figure 9.13 Big Bird and the First Lady—one legacy of the broadcast reform movement was an increasing emphasis on educational television for children through shows like *Sesame Street*. In this 1993 photo, Big Bird meets Hilary Clinton. (National Archives)

The year-to-year funding was an ongoing political problem for PBS. As early as 1971, President Richard Nixon vetoed a two-year authorization bill, and in 1981, President Ronald Reagan started making drastic cuts in CPB funding, but in 1984, the FCC loosened the rules for public broadcasting, allowing advertising under the name of "enhanced underwriting."

Other controversies included a variety of confrontations over liberal versus conservative social issues in programming. Conservatives objected to a 2004 cartoon called *Postcards from Buster* in which the child has "two mommies." They claimed that PBS documentary producer Bill Moyers was too liberal, pressuring him to resign in 2005. (He did, but returned when PBS invited him back in 2007.)

In the twenty-first century, about half of PBS revenues come from state and federal taxes and another half come from private donations. Some believe that public broadcasting has outlived its usefulness, since it started as an alternative to the three major networks. Others point to a long history of educational and public broadcasting and maintain that commercial television is not capable of consistently producing educational programming.

Television advertising

Tobacco advertising

Television advertising is powerful, more so than radio or print, and the images it presents can be highly influential. When the US Surgeon General issued a report in 1964 summarizing 7,000 studies on the destructive effects of tobacco smoking on health, some of the first recommendations involved warning labels on cigarettes and a ban on television advertising.

The Federal Communications Commission considered that since the topic of smoking was controversial, broadcasters were breaking the Fairness Doctrine when they aired cigarette commercials since they didn't provide air time for opposing viewpoints. Although anti-smoking ads stared appearing on television in the late 1960s, the glamorization of smoking was itself controversial. This included advertising campaigns featuring the "Marlboro Man"—a rugged cowboy depicted in a Western setting smoking a cigarette—and even children's cartoon characters like the Flintstones. Congress passed the Public Health Cigarette Smoking Act, banning cigarette advertising on television on January 2, 1971.

Tobacco companies shifted advertising to magazines and sports events, but new US laws and regulations in 2010 prohibit companies from sponsoring sports, music and other cultural events.

An international treaty banning all tobacco advertising was approved by 168 nations, not including the United States, in 2005. The treaty, called the World Health Organization Framework Convention on Tobacco Control, is seen as a watershed moment for global public health.

Advertising to children

A variety of controversies over television advertising to children emerged in the 1970s and continue to the present. Among them are the sheer volume of advertising; the advertising of unhealthy foods; and the psychological and programming approaches used by advertisers to engage children.

The average child watches about 25,000 TV commercials a year (Holt, 2007) and the rate has risen slightly since the 1970s. Ads for foods with high amounts of sugar and fat are the most troubling to consumer advocates, who have seen a connection to childhood obesity.

Consumer advocates argued that children are trusting and vulnerable, and that advertisers were taking advantage of that innocent frame of mind. In 1974, the FCC issued new guidelines for children's advertising that separated program content from commercial messages and limited the number of commercials. "If our policy against over-commercialization is an important one," the FCC said, "it is particularly important in programs designed for children." The same year the advertising industry put together the Children's Advertising Review Unit (CARU), a voluntary regulation agency that dealt with complaints and made recommendations to advertisers.

Organizations and grass-roots groups concerned about advertising asked the FCC for tightened regulations. But in the 1980s, with the Reagan administration's deregulatory approach, the FCC took the opposite stand and began deregulating all advertising, saying "the market will regulate itself." One of the groups, Action for Children's Television (ACT) petitioned the FCC for a re-hearing about the specific question of children's advertising, presenting evidence that the market had already failed to regulate advertising for children. The FCC refused to reconsider children's advertising, and ACT filed a federal lawsuit.

A federal court examined the issue and found that the FCC had changed the regulations without considering the problem at all, which it found "profoundly wrong." (*ACT v. FCC*, 1987). In 1990, Congress passed the Children's Television Act, noting that market forces alone had not created an adequate amount of children's educational programming and that government action was needed. The act limited ads to 12 minutes per hour on weekdays and 10.5 minutes per hour on weekends, along with limiting program length advertising (shows that depicted a character also being sold as a toy).

Since the 1990 act, media choices exploded, with cable satellite and internet services. But advocates say the amount and quality of educational programming has not really increased (Conley, 2010).

One effect of top-down regulation has been an increase in alternative advertising approaches, such as running contests and events where the advertiser has only a subtle presence. This was "exactly the opposite of what some of the advocacy groups were aiming for," a *New York Times* article noted (Clifford, 2010).

Controversy over television violence and indecency

The question of whether television influences people, especially children, to commit violent acts has been hotly debated for decades. Hundreds of commissions, studies, lobbying groups, and regulations emerged since then, with two major recommendations: better approaches to the way television is produced for young children; and the development of a rating system that parents can use to evaluate programs that may be unsuitable.

The regulatory saga began with the Commission on the Causes and Effects of Violence, started in 1968 by President Johnson. A panel of industry and academic experts studied previous studies and commissioned 23 more social science and psychological studies of the effects of television. The panel's report in 1972 was controversial, as industry struggled against academics to tone down the report's conclusions.

The National Association of Broadcasters code prohibited gratuitous violence or pandering to morbid curiosity, but the public appetite for violent programs brought home a longstanding dilemma: what's in the public interest is often not what the public is interested in.

The gravity of the problem of violence on TV was reinforced with a 2002 report by the American Academy of Child and Adolescent Psychiatry. The report said that violence on TV was not the only cause of violent behavior, but that hundreds of studies had shown that children were becoming numb to the horror of violence;

were gradually accepting violence as a way to solve problems; and were imitating what they saw on TV (AACAP, 2002).

Also in the latter decades of the twentieth century, as indecent talk shows and comedy routines became increasingly popular, the problem of children's exposure to casual indecency on the air remained.

Two approaches were taken to address the problems. First, under the "safe harbor" concept, FCC regulations are intended to keep patently offensive material off the air from 6 a.m. to 10 p.m.

Secondly, the idea of using technology to allow parents to block objectionable programming was written into the Telecommunications Act of 1996. Television receivers sold since 1999 have to have "V-Chip" as part of the circuitry. V-Chips can detect information about a program's rating and block it if parents desire. Yet according to a 2007 FCC survey, only 27 percent of parents could figure out how to program the V-Chip. And in a separate poll that year, only 12 percent of parents were using parental controls such as the V-Chip, and the conservative Parents Television Council called it a failure.

Broadcast deregulation: the end of the media reform era

The big change in broadcasting policy from the 1980s to the twenty-first century was a greater emphasis on marketplace competition and reduced emphasis on social responsibility theory. The milestone was the Telecommunications Act of 1996, which deregulated ownership rules for radio, television and cable companies, leading to a host of mergers and consolidations that concentrated the broadcast industry.

The advent of new technologies like cable and satellite television challenged the original reason for FCC regulations , which was the idea that broadcasting depended on government allocation of the broadcast frequency spectrum—a limited public resource. In other words, now that the resource was not so scarce, the "scarcity rationale" that justified government regulation had been undermined. What this meant was that broadcasters pushed for—and got—a deregulation of the content and the structure of broadcasting.

One casualty of the new market approach was the Fairness Doctrine. Originally created by the FCC to ensure that all sides of controversial issues could be heard, the doctrine was used to assure that anti-smoking advertising balanced tobacco advertising in the 1960s. The doctrine was affirmed by the Supreme Court in cases like *Red Lion Broadcasting v. FCC*, 1969, which involved a station's attack on an individual book author. But the courts did not agree that environmental issues such as leaded gasoline advertising deserved balance from the environmental perspective (*Friends of the Earth v. FCC*, 33 FCC 2nd 648 1972).

By the 1980s, the view of broadcasters as community trustees was replaced by a conservative view of broadcasters as marketplace participants. The courts also noted the complexities of enforcing balance emerged in a case involving the League of Women Voters, and a few years later, the FCC said it would no longer enforce the doctrine.

Calls for a return of the Fairness Doctrine are frequently heard, such as one from environmental lawyer Robert F. Kennedy Jr:

> The airwaves belong to the public. They were public-trust assets, just like our air and water, and broadcasters could be licensed to use them but only with the proviso that they use them to promote the public interest and to advance American democracy . . . Today six giant multinational corporations now control all 14,000 radio stations in our country, almost all 6,000 TV stations, 80 percent of our newspapers, all of our billboards, and now most of the Internet information services. So you have six guys who dictate what Americans have as information and what we see as news. The news departments have become corporate profit centers. They no longer have any obligation to benefit the public interest; their only obligation is to their shareholders. (Kennedy, 2004)

Another casualty of the market-oriented approach was the "News Distortion Rule," which says that as public trustees, broadcast licensees may not intentionally distort the news, and that "rigging or slanting the news is a most heinous act against the public interest." However, in cases where the rule was invoked, the FCC took no action. For example, in 1997, two Florida reporters said their investigation on the dangers of a synthetic growth hormone (BGH) used by dairies was distorted, but complaints to the FCC were not upheld.

New realities in the global village

The larger impact of global satellite communications was highly unsetting to old political systems. One of the most important impacts was, according to many Eastern Europeans, the end of Soviet domination of Eastern Europe and the dismantling of the Berlin Wall.

In a 2002 interview with *Wired* magazine, Lech Walesa said:

> " . . . Rapid development of satellite television and cell phones . . . helped end communism by bringing in information from the outside. It was possible to get news from independent sources; stations like the BBC (British Broadcasting System) and VOA (Voice of America) were beyond government control. During '50s and '60s, the Communist government put people accused of listening to these stations in prison . . . It's hard to believe that things like that actually happened from today's perspective." (Scheeres, 2002)

The possibilities had dawned on many others. Technologies to organize intelligence and communication could be liberating as well as tyrannical. Ithiel de Sola Pool noted this trend in the converging telecommunications industry in *Technologies of Freedom*, and Ray Kurzweil predicted in 1987 that that the Soviet Union "would be swept away by this growth of decentralized communication."

The technological improvements in communication have not always been welcome, nor have they been without controversy. Perhaps the biggest international controversy over communication involved a 1980 report Many Voices, One World, by a Commission on International Communication for United Nations Educational,

Scientific and Cultural Organization (UNESCO) chaired by Nobel Laureate Seán MacBride.

The commission said that the communications revolution had created dangers as well as opportunities. The unequal flow of communication was making developing nations dependent on the cultural products of the industrial West. Centuries-old customs, time-honored cultural practices and simple life styles were being threatened.

The one-way flow of information from industrial nations to developing nations was also a problem, the report said. News about the developing world in North American and Europe was dominated by spot reports on disasters and military coups, but the underlying realities and developments were ignored. One recommendation was for more professional international training for journalists on both sides of the divide between industrial and developing nations. Another recommendation involved protection of journalists and freedom of the press.

Another recommendation was that small nations should foster internal media development, have more control over the cultural processes of modernization and find ways to reduce the commercialization of communication. These recommendations amounted to an international theory of social responsibility for the media—a Hutchins Commission report on a global scale.

But the recommendations, and subsequent proposals for a New World Information and Communication Order were seen as opening the door to increased media regulation by non-democratic nations, and the International Federation of Newspaper Publishers (FIEJ), among others, issued strong denunciations of the NWICO. The US and Britain withdrew from UNESCO in protest in 1984 and 1985 (although they later rejoined in 2003 and 1997, respectively).

The MacBride report's authors "had the foresight to hope for a kind of 'globalization' that, rather than signify divisions among citizens of the world, acknowledged our common humanity," said Andrew Calabrese in a 25th anniversary article on the report. "With all of its flaws, for which progressive communication activists understandably have distanced themselves over the past twenty-five years, the MacBride Report projects a spirit of hopefulness about how a better world is possible, (and) about the continued importance of public institutions as means to ensure global justice" (Calabrese, 2005).

Satellites increase tensions between Islamic, Asian and Western cultures

As satellite communications brings cultures together, tensions are inevitable. One of the areas most prone to divisiveness is the representation of Islam in Western societies with a tradition of free speech and criticism of religion.

Salmon Rushdie, a British-Indian novelist and essayist, was sentenced to death in absentia for his 1988 book, *The Satanic Verses*, which contained a storyline that many Muslims believed was blasphemous. As the world moved ever closer, even small incidents provoked violent controversy. In September of 2005, for instance, violent reactions followed news that a Danish newspaper, *Jyllands-Posten*, had printed editorial cartoons depicting the Islamic prophet Muhammad in an unfavorable light. And riots broke out in 2011 when a Florida minister burned copies of the Qur'an.

New voices from Islamic nations, now available through satellite, may eventually lead to more international understanding, although there has been considerable controversy. One new satellite news network, Al Jazeera, was founded in Qatar in 1996 and presents news from an Islamic viewpoint. The network is frequently at odds with conservative US policies, and objections to "incitements to violence" have been made at many levels by US officials. However, Al Jazeera presents legitimate journalism and is just as controversial in Arab nations. Moreover, the network has vehemently denied allegations that it showed gruesome videos glorifying terrorist violence.

Another controversy emerged around the joint Chinese-American development, the Phoenix satellite system. The US-based News Corporation, headed by publisher Rupert Murdoch, sent the satellite up in 1996. Access was shut down by the Chinese government in 1999, but a Phoenix InfoNews Channel was established in 2001 as a joint venture with state-owned China Central Television (CCTV). Critics accused Murdoch of bowing to censorship, but his partner in the venture, Chinese businessman Liu Changle, believes that taking a cautious and deliberate approach is best. "China is opening up step by step," Liu said. "Opening up news and media should be slower than the overall economy. It will probably be the last to open. We and the Western media should be prepared for this and not expect too much" (McDonald, 2005).

In *The World is Flat*, columnist Thomas Friedman noted the sense of humiliation and relative depravation that people in highly traditional cultures have felt when confronted with advances in the other regions of the world. It's impossible to return to a time when cultures had less contact, he concludes. The answers will have to come from progressive forces within Arab and Asian cultures, based on their historical traditions. It's not impossible for that to happen, Friedman believes. Arab culture was the original source of the higher mathematics on which the digital revolution now depends. "The entire modern information revolution . . . can trace its roots all the way back to Arab-Muslim civilization," said Nayan Chanda, a Yale Global Online editor (Friedman, 2008). Again, the value of history in helping us understand paths forward into the future cannot be underestimated.

As Marshall McLuhan observed, the global village "doesn't necessarily mean harmony and peace and quiet, but it does mean huge involvement in everybody else's affairs."

Cable and satellite home television

Cable television was originally created in the 1940s to serve remote communities where broadcast signals were weak. When the cable systems began to use microwave relays in the 1960s to import more programming, independent non-network stations operating on the UHF bands were afraid that would be driven out of business.

Broadcasters mounted a "fight pay TV" campaign, and the FCC effectively blocked the expansion of cable systems.

When satellite communications became available in the early 1970s, thousands of community cable systems began merging to take advantage of new channels such as Home Box Office (HBO) and Music Television (MTV). "Superstations" such as WTBS in Atlanta began serving more of the cable market through satellites. They grew into larger organizations such as Cable News Network (CNN). In the process, cable service had an overall market penetration of 60 percent by the year 2000.

The majority of cable TV services were owned by five or six large integrated companies, ranging from Comcast and Time Warner to Cox and Charter. But local franchises are administered by cities and counties, which have not been prepared to deal with major corporations. Cable companies took advantage of their monopoly status, according to the Consumer Federation of America, noting that deregulation of cable in the Telecommunications Act of 1996 meant that cable rates rose at three times the rate of inflation.

Meanwhile, hobbyists who did not want to pay for cable TV in the 1980s could order kits to build a large (three meter) satellite dish and pick up some unscrambled transmissions from satellites. At one point the market was growing so quickly that a Congressman joked that they had become the "state flower of West Virginia."

Small dish direct broadcasting (DBS) home satellite TV, introduced in 1994 by Hughes DirecTV, was followed in 1996 by EchoStar. Proposals to merge the two satellite TV companies were rejected by the FCC in 2002 because television audiences would then only have the choice between a local cable monopoly and a satellite TV monopoly.

By 2010, cable TV had peaked at about 60 percent of all US homes, while satellite TV had about 30 percent of the market. New digital systems would quickly undermine the old monopolies.

Hard times for traditional media

Television networks and other content providers went into a tail spin similar to that of newspapers in the first decade of the twenty-first century. Smaller audiences meant declining profits, which led lower quality programs, which led to smaller audiences.

At its peak in 1976, the three US networks (ABC, CBS and NBC) attracted 92 percent of all viewers. By 2008, the four main networks (including Fox) attracted only 46 percent of viewers. Over the previous decade, NBC's ratings dropped 37 percent, ABC's 35 percent, CBS's 33 percent and PBS dropped 37 percent.

Network news was especially hard hit, overwhelmed by the financial demands of corporate owners who have "little appreciation for the sacred trust that goes with owning a news organization," said Philip S. Balboni in *Nieman Reports*, noting the "near extinction" of the kinds of television documentaries produced by Edward R. Murrow and others in the 1950s and 60s (Balboni, 2001).

Staffs cuts of half or more of a newsroom made once-thriving network news offices look empty, and news bureaus closed down in most cities outside Washington and New York. The new austerity meant that the reporters who managed to keep their jobs had to perform at a higher level. They would no longer be accompanied by a producer or camera crew, but would now set up their own camera, record their own news story, edit it, and send it back to the newsroom on their own. While the technology made this process easier, it didn't make it any less time-consuming. "They're getting away from substance," said one journalist. "They're not covering the statehouse, the city council, the county board. They do whatever's quick and easy" (Kurtz, 2010).

One of the quickest and easiest ways to attract audiences was through television talk programs. Usually TV talk shows are hosted by a celebrity, conducted in the present tense, and highly structured. They are fairly inexpensive to produce, compared to network dramas, and can bring in high returns for networks (Timberg, 2002). They also involved a relatively neutral figure moderating the conflict.

The US political debate became less moderated as audiences and channels fragmented in the late twentieth and early twenty-first centuries. On the one hand, more channels meant that viewers could simply click the remote to hear a different point of view. And because there were more channels, there was no "scarcity rationale" for government-imposed content boundaries, such as the Fairness Doctrine. Under heavy commercial pressures, network news and public affairs became increasingly shrill and partisan.

Traditional television networks, losing audiences and desperate for a return to their once-lucrative market positions, retreated into a level of vitriolic partisanship not seen for a century. Fired up by the deregulation of political advertising, partisan television especially seemed to be fragmenting the political center in the United States.

In a speech reminiscent of Edward R. Murrow's NAB address (quoted above), John Stewart, a television comedy show host, noted:

> "The press can hold its magnifying glass up to our problems, bringing them into focus, illuminating issues heretofore unseen, or it can use its magnifying glass to light ants on fire, and then perhaps host a week of shows on the sudden, unexpected dangerous flaming-ant epidemic. If we amplify everything, we hear nothing . . . The press is our immune system. If it overreacts to everything, we actually get sicker . . . And yet, with that being said, I feel good. Strangely, calmly good, because the image of Americans that is reflected back to us by our political and media process is false. It is us through a funhouse mirror." (Burnett, 2010)

The image was false, Stewart said, because in everyday life, people cooperate and work together in ways that belie the media image of constant partisan politics.

The impact of digital networks and tv

As usual in the history of media technology, the reaction to a monopoly is the development of new technologies. We've seen the trend in printing, for example, when magazines led the Progressive era charge for broad social reforms at a time when newspapers were too monopolized to take risks. We've seen it in the intent to replace the telegraph monopoly with the telephone, which itself became a monopoly. We've seen it in home satellite delivery television that was intended to circumvent local monopolies of cable television systems.

Similarly, in the second decade of the twenty-first century, home broadband internet technologies expanded to the point where consumers could access television programs without paying high satellite or cable fees, as a wide variety of news and entertainment programs became available on computers. But the economic impacts of connecting the internet to the home television posed problems for both delivery systems and content providers.

New types of delivery systems included Netflix, a subscriber service which offered instant movies by internet access; and Hulu, an advertising-supported experiment by three big networks (NBC, ABC and Fox) to deliver their content over the internet.

Technically, it was easy around 2010 to begin distributing television through the internet to home television sets. Set-top boxes from providers Apple TV, Google TV and Boxee became available around 2010. However, content providers like NBC, ABC, Fox and others, worried about profits, blocked the new set-tops from carrying their programming. The largest cable provider in the United States, Comcast, bet on creating its own on-demand programs in a bid to compete with on-demand models like Netflix and Google TV.

Broadcasters in Europe were much quicker to embrace the internet TV model, offering "catch-up" television where the original broadcast would be available for a week or on the internet through services like itvPlayer in the UK and M6 in France.

Audiences found they didn't need to pay for a bundle of network programming when what they really wanted was just a few favorite programs. The ability of to unbundle news, sports and entertainment had impacts in other areas, such as newspaper readership, as we have seen. Yet by 2010, it seemed inevitable that cable and satellite television would shift, in part, to the internet, breaking up old monopolies and allowing new forms of competition.

Broadcasting as re-tribalization

One interesting issue was the possibility that social evolution had taken a turn toward what Marshall McLuhan called "re-tribalization" through broadcasting. McLuhan used the term as a way to describe the tendency of radio and television to enhance the post-literate culture, making it more passionate while, at the same time, craving a harmonious and unified sense of social balance. In a 1969 interview, McLuhan said:

> The instant nature of electric-information movement is decentralizing—rather than enlarging—the family of man into a new state of multitudinous tribal existences. Particularly in countries where literate values are deeply institutionalized, this is a highly traumatic process, since the clash of the old segmented visual culture and the new integral electronic culture creates a crisis of identity, a vacuum of the self, which generates tremendous violence—violence that is simply an identity quest, private or corporate, social or commercial.

Although McLuhan observed the trend with concern for violence, there are others who have seen changes in the individual ties to society as simply emerging in new forms. Tribes, according to Business writer Seth Godin, have always been a natural focus for social change. What the internet has done, and what mass marketing through one-way broadcasting media never could do, is allow the development of small groups that could lead social change (Godin, 2008).

"Narrowcasting" of video through the Web can empower global innovation, according to Chris Anderson, a media entrepreneur behind the TED conference (Technology, Education and Design). Anderson believes that the expansion of video on the Web will make up for the decline in public information from network television and printed media.

"This is the technology that's going to allow the rest of the world's talents to be shared digitally, thereby launching a whole new cycle of crowd-accelerated innovation," he said in a 2010 TED talk. Noting that 80 million hours of YouTube are seen every day, it's possible to imagine an internet-fueled learning cycle "capable of carrying all of us to a smarter, wiser, more beautiful place."

"If it's all puppies, porn and piracy, we're doomed," Anderson said. "I don't think it will be. Video is high-bandwidth for a reason. It packs a huge amount of data, and our brains are uniquely wired to decode it" (Anderson and Wolf, 2010).

Section IV

The Digital Revolution

Introduction to Section IV

The power of the digital revolution was only dimly foreseen in the decades before computers graced every desktop and "desktops" opened every computer.

The popular early visions of computers featured machines that were cunning, inhuman, dangerous or seductive.

- George Orwell's *1984* (published in 1948) described a totalitarian state where history is erased on demand and where people are constantly monitored.
- Stanley Kubrick's *2001: A Space Odyssey* (produced in 1969) is a film in which a computer takes over a spaceship and kills most of the crew.
- William Gibson's *Neuromancer* (published in 1984) described a nightmarish world of totalitarian control over human–computer interfaces.

It might have been easy to dismiss these as fantasies at the beginning of the digital revolution; after all, they were projected on a technology that nobody quite understood. But the fears were taken very seriously, and that played a cautionary role in the way that digital technology was envisioned.

As we will see in this fourth section of *Revolutions in Communication*, computer technology was conceived early in the nineteenth century Industrial Revolution and born in the twentieth century chaos of World War II. Technically, early digital computers were a cross between mathematics and radio electronics. They were originally meant to serve code-breakers, weapons designers and rocket scientists who needed to manipulate complex calculations. The networks that linked them were originally meant to warn of pending nuclear attacks and provide the capability to launch retaliatory strikes.

Early computer engineers thought their machines were capable of greater things, and they tended to have a far more positive vision than writers and artists like Orwell, Kubrick or Gibson. They saw an enabling technology that could help reorganize the way people used information. Their vision spread slowly across the decades, from nerd engineers with pocket protectors in the 1960s to hipster hardware developers in the 1970s to the rebellious cyberpunk programmers of the 1980s and 90s.

What gave these visionaries hope was that the technology itself seemed to be so malleable that it had no single or obvious trajectory. Unlike most other technologies, computing could have gone in a million different directions. Perhaps it could have been used to help build a nightmarish totalitarian society; perhaps it still can be. Some historians don't believe that computing so easily adapts to the service of totalitarianism, but few would dispute that social construction (rather than determinism) had a major influence in the current state of computing and digital media.

So the story of computers and digital media is the story of creative cultures patching together an improbable system. It's the story of innovation and cooperation over competition and hierarchy. It's also the story of how the world's largest computer and media businesses missed their moments and how the smallest companies, guided by a larger vision, created a vehicle for a global culture and media with a new ideal of service.

Traditional media miss the curves in the road

Some in the traditional media saw the implications of digital technology Derek Daniels, chief editor of the Knight newspapers (*Miami Herald*, *Detroit Free Press*) predicted in 1970 that multimedia technologies would be the future of the media business (Daniels, 1970). But most other media executives just didn't get it. As late as 1994, Viacom CEO Sumner Redstone said the emerging internet was "a road to fantasyland"—and not a game changer. "To me it seems apparent that the information superhighway . . . is a long way coming if it comes at all" (Auletta, 2010).

Even as late as 1998, a consortium of the nation's largest newspaper publishers abandoned a project called New Century Media because (as noted in Chapter 3) they thought the competition was not emerging. As it turned out, the competition came from an unexpected direction, and the publishing industry kept on with business as usual. A frequently-used metaphor is that the industry kept "driving" in a straight line and "missed the curve in the road."

On occasions when big media attempted to cope with the digital revolution, it somehow managed to miss the mark. Knight-Ridder's experiments with "Viewtron" belly-flopped in 1986. Microsoft's attempt to set up a Microsoft Network, in competition with the Web, fell apart in 1996—although an old-media cable TV channel survived as MSNBC. When Rupert Murdoch's News Corp. bought MySpace in 2005, mainstream media had become so deeply unpopular that many saw the purchase itself as the kiss of death.

The unpopularity of mainstream media in the twenty-first century is worth noting, since a major motivation for new media technologies has been to circumvent the old, dominant media technologies. As we have seen, telephone technology was financed by people who hoped to get around the telegraph monopoly; radio and film were attractive new media in their day because newspapers (as Will Irwin famously said) spoke in the voice of the older generation. The new digital media did not only speak to a new generation—it allowed an entire generation to speak together. A 1993 article in *Rolling Stone* magazine made this point when (it said) "the new medium still doesn't really have a name."

"For generations, the leading newspapers, networks and magazines have served as the nation's information gatekeepers, deciding which of the many millions of news stories will move through the gate and out into the country. Armed with relatively inexpensive new technology, millions of Americans are now finding that they don't need the gatekeepers any more." (Katz, 1993)

It took almost 20 years for this idea, and many more like it, to work its way through the social and technological system. When it did, the publishing business was in collapse and the profession of journalism so out of fashion that universities started closing down journalism schools, apparently not recognizing that the problem had nothing to do with the production of information and everything to do with controls over the way traditional media spoke to a new generation.

Traditional business and the curves in the road

Like big media, big corporations also missed many of the curves in the road. As we will see in this section:

- AT&T engineers disliked idea of data transmission interfering with their voice telephone lines in the early 1970s. The company refused the Defense Department's request that they own and administer the internet. Instead, a consortium of universities ran the network haphazardly and kept it open to innovation.
- IBM was not prepared for the personal computer market, and allowed Microsoft to develop an operating system that could be used in "clone" computers.
- Xerox didn't appreciate its own research at the Palo Alto research center and lost creative staff and big ideas to Apple Corp. in the early 1980s.

The digital revolution proved amazingly fluid and very difficult to predict, let alone control. It allowed the creation of new forms of information at the center of new kinds of communities. No single person can be credited with kicking off the digital revolution. Instead, hundreds of thousands of engineers, programmers and visionaries shared the idea of liberation through concepts like "open source" software, "crowdsourcing," and individuals as information producers as well as consumers.

How that happened, and why, is the historical question. Was it something fundamental in the digital technology itself, or was this a case where social construction mattered more? Or was it both? Did the social construction, the vision, change the path of what could have been a more controlling technology?

J. David Bolter chose the technologically deterministic answer when he wrote in *Turing's Man*:

The premise of George Orwell's 1984 was the marriage of totalitarian purpose with modern technology. But . . . computer technology may well be incompatible with the totalitarian monster . . . Computers make hierarchical communication and control far easier, but they also work against . . . the absolute dedication to the party line. (Bolter, 1984)

Inside the computer revolution, the idea of social construction dominated, as we will see. Steve Jobs of Apple often said his mission was to "change the world." In 1993, *Wired* magazine's editor said this about the cyberpunk revolution:

> . . . I will bet that the digital counterculture will reject (the old) bleak vision for a future where technology enlarges the human spirit as a new tool for consciousness . . . This new movement will be cyberpunk imbued with human warmth, substituting a deep sense of interdependence in place of lone-wolf isolation . . . The gospel of this new movement will be one of machines in the service of enlarging our humanity. . . . Watch the skies for a new comet—it will be digital, and its tail is likely to glow in technicolor swirls. Its arrival will change all of our lives forever. (Rossetto, 1993)

It's possible to find similar rhetoric about other breakthrough media technologies such as the telegraph: "One feeling and one impulse are created from the center of the land to the utmost extremity," said an enthusiast in the 1840s. It's also possible to find historians who think that the telegraph had more impact in its day than the computer will have in the twenty-first century. This seems doubtful, given the pace of change, but the question is why: Why did a machine that was originally designed to compute artillery trajectories and bank deposits turn up as the Thomas Paine of the media revolution?

In Chapter 10, we'll consider that machine—where it came from, how it was developed and how computers organized information in new ways.

In Chapter 11, we'll look at the networks that link those machines together and consider how they emerged from the defense system and how they linked personal computers together by the 1990s. The combination of personal computers and digital networks has created new kinds of businesses like Amazon and Netflix, along with new ways to distribute news from top-down, one-to-many platforms.

In Chapter 12, we'll look at some of the new kinds of civic and social networks that computers and networks made possible, such as Wikipedia and Facebook. We'll also consider questions still hanging in the balance: For instance, whether the digital revolution will ultimately prove to be a liberating technology, or whether its enormous power will be harnessed for less noble purposes.

One thing to observe is how social construction of technology played a major role in the vision for computing and how the media experience stands in sharp contrast to other areas of technology. In energy and environmental debates for instance, a constant comment from traditional utilities and fossilized industries is that "you don't get to pick and choose" technologies. But why not? What is a democracy if the fundamental technological foundations of a society are so far removed from popular choice?

If there is any lesson of history to be appreciated from the digital revolution and media history in general, it is that without a positive vision for a technology, dystopian tendencies can become self-fulfilling prophecies. People with a positive vision, despite the odds, can—as computer pioneers predicted—change the world.

For additional reading, discussion questions, links to video and other suggestions, see www.revolutionsincommunications.com.

10 The advent of computers

The Digital Revolution is whipping through our lives like a Bengali typhoon. (Louis Rossetto, Wired magazine, 1993)

Changes in the information age will be as dramatic as those in the Middle Ages in Europe. (James A. Dewar, 1998)

Charles Babbage's Victorian-era computer

It began with a shock. Charles Babbage, a mathematician working at the Greenwich Observatory in 1821, found an error in a set of astronomical tables that navigators used to fix the position of ships at sea. And then another error. And then dozens more.

In the process of correcting the tables, it occurred to Babbage that a mechanical device might avoid the errors. The idea took shape as a "difference engine," the world's first computer, a machine that could create tables of astronomical calculations and print them out with unerring accuracy.

Babbage spent the rest of his life working on the project, which was blueprinted but never completed. He claimed that the final design developed between 1847 and 1849, could solve complex equations with answers of up to 31 decimal places. But the historical mystery was whether it could have actually worked and whether it could have been built in his time.

For years, experts said it could not. "His idea was sound enough, but construction and maintenance costs were then too heavy," said Vannevar Bush.

Figure 10.1 Victorian-era computer designer—Charles Babbage felt that he was born in the wrong century, but his ideas about computing had an influence on the future. The Babbage "difference engine," designed in 1847 but never fully built, was no simple adding machine. It had 8,000 cams and cogwheels, could handle polynomial equations, and could calculate to 31 decimal places.

Figure 10.2 Reconstructing Babbage's difference engine—Doron Swade, a curator at the Science Museum of London, stands next to a reconstruction of Charles Babbage's difference engine, built from architectural drawings for the Science Museum of London. (Photo by David Exton, courtesy of the Computer History Museum, Mountain View, California)

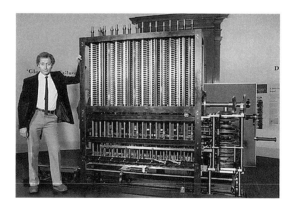

"Babbage remained a brilliant aberration, a prophet of the electronic age in the heyday of the steam engine," said historian J. David Bolter.

Then, in late 1980s, London Science Museum curator Doron Swade built the Babbage machine, taking care to specifically use machining techniques available in Babbage's time. Working from 20 drawings, Swade built the 5-ton, 11-foot long machine with 8,000 cams and cogwheels made from bronze, cast iron and steel. "It's a design of extraordinary elegance and economy," he said. The solutions to polynomial equations could not only be printed in hard copy but also punched into a soft card for hot lead stereotypes in order to completely eliminate typographical errors.

"We know he could have built it in that time," said Nathan Myhrvold, a former Microsoft executive whose interest in history led him to help finance the computer's re-creation. The problem, he said, was that Babbage "didn't know how to manage a large complicated project." Even so, the historical issue was settled when the final version of the Babbage machine showed that basic principles of computing were well understood long before electronic computers were built in the 1940s.

There had been other attempts at mechanical devices to help with calculations. One of these was an ancient Greek astronomical device brought up from the Aegean Sea off the island of Antikythera in 1900. The device turned out to be a modestly accurate model of the solar system that would have been useful for navigation (Price, 1959).

French scientist Blaise Pascal also created a mechanical adding machine in 1642, and German mathematician Gottfried Leibniz' 1694 "stepped reckoner." The Leibniz machine was an improvement over Pascal's since it could not only add, but also multiply, divide and extract square roots. Leibniz used a binary system, typical of electronic computers of a later age, rather than Pascal's decimal system.

However, Babbage is often called the "father of computing" because his system could handle polynomial equations needed for astronomical tables and artillery ballistics calculations. He not only created a processing system using gears and cog wheels, but he also designed an input device, a memory system and other features of a modern computer. On the broad scale, Babbage wanted to mechanize intellectual work with his difference engine in the same way that manufacturing operations were being mechanized with steam engines during the Industrial Revolution.

It's interesting that one of his associates, Countess Ada Lovelace (1815–1852), was a mathematician who helped develop the first algorithm for one of Babbage's designs. The daughter of the famous poet Lord Byron, she was called "The Enchantress of Numbers," by Babbage. She is remembered as the first computer programmer and also with a programming language, Ada, that was named in her honor.

In the end, Babbage felt frustrated that his vision of a computer seemed so far away. He once said he would give the rest of his life just to spend three days in the future 500 years away. As it turned out, he would not have had to travel quite so far ahead in time to see his device widely accepted.

Figure 10.3 The first programmer—Countess Ada Lovelace, daughter of famed poet Lord Byron, was a mathematician who developed algorithms for Charles Babbage's early computers. She is remembered today with a programming language, Ada, named in her honor. (Science Museum, London; Wikimedia Commons)

Moving beyond mechanical computers

The first large-scale use of a mechanical computer was in 1890, when Herman Hollerith, a mathematician working for the US Census, created a computer to accurately sort and manipulate numbers generated by census workers.

The computer was not as sophisticated as Babbage's difference engine. It used a system of punch cards as input devices—an idea borrowed from the textile industry. Hollerith went on to improve mechanical computers and create the Tabulating Machine Company in 1896, which became International Business Machines (IBM) in 1924.

The company focused on large-scale projects for government and business, including census, Social Security, military, insurance and banking operations.

IBM's electro-mechanical tabulators from this period were extremely useful in keeping track of many numbers, but they were not programmable computers.

IBM machinery was sold around the world, but the most controversial use of census tabulators involved the company's German subsidiary, which in the 1930s played a role helping the Nazi government of Germany identify Jews and organize the Holocaust. Evidence exists that technical support also came from US headquarters (Black, 2002), but IBM officially denies the inference (IBM, 2001). Researchers have not accessed IBM archives, and the controversy remains unsettled.

IBM's initial foray into digital computers took place at Harvard University in 1939. Called the Mark I, the machine used both electronic and mechanical means to take input from cards and calculate tables of data.

Figure 10.4 Computing pioneer—Herman Hollerith, a US Census employee in 1890, developed a tabulating machine to more accurately read and sort census data. (Library of Congress)

Figure 10.5 Hollerith machine—Ann Oliver of the US Census demonstrates the Hollerith machine in this 1940 picture. The machine was fed cards containing census information at the rate of 400 a minute and from these, 12 separate bits of statistical information were extracted. (Library of Congress)

Experiments in fully digital computer design began accelerating with the war years and the need for higher levels of computing power. In Britain, engineers built a computer called Colossus to decipher German military commands which were sent in code.

Among the veterans of the Colossus project was Alan Turing (1912–1954), a British mathematician and cryptographer, who was a key figure in designing computing systems on mathematical principles. Turing would later go on to envision what's called the "Turing test"—a situation where a person communicates with what may be a computer, and the computer is responsive enough and apparently intelligent enough that it can be mistaken for another human in a blind test. Interestingly, another set of veterans from the Colossus project were the parents of Tim Berners-Lee, the visionary who developed the idea of the World Wide Web in the early 1990s (see Chapter 11).

The largest computer developed during the war years was the ENIAC, the electronic numerical integrator and calculator. Built at the University of Pennsylvania, the ENIAC used 17,468 radio tubes, weighed 30 tons, measured 100 feet long and eight feet high, and, on a good day, could perform 100,000 calculations per second. Technically, the ENIAC has been described as a processor with 20 register positions. Yet in two hours it did the work of 100 human mathematicians working one year.

Harry Reed, who worked with ballistics lab in the early 1950s, thought of the ENIAC as very personal computer. "Now we think of a personal computer as one which you carry around with you. The ENIAC was one that you kind of lived inside . . . You could wander around inside it and watch the program being executed . . . So instead of you holding a computer, this computer held you" (Reed, 1996).

Another important figure in early military computing was Grace Hopper, a US Navy computer scientist who worked on the Mark I computer at Harvard and developed the COBOL computer language.

Before this time, mathematicians working on ballistics tables were themselves called "computers" because their job was to compute the tables, in the same way that a person might be a baker because their job was to bake bread. After the ENIAC, the role of a computer was mechanized in an industrial device—just as Charles Babbage intended a century beforehand.

Figure 10.6 THE ENIAC—the first large-scale electronic computer in the US was made for the Army Ballistics Research Lab at the University of Pennsylvania. Here, Glen Beck checks wiring to the some of the 17,486 vacuum tubes while Frances Snyder Holberton stands in front of a set of function tables on wheels. As ungainly as it looks, in an hour the Electronic Numerical Integrator and Computer could perform the tasks of 50 human "computers" (mathematicians) working for a year. (US Army Photo)

Figure 10.7 Navy programmer—Grace Hopper, a computer programmer and (by her retirement) Admiral in the US Navy, developed the COBOL computer language and worked on defense department computing during a long career. She also came up with the term "debugging" computer programs after a moth got stuck in the Harvard computer in 1947. "It's easier to ask forgiveness than it is to get permission," is an aphorism often attributed to her. (Photo Courtesy of the Computer History Museum)

The new frontiers for science

One of the most important figures in the long-term development of the computer was President Franklin Roosevelt's science advisor, Vannevar Bush. In the years after World War II, Bush outlined the relationship between science and the democratic system and suggested new goals for scientists who had been freed from wartime research needs.

It was important to think about the problem, he said. While the discussions about politics and crops at the corner store might not explicitly involve democracy and its relationship to science and technology, those elements are constantly in the background. "They determine our destiny, and well we know it," he said.

He expressed hope for democratic influences on science and technology. "In a free country, in a democracy, this [path taken] is the path that public opinion wishes to have pursued, whether it leads to new cures for man's ills, or new sources of a raised standard of living . . . In a dictatorship the path is the one that is dictated, whether the dictator be an individual or part of a self-perpetuating group" (Bush, 1949).

Bush was specifically concerned with the problem of information overload and suggested a high priority for new information systems to extend human wisdom. In a 1946 article published in *Atlantic* Magazine, Bush predicted the development of a computer that he called a "memex."

It consists of a desk, and while it can presumably be operated from a distance, it is primarily the piece of furniture at which [a person] works. On the top are slanting translucent screens, on which material can be projected for convenient reading. There is a keyboard, and sets of buttons and levers . . .

Wholly new forms of encyclopedias will appear, ready made with a mesh of associative trails running through them, ready to be dropped into the memex and there amplified. The lawyer has at his touch the associated opinions and decisions of his whole experience, and of the experience of friends and authorities. The patent attorney has on call the millions of issued patents, with familiar trails to every point of his client's interest. The physician, puzzled by a patient's reactions, strikes the trail established in studying an earlier similar case, and runs rapidly through analogous case histories, with side references to the classics for the pertinent anatomy and histology . . . The historian, with a vast chronological account of a people, parallels it with a skip trail which stops only on the salient items, and can follow at any time contemporary trails which lead him all over civilization at a particular epoch.

There is a new profession of trail blazers, those who find delight in the task of establishing useful trails through the enormous mass of the common record. The inheritance from the master becomes, not only his additions to the world's record, but for his disciples the entire scaffolding by which they were erected . . . The applications of science . . . may yet allow [mankind] truly to

Figure 10.8 Science and democracy—Vannevar Bush, science advisor to President Franklin D. Roosevelt, was at the center of revolution in computing in the 1940s and 50s. His widely shared perspective was that the technological path taken in a democracy is the one that is led by public opinion. (Library of Congress)

encompass the great record and to grow in the wisdom of racial experience. (Bush, 1946)

The essay had a profound influence on scientists and engineers at the time, particularly J. C. R. Licklider, who envisioned the internet and better human–computer interfaces at MIT, and Doug Engelbart, who invented the computer mouse and the graphical user interface at Stanford Research Institute.

First public test of a computer

By 1952, the ENIAC had spun off into a private company and was dubbed the Sperry-Rand Univac computer. Its public debut was on election night, 1952, on CBS television.

With early election returns from key precincts, the Univac was able to project that Dwight Eisenhower would win 438 electoral votes and his opponent, Adlai Stevenson, would win 93. The official count would turn out to be 442 and 89 electoral votes (Goff, 1999). Although Eisenhower seemed likely to win at the time, the landslide was unexpected. The data seemed so out of line with other predictions that the CBS network news team and the computer programmers held it back, claiming that they had some kind of computer malfunction.

The next morning, reviewers found it charming that computers had such a hard time replacing humans. "The CBS pride was called the Univac, which at a critical moment refused to work with anything like the efficiency of a human being," TV reviewer Jack Gould wrote in *The New York Times* the morning after the election. "This mishap caused the CBS stars, Walter Cronkite, Ed Murrow and Eric Sevareid to give Univac a rough ride for the rest of the evening, in a most amusing sidelight to the CBS coverage."

Actually, the computer's projections were so accurate that it frightened not only the CBS news producers but also the Univac programmers. According to the National Academy of Engineering, the projection was so unequivocal that Univac's operators grew nervous and altered the program to produce a different result. "They later confessed that the initial projection of electoral votes had been right on the mark," the NAE said (NAE, 2010).

Computer problems also popped up on subsequent election nights, and the wonder is that the Univac did so well under deadline pressure. It used radio tubes that were fragile, failing at the rate of one every 7 minutes. Another problem was that the warmth of the radio tubes sometimes attracted moths, and in the early years, programmers occasionally had to "de-bug" the machine. Later, the term "bug" became a synonym for a problem with the program.

Figure 10.9 Computer of the future—CBS news anchor Walter Cronkite demonstrates a prototype of a "television communication set" that was a prototype for "a globally connected library system" in 1967. (Library of Congress)

From tubes to transistors

Since radio tubes were acting as nothing more than electronic switches, considerable research went into the idea of creating smaller and more efficient switches. This could be done if the switches were placed in a "semi-conductor" environment such as silicon. William Shockley and others at Bell Labs invented the semiconductor transistor as a way to miniaturize the radio tube in 1947. This made computers, radios and other electronic devices much smaller and easier to manage.

A transistor-based computer called the TRADIC (for TRAnsistor DIgital Computer or TRansistorized Airborne DIgital Computer) was developed for the military in the 1950s. It processed a million operations per second and was far more compact than the ENIAC. At the time, a transistor cost $20 and a radio tube cost about one dollar, so it was an expensive machine. But it could perform thousands more calculations without failing and it was light enough to be used in aircraft.

By the 1950s, Texas Instruments Company had developed a cheaper transistor, making possible portable radios along with far more powerful computers. But transistors were destined to remain expensive, since all of the circuitry was created by individually hand-soldering processes, and flaws were bound to emerge somewhere as computers became more complex.

IBM continued to dominate the market for mechanical adding machines, typewriters and other business equipment, and it was coming to dominate the computer market as well. IBM's computers had become vital to the insurance and banking industries as well as the military. IBM's first computer using an integrated processor, the IBM 360, was marketed in 1964 and has been mentioned alongside the Boeing 707 and the Ford Model T as a technological milestone.

One reason for the success of the IBM 360 was that it was based on the idea of scalable architecture, which means that a variety of capabilities and add-ons could run on one software system. According to Bill Gates of Microsoft, the concept drove away many of IBM's competitors until other companies like Amdahl, Control Data, Hitachi and Intel also delivered computers in the 1970s that could run on IBM system software (Gates, 1995).

Along with the military, IBM's computers served the insurance and banking industries, which had a need to create actuarial tables and complex reconciliation statements. As computing power grew, and the cost of computers declined, other industries began sharing time on computers to run their numbers and calculations.

Not many people saw anything revolutionary in these developments, least of all IBM. Their business culture was one of strict conformity. Precise haircuts, dark suits, narrow black ties and a strong sense of company loyalty made the IBM world, for some, a harrowing glimpse into the totalitarian future of computing. For others, the problem was that the old-fashioned IBM culture simply failed to glimpse the possibilities of the technology it dominated.

From transistors to integrated circuits

In the late 1950s, engineers realized that there was no need for transistors to be separately soldered onto circuit boards. The idea of the integrated processor, or "chip," occurred independently to Jack Kilby of Texas Instruments and Robert Noyce of Fairchild Semiconductors at around the same time.

In 1958, Kilby used a germanium slab and interconnecting wires to create an integrated chip. The following year, Noyce developed a set of circuits and transistors that could be printed onto each layer of a silicon chip. The ability to print circuits and transistors allowed mass production. Like Gutenberg's original printing system, mass production brought costs down and helped spark a communications revolution (Reid, 2001).

In 2000, Kilby was awarded the Nobel Prize in Physics. Noyce went on to establish a company with Gordon Moore in 1968 that set the pace for Silicon Valley: Intel. From the beginning, Intel was a different kind of company. The bottom line for Intel would be excellence in engineering, and that meant that the people with the power to make business decisions would be engineers and not professional managers. Intel was known for creating a new kind of corporate culture, one where offices had no doors and where managers stayed in touch with researchers by working part of the year in the labs or on the factory floor.

One early client was NASA and the Defense Department. Rockets needed guidance systems, and integrated chips made it possible. Even paying several thousand dollars just for a small chip was no problem. By 1971, Intel sold the first commercial microprocessor called the 4004. It used four-bit processing, and it contained the equivalent of 2300 transistors operating at around 60,000 interactions per second (0.06 MIPs) at a speed of 108KHz.

Rapid increases in the power of the computer chip seemed to follow a predictable path, and in 1965, Gordon Moore published a paper predicting that computer power would keep doubling about every year. This was later called "Moore's Law." It was greeted with skepticism in the 1960s but soon proved to be accurate, or even slightly pessimistic, as the computer industry boomed (Moore, 1965).

In 1978, Intel introduced the 8086 and the 8088, the first commercially successful 16-bit and 8-bit processers which were to power the first IBM personal computers. The 8088 contained 29,000 transistors and achieved 0.8 MIPS at 3 to 5 MHz.

Competitors included Motorola and MOS Technologies, which produced the 6502 chip, at the heart of the Apple II and Atari game consoles. MOS introduced a quality control approach to printing computer chips that greatly reduced costs.

Within five years, a 2.7 MIPs processor with 134,000 transistors running at 12.5 MHz was introduced, and by 1989, Intel released the 80486 DX. It contained the equivalent of about 1.2 million transistors running at 25 MHz and achieved up to 20 MIPs. By 2010, computers capable

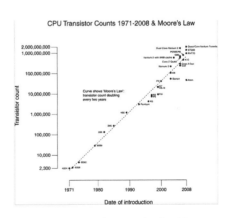

Figure 10.10 Moore's Law—Gordon Moore of Intel observed that computer power was rising quickly in 1965, and projected the trajectory of improvements in processing power. The prediction proved amazingly accurate. (Wikimedia Commons)

of over 500 trillion calculations per second, running at 6,000 MHz (or 6 Gigahertz) had become standard.

Social reaction: fear of 1984

Ballistics, accounting and astrophysics were not the first things that came to mind when people thought about computers in the 1960s and 70s. Instead, there was a sense of unease that accompanied the increasing power of "super-brain" computers. They became associated with totalitarian governments and George Orwell's book *1984*, which described government monitoring people through their "telescreens."

Another idea about computers was that artificial intelligence would threaten humanity. That theme found an early expression in Stanley Kubrick's 1960 film *2001: A Space Odyssey*, in which the HAL computer (for IBM) begins killing the astronauts on a space mission.

"In the 1950s and 1960s there existed the notion that the computer not only could but would control all aspects of our lives," said MIT management expert Edgar H. Schein. "Images of the fully computerized home that automatically turned the lights on and off and that prepared meals and controlled daily diets were popular. And the fear that computers might, as in the movie 2001: A Space Odyssey, even try to take charge altogether was widely experienced" (Shein, 2004).

Realistic or not, these fears led to a social reaction that influenced a generation of programmers and engineers to attempt to push the technology into directions that were less about control and more about individual empowerment. Computers had to be liberated from the IBM way of life, according to the Stewart Brand (publisher of the Whole Earth Catalog) and Ted Nelson, the "Don Quixote of computing."

Nelson, in a series of books starting in 1973, was among those advocating "Computer Lib" (liberation) through socially conscious engineering. Nelson advocated a vision of a network of computers that would inform, entertain and make information sharing possible in ways that had never been considered before. His thinking influenced many up and coming programmers in the 1970s, including Steve Jobs of Apple. But it also reflected thinking that was coming from inside the Department of Defense, as we will see in the next chapter, and the idea among satellite engineers and communications specialists that they, too, had been advancing "technologies of freedom" (de Sola Pool, 1984).

The computer had a special place in all this, according to historian James Burke. In a 1979 BBC documentary, Burke said that innovative people have always had to struggle against oppressive systems. Yet, ironically, a product of that system

> could blow everything wide open . . . With this [microchip] . . . we might be able to lift the limitations of conforming to any centralized representational form of government—originally invented, because there was no way for everybody's voice to be heard. [But] with it, we could operate on the basis that values and standards—and ethics and facts and truth—all depend on what your view of the world is—and that there may be as many views of that, as there are people.

So the focus on personal computers—as opposed to mainframe computers—was a social construction as much as it was a natural part of the technology's trajectory. A personal computer was one that you could use without "big brother" looking over your shoulder.

For computer nerds, however, the personal computer was a way to actually access computers and develop software. Many hobbyists who later became software developers were happy to have a more user-friendly machine that they could access. After all, it was hard to get computer time on a mainframe, regardless of "big brother."

New business cultures and the personal computer

The idea that computers could liberate and not tyrannize was shared across several innovative centers that sprouted up at the time. One was located in Cambridge, MA and associated with the Massachusetts Institute of Technology (MIT). Another culture emerged in the 1970s around Stanford University in Palo Alto, California—a region also known as "Silicon Valley."

Among the many problems these two different centers encountered was the human computer interface. J. C. R. Licklider, an MIT professor who became head of the Defense Department's research team for information processing in the 1960s, was fascinated by the problem. His 1960 paper, *Man-Computer Symbiosis* discussed the need for interactive computing.

The significance of interactive computing is easy to grasp. In the 1960s, computers processed programs in batches. A programmer would punch holes in paper tape or cards and these would be taken to the computer room and turned over to someone wearing a white lab coat. Licklider's idea was that computing should be interactive. When a person would type something into a terminal, the computer should come back with an instant response.

Licklider is considered one of the most important figures in computer history because, like a kind of intellectual Johnny Appleseed, he planted the ideas and inspired dozens of young protégés with a vision for the future. He also envisioned the development of something he called the "intergalactic computer network," which we will explore in Chapter 11.

When Licklider moved to the Department of Defense, he was able to fund early efforts in time-sharing, which helped mainframe computers be more interactive. He also had a hand in starting the Augmentation Research Center at Stanford Research Institute in Silicon Valley.

The human–computer interface problem also fascinated researchers in Silicon Valley, especially Douglas Engelbart, who, like Licklider, thought computers had a potential to change the world for the better. (He was told while he was a graduate student at the University of California, Berkeley, to be very careful about who he talked to about such wild ideas.)

Engelbart joined SRI and in 1962, wrote *Augmenting Human Intellect: A Conceptual Framework*, that contained ideas inspired by Vannevar Bush and J. C. R. Licklider. By augmenting human intellect, Engelbart did not mean isolated

clever tricks that help in particular situations. "We refer to a way of life in an integrated domain where hunches, cut-and-try, intangibles, and the human 'feel for a situation' usefully co-exist with powerful concepts, streamlined terminology and notation, sophisticated methods, and high-powered electronic aids."

These gains in human thinking could be as significant, he said, as the gains made in personal geographic mobility since horseback and sailboat days. He presented a plan for research that would look into ways to improve interactivity with computers. The paper led to funding from Licklider's office at the Advanced Research Projects Agency to launch Engelbart's work at the Associative Research Center.

Figure 10.11 The Xerox Alto—the first working personal computer was developed at Xerox Palo Alto Research Center (PARC) in 1974. Thousands of prototypes were manufactured. Although never a commercial product, the Alto had an enormous influence on personal computing with attributes like a graphical user interface and a computer "mouse." (Photo by Linda Burton)

On December 9, 1968, the previously unknown Engelbart launched into history with a 100-minute multimedia presentation of the mouse, the GUI and the underlying network philosophy for a computer conference in San Francisco. Most impressive was Engelbart's implementation of Bush's Memex, showing how a user could select a word in one document and bring up a second relevant document instantly—a forerunner of the hypertext link. The 1,000 computer engineers assembled at the conference gave Engelbart a standing ovation.

Particularly instrumental in organizing the path-breaking presentation was William K. English, who left SRI and moved, in 1971, to Xerox PARC, taking a dozen researchers with him, to develop other new advanced applications including the "what you see is what you get" (wysiwyg) interface, the desktop, Ethernet and object oriented programming. PARC put the concepts together into the first working personal computer—the Alto—developed in 1974. Thousands were manufactured and used in corporate offices and universities, but never sold commercially.

Apple takes a bite out of the market

The excitement surrounding the work at MIT, SRI and PARC spilled over into Stanford University in Palo Alto, California. One of the informal groups that sprang up was the eclectic "Homebrew Computer Club," a learning club which would meet weekly to hear lectures and share ideas about computing at Stanford.

Steve Wozniak and Steve Jobs were among the computer enthusiasts who attended these early meetings. They were originally motivated by a desire to use their knowledge of electronics as a way to make free phone calls, but Wozniak found he was fascinated by the intricacies of electronics. He became the "Mozart of computer engineers" (Cringley, 1996).

Teaming up with Steve Jobs, a technically adept and dynamic leader, the two founded Apple computers in 1977. The name Apple was chosen at random, probably after working on a California farm, Wozniak said, and they just never came up with anything better (Linzmahyer, 2004). Apple's first personal computer sold 50 units, and with venture capital, they marketed the Apple II, the first personal computer designed to look like a consumer product that could be used in a small business. Primitive by modern standards, the Apple II was nevertheless an instant hit, and eventually five to six million units were sold. Meanwhile, Jobs and Wozniak were multimillionaires by the time they celebrated their 25th birthdays.

Apple hit the market at exactly the right time with a good product that was several steps ahead of the competition. The Apple II looked like a home appliance, not a piece of electronic equipment. It was like a typewriter, but it was also programmable, like the IBM 360. And anyone could write software for it.

One of the independent software innovations for the Apple II was a spreadsheet program called VisiCalc, created by Dan Bricklin, then business graduate student at

Figure 10.12 Apple founders—Steve Wozniak (left) and Steve Jobs, around 1978, examine an Apple I computer. The design was elegant and the product flew off the shelves, helping to start the personal computer revolution. (Photo by Joe Melina, courtesy of the Computer History Museum)

Figure 10.13 Apple II—the Apple II computer had dual disk drives (one for the application and one for storage), along with a built-in keyboard and an auxiliary number pad. (Photo by Linda Burton)

Harvard. The idea was to create a "visible calculator" that would help small businesses "run the numbers" for the weekly payroll or inventory or supplies. The spreadsheet cut the work load dramatically. It was copyrighted but, due to issues with the legal system at the time, not patented (Bricklin, 2010).

The spreadsheet was the first "killer application"—a term that means that a software application is so useful that it would lead people to buy the computer just to be able to run the software (Cringley, 1996). It sold 700,000 copies in six years, and it helped make the Apple II a success.

Apple and the curve in the road at Xerox

One of the enduring legends of the computer industry is the way that Xerox missed the "curve in the road" by allowing Steve Jobs of Apple Computers to "steal" the research products from Xerox PARC. The reality is far more complex, as Michael Hiltzik's history, "Dealers of Lightning," points out.

Xerox established the Palo Alto Research Center next to Stanford University in January, 1970 to pursue research in computing and physics. The Xerox company itself was originally founded in 1906 as a photographic paper and chemicals supplier from Rochester, NY called Haloid Photographic Co. It became Xerox in 1958, and it introduced plain paper photocopying in 1962. The copiers were useful and very profitable, and the company dominated the market until 1970, when IBM introduced a plain paper copier. Other competitors were following quickly, including Haloid's old nemesis, Kodak. Some far-sighted Xerox executives hoped that PARC would help the company find new products.

With a strong research budget and an extraordinary staff, PARC was a hothouse of innovation. Most of the shape of the modern personal computer industry was first envisioned by engineers sitting in the famous PARC bean-bag chairs, sipping coffee, talking, and jumping up to scribble new ideas on whiteboards.

Despite all the excitement, PARC became isolated, like an island of innovation in a sea of stranded ideas. Proposals for a small business and personal computer called the Alto were not well received by Xerox managers. A plan to market the Alto III had been put on hold and an electro-mechanical typewriter with a small amount of correctable memory was marketed instead. Senior management were not convinced that PARC's highly advanced computer would make the company money. "If there's no paper to be copied . . . how will I get paid?" That was the thinking inside management (Hiltzik, 2000, p. 264).

When Jobs and the Apple engineering team were invited to a Xerox PARC presentation in December, 1979, they were widely hailed as the kids who had hit the big time. But their Apple II computer had a build-in keyboard, no mouse, a poor word processing interface and low resolution graphics. They had began working on a project called "Lisa," a next step in personal computing that would make it easier and more useful, and they were looking for ideas.

The invitation to visit PARC was not unusual. PARC engineers often hosted tours and briefings for potential customers. But some of the engineers inside PARC worried that Apple was a potential competitor, not a customer. This worry seemed a little misplaced at the time—Xerox had invested in Apple earlier that year, with the understanding that Apple would look at its technology, give advice on its marketability and possibly license some of its products. Nevertheless, it is grain of truth behind the legend.

Jobs and company were given a short demonstration in December, 1979 and went away apparently satisfied. But Jobs, often described as a man with an intense and demanding personality, returned a few days later, unannounced, insisting on the full briefing. After hurried calls to headquarters in New York, and hand-wringing by some of the staff, Jobs and the Apple team got their briefing (Hiltzik, 2000).

Jobs and the Apple engineers saw four important concepts:

1. Ethernet, a system for a networked office, with email and links to printers and copiers;
2. A graphical user interface (a "GUI") with a "desktop" and windows arrangements for different files, using a mouse that points at anything on the screen;
3. "Wysiwyg" text editor (What you see is what you get), a computer screen that shows how the printed product will look
4. An object-oriented programming language called Smalltalk that made it easy to create a GUI with bitmapped graphics on the computer screen.

"After an hour looking at demos, [Jobs] understood our technology and what it meant more than any Xerox executive understood it after years of showing it to them," said Larry Tesler, who worked for Xerox PARC at the time but soon moved to Apple.

Within four years, all except the object-oriented programming language would be part of the Apple Mac. Falling back on the theme that set the personal computer revolution in gear, Apple introduced the Macintosh with a Super-Bowl television ad that depicted an athletic woman eluding masked police while everyone else is marching in

Figure 10.14 Why 1984 won't be like 1984—this award-winning advertisement for the Apple Macintosh played off the association of computers with totalitarianism as depicted in George Orwell's book *1984*. The Mac, and this ad, were introduced in the year 1984. With a graphical user interface and a mouse, the Mac changed personal computing.

step. The woman throws an athletic hammer and smashes a giant telescreen while workers in identical uniforms gape in astonishment. "You'll see why 1984 won't be like '1984'," the ad promised.

The Apple Mac, with its GUI, wysiwyg desktop and mouse, featured the second "killer application" to hit the market: Desktop Publishing.

With desktop publishing, users could set type, create graphics, design newsletters and newspapers. In effect, anyone could enter the publishing business for less than the cost of the chemicals needed to run photo-optical systems in the big newspaper and publishing companies.

Sales soared at first, but flattened out later when consumers balked at the $4,000 price tag. Meanwhile, Apple's board of directors, unhappy with Steve Jobs' manic management style, decided to relieve Jobs of his position at the head of the Macintosh division. Jobs went to work on a new Unix-based computer system called NeXt and on digital animation techniques by helping form the Pixar Corp until he returned to Apple in 1996.

IBM, Microsoft and the clones

Meanwhile, alarmed that it had missed an important market for personal computers, IBM began developing personal computers and introduced the first model in 1981. In their haste to market a competitive product, IBM approached a small Seattle software company called Microsoft to write the underlying operating system.

Figure 10.15 The IBM Personal Computer, introduced in 1981, was followed by hardware clones that still needed the Microsoft operating system and other spreadsheet and word processing applications. (Photo by Linda Burton)

The moment, like the Apple–Xerox saga, has been called Microsoft's "coup," and point where IBM "missed the curve in the road" (Segaller, 1998). "The Microsoft connection made the IBM PC possible, and the IBM connection ensured Microsoft's long term success as a company," said Robert X. Cringley (Cringley, 1996, p. 134). It was the deal of the century.

But as Microsoft founder and president Bill Gates described it: "We gave IBM a fabulous deal—A low, one-time fee that granted the company the right to use Microsoft's operating system on as many computers as it could sell." Two other computer systems were also available for the PC then, but the Microsoft system, at $50, was by far the cheapest. (Gates, 1995)

The main goal for Microsoft at the time was to establish a software standard that would reach a tipping point, just as VHS tapes had helped standardize the video rental industry.

"Our goal was not to make money directly from IBM, but to profit from licensing MS-DOS to other companies," Gates said. "It has become popular for certain revisionist historians to conclude that IBM made a mistake working with Intel and Microsoft to create its PC." But if IBM was "king of the hill" in the mainframe market, in the volatile world of the personal computer, IBM's position was more like a front runner in a marathon (Gates, 1995).

IBM thought that the sale of hardware would be the key to the future of the business, but they had not counted on "reverse engineering," which is the legal ability to take a product apart, write exact specifications for it, and build a similar product from scratch. Only two years after the IBM PC was introduced, Compaq computers introduced the first PC "clone" that could run any software that an IBM PC could run.

That didn't detract from IBM's success at first. In 1984, IBM's PC sales reached two million, instead of the half million projected, and the PC team was euphoric (Segaller, 1998). IBM had reached the height of its corporate power, with record profits of $6.6 billion on sales of $46 billion. But sales peaked in 1990, stock prices fell, and in the coming years, over a hundred thousand employees left the firm.

And so, IBM lost the race by competing with its hardware and did not have revenues from its software to support it. The "suit" culture of IBM had lost to the nerd engineers. Like Samuel Morse, Bill Gates and Steve Jobs realized that code—or software, in this case—was the key to technological success.

Desktop publishing and nonlinear editing

Mechanized typesetting reached its technical peak in the 1950s with a "hot" type system called a Linotype (see Chapter 3). Copy would be typed out on paper and then handed over the copy desk, where it would be proofread and sent down to typesetting. "Copy over" and "copy down" were frequently heard calls in a busy newspaper or magazine organization.

A Linotype operator would key in a line of reversed type and then release a stream of molten lead. The lead would form a positive raised impression from the reversed type and, after trimming, would fall into a stick just like hand-set type. From there it would be composed on a page that would then be prepared for printing.

The linotype machines were based on a century of experimentation with mechanized typesetting technology and cost around $50,000 each in the 1950s. These "hot type" machines were hot, dirty and dangerous, and lead poisoning was a frequent problem in the publishing trades.

Two French inventors, Rene Higonnet and Louis Moyroud, thought hot-lead Linotypes were archaic technologies. With the help of Vannevar Bush and a publishers' cooperative, they developed a photo-mechanical process in the 1950s that set type six times faster than Linotypes at a cost of about $10,000 for a small unit. The photo-mechanical process eventually took on more and more computerized controls, and eventually digital systems like Compugraphic, Atex and SII used transistors to control light exposure on photosensitive paper.

The paper was developed through a photographic process, cut and then pasted onto a page. Large news organizations saved money using this photo-mechanical process but found the "cold type" system unpredictable and difficult to maintain. In the words of one Virginia publisher, it took "a bishop, five priests and a dozen acolytes to keep the things running."

The "desktop publishing" revolution involved much simpler technology for setting type. The Apple Mac, introduced in 1984, and other PC systems later in the 1980s, made it possible to set type in wysiwyg format using laser printers and Postscript technology developed by Xerox PARC researcher John Warnock, who founded Adobe Systems in 1983.

Less than 20 years after the last linotype machine was sold for $50,000, and ten years after a Compugraphic sold for $10,000, it was possible to produce camera-ready pages for printing with an investment of $5,000 in a computer and a laser printer.

When the Berlin Wall came down in 1989, newspapers across the Eastern Block rushed to set up their own typesetting operations, which had been centrally controlled by the communist publishing system. News organizations like the *Washington Post* offered their older ATEX and SII systems without charge to newspapers like *Lidové Noviny* in Prague. But it was actually cheaper to buy new desktop publishing systems than to keep the old behemoths going (Kovarik, 1990).

Nonlinear video editing systems also changed the movie and television news business. Although experimental units were available as early as the 1970s, the breakthrough came with the Lucasfilm EditDroid, developed in the mid-1980s to replace film editors like the Moviola system. EditDroid used laserdiscs and lacked processing power to deliver clean edits, but it was a harbinger of high quality editing systems that would be developed in the 1990s, such as Sun and Silicon Graphics, and later, the Avid and Media100 applications for Macintosh and PC computers.

Sun Microsystems and early workstation computers

Personal computers caught on quickly in the 1980s, but generally they were not powerful enough to handle complex tasks such as three-dimensional mechanical designs, engineering simulations and medical imaging.

Such tasks could be performed by a mainframe computer before PCs, but that was expensive. Since the 1960s there had been a niche for another kind of computer called a workstation that was smaller in scale and suited to scientific and technical work.

The earliest workstation was a 1959 unit by IBM called the Cadet, and it rented for $1,000 a month—far less than a mainframe but still far more than any average person could afford. It lacked logic circuitry, leading some to claim that that Cadet meant: "Can't Add, Doesn't Even Try."

IBM also developed several other small-scale scientific computers, but the leader in the workstation field was the Digital Equipment Corp's PDP-8. Even the Xerox Corp's Palo Alto Research Center (PARC) used a PDP-8 in preference to Xerox's own Sigma computers in the 1970s.

All in all, about 25 companies competed for the workstation market in the 1980s and 90s. One of the most successful was Sun Microsystems. The company was founded in 1982 by four Stanford University students, Scott McNealy, Vinod Khosla, Bill Joy and Andy Bechtolsheim. They created the Sun computer as part of the second wave of successful start-ups (after the Apple/Microsoft wave) that included Silicon Graphics, 3COM, and Oracle Corporation.

The Sun workstation was among the first to reach the "3M" goal—1 MPS (million instructions per second); 1 Megabyte of RAM and 1 Megapixel of display (1280 x 800). While this is standard for twenty-first century home computers, at the time, the IBM personal computer had only 16 Kilobytes of memory, a text-only display, about 1 kiloflop/second performance, and a 320 x 200 pixel display.

So in other words, the Sun workstation ran rings around the personal computer, performing 63 times faster with displays that were 16 times more complex. It also had networked file sharing and graphics acceleration, which meant that it was useful for computer animation and special effects that were coming to dominate movies. Sun workstations animated the popular movie *Toy Story*, for example.

Sun's Sparc workstation sold for three to four times more than personal computers. By 1993, over a million units were shipped and Sun had taken its place next to Apple and Microsoft as an enormously successful system. By 1995, Sun introduced a software package called Java, with the motto "write once, run anywhere." It was a software system that allowed interactive graphics to be shown on the Web on any platform. And Sun partnered with Netscape to make web browsers Java compatible (see Chapter 11).

The company was also a proponent of open systems in general and Unix system software, and was a major contributor to the open source movement. Despite their advantages and contributions, Sun workstations became less useful in comparison to the increasing power of the personal computer, and the company moved increasingly into proving Unix-adapted mainframe hardware for networked systems. In 2010, Sun was acquired by Oracle Corporation for US $7.4 billion.

Apple and Microsoft in the new century

Just as Microsoft seemed to be getting an edge in the race against IBM in the late 1980s, the competition between Apple and Microsoft flared up with a lawsuit brought by Apple over copyright infringement. Apple contended that the Microsoft Windows system copied the "look and feel" of the Apple system. Microsoft responded that the Windows idea really came from Xerox PARC and was never licensed to Apple, although Xerox was an investor. Apple lost the suit in 1993 and the company teetered on bankruptcy.

At one point around 1995, Apple was so desperate that it experimented with licensing its operating system to clone manufacturers. Power Computing was one company that made lower-priced Apple clones. But in 1997, with the end in sight, Apple brought back Steve Jobs, who ended the licensing program. When Apple clone maker Psystar attempted to use Apple software a decade later, a federal judge ruled that it was a copyright violation, and Apple's operating system was secured (Wildstrom, 2009).

The key to market success for computer rivals Apple and Micro-

Figure 10.16 Former rivals—Steve Jobs, CEO of Apple Computers, and Bill Gates, former CEO of Microsoft, enjoy a moment at D5:All Things Digital, a 2007 forum. More than any others, Jobs and Gates have shaped personal computing technology in the twentieth and twenty-first centuries. (Photo by Joi Ito—licensed under a Creative Commons Attribution)

soft was complicated in the first decade of the twenty-first century by the fact that the dot-com market "bubble" had burst. Silicon Valley startup companies, once the darlings of Wall Street, went bankrupt by the dozen. Even the once-mighty Microsoft descended from the lofty heights of nearly $600 billion in market capitalization to around $300 billion for most of the decade, and then under $200 billion during the financial crisis of 2009–2011.

In 2001, Microsoft diversified into computer games with the Xbox, while Apple held steady with its iMac line of computers, incorporating an Intel-based system that could also run the Microsoft Windows system and software.

The game changer that put Apple back in the money was a gadget called the iPod, a pocket sized music player that sold over 200 million units during the decade. By 2010, Apple's market capitalization was approaching $200 billion just as Microsoft's was falling.

Apple's release of the iPhone in 2007 and the iPad in 2010 also showed that innovation and mobility were prized by consumers.

Yet concerns grew that iPhone and iPad had been closed to "apps" that did not meet the company's political approval. Like Thomas Edison and Guglielmo Marconi's attempts to control film and the radio, Jobs appeared to be trying to control the content delivered through Apple products.

Open-architecture systems, such as the Google Android for mobile phone/information devices, also under development in the first decade of the twenty-first century, seemed to hold the promise of a more flexible system.

Figure 10.17 Computer of the future?—the caption on the photo reads: "Scientists from the RAND Corporation have created this model to illustrate how a 'home computer' could look like in the year 2004. However the needed technology will not be economically feasible for the average home. Also the scientists readily admit that the computer will require not yet invented technology to actually work, but 50 years from now scientific progress is expected to solve these problems. With teletype interface and Fortran language, the computer will be easy to use."

Thinking about the "Computer of the Future" photo

According to historian John Tosh, there are three components of analysis when examining an historical document: textual authentication; validity of factual information; and weighing alternative interpretations (Tosh, 2000).

1. Textual authentication—The photo and the text are part of the same image, as would be typical of a wire service photo sent to news organizations. However, checking the Associated Press photo transmission guide, we see that many elements are missing, including: date, location, photographer name, photo agency, and meta data about the transmission itself and intended publication date range. There are also grammar issues—"how a home computer could look like . . . "

2. Validity of factual information—It's possible that scientists from RAND Corp. were working on computers of the future, since as we learn from a simple Google Search, the RAND Corp. was founded in 1945 as a policy and technology institute. But we don't know that they anticipated, or even could have anticipated, a home computer. Most of the work on computers had been taking place at MIT and the University of Pennsylvania with the Univac system.

3. Alternative information—Rather than a news agency photo of a home computer being demonstrated at the RAND Corp., could this photo and caption be something else? The visual information seems less than valid, for instance, why would a computer have a steering wheel? This leads us to ask whether this could this be a control panel for something other than a computer.

4. Re-Evaluate—Using search engines to find this image, we learn that it is not a vision of computer of the future from the year 1954, but actually a caricature from the present poking fun at supposed miscalculations of the past—a classic blunder in understanding history.

This supposed vision of twenty-first century home computer is in fact a full-scale mock-up of a control room in a nuclear submarine from the 1950s. The original photograph was taken at a Smithsonian Institution exhibit called "Fast Attacks and Boomers: Submarines of the Cold War." It became the basis of a Fark.com Photoshop contest in September 2004.

11 Networks

The message that changed the world

By the power vested in me by nobody in particular, alpha/beta version 0.5 of NCSA's Motif-based networked information systems and World Wide Web browser, X Mosaic, is hereby released . . . (Marc Andreessen, Saturday, January 23, 1993 at 7.21 a.m. sent from the University of Illinois supercomputing center)

Marc Andreessen, a young graduate student in computer science, was only half joking when he said that the power was vested "by nobody in particular." Actually, Andreessen's group was funded by the National Center for Supercomputing Applications, which was trying to develop noncommercial software to aid scientific research. Releasing software was routine, but no one had any idea what the impact of Mosaic would be.

Tim Berners-Lee, a computer engineer at a major European physics project, had written code for something he called a World Wide Web a few years before. He distributed Andreessen's message through an international academic email system with this comment: "An exciting new World-Wide Web browser has come out, written by Marc Andreessen of NCSA. Using X/Motif, and full of good features, it installs very easily . . . "

Mosaic was the first easily available web browser that could be used to view websites, but it was remarkable in that it was also released with a web server. It was as if Andreessen distributed free eyeglasses to help read books, and then threw in a printing press as well.

Computer users who had grown accustomed to network screens full of green text now had what looked like a book page in front of them, with formatted text, pictures and—coolest of all—clickable hyperlinks to an infinite number of pages in a rapidly expanding world library.

Berners-Lee's World Wide Web was a "generative" technology, enabling people to do far more than just passively receive media from centrally produced sources.

Andreessen's Mosaic was the key that opened the door, making it easy for everyone to access and generate content for an open and unregulated World Wide Web. By the mid-1990s, with a little expertise in html coding, anyone could be a publisher.

The Web exploded: by 1998 there were 26 million pages. By 2000 there were a billion. And by 2008 there were one trillion unique web addresses, and the number of individual web pages was growing by several billion per day (Alpert and Hajaj, 2008).

Early visions of a World Wide Web

H. G. Wells, science fiction author

Both the assembling and the distribution of knowledge in the world at present are extremely ineffective . . . [We] are beginning to realize that the most hopeful line for the development of our racial intelligence lies rather in the direction of creating a new world organ for the collection, indexing, summarizing and release of knowledge, than in any further tinkering with the highly conservative and resistant university system. (Wells, 1937)

Vannevar Bush, White House Science Advisor, MIT president

Consider a future device for individual use, which is a sort of mechanized private file and library . . . A "memex" is a device in which an individual stores all his books, records, and communications [which] may be consulted with exceeding speed and flexibility. . . . Wholly new forms of encyclopedias will appear, ready made with a mesh of associative trails running through them . . . There [will be] a new profession of trail blazers . . . who find delight in the task of establishing useful trails through the enormous mass of the common record. (Bush, 1946).

J. C. R. Licklider, MIT and ARPA, 1960

"It seems reasonable to envision, for a time ten or fifteen years hence, a thinking center that will incorporate the functions of present day libraries together with anticipated advances in information storage and retrieval." (Larry Roberts said: "Lick had this concept of the 'intergalactic network' in which . . . everybody could use computers anywhere and get at data anywhere in the world. He didn't envision the number of computers we have today by any means, but he had the same concept.) (Segaller, 1998)

Martin Greenberger, computer science professor

Barring unforeseen obstacles, an on-line interactive computer service, provided commercially by an information utility, may be as commonplace by 2000 AD as telephone service is today. By 2000 AD man should have a much better comprehension of himself and his system, not because he will be innately any smarter than he is today, but because he will have learned to use imaginatively the most powerful amplifier of intelligence yet devised. (Greenberger, 1964)

Ted Nelson, Xanadu Network designer

Forty years from now (if the human species survives), there will be hundreds of thousands of files servers. And there will be hundreds of millions of simultaneous users. All this is manifest destiny. There is no point in arguing it, either you see it or you don't. (Nelson, *Literary Machines*, 1981)

By "hypertext" I mean non-sequential writing—text that branches and allows choice to the reader, best read at an interactive screen. (Nelson, Computer Lib, 1987/1974)

The vision precedes the reality

Often the idea of what a technology could become precedes the useable hardware by many decades. That was the case with the airplane, the automobile, the television and many other technologies. And it was also the case with the internet and World Wide Web: Engineers and scientists imagined ways to solve their communication problems. Where a path was envisioned, a highway might eventually follow. In fact, for a while, the internet was called the "information super-highway," a nickname typical of the high-flown rhetoric that accompanies the introduction of new technologies.

The problems of communication that early visionaries wanted to overcome mostly involved the storage and retrieval of reference information. The computer networks that solved these problems could have taken any one of a number of technological paths. Like other communications revolutions, there were curves in the road where giant companies bought up small organizations, and other instances where the giants lost to smaller visionaries.

The networking revolution was unusual in the history of technology. It did not just emerge from big top-down media companies, but rather, it enabled bottom-up, user-to-user communication. It was an "enabling" or "generative" technology. It let people do things that had never been done before. Its capabilities stretched far beyond the original idea of a giant reference library.

In the early years of the late 1980s and early 1990s, the big question seemed to be which Internet Service Provider (ISP) would come out on top. But ISPs were like gated communities for information, and in the end, they all lost. "They were crushed by a network built by government researchers and computer scientists who had no CEO, no master business plan, no paying subscribers, no investment in content, and no financial interest in accumulating subscribers," observed Jonathan Zittrain (2006).

Attempts to control the internet through the Federal Communications Commission were also defeated. "The interest in encouraging freedom of expression in a democratic society outweighs any theoretical but unproven benefit of censorship," said the Supreme Court in a 1997 decision that ensured the freedom of the internet (*Reno v. ACLU*, 1997). It's worth noting that we did not end up with a Federal Internet Commission that endlessly debated social responsibility issues with consumer organizations, as was typical with the broadcasting industry.

The story of networked computing is a story of the link between an enabling technology and the moments in history when people try to unite around a common vision.

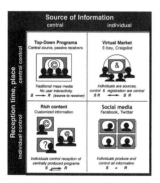

Figure 11.6 Changes in media traffic—digital networks have enabled revolutionary changes in the flow of communication, as this chart shows. Traditional media (upper left) is characterized by central control of production at the source as well as central control of the time and place of reception. Other forms of media traffic are characterized by some level of individual control. (Graphic by Bill Kovarik).

The US Pentagon
creates the first network

Just as massive electronic computers were a product of World War II, computer networks grew up in the cold war atmosphere in which scientific research had access to unlimited funds. One of the top priorities was to use computers to link radar systems across the Canadian and Alaskan north to anticipate Russian warplanes. The system was called the "Defense Early Warning" (or DEW) line. Another priority was to develop a system that could retaliate after a Russian nuclear attack.

When the Advanced Research Projects Agency was established in 1958, engineers began considering how to improve communication systems. One idea was to use phone lines for digital signals—an idea that AT&T resisted as too competitive with the then-monopoly Bell System (Segaller, 1998). Instead, the research focused on analog signals. But digital signals had many advantages, among them, that they could be sent in "packets" through a distributed network and could be automatically re-routed around trouble spots, stored and then reassembled in case of network problems. In case of a nuclear war, a digital network could be more flexible and durable than a centralized analog network.

Networking could also solve other technical problems, according to J. C. R. Licklider, the legendary computer information chief at the Defense Department's Advanced Research Projects Agency (ARPA).

First, digital networks would allow computers to work in real time, continuously rather than processing batches of instructions on cards; and secondly, a network could allow "time sharing" on computers to maximize their efficiency. As a bonus, networks could also create an advanced library, according to Licklider.

Licklider's colleague at ARPA was Rob Taylor whose Washington D.C. office in the mid-1960s had three computer terminals: one for the computer at the University of California, Berkeley, one for a computer at MIT in Massachusetts, and a third for a computer at Systems Development Corp. in Santa Monica, CA. "To talk to MIT I had to sit at the MIT terminal," Taylor said. "To bring in someone from Berkeley, I had to change chairs to another terminal. I wished I could connect someone at MIT directly with someone at Berkeley. Out of that came the idea: Why not have one terminal that connects with all of them? That's why we built ARPAnet" (Softky, 2000).

To move forward with the networked computing idea, ARPA sent out a request for proposals in 1968. The winner was a small Cambridge, MA company called BBN that had the idea of creating an Interface Message Processor (IMP) between the different kinds of computer systems. Within a year, BBN connected four universities' computer systems to create the first computer network called ARPANET. Only a few people saw the revolutionary impact of this achievement when it was completed, relatively quickly, in December, 1969.

One of the contractors for ARPA, Len Klienrock, predicted that with more sophisticated computer networks, "we will probably see the spread of computer utilities . . . like the present electric and telephone utilities." (Segaller, 1998).

An important milestone was the development of electronic mail (email) in 1972. Electronic messages were not new, of course. Operators of mainframe computers were able to place electronic messages to other operators of the same computer since the 1960s. Ray Tomlinson at BBN wanted to extend this capability to the expanding ARPA network, and wrote a program allowing computers to send and store individual messages. In order to individualize the message address, Tomlinson selected an obscure symbol used for accounting—the @ symbol—to indicate the destination domain of the email.

Scientists and academics who first used email in the 1970s started to enjoy the free and fast information exchanges. They found it easy to keep up with distant colleagues, arrange conferences, exchange ideas and collaborate on research. And they also started having fun writing to friends and trading advice and jokes. Email quickly became the "killer application" of networked computers, but in the early 1970s, preliminary designs for email applications were too weak to handle the growing network. Better packet sharing protocols and standardized systems were needed.

TCP/ IP and the Ethernet

Some computer scientists believe that the development of a common computer data transfer protocol was far more significant than ARPANET itself. They also say that it was an international effort, and that the collaboration of researchers from Europe as well as the United States was crucial to its success (Hauben, 2010).

The need to standardize packet switching networks was recognized early on by Vint Cerf, at Stanford University, and Robert Kahn at ARPA. They began envisioning a system of protocols that would link both satellite and ground-based data networks together.

Networking issues were also recognized by other researchers at the same time. Louis Pouzin was developing the French packet switching Cyclades/Cigale network. In Britain, Donald Davies and others were working on the NPL network. "The question became how could these networks be interconnected, i.e., how would communication be possible across the boundaries of these dissimilar networks," said Ronda Hauben. International conferences not only brought many together to discuss their work, but also showed how collaboration could make incremental improvements in what became TCP/IP (Hauben, 2004).

The TCP system that emerged allowed the network itself to route only the data from "nodes" and have no central control function. The "IP" or Internet Protocol would provide the address that allowed packets to be transmitted. The system was supposed to be simple enough that it would run through "two tin cans and a string."

Making the system work for personal computers was Bob Metcalfe's contribution. Metcalf had worked at BBN and helped tie MIT's computer into the ARPANET in 1969. By 1972 he was at Xerox PARC working on the same problem that Cerf and Kahn had been navigating. Metcalf's answer was Ethernet, a term he coined in 1973, envisioning a network that used cable to route a local area network of personal computers together.

PARC had developed a small personal computer call the Alto with graphical user interface and used the computer "mouse" developed by Doug Engelbart at SRI. Using an "Ethernet" made the system a prototype of computers to come.

It was clear that the academics from Palo Alto and Stanford University had a different idea of where computing could go than the US Dept. of Defense. For example, ARPA asked AT&T to take over ARPANET, more or less at cost. Out of fear that data networks would somehow create problems in the phone system, AT&T refused. This would later be seen as another instance of a big company missing the "curve in the road." As it turned out, and the engineering work on what was to become the internet remained embedded in small academically affiliated research groups rather than large corporations. It was accomplished by people who did not have the usual corporate loyalties, freeing them to create a system that was unlike anything that had been seen before.

Ethernet and TCP/IP had short-term commercial impacts as well. High quality printers, such as laser printers developed at Adobe systems in the 1980s, were three to four times more expensive than the computers they served. Few people would buy a $2000 computer and then add on a $6,000 laser printer. But in a small office with a network users could share a laser printer, and the expense made sense.

Networks expand in United States and Europe

In the late 1970s, various pieces of the academic and military networks were brought together into the National Science Foundation network and merged with a university network called "Bitnet." Both were really patchworks of several dozen networks that were able to join together using TCP/IP.

From this patchwork, two major types of network activity emerged in the 1980s: university internet systems, where users had email, ftp and text-only files accessed through "gopher" servers; and commercial Internet Service Providers (ISPs), again, a text-only system, designed for non-academics and hobbyists to exchange email and use chat rooms, and for games played in "multi-user dungeons."

While university computers were usually hard-wired into the network, ISPs offered a service that was not available from the phone companies at the time. A home computer user would connect a computer modem with a telephone line, call a local number, and then connect to the internet with a series of bell-like noises surrounded by static.

Text was the only communication method possible in the early days of the internet. Images, audio and video files were far too large to send through network connections. Early modems ran at very low speeds—around 300 bits per second, and by the year 2000, modem

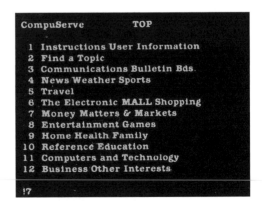

Figure 11.7 Early internet—this screen from the Compuserv ISP around 1984 shows the interface of the early text-only internet.

speeds still remained as low as 28,000 bits per second (or 28.8 kilobits). It wasn't until around 2004 that DSL modems with speeds of millions of bits per second became commercially available.

By 1978 the basic framework of the internet system was in place. When IBM began planning a personal computer that year, the IBM executive in charge, William Lowe, asked Ted Nelson and Doug Engelbart to talk with computer executives. According to computer historian John Markoff, the two network designers "sketched out a world in which computer users would be able to retrieve information wherever they were, came as a shock to the blue-suited I.B.M. executives . . . It gave a hint of the world that the PC would bring, and even though the I.B.M.-ers were getting ready to transform a hobbyist business into one of the world's major industries, they had no clue of the broader social implications" (Markoff, 2007).

University-based computer networks

By the early 1980s, the center of gravity for the digital communications revolution had shifted over to an extensive set of networks linking major US and European universities. The network accounts were free to students and faculty, offered unlimited time online, and were useful for communication within disciplines. The network also allowed computer science students to share their software projects.

One of the first innovations was a method to send a group email called a "listserv." (The limit of eight characters for file names in early computers explains some of the strange spellings of terms like "listserv" and "videotex.") Users could "subscribe" to any discussion group, and hundreds formed around topics from network protocols to science fiction. Anyone could start a listserv on any discussion topic. Another network function was FTP (file transfer protocol), used for downloading all kinds of programs and documents.

Adventurous internet users could join "Internet Relay Chat," a real-time text exchange where anyone could set up a "channel" on any topic at any time. In its heyday you could find a thousand channels going with participants from Australia to Sweden holding forth on topics ranging from world politics to bowling. There was even an IRC channel called "hot tub" for those who enjoyed racy and sexually suggestive talk.

Another development that shook some media professionals was the Usenet "news group" system. It usually involved collections of email threaded by topics ranging from recreation to computing to professional interests. Few topics had anything to do with traditional news. Discussion group topics were dominated by computing and networking issues but also included topics from archery to zoology. Usenet postings usually took a day to be distributed because the network was designed to operate at night and take advantage of computer downtime. Anyone with access to university networks could start their own group.

One system that closely anticipated the Web was a hierarchical structure of read-only files called the "gopher" system, developed at the University of Minnesota. Between 1990 and 1994, hundreds of thousands of gopher sites served up text files in a way that was similar to what would become the Web.

Interactivity, new technology and the mass media

The mainstream mass media attempted to keep up with all the changes, but digital technologies had already caused painful transitions in the business. These included the switch from "hot" lead typesetting to "cold" computer-set type and an expensive switch from film cameras to videotape in the broadcasting business. As a result, publishers were cautious about new technology investments despite the high profits the mainstream media enjoyed at the time.

In the 1980s, two kinds of experiments in new interactive media backed by news organizations turned out to be expensive failures: teletext and videotex. Around 1978, television networks experimented with the idea of inserting text and graphics into the TV signal (technically, into the vertical blanking interval). Several hundred pages could be broadcast in sequence to viewers who owned a special receiver and a small keypad. Stations and networks in the United States, Japan and Europe experimented with the teletext system, but the system was slow and highly limited.

Another approach involved what was generically called videotex Early prototypes included an Associated Press/CompuServe partnership in 1980 and the Times Mirror "Gateway" and Knight Ridder "Viewtron" experiments of 1982–1986. Viewtron was ahead of its time with electronic banking, games, chats, and other non-news services. Another experiment was the CBS-IBM-Sears venture called Trinitex, which started in 1984, ended in 1988. It was revived in 1989 as Prodigy without CBS as a partner.

The US experiments did not succeed partly because the technology was expensive. Users had to buy the Viewtron terminal, at a cost of $600, and then pay monthly fees of over $20. Viewtron tried to bring down the expense with advertising, but poor graphics were not attractive to advertisers or users.

By the end of the 1980s, news media analysts concluded that videotex was "not a threat" to the news business. Editors in the traditional media said that they were in the news business, not in business to help users connect or chat with each other. And traditional news wasn't that important to those who subscribed to ISPs like Compuserv, Prodigy and America On Line.

Times Mirror company, still bruised from the Gateway experiment, and others like Cox Communications in Atlanta, GA partnered with the Prodigy between 1992 and 1995. But editors worried that computer experts and site designers were more in control of the news than they were. They believed that with the complexity of the technology, quality news was taking second place to packaging.

One of the publishing industry's last attempts to anticipate market changes was launched at Knight Ridder's Information Design Lab in Boulder, CO, in 1992. The idea was to create "touch-tablet" technology with a look and feel similar to a newspaper. "For the first time, we're going to be seeing an alternative to ink on paper," said lab director Roger Fidler. "It may be difficult to conceptualize the idea of digital paper, but in fact, we believe that's what's going to happen." But the concept was ahead of its time, and the lab closed in 1996. "Fidler's dream never quite got airborne before the hurricane blowing through the American newspaper industry killed off the Knight Ridder lab and all its hopes," said Alan Rusbridger (Rusbridger, 2010).

Valuable lessons came out of these experiments:

- *Navigation is important.* The back button and site history lists, standard on web browsers in the 1990s, came from the confusion of having to navigate endless chains of numbered topics in the 1980s.

- *News was not enough.* People wanted to be able to communicate in small groups and generate their own content.

- *Graphics mattered.* Users wanted a graphical display for networked communications to match new GUI interfaces on their computer desktops. People wanted, at the very least, to experience the first two media revolutions—movable type and visual communication— through their computer networks.

European networks

Interactive networks caught on in Europe much more quickly than the United States, since they were backed by governments that had a tradition of running subsidized and more reliable telecommunications services.

In the early 1970s, the British Broadcasting Corp. (BBC) began offering a service called Teletext, a closed-caption interactive news service carried over the television broadcast signal in the vertical blanking interval. In 1980, the British Post Office launched a videotex computer service called "Prestel" amid a chorus of enthusiastic predictions. Prestel offered online news and services such as banking and travel ticket sales. It was linked directly to television sets. However, it was expensive and Conservative British politicians in the 1980s were not inclined to continue subsidies. When attempts to market the service to business did not pan out, it was finally suspended in 1994.

The French telecommunications ministry was far more successful with an ambitious project called Minitel, launched in 1980. Minitel featured a small, low-resolution

Figure 11.8 Early British internet— Teletext, a closed-captioned text service delivered through television broadcast signals, was available from the 1970s through the BBC. About two million Teletext sets were in use in 1982. But the system was slow to respond and not capable of high resolution graphics, as this screen shot from July 1990 shows. (Photo courtesy Bill Johnston)

Figure 11.9 Early French internet—an ambitious telephone-based information service called Minitel was used by about 25 million people in the 1980s and 90s for business services, advertising and telephone directories. Minitel also had chat features available that allowed the creation of virtual communities. The system was an early demonstration of the value of large-scale networks when prices were within reach of most people.

terminal available at little or no cost to all telephone customers. It had a phone modem that could also double as a regular telephone. In the beginning, Minitel carried online phone listings and saved the cost of publishing some phone directories. But by the mid-1980s, Minitel blossomed into the world's largest e-commerce marketplace, with banking, shopping and all kinds of services.

The Minitel experience was early proof that interactive media could catch on. Surprisingly, Minitel's low resolution terminals became a fixture in France, and despite a migration to the World Wide Web, Minitel was still generating about a million directory assistance page views a month in 2009 (RFI, 2009).

The internet takes off with ISPs

The telephone company did not provide internet service in the early years of the internet, so individual bulletin boards and ISPs emerged to fill the gap. Computer users would "dial-up" a local phone number to connect with the bulletin board or ISP's computer. These were usually stand-alone services, in effect, gated information communities. Not until the mid- to late 1990s would these ISP services connected to the broader internet or the Web.

About 70,000 independently operated small bulletin boards were operating in the United States in the early 1990s (Rheingold, 1996). Each of these had to be accessed through a separate procedure, by dialing a phone number through a computer modem, rather than directly through the internet.

Part of the problem was that the backbone of the internet at the time was the National Science Foundation's data network. Access was limited by the NSF's Acceptable Use Policy that prohibited commercial traffic, requiring that all information have educational, scientific or research value. Legislation to open the NSFnet to links with commercial networks, called the Scientific and Advanced-Technology Act, was introduced by Sen. Al Gore and Rep. Rick Boucher in 1992.

The first large ISP was CompuServe, which grew from several hundred thousand subscribers in the late 1970s to about four million in the early 1990s. Users paid an

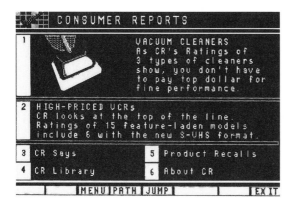

Figure 11.10 Prodigy service in the United States—in an attempt to cut costs to consumers, IBM and Sears invested in Prodigy, an information service supported by advertising. Prodigy screens such as this one had low-resolution graphics and better navigational controls than most other services at the time.

access fee and an hourly rate. An hour online every day could cost over $100 a month.

One of the lessons from an early 1981 partnership between CompuServe and the Associated Press was that not many people were interested in paying a premium fee for news. Only about five percent of the demand involved information needs; most of the rest involved person-to-person communication about personal interests and games.

An early experimental dial-up "bulletin board" network was the Whole Earth 'Lectronic Link (WELL), a computerized counterculture meet-up started by Whole Earth Catalog publisher Stuart Brand in 1985. One of the early advantages of WELL membership was the ability to keep track of concerts by music groups like the Grateful Dead, sharing travel plans and bootlegged music tapes. But all kinds of other exchanges were taking place, from jokes to political activism.

In 1989, a commercial ISP named Prodigy attempted to cut the high cost of online services with a new business model that included advertising. IBM and Sears invested over a billion dollars in Prodigy with the idea that it would be the litmus test for the online industry.

Prodigy billed itself as a family-oriented ISP and used editors to screen sexual and other potentially offensive content. As a result, the courts held that Prodigy was responsible for everything published on its websites, and the company lost an expensive libel case as a result (*Stratton-Oakmont v. Prodigy Services*, 1995). Prodigy eventually merged with CompuServe, which in turn merged with America Online.

One problem that ISPs faced in the early 1990s, before the introduction of the World Wide Web, involved low-resolution graphics due in part to very slow networks then in existence.

America Online, founded in 1992, was the most successful ISP in part because it had the best graphical interface. In effect, the company found a "workaround" to the slow transfer of graphics through networks. AOL using the regular US mail to deliver CDs (compact disks) that updated users' graphics data, putting permanent frames and navigation buttons around the interactive text windows. AOL also made the process of connecting to an email system easy for consumers who had few other

Figure 11.11 America Online—one of the most innovative early Internet Service Providers was America Online (AOL), a company started in 1992 and merged with Time-Warner in 2000. AOL's graphics and fixed navigational buttons were pre-loaded from disks sent through the mail. The approach was highly successful in the 1990s but the company failed to keep up with changes in technology in the early twenty-first century.

options. The number of subscribers grew from half a million in 1993 to a peak of around 27 million by the year 2000.

The arrival of the World Wide Web

Tim Berners-Lee said he never really had a "Eureka" moment about the World Wide Web. Instead, the idea grew and coalesced over the years as he worked at CERN, the European Laboratory for Particle Physics based in Switzerland.

"Suppose all the information stored on computers everywhere was linked," he thought. "Suppose I could program my computer to create a space in which anything could be linked to anything" (Berners-Lee, 1999).

Berners-Lee was aware of a previous attempt at network building called Xanadu by Ted Nelson. Like many projects, it was too early and too complex, but it had valuable ideas. One of these was "hypertext," the now-familiar idea that text could have embedded links, and that those links could lead away from a linear document toward references or related paths. Berners-Lee called the basic protocol for the Web a "hyper-text transfer protocol," also known as "http." Another important idea was the Universal Resource Locator, "URL," that would help locate web pages.

The first website built was at the European Organization for Nuclear Research (CERN), and was first put "on line" on August 6, 1991.

The idea was to exchange charts and other graphic data more easily by using a computer program that interpreted text and pictures in one window. It was originally developed for scientists to collaborate on high-energy physics projects as they worked at different universities and institutes all over the world, but Berners-Lee believed it could also be useful for all kinds of communication. The program could read pages of text which had special commands or "tags" that automatically brought pictures into the browser window. Several different kinds of tags were used initially, but HTML (Hyper Text Markup Language) was what caught on. Berners-Lee shared his idea freely with users around the world and a number of early browsers emerged.

Figure 11.12 World Wide Web pioneer—Tim Berners-Lee, as an employee at the European Organization for Nuclear Research, conceived the idea of using hypertext with a code that combined text formatting and a graphical user interface. His idea went online in August, 1991, but took off in 1993 when the Mosaic browser and server software, developed by Marc Andreessen at the University of Illinois, became freely available in 1993. The Web allowed anyone to publish virtually anything, revolutionizing international communications in a few years. (Photo taken in 2010 by Paul Clarke, licensed under a Creative Commons Attribution)

The most popular early web browser was Mosaic, created between 1992 and 1993 by Marc Andreessen and fellow computer students at the National Center for Supercomputing Applications (NCSA) at the University of Illinois. Mosaic could run on Windows, Unix, and Mac platforms and it had navigation buttons, a memory and seamless graphics. It also came with server software, which allowed anyone to not only read but also publish on the World Wide Web.

Because Andreessen's research project was funded specifically for developing free scientific applications, he gave Mosaic away, and in the process fueled a surge of interest in this new form of communication. The original Mosaic browser was rather clunky and network connections were still fairly slow, but the combination of text and visual communications was instantly recognized as revolutionary. By March, 1994, the phenomenal success of Mosaic led Andreessen and others to create a company that became Netscape. Among the early investors were news media giants like Knight Ridder.

As it turned out, a handful of visionaries at universities and research institutions had transformed the internet from a valuable but limited text delivery service into a new window on the world.

As Berners-Lee said: "We are slowly learning the value of decentralized, diverse systems and of mutual respect and tolerance. . . . My hope and faith that we are headed somewhere stem in part from the repeatedly proven observation that people seem to be naturally built to interact with others as part of a greater system" (Berners-Lee, 1999).

News on the Web

The news media does not usually get credit for a quick response to the Web, but in some cases it should. Knight Ridder and NBC, for example, jumped in with both feet in 1994 and 1995.

"They brought [Mosaic] up on the screen—graphics, text, data. I was blown away. It didn't take long to see that this was going to be a revolution," Chris Jennewein, Knight Ridder News Media vice president for technology and operations told *American Journalism Review* in an article about the Web. In January of 1994, Jennewein was working with Knight Ridder's *San Jose Mercury News*. Since the *Mercury* is located in the heart of Silicon Valley, its editors and reporters had been more aware than most of the digital revolution. They had already developed a faxed newspaper and an internet bulletin board.

In 1994 the paper had a news site available through America Online, but the disadvantage was that readers had to subscribe to AOL. Also, the graphics were pre-downloaded from a disk weeks or months in advance, not from the site update. News photos could not be sent through the network.

And so, Jennewein said, developing a website was the logical next step. In fact, Knight Ridder also became one of the original investors in Netscape as Marc Andreessen and the other inventors of the Mosaic browser broke off to form their own browser company. Following the *Mercury* by early 1995 were the *Washington Post*, the *Raleigh News & Observer*, and many others. By 1996, every major publication and broadcast network had a website.

Most of them didn't do much more than shovel the same news from the paper or broadcast onto their pages. But within a few years they also began to innovate with interactive forums, audio and video clips, and other services. The idea that new media could help traditional media deliver better services, faster, to a growing audience made sense at the time.

Figure 11.13 First news web page— The *San Jose Mercury News* put the first news web page online in May of 1994. While the graphics capabilities were limited, at least the entire content of the Web page could be downloaded at once, unlike America Online, the dominant ISP at the time. (Screenshot courtesy *San Jose Mercury News*)

When content was king

A joint partnership between NBC and Microsoft to create a new MSNBC cable channel and the msnbc.com website started off with high hopes in December, 1995 and floundered, for a time, as ratings remained low. Critics quipped that CNN and Fox were broadcast channels with websites, while MSNBC was a website with a cable channel.

The website/cable channel idea was based on widely accepted idea, best articulated by Bill Gates, that "Content is King." This means that quality programming is what both viewers and internet users want, and therefore future of the internet would be in combined efforts with traditional content producing media.

Introducing the Microsoft-NBC partnership, Gates said:

> Content is where I expect much of the real money will be made on the Internet, just as it was in broadcasting. The television revolution that began half a century ago spawned a number of industries, including the manufacturing of TV sets, but the long-term winners were those who used the medium to deliver information and entertainment . . .

The Internet also allows information to be distributed worldwide at basically zero marginal cost to the publisher. Opportunities are remarkable . . . For example, the television network NBC and Microsoft recently agreed to enter the interactive news business together. Our companies will jointly own a cable news network, MSNBC, and an interactive news service on the Internet. NBC will maintain editorial control over the joint venture . . .

Figure 11.14 Independence in cyberspace—John Perry Barlow, lyricist for the Grateful Dead music group, wrote a widely circulated call for independence in cyberspace as a reaction to Congressional attempts to control internet content in the 1996 Communications Decency Act. (Photo by Joi Ito—licensed under a Creative Commons license).

Many computer hackers strongly disagreed with the idea of a marriage between the internet and traditional media. As we will see in Chapter 12, they hoped for a more inclusive future for digital media. One of the leaders of this movement was John Perry Barlow, a Grateful Dead lyricist and one of the founders of the Electronic Frontier Foundation. Barlow wrote "A Declaration of the Independence of Cyberspace" a month after Gates' speech.

Governments of the Industrial World, you weary giants of flesh and steel, I come from Cyberspace, the new home of Mind. On behalf of the future, I ask you of the past to leave us alone. You are not welcome among us. You have no sovereignty where we gather. We have no elected government, nor are we likely to have one, so I address you with no greater authority than that with which liberty itself always speaks.

I declare the global social space we are building to be naturally independent of the tyrannies you seek to impose on us. You have no moral right to rule us nor do you possess any methods of enforcement we have true reason to fear . . .

Barlow's argument for free speech on the internet and the Web struck a strong chord in a new generation. Barlow was particularly incensed by the 1996 Telecommunications Act, especially the portion called Communications Decency Act (CDA), which attempted to impose heavy content restrictions on indecent language and images on the internet and the Web. Under the law, the word "breast" could have been illegal, even if it referred to cancer research.

In court testimony about the value of free speech on the internet, Howard Rheingold noted the importance of virtual communities to people who felt socially isolated by their values or orientations. "If you were, for example, a gay teenager in a small town who felt that maybe you were the only person in the world who had certain feelings . . . [you would be among] a number of people like that who are at risk of suicide and depression." Heavy regulation of the internet would mean that "they might be unable to participate in discussions with others who might be able to tell them that they're not alone" (Rheingold, 1996).

In 1997, the US Supreme Court endorsed the idea of free speech and struck down the CDA in the *Reno v. ACLU* case. They said:

> "... Unlike the conditions that prevailed when Congress first authorized regulation of the broadcast spectrum [for radio and television], the Internet can hardly be considered a "scarce" expressive commodity. It provides relatively unlimited, low cost capacity for communication of all kinds. Through the use of chat rooms, any person with a phone line can become a town crier with a voice that resonates farther than it could from any soapbox. Through the use of Web pages, mail exploders, and newsgroups, the same individual can become a pamphleteer ... "

The result was that the internet and the Web were considered to be protected by the First Amendment, which meant that they were free and open to nearly all content, like print, photography and film media, and not regulated by a federal agency, like radio and television.

The CNN-AOL disaster

The idea that "content is king"—an idea that animated the Microsoft-NBC venture—was an underlying rationale in the high-stakes bet on a partnership between America Online and Time Warner CNN. In 2000, the stock value of AOL had inflated to the point where it was used to buy Time Warner CNN, then one of the word's largest media content companies and owner of Warner Brothers studio, Cable News Network (CNN) and the *Time* publishing empire. It was the largest merger in business history, and it was made just two months before the "dot-com bubble" peak.

Company executives saw themselves creating "the world's first fully integrated media and communications company for the Internet Century, in an all-stock combination valued at $350 billion." AOL's chairman, Steve Case, took charge of the gigantic new company (Time-Warner, 2000).

The train wreck that followed is the stuff of legend. First, the "dot-com bubble" burst March 13, 2000, probably caused by a coincidental influx of sell orders processed that day. The sell orders triggered a chain reaction of selling that fed on itself as investors bailed out of speculative bets on information technology stocks. Contributing to the panic was a court finding that Microsoft was operating as a monopoly. Around the same time, a federal investigation showed that

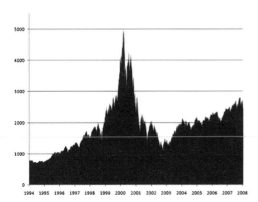

Figure 11.15 Dot-com bubble—the rise and fall of internet stocks is seen clearly in this graphic of the rise and fall of the technology-heavy NASDAQ composite stock index. (Graphic by Little Professor—released to public domain through Wikipedia)

AOL had been inflating earnings statements in order to get into position to buy Time-Warner.

When the dust cleared, Case had left the building. Analysts blamed the disaster on the clash of business cultures, AOL's financial irregularities and Time-Warner's inability to carry out the vision. Yet the disaster wasn't entirely unpredictable. AOL was already becoming obsolete at the time, since after 2000, most consumers didn't need an ISP to access the internet—regular phone companies were providing direct connections to the open web.

Another problem with the merger was that computer users were not so interested in simply extending their television habits into some sort of web interactivity. While AOL offered hobby groups, online markets and other community oriented resources, many users did not find the network worth the $30 per month subscription price. AOL was often compared to a "walled garden" on the edge of the enormous World Wide Web frontier.

In 2009, Time-Warner sold off AOL for a fraction of its original value, and by 2010, the combined value of both companies was about one-seventh of what it had been (Arango, 2010). Content may have been noble, but it had been deposed as "king" in the twenty-first century.

Browser "Wars"

When the World Wide Web became widely available to consumers in the mid-1990s, a dozen browsers were available: among them were Opera, Arachne, Cyberdog, HotJava, Lotus and the popular Mosaic. After Marc Andreessen left the University of Illinois, he founded Netscape Corp. with venture capital expert Jim Clark in 1994. Netscape's Navigator browser became the most popular on the Web in the mid-1990s, but trouble was on the horizon.

Microsoft licensed Mosaic from the University of Illinois in 1995 and released their version of it as Internet Explorer 1.0 with the first Microsoft Windows operating system. Microsoft's browser caught up with Netscape around 1998 and took about two-thirds of the market by 2000. Finding it difficult to compete, Netscape was acquired by America OnLine (AOL) in 1998, and the browser software code was released to the Mozilla Foundation, which opened the code to all programmers.

Microsoft's Internet Explorer was widely used because it was bundled with Microsoft Windows. Even though Microsoft gave Explorer away, a complex new twist on century-old laws against "tying" and "refusal to deal" became evident. With around 90 percent of all computer system software, Microsoft was already a monopoly in fact. By "tying" of products together, Microsoft allegedly violated antitrust laws. Another serious allegation involved Microsoft's alleged altering of application programming interfaces (APIs) to favor Internet Explorer over other web browsers when used with Microsoft's system software. This was seen as a "refusal to deal," similar to the way newspapers once refused to carry radio ads in the 1950s (as noted in Chapter 3).

The US Justice Dept. sued Microsoft in 1998, alleging that the company abused its monopoly power, but as the Justice Dept. dropped most of the lawsuit when the

Republican administration of George W. Bush took office in 2001. A similar lawsuit was settled in Europe. Meanwhile, the Mozilla Foundation took Netscape's basic code and, through the open-source process created the Thunderbird and Firefox browsers in 2004.

The overall problem, according to some observers, was that Microsoft was composed of technological idealists who were slow to appreciate the political implications of some of its technology decisions (Auletta, 2010). The lesson for large engineering-oriented companies that become protective was that they may find that they have overstepped legal or ethical boundaries without always knowing how serious those boundaries were for traditional media.

The long tail of the Web

One of the most significant innovations that the World Wide Web made possible involved serving special needs and niche markets. This is known as "long tail marketing," a concept that can be applied to mass media, products, services and social networks.

Long tail marketing is more or less the opposite of mass marketing or mass media. In order to appeal to a mass market, the most popular 20 percent of items must be available in volume to the buying public. For a retail bookstore, this can mean stocking the shelves with best-sellers and popular books but not serving smaller niche markets.

Two important examples of successful long-tail marketing in mass media are Amazon.com and Netflix. Jeff Bezos, a financial analyst who left his job with just an idea of an online book company, started Amazon.com in 1994 at a time when selling books through the Web was difficult. "Investors thought he was crazy," said a *Time* magazine profile (Ramo, 1999). By 2009, Amazon revenue was $24.5 billion. A similar long-tail venture was started by Reed Hastings, a computer engineer who left the Marines for the Peace Corps. Hastings founded Netflix in 1998 after being laid off from his job and worrying about overdue fees at a local video store. By 2009 the company was bringing in $1.7 billion in revenue and providing on-demand video movie services.

While niche marketing is nothing new, the internet presents new kinds of opportunities for people who see the potential. Chris Anderson, editor for *Wired* Magazine, sees the future of business in long tail marketing through the internet since the volume of all the low popularity items can be greater than volume of highly popular items (Anderson, 2008).

Figure 11.16 Amazon Books founder—Jeff Bezos founded Amazon.com online bookstore as an early test of "long-tail" marketing to serve large numbers of small niche markets. (Photo by James Duncan Davidson, licensed under a Creative Commons Attribution)

Search engines

In 1996, a pair of young Stanford University computer students, Larry Page and Sergey Brin, started research on the link structure of the World Wide Web. In the process, they created a search engine that would become Google by 1998.

Most web search engines at the time, such as Excite or Yahoo, were based on the number of times the search term was found on a web page, and it was easy to optimize web pages for searches by simply repeating the terms over and over again in the text or meta tags.

On the other hand, links were in effect votes by other users for the content of the web page, Page and Brin realized. By creating a map of weblinks, they had created the basis of a new kind of search engine that would be more likely to turn up useful information than competing search engines. At the time, other search engines like Yahoo and AskJeeves were positioned as "portals" to the Web. Their strategy was to be "sticky," to slow users down so they would find other items of interest (and advertising) on the way to getting the information the users needed. Google, with a rapidly responding, low-graphics front end, was designed to speed users on their way to the pages they wanted to find.

By 2010, Google was by far the world's leading search engine with one million servers in data centers around the world, over a billion hits per day and two-thirds of US search engine traffic. The Google phenomena includes dozens of other products, such as YouTube (see Chapter 12), and auxiliary services such as translation and collaborative documents.

Google's $22 billion dollar income in 2009 came mostly from advertisers who want to reach people already in the market. For example, retailers can advertise on search pages that come up for people who are looking for specific products. The entire process is automatic through Google Ad Sense. There are no advertising salesman, no middle-men, no contracts.

"There are sound reasons for traditional media to fear Google," said Ken Auletta in his book about Google. "Today, Google's software initiatives encroach on every media industry from telephone to television to advertising to newspapers to magazines to book publishers to Hollywood studios to digital companies like Microsoft, Amazon, Apple and eBay" (Auletta, 2010).

Internet freedom

One of the most significant issues for Google involves its use in China and other countries where governments place heavy controls on information. In 2000, Google began offering Chinese language web searches from its US base, but found it was being slowed or blocked by border routers, also known as the "Great Firewall of China."

Google began offering search engine services on Google.cn in 2006. The company was criticized in the United States and Europe for cooperating with Chinese censors but a spokesman said the product was "faster and more reliable, and . . .

provide[d] more and better search results for all but a handful of politically sensitive subjects . . . Self-censorship, like that which we are now required to perform in China, is something that conflicts deeply with our core principles," said Google spokesman Elliot Schrage in Congressional testimony. "This was not something we did enthusiastically or something that we're proud of at all" (Schrage, 2006; Martin, 2007).

In January 2010, Google said it had come under a highly sophisticated hacking attack in China and would no longer cooperate with censors. It redirected searches to Google.hk (Hong Kong), which is part of China but under a somewhat different legal system.

Figure 11.17 Google founder—Sergey Brin and Google co-founder Larry Page were interested in mapping the Web as a Stanford University graduate project in computer engineering when they realized that their web maps provided a better basis for a search engine (Photo by Joi Ito—licensed under a Creative Commons Attribution)

China's use of 30,000 internet police, its blocking of "harmful" content like the words "freedom" and anti-government protests, and its imprisonment of journalists and dissidents are well known abuses of internationally guaranteed freedoms.

China is not the only country with a "great wall" around the internet. Many countries block websites that are deemed illegal. For example, Saudi Arabia has two firewalls, one for indecent content and the other for politically offensive content. According to Reporters Without Borders report, *Enemies of the Internet,* the worst violators of freedom of expression are Saudi Arabia, Burma, China, North Korea, Cuba, Egypt, Iran, Uzbekistan, Syria, Tunisia, Turkmenistan and Vietnam.

Unlike these countries, most of the world rejects political repression. Yet there are kinds of communication that most people would not want to tolerate, for example, child pornography and open incitements to violence. And there are gray areas that various cultures define for themselves. In Europe, laws against "hate speech" make it illegal to advocate racist causes or sell Nazi paraphernalia, and websites with Nazi materials have been blocked at Yahoo and eBay. And in Asia and most Arab nations, laws against pornography are much more strictly enforced than in the United States, Europe or Latin America.

Harmonization of communications law between various systems does not mean forcing the same laws on every country, but rather, reducing the differences and creating minimum standards. And yet, given the enormous differences between political and cultural systems in the world, the current potential to minimize conflict seems small compared to the potential to generate it.

Laws of network value

A "law" in economics or technology is simply a theory based on observations about repeating patterns. It's not to be confused with the kind of law made by a legislature or parliament.

There are several "laws" of networks that have been warmly debated, but the recent ones show that the one-to-many relationship of the broadcaster to the audience (Sarnoff's law) is less valuable than the new relationships between a computer network and its users in the many-to-many systems.

> *Sarnoff's law*—David Sarnoff, the president of NBC radio and RCA from the 1920s to the 1950s, said that a broadcast network is valuable in proportion to the number of people in its audience. This "top-down" model values each individual once. A network of 5 would be half as valuable as a network of 10.

> *Metcalfe's law*—Robert Metcalfe, inventor of Ethernet, said the value of a network was the square of the number of users. A network of 10 users would be four times more valuable than a network of 5 users (e.g., 5x5=25; 10x10=100).

> *Reed's law*—David P. Reed said the value of a network doubles every time a user is added. A network of 5 users would have a value of 32, while a network of 6 users would have a proportional value of 64, and a network of 10 people would have a value of 1024.

> *Beckstrom's law*—Rod Beckstrom said the value of a network is in the way it saves on the costs of transactions. A more concrete economic law than Metcalf or Reed's laws, Beckstrom's idea is simply that the money a person saves in a network transaction is the value of that network to that person. If a book costs $25, but it can be purchased for $15 on a network, then the network is worth $10 to that person based on that one transaction. The overall value of the network is how it saves money in all transactions.

12 Global digital media culture

No experiment can be more interesting than that we are now trying, and which we trust will end in establishing the fact that man may be governed by reason and truth. Our first object should therefore be to leave open to him all the avenues to truth. The most effectual hitherto found is the freedom of the press. It is, therefore, the first shut up by those who fear the investigation of their actions. (Thomas Jefferson, 1804)

The digital media revolution was well under way, creating major shifts in media structures and sparking dramatic social change, as the twenty first century passed its first decade.

For the first time in human history, digital networks allowed billions of people to communicate across national boundaries, instantly, at no cost, in any media format—from text to video. Within this new global media culture, information about an earthquake in China, violence in Kenya or a protest in the Middle East could be shared between people with only a few hundred dollars worth of technology. The information did not have to be generated by professional news organizations; instead, participants and observers could post information into personal networks which could then be passed along to broader networks. If the information was significant and verified, it would be passed along to the global media. The dramatic differences in communication in only a few short decades meant that even closed kingdoms and cloistered societies had become open books to the world.

The digital media revolution also continued to spawn new consumer devices, such as highly portable readers and video cell phones. These "information appliances" were built on systems capable of using closed and tightly controlled "apps" (small applications). As a business model, they provided a small ray of hope for professional media operations on the brink of bankruptcy, but critics said they could close off the creative frontier of the Web.

That frontier was seen in new forms of media creating new communities and new marketplaces of ideas. Social and collaborative information structures such as Wikipedia, Facebook and Twitter provided early examples of the sense of community that could be achieved. Meanwhile, the new media also generated controversy over issues like copyright, personal privacy and accuracy in publications.

Perhaps the most important question about the digital media revolution involved challenges to longstanding principles of freedom of expression. Governments tried to contain popular revolts sparked by information spread through the internet, but repression usually just spread the anger. Increasing tensions between the world's cultural systems were another consequence of unprecedented forms of freedom of expression. One website in particular, an international nonprofit organization called WikiLeaks, accepted and published secret diplomatic memos from anonymous sources that revealed deep corruption in Middle Eastern governments. The new information was a major factor in triggering popular uprisings across the region.

While supporting internet freedom in broad terms, the United States and European nations attempted to control WikiLeaks and similar spin-off sites. Computer hacker activists, meanwhile, said they were determined to use the new media as a lever to compel reform, just as earlier generations of political revolutionaries used newspapers and muckraking reformers used independent magazines.

Social and collaborative media

Throughout human history, people have needed small group communication to plan collaborative activities like hunting and farming. In oral cultures, traveling minstrels, town criers and civic meetings were the social media. In emerging literate cultures, such as the Egyptian, Indian, Chinese, Greek and Roman empires two to four millennia ago, handwritten newsletters were the social media for small and usually elite groups. Other historical examples of social media include newsletters circulated by banking houses in early modern Europe and letters exchanged by the Committees of Correspondence before the American Revolution.

Digital social media began with email networks called listservs and Usenet groups, which became popular in universities, while internet service providers like America Online and the Whole Earth 'Lectronic Link (WELL) opened commercial markets, as we have seen in Chapter 11. In the early twenty-first century, digital social media expanded through the use of web browsers and apps, enabling a more democratic, accessible and responsive way to form more intricate personal networks.

Social media served several kinds of functions. They allowed person-to-person communication where people could socialize, extend their personal lives, share photos and find avenues for self-expression. Some allowed free classified advertising for jobs, used cars, real estate and garage sales, replacing the way newspapers had once served as a central bulletin board for small-scale community commerce.

There was fun in discovering all these new functions; people enjoyed becoming part of a virtual community. Journalist and author Howard Rheingold was so fond of social networks in the 1980s that he described the excitement in his book *The Virtual Community*:

> Finding the WELL was like discovering a cozy little world that had been flourishing without me, hidden within the walls of my house; an entire cast of characters welcomed me to the troupe with great merriment as soon as I found the secret door. Like others who fell into the WELL, I soon discovered that I was audience, performer, and scriptwriter, along with my companions, in an ongoing improvisation.

Figure 12.1 Falling into the WELL—journalist Howard Rheingold fell into the Whole Earth 'Lectronic Link (the WELL) in 1985 and described in his book *The Virtual Community*. "An entire cast of characters welcomed me to the troupe . . . " he wrote. (Photo by Joi Ito—licensed under a Creative Commons Attribution)

> A full-scale subculture was growing on the other side of my telephone jack, and they invited me to help create something new. (Rheingold, 1993)

The excitement of the WELL experience had counterparts in other easy-to-use social utilities like Compuserv, Prodigy and AOL, but as we have seen, all of these "walled garden" networks went bankrupt as they attempted to compete with the wide-open World Wide Web. "They were crushed by a network built by government researchers and computer scientists who had no CEO, no master business plan, no paying subscribers, no investment in content, and no financial interest in accumulating subscribers," observed Jonathan Zittrain (Zittrain, 2008).

The free software movement

Computer hackers of the 1970s and 80s were noted both for their idealism and their anti-authoritarian culture. One important idea was that digital media had unique characteristics, and trying to make it follow old media rules would just hold it back. "Information wants to be free" was their motto; working together on information distributing software was their obsession.

In the words of free software advocate Richard Stallman:

> The copyright system grew up with printing—a technology for mass-production copying. Copyright fit in well with this technology because it restricted only the mass producers of copies. It did not take freedom away from readers of books. An ordinary reader, who did not own a printing press, could copy books only with pen and ink, and few readers were sued for that. Digital technology is more flexible than the printing press: when information has digital form, you can easily copy it to share it with others. This very flexibility makes a bad fit with a system like copyright. That's the reason for the increasingly nasty and draconian measures now used to enforce software copyright.

The idea of open-source software may seem idealistic and farfetched at first, since it lacks even the most rudimentary business model, but some of the most important software applications in computing—for instance, the Unix operating system, the

Figure 12.2 Free software—some of the most important network and system software has emerged from the Free Software movement led by Richard Stallman, a leader of the hacker culture and a programmer who worked on artificial intelligence at MIT. (Photo by Sam Williams, from the O'Reilly book *Free as in Freedom: Richard Stallman's Crusade for Free Software*; Creative Commons)

Apache web server and the Mozilla (Firefox) browser—have been based on the open source concept. Unix, the application at the base of most mainframe computers, along with Apple system 10, Linux and others—was developed at the University of California, Berkeley, by Bill Joy, Kevin Thompson and others in the 1970s and 80s. The important contribution was not just the software, according to tech writer and historian Andrew Leonard. "It was the way Berkeley created software," he said. A core group would coordinate the contributions of a far-flung network of hackers, creating a template for open-source software development. "The Berkeley hackers set up a system for creating free software," he said (Leonard, 2000).

This was the same approach taken in the mid-1990s when the Web started outgrowing the NCSA web server developed by the Mosaic team. A group of developers around the San Francisco Bay area formed a group to patch the NCSA web server software, and the original name "A patchy" sever, quickly evolved into Apache. Today the software is used by at least 50 percent of web servers, leading Microsoft and other proprietary servers. It was developed using the same open-source approach. Apache developers said:

> "We believe the tools of online publishing should be in the hands of everyone . . . We realize that it is often seen as an economic advantage for one company to 'own' a market . . . This is typically done by 'owning' the protocols through which [software] companies conduct business, at the expense of all those other companies. To the extent that the protocols of the World Wide Web remain 'unowned' by a single company, the Web will remain a level playing field for companies large and small."

Another open source approach involved software designed to help people in developing nations where intercommunication is needed but traditional software costs are prohibitive. An example was Dynebolic, a photo, audio and video sharing application developed by Rasta Software, which says it is all about "resistance in a Babylon world which tries to control the way we communicate . . . "

The Free Software Foundation, founded in 1985, continues to advocate free software, free media formats, the GNU system and open "general public license," also known as "copyleft." It also organizes activist campaigns against what it sees as threats to user freedom in traditional computer operating systems and digital rights management of eBooks and movies.

"The free software movement is one of the most successful social movements to emerge in the past 25 years, driven by a worldwide community of ethical programmers dedicated to the cause of freedom and sharing . . . and teaching . . . about the danger of a society losing control over its computing," said Peter Brown of the foundation (Brown, 2010). Not surprisingly, the Free Software Foundation is frequently at odds with the Business Software Alliance, which represents Microsoft, IBM, Dell and other electronics firms in large-scale networking standards issues.

Copyright and music on the internet

Organizations that set international standards for communication go back to the era of the telegraph. Usually operating without fanfare, their decisions can have enormous impacts. Take the MP3 audio compression standard.

In 1993, the International Standards Organization's subgroup on video and audio standards, known as the Motion Picture Experts Group, developed the MP-1 Audio Layer 3 technology, also known as MP3. This audio standard allowed the reduction of audio file sizes by 11 times without much loss of apparent quality to most listeners. As a result, it became far easier to digitally store, rearrange and share audio files.

One effect was to un-bundle songs that had been thrown together into standard 70 minute "album" sets that were sold on CDs. With MP3 technology, listeners could isolate their favorite songs and play them in whatever order they wanted. At the same time, musicians did not have to conform to a list of 10 to 12 songs. They could have more flexibility and control over how their music was created and when and where their songs were released.

"There is a whole universe that already exists on line, built around the MP3," said Neil Strauss in *The New York Times*. "It is not a world of pirated music, as the record industry would have you believe, but one in which you can choose and design the look and feel of your music" (Strauss, 1999). Yet "piracy"—the illegal sharing of music— did become a problem for the industry, which began the debate in 1999 by insisting on full digital rights management (DRM) so that MP3 players could not be used for copied songs. Consumers rejected DRM, and younger music lovers began sharing music files by the millions over the internet.

Napster was one of the first sites to freely share copyrighted music. It was developed by Shawn Fanning while at Northeastern University in Boston in 1999. By 2001, Napster had over 26 million users worldwide, but lost a copyright suit brought by A&M Records and other music companies. By 2002 Napster was bankrupt. While some estab-

Figure 12.3 Controversial P2P programmer—computer programmer Shawn Fanning achieved fame, if little else, with his Napster "point-to-point" file sharing program. A federal court found that Napster was infringing copyright and ordered the servers shut down in 2001. Fanning has since worked on a mobile application for social networking and photo sharing called Path. (Photo by Joi Ito—licensed under a Creative Commons Attribution)

lished musicians, including Dr. Dre and Metallica, were vehemently opposed to having their music given away for free, other emerging musicians, such as Radiohead and KidA, found that the exposure helped their sales and concerts.

Once Napster was shut down, other point-to-point music sharing sites, such as Limewire, Gnutella, Kazaa and Pirate Bay emerged between 2000 and 2010. Most were closed down after various legal battles; the owners of Pirate Bay, for instance, were sentenced to one year in jail in Sweden in 2010.

Meanwhile, legal music websites, especially iTunes by Apple, emerged to take advantage of music sales through the internet. Apple also managed to pull back from near-bankruptcy with its popular iPod, a player for digital music in MP3 and other formats. By 2010, iTunes was selling 312 million songs per year for one dollar each. But the music industry notes that this was only a fraction of its $10 billion US annual (and $27 billion international) revenue in 2008—a figure that had come down 25 percent from the recording industry's peak sales ten years earlier.

The Recording Industry Association of America (RIAA) said that musicians were suffering. "Piracy doesn't even begin to adequately describe the toll" that music theft takes on the industry, it said, claiming that global music theft "causes $12.5 billion of economic losses every year" (RIAA, 2010).

To reduce the losses, the RIAA sued 17,000 individuals who simply downloaded music in the decade between 2000 and 2010. Only a few chose to fight the lawsuits; most settled with the RIAA and paid a few thousand dollars. Those who did fight faced serious consequences. In one 2009 case, *Capitol Records v. Jammie Thomas-Rasset*, the RIAA persisted through a jury trial and was awarded a fine of $80,000 per song or $1.9 million for 24 songs. Later, the judge cut the fine to $54,000 for Thomas-Rasset, a working mother with four children. In another case, *Sony v. Tenenbaum*, courts upheld a verdict of $675,000 for a young man illegally downloading 30 copyrighted songs. Neither defendant has any hope of paying the fines, which were widely seen as out of proportion to the individual impacts of the infringements.

Critics said the existing copyright system was flawed, and that excessive fines and overly long copyright terms should not be imposed on new digital media. Lawmakers, out of touch with younger music-lovers, maintained stiff fines for infringements without regard for the harm it caused relatively innocent people, critics said. The debate had the familiar sound of previous media controversies.

Figure 12.4 Free culture advocates—Jonathan Zittrain and Lawrence Lessig, both professors at Harvard University law school, question the way copyright and communications law often stifles creativity and freedom. (Photo by Andrew Feinberg, Capitol Valley Media)

Two prominent critics of the copyright law, Harvard University law professors Lawrence Lessig and Jonathan Zittrain, questioned the way copyright and communications law affected creativity and freedom. Lessig compared copyright law to the original idea of property ownership that extended from the ground all the way out into space. That idea was fine until the invention of the airplane, he said. At that point, a new technology made the old law irrelevant.

> We come from a tradition of free culture. Not "free" as in "free beer" . . . but "free" as in "free speech," "free markets," "free trade," "free enterprise," "free will," and "free elections." . . . A free culture is not a culture without property, just as a free market is not a market in which everything is free. The opposite of a free culture is a "permission culture"—a culture in which creators get to create only with the permission of the powerful, or of creators from the past. (Lessig, 2005)

One of the impacts of digital media technology on the music recording industry was the reduced support that recording companies were able to give their musicians. This change in media structure was rather similar to the way the Hollywood studio system collapsed with the advent of television. As they began to lose constant, dependable income, the broad based systems began shrinking, which opened the way for a more independent productions. In other words, the free market started to come alive again.

YouTube, music and cultural curators

Although MP3 technology allowed music sharing in the late 1990s, video sharing was not easy until after around 2005, when a site called YouTube allowed free video uploads to the Web. At that point, people with small cameras or camera phones could directly upload unedited clips.

The idea for YouTube came from the difficulty several of its founders had in sharing video files over email. By 2011, it was the third most accessed website in the world after Google and Facebook (Alexa, 2011). While most of YouTube's videos are uploaded by individuals, many music videos are professionally produced.

In some cases, musicians who are happy to encourage fans have come in conflict with their record labels. For example, in 2006, a rock band named OK Go uploaded "Here It Goes Again," a song with a humorous video. The video became popular (or "went viral" as people said), bringing in 10,000 hits per day. This happened because fans put the video's <embed> code on their own web pages so that the video would play on their websites. The group's record label, Capitol/EMI, realized they were losing advertising money from the ads that are automatically placed by YouTube. So EMI pulled the plug on the embed tags. Fan hits quickly dropped from 10,000 to 1,000 per day, and EMI's revenue from YouTube dropped from about $80 a day to only $8 per day.

"This isn't how the Internet works," said Damian Kulash of OK Go. "Viral content doesn't spread just from primary sources like YouTube or Flickr. Blogs, Web sites and video aggregators serve as cultural curators, daily collecting the items that will interest their audiences the most. By ignoring the power of these tastemakers, our record company is cutting off its nose to spite its face" (Kulash, February 20, 2010).

Figure 12.5 Embedding Rube Goldberg—a disagreement over the way their record label allowed access to promotional videos on YouTube shows the disconnects that take place in the world of new media. The record label, EMI Inc., wanted to recover advertising revenue from a YouTube video produced by OK Go. So they removed embed tags from the video "Here It Goes Again." But advertising revenue in the neighborhood of $8 per day was the only reward for sacrificing more valuable promotion. That's a misunderstanding of the role of new media, said musician Damian Kulash. "Blogs, Web sites and video aggregators serve as cultural curators, daily collecting the items that will interest their audiences the most," he said. The music industry's response to the Web has been "like a corporate version of the Three Stooges." Here, in black and white but with embed tags restored, are OK Go's Andy Ross, Damian Kulash, Dan Konopka and Tim Norwind after a workout with the "This Too Shall Pass: Rube Goldberg" video on YouTube. (Photo courtesy Hornblow Group USA)

While respecting EMI's need to recover its investment in musicians through its studio system, Kulash also felt that the group's use of the new media was in the record company's long-term best interest. Eventually, the record label restored the embed code on the group's YouTube video, but the issue shows how difficult it can be for traditional media to anticipate the problems posed by new digital media. "It's been like a corporate version of the Three Stooges: absurd flailing, spectacular myopia and willful ignorance of reality," Kulash added. "Now that the big record companies have made themselves obsolete, bands such as mine can make a better living without their help than we can with it" (Kulash, August 29, 2010).

Digital community commerce: eBay and Craigslist

The world's largest garage sale is an online auction site founded by Pierre Omidyar, a computer programmer who worked at an Apple Computer subsidiary in San Jose, CA. He was inspired to write the basic code for what was first called AuctionWeb over a long weekend in 1995. According to some accounts, the first item sold on eBay was an apparently useless broken laser pointer at the price of $14.83. Worried about the transaction, Omidyar emailed the buyer to explain that the pointer was broken. But the buyer explained that he collected broken laser pointers.

The incident amazed Omidyar, who realized that millions of collectors were waiting for a service that would help them buy and sell their particular obsessions. In 1997, with an infusion of venture capital, the site's name was changed to eBay. Like Amazon or Netflix, eBay is a "long tail" marketing service, but with the difference that sales do not move from a central point to outlying buyers, but rather can be made between individuals across the network. Both buyers and sellers register products, negotiate bids and finalize sales through the site. By 2009, eBay was grossing nearly $9 billion in revenue per year and operating in 30 nations.

The eBay operation stands in sharp contrast to a website known as Craigslist, which receives a similar number of unique web visitors but operates on a minimalist nonprofit basis. Craig Newmark started Craigslist the same year as eBay, in 1995. An iconoclastic San Francisco programmer, Newmark began a free email list service in 1995 that featured local events, and a year later, wrote code to turn the emails into a web page. Within 15 years, Craigslist had become the world's leading site for what newspapers once called classified advertising: cars, pets, real estate and other items for sale. Most of these can be advertised for free on Craigslist. The organization's relatively low revenue stream comes from fees to post "help wanted" ads in major cities. With personals and discussion forums, Craigslist also qualifies as a social media site.

Craigslist is one reason for the precipitous drop in newspaper classified advertising revenue in the early twenty-first century. Newmark is not apologetic about his role in undermining newspaper publishing. He distrusts journalists and says that badly informed reporting led to the war in Iraq (Usborne, 2005). Ordinary people are "ready to take over the newsroom," he says, although at this point, Newmark has only gotten as far as the classified advertising department.

With sites for 570 cities in 50 countries, and a minimalist design reminiscent of the earliest web pages, Craigslist is by far the largest job and community bulletin board in the world. But the site is prone to spam Despite profits that probably range into the hundreds of millions per year, Craigslist has a light management style with only 32 employees (in contrast, eBay has 15,000 employees). *Wired* Magazine wrote about the "tragedy of Craigslist," equating the site's somewhat chaotic state with the "tragedy of the commons," a bio-ethical concept about overuse of common resources (Wolf, 2009). But Newmark's idea of a social service is to connect people and then step back. He doesn't want 15,000 employees.

Figure 12.6 Craigslist creator— Craig Newmark, founder of Craigslist, is proud to be providing a free service even if it has cut into newspaper advertising revenues. The site, running on twenty-first century servers in 570 cities worldwide, has retained its 1990s design and its 1960s peace sign logo. (Photo by Gene X Hwang, Orange Photography, San Francisco)

Perhaps the interesting thing about the new digital media is that both eBay and Craigslist auction sites are thriving, despite radically different approaches to business, with respective ranks of 9th and 10th (in the United States) and 22nd and 38th (worldwide) (Alexa, 2011).

From Friendster to Facebook

Universities once published a reverse yearbook with the photos, names, majors and hometowns of incoming freshmen in order to help them get accustomed to their new university homes. The generic name of the reverse yearbook was a "facebook" because it would have the portraits of freshmen to help identify them.

When universities starting putting their "facebooks" on line, entrepreneurs saw a chance to do the same on a popular level. SixDegrees and SocialNet were among the first in the 1990s, but both were ahead of the market. When computer programmers Jonathan Abrams and Chris Emmanuel founded Friendster in 2002, the name was a take-off on Napster. A year later, a group working in the same company as Friendster founded another social networking site called MySpace.

That same year, a Harvard student named Mark Zuckerberg created a "hot or not" ranking system for photos of female Harvard students. The joke was not appreciated, and the university called him on the carpet for unauthorized use of the photos. The next year, Zuckerberg dropped out of Harvard to create a website called "thefacebook. com." Within six years Facebook had grown to over 500 million users who could make "friends," share text or photos or video clips or games, and see what other people were thinking about.

The succession of these companies reflects the intense competition for what has become known as social networking software. One question is why Facebook has become so successful. Critics said Friendster's servers didn't perform well early out, and that Friendster editors imposed restrictions. Users started migrating to MySpace, where networks were often organized around music groups. Although MySpace was initially successful, the site went from nearly six million users per day down to one and a half between 2009 and 2011. Its purchase in 2005 by traditional media giant News Corporation might have improved the site's many coding and security problems, but the trend turned towards Facebook, where daily users grew from over 15 million to 40 million during the same time period.

Controversy and lawsuits surrounding the creation and success of Facebook were partly described in a 2010 movie called *The Social Network*. Questions about privacy policies for Facebook and other social media sites have also been raised by groups like the Electronic Privacy Information Center. It's not likely that Facebook will always dominate the market for social networking software. One question is whether the way users value a network can peak and then decline if the network's size or complexity makes it too unwieldy.

A different kind of social network is a twist on the old community bulletin board. Meetup.com involves setting up in-person meetings through meetup.com for music, sports, spiritual and artistic groups. LinkedIn is a similar social networking site oriented to business.

Other kinds of social media also emerged in the early twenty-first century. Photo sharing started in the early 2000s, picking up with services like Flickr, originally created in 2004 for an online game system and purchased by Yahoo in 2005. The business model for many sharing sites is to offer free accounts limited to several hundred megabytes and a range of prices for more storage space. YouTube (noted above) is a similar site for video sharing.

Collaborative media and Wikipedia

Another grass roots digital media phenomenon is the "wiki," a server application that allows many users to create and edit pages on a website through their browser windows. Software designer Ward Cunningham from Portland, Oregon came up with the first wiki in 1995 as way for lots of people to contribute to a software repository. He picked the word "wiki" as the Hawaiian language word for "fast," and the idea was that a wiki could be a quick and simple way for many people to make changes on web pages (Leuf, 2001).

Small-scale collaborative wikis proved useful for software designers and businesses, but they did not seem useful for bigger projects at first, since wide open editing could undermine a website. That openness would seem to be the last thing you might want for an encyclopedia, which is supposed to be a well-vetted reference guide produced by experts.

The story behind Wikipedia, the largest collaborative project of the early twenty-first century, is that a group of web entrepreneurs, led by economist Jimmy Wales and epistemologist Lawrence Sanger, was putting together an encyclopedia for the Web called "Nupedia" in 2000 when the dot-com bubble burst. Nupedia wasn't a wiki. In fact, contributors had to qualify by faxing in their diplomas, and their articles had to go through a seven-stage review process.

"As you might expect, it was a complete failure," Wales said. However, a side project that was originally meant to help Nupedia, an open wiki site, was attracting some interest. So Wales and Sanger decided Nupedia wasn't going to attract more investment during the dot-com bust and started focusing on the side project called Wikipedia. They had been watching the growth of open source software movement, Wales noted, so they decided to take a similar approach, remove the barriers and see what would happen (Blodget, 2010).

Within a decade, Wikipedia was a global phenomenon, the seventh most visited website and the world's largest encyclopedia, with over 3.4 million entries in English and 17 million in over 250 languages. "One of the most important keys to success," Wales said, "is to genuinely trust people, and give them the tools to do things they are proud of."

Over the long term, Wales and the Wikimedia Foundation hope to create a free encyclopedia for every person on earth. "It means a lot more than just building a cool website," Wales said. "We're really interested in all the issues of the digital divide poverty worldwide, empowering people everywhere to have the information that they need to make good decisions."

Other approaches to creating a common record have sprung up in the wake of Wikipedia, for example, in wiki-map sites, political wikis, health wikis, cookbooks, game wikis and many more. There are also collaborative sites where musicians in different locations can record separate tracks to a song that can then be put together in one place.

Why people would pitch in to create a definitive world encyclopedia, without any thought of reward, is a bit mysterious; it has been called the "Wikipedia effect." We usually think of crowd psychology as negative, but apparently there is also a strongly positive side, argues James Surowiecki in *The Wisdom of Crowds*. A diverse collection

Figure 12.7 Encyclopedic entrepreneur—what started as a use of new media to simplify communications among contributors turned into a collaborative encyclopedia where users and readers would make the contributions. According to co-founder Jimmy Wales, no one thought it would amount to much more than an experiment at first, but Wikipedia's volunteer spirit has made it the seventh most popular website in the world, with over 17 million articles (3.4 million in English) by 2010. (Photo by Manuel Archain, Buenos Aires, licensed under a Creative Commons Attribution)

of independent-minded people is likely to make certain types of decisions better than the experts (Surowiecki, 2004). Similarly, in *Smart Mobs*, Howard Rheingold noted that new digital technologies could help people assemble quickly to get things done (Rheingold, 2002).

The question of accuracy comes up frequently with Wikipedia. One 2005 study published in *Nature*, a scientific magazine, asked experts to review 42 articles in both Wikipedia and *Encyclopedia Britannica*. In both encyclopedias, four serious errors were found in each group, while Wikipedia had 32 percent more minor errors or omissions than Britannica (Giles, 2005). The editors of Britannica disputed the findings, especially the conclusion that the accuracy rates were close (*Encyclopedia Britannica*, 2005). In response, Wikipedia noted that its open digital technology makes it possible to quickly correct errors as well as make them.

One major Wikipedia error involved a biographical entry for journalist and *USA Today* editor John Seigenthaler. The entry falsely alleged that he had been involved in a plot to assassinate United States President John F. Kennedy and his brother Robert Kennedy in the 1960s. The information had been planted by a malicious prankster and stayed in place for four months. Seigenthaler saw it as an example of the weakness in the system. "I had heard for weeks from teachers, journalists and historians about 'the wonderful world of Wikipedia,' where millions of people worldwide visit daily for quick reference 'facts,' composed and posted by people with no special expertise or knowledge—and sometimes by people with malice . . . We live in a universe of new media with phenomenal opportunities for worldwide communications and research—but populated by volunteer vandals with poison-pen intellects" (Seigenthaler, 2005). In response, Wikipedia required registration for certain page edits and reinforced its civic technology framework to catch errors more quickly.

It's interesting that Denis Diderot, the editor of the *Encyclopédie* of 1751, said that his motivation was to facilitate access to all available knowledge and to change the way people thought about the world as a whole. Like Wikipedia and WikiLeaks, the *Encyclopédie* faced many controversies, such as whether religion should be a subcategory of philosophy and whether there could be a religious answer to a scientific question. Diderot's *Encyclopédie* set the stage for the Enlightenment in the eighteenth century, and the idea that Wikipedia will be accessible around the world in every language embodies a similar and far larger potential.

Twitter's culture of generosity

If the "Wikipedia effect" seems mysterious, consider the "culture of generosity" found within the Twitter universe. Twitter was originally a way for programmers to catch up with each other in the mad hacking environment of Silicon Valley, where it was typical to work non-stop for days on end, followed by a few days off.

In this environment, employees at Odeo, a start-up search engine for audio and video, were finding it difficult to plan meetings in 2006. They could text each other by phone, but that became confusing when more than a few people were involved. So they created a mini-blog where someone could post a short text message and anyone in a small group "following" that person could read it, either on the website or on a cell phone (Israel, 2009). By early 2010, over 50 million Twitter messages (tweets) were being posted daily. Once again, an accidental discovery paved the way for a communications innovation.

Twitter took off in 2007 when it proved useful at several conferences, notably the South by Southwest conference held every year in Austin, Texas. People in crowds found it easy to assemble small groups and compare notes with Twitter, and since the application was free, and easily used on any cell phone or digital assistant, its use quickly expanded at these conferences.

Twitter was originally named twttr, and was a takeoff on Flickr, the name of a photo-sharing website. An interesting feature of Twitter, according to writer Shel Israel, is the "culture of generosity" among its users. Twitter has been useful in situations ranging from life-threatening emergencies to simply chatting about the best restaurants in town, but in many cases, the willingness to share and to experience community seemed to be a hallmark of Twitter users, Israel said in his book *Twitterville* (Israel, 2009).

Citizen and collaborative journalism

If collaborative encyclopedias and mini-blogs can work, why not collaborative newspapers and television programs? Some have embraced the idea enthusiastically; others, well, not so much.

Originally, the hope for digital media technology was simply that people would have more choice in selecting news reports. In his 1995 book *Being Digital*, MIT Media Lab director Nicholas Negroponte said it would be possible to produce a "Daily Me" sort of newspaper where a personal agenda would guide the use of top-down information. Negroponte was right, of course, and today's web feeds and personal web portals are a triumph of nonlinear technology and personalization of information environments.

In the early years of the twenty-first century, the idea that information traffic should include the entire network, and not just flow from the top down, dawned on the once-cloistered profession of journalism. It seemed like a fairly good idea to those who had already been involved in discussions about being transparent and responsive to readers.

The new information traffic paradigm was called participatory or citizen journalism. A 2003 report called "We Media" that said citizens should play "an active role in the process of collecting, reporting, analyzing and disseminating news and information" (Bowman and Willis, 2003). Of course at that point, the bottom had not yet fallen out from under the news business, so the range of amateur involvement—from participating to collaborating to actually taking full responsibility for reporting—had not become an economic rationale.

Experiments in citizen journalism ranged from automatic blog sites for all subscribers (for instance, in the Bluffton, South Carolina, *Today*) to non-journalism volunteers recording civic meetings (in Deerfield, New Hampshire) to student and journalism school supported full-spectrum projects like *South LA Report* and *Local East Village*.

Some of the experiments have run into interesting obstacles, such as extraordinarily caustic commentary in Bluffton, South Carolina and at the *Voice of San Diego*, California, where editors ended anonymous commenting but encouraged more signed comments.

It's predicted that by 2021, half of the news will be produced by citizen journalists. Dozens of news organizations are engaged at some level; two major training initiatives, the Knight Citizen News Network and the Poynter Institute NewsU program, began training programs for citizen journalists in 2010.

Some are wary of the concept. "As a bit of a reality check, when was the last time you encountered a 'citizen doctor' . . . took off in a plane flown by a 'citizen pilot' or saw justice meted out by a 'citizen policeman'?" asked James Farmer in an article in *The Age*, an Australian newspaper (Farmer, 2006).

Actually, it's not hard to find free clinics, amateur pilots and neighborhood watch programs. All of these reflect the changing relationship between professionals and the public. And while medicine and piloting require licenses and performance to professional standards, the media is far different. People from all walks of life can write, perform music, shoot film, play sports and program computers at a professional level without having to work for professional pay. They're often called "Pro-Ams" or professional amateurs (Leadbeater and Miller, 2004).

By 2011, the mass media was leaving the cloistered world, for good or ill. The future for community news, presented in a more organized format such as a combination of wikis and blogs, might be an improvement over the old community newspapers. Many of these had become high-profit, low-quality publications that had abandoned any serious attempt at public service. Civic information volunteers can produce information just as accurately, and possibly with a greater sense of social responsibility, than low-paid community newspaper journalists.

"Face facts," said Jason Stverak in an *Online Journalism Review* article. "Traditional media have put journalism last for at least a decade, cutting thousands of jobs and [then] wondering why readers, viewers and listeners flee." America lost a generation of professional journalists, Stverak said, and that is a serious threat to self-government. "How will we replace them?" (Stverak, 2010).

Citizen journalism could be one part of the answer, but the larger goal is to generate conversations and build communities. Trained professional reporters to generate verified information will continue to be needed.

The future of digital media

A revolution, by definition, is a dramatic or wide-reaching change in conditions or an overthrow of the established social order. The first three media revolutions—printing, imaging and broadcasting—helped create social revolutions on a vast scale. Each revolution had an impact on the one beforehand. Imaging changed publishing, making it more visual and mass oriented; broadcasting changed both, co-opting visual media and pushing print publications into news cycles with more immediacy and geographic reach.

Digital media, as the fourth wave of revolutionary technology, made production and distribution far more flexible for the other media types. It also opened doors to new information functions and traffic patterns. Media was no longer a one-way deal, from top-down to mass markets. It was networked, allowing many-to-many conversations. It didn't have to be centrally produced. Users, readers and/or viewers all had highly individualized choices.

So why did that happen? Why did we end up with a kind of new media that entailed many new dimensions for information? Couldn't it just as easily have become a tightly controlled, top-down information system with a little bit more flexibility? What made the digital revolution different?

According to media analyst Jonathan Zittrain, digital technologies were shared while they were still incomplete, leaving open the potential for further improvements. That was the only way they could compete with the big computer and media companies. The Unix/GNU operating system and Apache server software are examples of collaborative open system approaches. The more these applications spread, the more they improved, until a virtuous circle pushed them from the creative margins into the mainstream.

"This is the story of the PC against information appliances, and it is the story of the Internet against the proprietary networks," Zittrain said. It's a legacy that Zittrain and others hope can be kept alive, a social construction of technology that is quite different from the static and deterministic corporate model.

What worries them is a new generation of "tethered" one-way information appliances, such as the Apple iPad, iPhone and other mobile units. "The iPhone is sterile," Zittrain said. "Rather than a platform that invites innovation, the iPhone comes preprogrammed. You are not allowed to add programs to the all-in-one device that Steve Jobs sells you. Its functionality is locked in." The iPad can't use more than one application at a time, and it doesn't play Flash videos. Attempts to "jailbreak" iPhones and iPads may turn them into "iBricks" (Zittrain, 2010).

For his part, Apple CEO Steve Jobs says the intent is to move beyond the PC market long dominated by rival Microsoft. "The iPad is clearly going to affect notebook computers . . . This is a new model of computing." Traditional media hope that it is a new business model for professionally produced top-down media as well.

Wired magazine's editor Chris Anderson sees the "app" economy helping to build value for publishers. "You can retain everything that makes the magazine great and then add these new things: the videos, the animations, the interactivity, a social media layer," Anderson said. "You can have more pages, and little things people don't think about—the idea of a jump page makes no sense in an app. A lot of the bugs in the linear medium get sort of fixed now in a two-dimensional or three-dimensional medium like the iPad" (Anderson, 2010).

> One of the most important shifts in the digital world has been the move from the wide-open Web to semi-closed platforms that use the Internet for transport but not the browser for display. It's driven primarily by the rise of the iPhone model of mobile computing. . . . And it's the world that consumers are increasingly choosing, not because they're rejecting the idea of the Web but because these dedicated platforms often just work better or fit better into their lives. (Anderson, 2010)

"You can only make money with scarcity," Anderson said. "In the 20th century, that scarcity was printing plants and trucks and crazed oligopolies over the powers of distribution. The rise of the specialized devices in the app economy is a way to . . . raise the barrier to entry, to create scarcity, both by taking content off and also more production going into the content you put on."

Traditional media enthusiasm for the "app" economy waned slightly in February, 2011, when Apple announced highly restrictive rules governing the use of their mobile technologies. Apple said it would allow publishers like *The New York Times* and the *Washington Post* to charge $4 a month to subscribe to their "apps" for the iPad, but only after Apple took a 30 percent share. News organizations would not be able to refer customers directly to their advertisers, nor would they know who their subscribers were (Kane, 2011). This did not make publishers happy. Meanwhile, Google announced a ten percent no-strings-attached deal, while electronics companies like Samsung, Motorola and Sony moved quickly to market pads using the open Android operating system developed by Google in 2005.

Figure 12.8 Apple iPad—portable and networked, a device like this Apple iPad was the subject of research by the newspaper industry in the 1990s, but the idea was ahead of its time. The iPad was introduced in 2009 and was an instant hit, and provided some hope that paid content models could succeed for the news business. But the iPad faced intense competition in the second decade of the twenty-first century. (Photo courtesy of Apple Computers)

By 2011, the digital revolution seemed to be moving in two directions. On the one hand, open source, net-neutral civic technologies had already shown that new digital media could be socially constructed in ways never before imagined. On the other hand, traditional media worked on ways to re-bundle content in dedicated mobile "apps" with information appliances like the iPad. The new business model would (theoretically) encourage more professional content and restore some profitability journalism organizations.

It's entirely possible that both approaches will co-exist in the new media of the twenty-first century. Yet however profitable the new walled gardens of Apples' "apps" may become, most experts believe that the open nature of the internet will not be overturned (Anderson, 2010).

Openness has its own virtues, and those who resist it will fall behind those who enable it. Users will rise up if there are too many restrictions that get in the way of the information they want and the content they want to create.

Technology and freedom

The popular uprisings in the Middle East of 2011 were widely attributed to new digital media technology, especially the ability to form crowds quickly and share video, photos and text instantly worldwide. "The Tunisian uprising was triggered by the WikiLeaks revelations, and fanned by the Internet," said *The Hindu*, a leading newspaper of India (*The Hindu,* February 23, 2011).

The historical role of the mass media has been evident in many other epochal upheavals, both violent and nonviolent. When Eastern Europe threw off Soviet Russian domination in 1989, the direct cause was the resentment simmering from years of oppression, but events were fueled by the rapid development of satellite TV and cell phones, as Polish President Lech Walesa noted (Scheeres, 2002). Similarly, the American civil rights movement accelerated under the gaze of television cameras, the new technology of the 1950s. Pamphlets and newspapers fanned the flames of political revolution throughout the eighteenth and nineteenth centuries, and when newspapers settled into a political equilibrium, magazines often took up the cause of reform. There are dozens of other examples: the legislative restructuring of the radio telegraph system following the Titanic disaster in 1912; the antitrust lawsuit of 1915 that stopped Thomas Edison's attempt to control film; the use of cable and satellites to circumvent limitations on broadcast licensing in the 1980s; the use of internet podcasting to circumvent the radio monopolies that emerged after 1996.

Every media revolution, then, is a circumvention of an old balance of power and a potential lever for social change. In many cases this is deliberate. Examples of change in media technology show that it tends to be the product of a "culture of improvement," as historian Robert Friedel observed. Occasionally, media changes may be driven by civic uses of technology (Zittrain, 2008), or a "culture of generosity" (Israel, 2009), or a "global defense of sources and press freedoms," as WikiLeaks proclaims in its motto (WikiLeaks, 2010).

Perhaps the most basic lesson of media history is that transitions in media technology do not take place simply because one new technology inevitably leads to another. Although the intrinsic properties of a technology influence its place in the market, technological determinism is only one part of the picture. In the case of media history, it may be only a small part of the picture.

What makes the digital media revolution unique is its tendency to create new communities and "flatten" global culture, as Thomas Friedman said. Digital media technologies have suddenly juxtaposed cultures that once existed in entirely separate worlds with very little influence over each other. For instance, it would have been unthinkable for devout Muslims to riot over what they saw as sacrilegious cartoons in a Danish newspaper in the nineteenth or twentieth centuries, but that is exactly what happened in September of 2005. The riots left more than 100 people dead, and they were only a harbinger of things to come.

In November, 2011, WikiLeaks published the first 200 over 250,000 secret diplomatic cables. Most world governments, including China, the United States and Europe, took serious steps to close down access to WikiLeaks after being embarrassed by the disclosures. Overt pressure on web hosts and covert attacks by data intelligence companies were among these steps.

"This is the first time we have seen an attempt at the international community level to censor a website dedicated to the principle of transparency," said global press freedom group Reporters Sans Frontiers. "We are shocked to find countries such as France and the United States suddenly bringing their policies on freedom of expression into line with those of China" (Apps, 2010).

Despite its general defense of internet freedom, the response of the United States to WikiLeaks was widely seen as contrary to its own traditions. American courts have long prevented the government from censoring leaks of classified information to major media, for example, in the Pentagon Papers case of 1971, *United States v. New York Times*. Similar cases, such as the courts refusal to allow former president Teddy Roosevelt to sue Joseph Pulitzer's *New York World* in 1909, are found throughout the country's history. The standard for prior restraint censorship has been the prevention of "imminent" violence. While many governments were deeply embarrassed by WikiLeaks, none of the leaked documents directly advocated violence. And WikiLeaks leader Julian Assange insists that he has offered to work with the United States government to edit materials that could harm to individuals.

Figure 12.9 WikiLeaks editor—Julian Assange, editor of the WikiLeaks whistleblower website, was both reviled and praised for enabling the release of hundreds of thousands of secret diplomatic cables in November, 2010 that triggered popular revolts in the Middle East a few months later. When a variety of private web providers refused to host WikiLeaks, open-access advocates began disseminating the documents across a wide spectrum of the internet in what was described as the outbreak of an "information war." Assange also faced a wide range of legal charges as a result of the release. (Photo by Espen Moe, licensed under a Creative Commons Attribution)

Without question, the WikiLeaks disclosures proved extremely damaging to the old political order in the Middle East. The cables showed, for instance, that ruthless corruption in Tunisia had concentrated the country's wealth in the hands of a very few people connected to former President Zine El Abidine Ben Ali and his wife's family. "In one incident of corruption revealed by WikiLeaks, the Son-in-Law of the President purchased a 17 percent share of a bank just before it was to be privatized and then sold the shares at a premium," said economics professor Basel Saleh. Other diplomatic cables showed that "success in the Tunisian economy [was] directly related to connection to the first family" (Saleh, 2011). The protests that followed the revelations drove Ben Ali from office and sparked similar uprisings in Egypt, Libya and other Arab nations.

In the early 20th century, W. E. B. DuBois predicted that the problem of the twentieth century would be the problem of the "color line," which is to say, the sharp distinction between races (DuBois, 1903). At the dawn of the twenty-first century, the problem and opportunity seems to be the blurring of lines and distances that once separated entire cultures around the world.

In that light, it's useful to recall the principles that guided the mass media from its inception in early modern Europe over five centuries ago. The principles of individual freedom of expression and access to uncensored information took many generations of bitter struggle before they formed the modern bedrock of global human rights policies. These principles are found in the First Amendment to the United States Constitution, the European Convention for the Protection of Human Rights and the United Nations Charter of Human Rights. While they are too often violated, they can never be repealed. Under democratic theory, human rights are natural rights that are not granted by governments but rather, are innate in human nature. They are, in the words of the American revolutionaries, "God-given rights." Thus, people will never stop defending and expanding their freedom, and no wholesale attempt to close down the marketplace of ideas can be rational or even effective in the long run.

The corollary to the principle of freedom of speech and press is the principle of social responsibility, as noted in the Nuremberg Principles following World War II, the Hutchins Commission in the United States in 1947, the United Nations MacBride Commission in 1980, and recent decisions by the United Nations International Court of Justice. Incitements to violence and hate speech directed against people or cultures are prime examples of a lack of social responsibility. Transparency in governments or disclosures of corruption, on the other hand, often serve the highest principles of social responsibility.

However, as is often the case, law and social conditions do not often kept pace with technology. Whether the internet and Web will remain free and continue to be liberating technologies is a question that the genius of the twenty-first century will need to address. The point is widely acknowledged. "The future of the new democracies will depend in part on the development and strengthening of free, independent and pluralist media in both the public and private sectors," said UNESCO Director Federico Mayor in 1997 (Demers, 2007).

At the start of this book, we noted Wilbur Schramm's idea that language and writing were the tuition paid by humanity for its own education. By the same token, we could view mass media as the open university of the world. Since the advent of printing, each media revolution has been characterized by internal tendencies that channeled its educational potential and by social constructions that shaped its impacts new medium. The global digital revolution is a quantum leap forward into this process, and it is quite possible that humankind was not entirely prepared. But it hardly matters now. The walls are down, and this university is wide open to both the lowest and the highest inspirations humanity can create.

With the future at our feet, where will we go? With a vast new power of worldwide networking, how will we envision the future? Will we use the media to lift and protect and diversify the human spirit? What will global culture become in a century or two?

It's a question of social construction, not simply one of technological momentum. The ability to shape the way technology is used, to serve the public interest, is the twenty-first century's truest badge of freedom.

Bibliography

For additional reading, discussion questions and suggestions for video and multimedia links, go to www.revolutionsincommunications.com

Abramowitz, Rachel. "Avatar's Animated Acting," *Los Angeles Times*, February 18, 2010.

Action for Children's Television v. FCC, 821 F.2d 741, 1987.

Adams, Samuel Hopkins. "The Great American Fraud," *Collier's Weekly*, October 7, 1905.

Aitken, Hugh. *Syntony and Spark: The Origins of Radio* (Princeton, NJ: Princeton University Press, 1992).

Alexa, "The Top 500 sites on the Web," www.alexa.com, accessed on the Web on February 18, 2011.

Alpert, Jesse and Nissan Hajaj. "We Knew the Web Was Big . . . " *The Official Google Blog,* 2008, on the Web at: http://googleblog.blogspot.com/2008/07/we-knew-web-was-big.html

American Academy of Child and Adolescent Psychiatry. "Children and TV Violence," November 2002. Published on the Web at: http://www.aacap.org/cs/root/facts_for_families/children_and_tv_violence

Anderson, Chris. *The Long Tail: Why the Future of Business is Selling Less of More* (New York: Hyperion, 2008).

Anderson, Chris and Michael Wolf. "The Web is Dead," *Wired* magazine, August 2010, on the Web at: http://www.wired.com/magazine/2010/08/ff_webrip/

Anderson, Janna and Lee Rainie. "The Future of the Internet," *Pew Internet and American Life Project,* February 19, 2010.

Anderson, Kevin B. and Peter Hudis. *The Rosa Luxemburg Reader* (New York: Monthly Review, 2004).

Andreessen, Marc. Message forwarded by Tim Berners-Lee, New "XMosaic" World-Wide Web browser from NCSA, message to comp.infosystems, February 11, 1993, on the Web at: http://www.bio.net/bionet/mm/bio-soft/1993-February/003879.html

Apache Software Foundation. "Apache http sever project," 2010, Published on the Web at: http://httpd.apache.org/ABOUT_APACHE.html

Appel, Joseph H. "A Case Study of an Advertising Agency and Some Observations on Advertising in General," *Bulletin of the Business Historical Society*, Vol. 13, No. 4 (October, 1939), pp. 49–57.

Apple, R.W. "Lessons From the Pentagon Papers," *The New York Times*, June 23, 1996.

Apps, Peter. "Wikileaks Stirs Debate on Info Revolution," Reuters, December 6, 2010, on the Web at: http://www.reuters.com/article/idUSTRE6B52DE20101206?pageNumber=1

Arango, Tim. "How the AOL-Time Warner Merger Went So Wrong," *The New York Times*, January 10, 2010, on the Web at: http://www.nytimes.com/2010/01/11/business/media/11merger.html?pagewanted=all

Arthur, W. Brian. *The Nature of Technology: What It Is and How It Evolves* (New York: Free Press, 2009).

Auletta, Ken. *Googled: The End of the World as We Know It* (New York: Penguin, 2010).

Axelrod, Toby. *Hans and Sophie Scholl: German Resisters of the White Rose* (New York: Rosen Publishing Group, 2001).

Bacon, Francis. "Novum Organum," 1620; trans. James Spedding et al., in *The Works* Vol. VIII (Boston, MA: Taggard and Thompson, 1863), on the Web at: http://www.constitution.org/bacon/nov_org.htm

Bagdikian, Ben. "The Lords of the Global Village: Cornering Hearts and Minds," *The Nation,* June 12, 1989.

Baker, Carlos. *Hemingway* (Princeton, NJ: Princeton University Press, 1972).

Baker, Kevin. "Stabbed in the Back! The Past and Future of a Right-wing Myth," *Harpers,* June 2006, on the Web at: http://www.harpers.org/archive/2006/06/0081080

Balboni, Philip S. "Documentary Journalism Vanishes from Network and Local Television," *Nieman Reports*, Fall, 2001.

Balio, Tino. *United Artists: The Company That Changed the Film Industry* (Madison, WI: University of Wisconsin Press, 1987).

Barbrook, Richard. *Imaginary Futures* (London: Pluto Press, 2007), on the Web at: http://www.imaginaryfutures.net/book/

Barnouw, Eric. *The Image Empire: A History of Broadcasting in the United States* (New York: Oxford University Press, 1970).

Barton, Bruce. *The Man Nobody Knows* (Indianapolis, IN: Bobbs-Merill Co., 1925).

Baudrillard, Jean. *The Illusion of the End* (Palo Alto, CA: Stanford University Press, 1994).

Beasley, Maurine H. and Sheila J. Gibbons. *Taking Their Place: A Documentary History of Women and Journalism* (College Park, PA: Strata, 2003).

Benjamin, Walter, Michael W. Jennings, Brigid Doherty and Thomas Y. Levin. *The Work of Art in the Age of Its Technological Reproducibility, and Other Writings on Media* (Cambridge: Harvard University Press, 2008).

Benkler, Yochai. *The Wealth of Networks: How Social Production Transforms Markets and Freedom* (New Haven, CT: Yale University Press, 2006), on the Web at: http://cyber.law.harvard.edu/wealth_of_networks/

Bently, L. and M. Kretschmer, eds. Court of Cassation (Supreme Court) on Photography (1863), Primary Sources on Copyright (1450–1900), on the Web at: www.copyrighthistory.org (accessed May, 2010).

Berners-Lee, Tim with Mark Fischetti. *Weaving the Web: The Original Design and Ultimate Destiny of the World Wide Web* (New York: Harper, 1999).

Berry, S. Torriano and Venise T. Berry. *Historical Dictionary of African American Cinema* (Lanham, MD: Scarecrow Press, 2007).

Billington, James. *Fire in the Minds of Men* (Piscataway, NJ: Transaction Press, 1999).

Black, Edwin. *IBM and the Holocaust* (New York: Time Warner Paperbacks, 2002).

Blackwood, William. "The Press," *London Times,* July 23, 1834, p. 7.

—. "The New Art of Printing," *Blackwoods's Edinburgh Magazine*, January 1844, p. 45, on the Web at: http://www.bodley.ox.ac.uk/cgi-bin/ilej/image1.pl?item=page&seq =3&size=1&id=bm.1844.x.x.55.x.x.u3

Blodget, Henry. "Interview with Jimmy Wales: How Wikipedia Became a Monster," *Business Insider*, May 3, 2010, on the Web at: http://www.businessinsider.com/ henry-blodget-jimmy-wales-wikipedia-2010-5

Blondheim, Menahem. "Rehearsal for Media Regulation: Congress versus the Telegraph-News Monopoly, 1866–1900," 56 *Fed. Comm. Law Journal*, 303 (2003–2004).

Bly, Nelly. *Around the World in 72 Days* (New York: Pictorial Weeklies, 1890), on the Web at: http://digital.library.upenn.edu/women/bly/world/world.html

—. *Ten Days Inside a Madhouse* (New York: Ian L. Munro, 1890), on the Web at: http://digital.library.upenn.edu/women/bly/madhouse/madhouse.html

Boehlert, Eric. "One Big Happy Channel?" *Salon*, 2001.

Bogart, Humphrey. "I'm No Communist," *Photoplay*, March 1948, on the Web at: http://docs.google.com/View?docid=dg6n6657_103f7bsqj

Bogart, Leo. *Commercial Culture and the Public Interest* (New York: Oxford University Press, 1995).

Bolter, J. David. *Turing's Man: Western Culture in the Computer Age* (Chapel Hill, NC: University of North Carolina Press, 1984).

Boorstin, Daniel J. *The Image: A Guide to Pseudo-Events in America* (New York: Harper Colophone, 1961).

Borkin, Joseph. *The Crime and Punishment of I.G. Farben* (New York: Free Press, 1978).

Bowman, Shayne and Chris Willis. *We Media: How Audiences Are Shaping the Future of News and Information* (Reston, VA: American Press Institute, 2003).

Brendon, Piers. *The Life and Death of the Press Barons* (New York: Atheneum, 1983).

Brian, Dennis. *Pulitzer: A Life* (Hoboken, NJ: John Wiley and Sons, 2001).

Bricklin, Dan. VisiCalc: *Information from its Creators, Dan Bricklin and Bob Frankston,* published on the Web: http://www.bricklin.com/visicalc.htm

Brinkley, Alan. *The Publisher: Henry Luce and His American Century* (New York: Knopf, 2010).

Brown, John Crosby. "American Isolation: Propaganda Pro and Con," *Foreign Affairs*, Oct. 1939, pp. 29–44.

Brown, Peter. "Free software is a Matter of Liberty, Not Price," Free Software Foundation, December 27, 2010, on the Web at http://www.fsf.org/about

Brown, Robert E. and Katherine Brown. *Virginia 1705–1786: Democracy or Aristocracy?* (East Lansing, MI: Michigan State University Press, 1964).

Browne, Malcolm W. "The Fighting Words of Homer Bigart: A War Correspondent Is Never a Cheerleader," *The New York Times*, April 11, 1993, on the Web at: http://www.pbs.org/weta/reportingamericaatwar/reporters/bigart

Bryce, James. Report of the Committee on Alleged German Outrages, 1914, originally published by the British government, on the Web at: http://www.gwpda.org/wwi-www/BryceReport/bryce_r.html

Bucholz, Robert O. and Newton Key. *Early Modern England 1485–1714: A Narrative History* (Hoboken, NJ: Wiley, 2009).

Burnett, James. "Stewart Closes Rally with Biting Critique of Media," *Rolling Stone*, October 30, 2010, on the Web at: http://www.rollingstone.com/culture/news/17389/228438

Burrough, Bryan and John Helyar. *Barbarians at the Gate: The Rise and Fall of RJR Nabisco* (New York: Harper & Row, 1990).

Burrows, Edwin G. and Mike Wallace. *Gotham: A History of New York City to 1898* (New York: Oxford University Press, 1999).

Bush, Vannevar. "As We May Think," *Atlantic*, August 1946.

—. *Modern Arms and Free Men: A Discussion of the Role of Science in Preserving Democracy* (New York: Simon and Schuster, 1949).

Bytwerk, Randall L. *Julius Streicher: Nazi Editor of the Notorious Anti-Semitic Newspaper* Der Sturmer (New York: Cooper Square Press, 2001).

Calabrese, Andrew. "The MacBride Report: Its Value to a New Generation," 25 Years of the MacBride Report: International Communication and Communication Policies, *Quaderns del CAC*, University of Barcelona, 2005

Cambeau, Don. "Modern Marvels: The Telephone," History Channel documentary, 2006.

Campbell, W. Joseph. *Yellow Journalism: Puncturing the Myths, Defining the Legacies* (Santa Barbara, CA: Praeger, 2003).

—. *Getting It Wrong* (Los Angeles, CA: University of California Press, 2010).

Cappo, Joe. *The Future of Advertising: New Media, New Clients, New Consumers in the Post-Television Age* (New York: McGraw Hill, 2005).

Carey, James W. *Communication as Culture: Essays on Media and Society* (New York: Routledge, 1992).

Carr, David. "So Plentiful So Cheap," *The New York Times*, February 7, 2010.

Cha, Ariana Eunjung. "Mobile Coupons Help Retailers Track Customers," *Washington Post*, June 27, 2010.

Chakravorti, Robi. "Marx the Journalist," *Economic and Political Weekly,* September 4, 1993, pp. 1856–9, on the Web at: http://www2.cddc.vt.edu/marxists/archive/marx/works/download/Marx_On_freedom_of_the_Press.pdf

Chaplin, Charlie. *My Autobiography* (New York: Simon and Schuster, 1964).

Christensen, Thomas. "Gutenberg and the Koreans: Did East Asian Printing Traditions Influence the European Renaissance?" on the Web at: http://www.rightreading.com/printing/gutenberg.asia/gutenberg-asia-1-introduction.htm

Clark, Stuart B. *The Sun Kings: The Unexpected Tragedy of Richard Carrington and the Tale of How Modern Astronomy Began* (Princeton, NJ: Princeton University Press, 2007).

Clifford, Stephanie. "A Fine Line When Ads and Children Mix," *The New York Times*, February 14, 2010.

Coke, V. D. *The Painter and the Photograph* (Albuquerque, NM: University of New Mexico Press, 1972).

Conley, Scott R. "The Children's Television Act: Reasons and Practice," *Syracuse Law Review*, Vol. 61 No. 1, 2010.

Conquest, Robert. *The Great Terror: A Reassessment* (New York: Oxford University Press, 1990).

Cousteau, Jacques. *The Silent World* (New York: Harper Brothers, 1953).

Cramer, Richard Ben and Thomas Lennon. "The Battle Over Citizen Kane," Frontline Documentary, Public Broadcasting System, 2000.

Crandol, Michael. "The History of Animation: Advantages and Disadvantages of the Studio System in the Production of an Art Form, Digital Media FX," accessed 2010 on the Web at: http://www.digitalmediafx.com/Features/animationhistory.html

Creelman, James. "The Real Mr. Hearst," *Pearson's Magazine*, May 1906, p. 257.

Cringley, Robert X. *Accidental Empires: How the Boys of Silicon Valley Make Their Millions, Battle Foreign Competition, and Still Can't Get a Date* (New York: Harper Paperbacks, 1996).

Csillag, András. "Born in Hungary 160 Years Ago: Joseph Pulitzer and the Hungarians," *Americana*, Vol. VI, No. 2, Fall, 2008, on the Web at: http://americanaejournal.hu/vol4no2/csillag

Curtis, James. *Mind's Eye, Mind's Truth: FSA Photography Reconsidered* (Philadelphia, PA: Temple University Press, 1991).

Czitrom, Daniel. *Media and the American Mind: From Morse to McLuhan* (Chapel Hill, NC: University of North Carolina Press, 1983).

Daniels, Derick. "The World of Multi-media," speech at University of West Virginia, April 7, 1970. Unpublished, Daniels family papers.

Darnton, Robert and Daniel Roche, *Revolution in Print: The Press in France 1775–1800* (Berkeley, CA: University of California Press, 1989).

de Bord, Matthew. "The Crisis in Crisis PR, Why the Dark Art Is in Meltdown," *The Big Money*, July 20, 2010, on the Web at: http://www.thebigmoney.com/articles/judgments/2010/07/20/crisis-crisis-pr?xs_wp_0004

de la Motte, Dean. *Making the News: Modernity & the Mass Press in Nineteenth-century France* (Boston, MA: University of Massachusetts Press, 1999).

Demers, David. *History and Future of Mass Media: An Integrated Perspective* (Cresskill, NJ: Hampton Press, 2007).

de Sola Pool, Ithiel. *Technologies of Freedom* (Boston, MA: Belknap Press of Harvard University Press, 1984).

de Tocqueville, Alexis. "Democracy in America, 1835," full text on the Web at: http://xroads.virginia.edu/~HYPER/DETOC/home.html

Dewar, James A. "The Information Age and the Printing Press: Looking Backward to See Ahead," (Palo Alto, CA: Rand Corp., 1998), on the Web at: http://www.rand.org/pubs/papers/P8014.html

Douglass, Frederick. "The Destiny of Colored Americans," *The North Star*, November 16, 1849.

Dregni, Eric and Jonathan Dregni. *Follies of Science: 20th Century Visions of Our Fantastic Future* (Golden, CO: Speck Press, 2006).

Drout, Michael. *Rings, Swords and Monsters: Exploring Fantasy Literature*, Modern Scholar series, Recorded Books, 2006.

DuBois, W. E. B. *The Souls of Black Folks* (Chicago, IL: A. C. McClurg, 1903).

Dunne, Finley Peter. *Observations by Mr. Dooley* (New York: R. H. Russell, 1902).

Ebert, Roger. "Casablanca," *Chicago Sun-Times*, September 15, 1996, on the Web at: http://rogerebert.suntimes.com/apps/pbcs.dll/article?AID=/19960915/REVIEWS08/401010308/1023

—. "Birth of a Nation," *Chicago Sun-Times*, March 30, 2003, on the Web at: http://rogerebert.suntimes.com/apps/pbcs.dll/article?AID=/20030330/REVIEWS08/303300301/1023

Editor & Publisher, "Generally Upbeat World Press Trends Report Highlights Regional Differences," *Editor & Publisher*, August 10, 2010.

Eisenstein, Elizabeth. "The Advent of Printing and the Protestant Revolt: A New Approach to the Disruption of Western Christendom", in Robert Kingdon, ed., *Transition and Revolution. Problems and Issues of European Renaissance and Reformation History* (Minneapolis, MN: Burgess Publishing Co., 1974).

—. *The Printing Press as an Agent of Change* (Cambridge: Cambridge University Press, 1980).

—. *The Printing Revolution in Early Modern Europe* (Cambridge: Cambridge University Press, 1990).

Elders, M. Joycelyn. Preventing Tobacco Use among Young People, Report of the Surgeon General, US Government Printing Office, 1994.

Ellett, Ryan. "Amos n' Andy: The Chicago Defenders Response," *Old Time Radio Researchers*, on the Web at: http://otrr.org

Emery, Michael and Edwin Emery. *The Press and America: An Interpretive History of the Mass Media* (Englewood Cliffs, NJ: Prentice Hall, 1988).

Encyclopedia Britannica Inc., "Fatally Flawed: Refuting the Recent Study on Encyclopedic Accuracy by the Journal *Nature*," *Nature,* March 2006.

Engelbart, Douglas C. "Augmenting Human Intellect: A Conceptual Framework," SRI Summary Report AFOSR-3223, 1962, on the Web at: http://www.dougengelbart.org/pubs/augment-3906.html

Epstein, Edward Jay. "The Vanishing Box Office: A Terminal Condition," *Slate* magazine, July 5, 2005, on the Web at: http://www.slate.com/id/2122000/ Also see http://www.edwardjayepstein.com

—. *The Big Picture: Money and Power in Hollywood* (New York: Random House, 2006).

Eyman, Scott. *The Speed of Sound: Hollywood and the Talkie Revolution, 1926–1930* (New York, Simon and Schuster, 1997).

Fallows, James. "How to Save the News," *The Atlantic* magazine, June 2010, on the Web at: http://www.theatlantic.com/magazine/archive/2010/06/how-to-save-the-news/8095/1/

Farmer, James. "Citizen Journalism Sucks," *The Age* (Melbourne, Australia), October 5, 2006.

Farnsworth, Stephen J. and S. Robert Lichter. *The Nightly News Nightmare: Television's Coverage of US Presidential Elections 1988–2004* (Lanham, MD: Rowman & Littlefield, 2007).

Febvre, Lucien and Henri-Jean Martin. *The Coming of the Book* (London: Verso, 1976).

Feldstein, Mark. "A Muckraking Model: Investigative Reporting Cycles in American History," *Harvard International Journal of Press/Politics*, Spring 2006.

Fenster, Julie M. "Inventing the Telephone—and Triggering All-Out Patent War," *American Heritage*, March 7, 2006.

Ferriman, Annabel. "Advertising Standards Authority finds against Nestlé," *British Medical Journal* 318 (7181), February 13, 1999.

Fidler, Roger. *Mediamorphosis: Understanding New Media* (Newbery Park, CA: Pine Forge Press, 1997).

Fine, Barrett. *A Giant of the Press: Carr Van Anda* (Oakland, CA: Acme Books, 1968).

Folkerts, Jean et al. *Voices of a Nation: A History of Mass Media in the United States* (Boston, MA: Allyn & Bacon, 2008).

Forbes, Jill and Sarah Street. *European Cinema: An Introduction* (Houndmills, Basingstoke: Palgrave Macmillan, 2001).

Franklin, Benjamin. "An Apology for Printers," *Pennsylvania Gazette*, June 10, 1731.

Freund, Gisele. *Photography and Society* (Boston, MA: Godine, 1980).

Friedel, Robert. *The Culture of Improvement* (Boston, MA: MIT Press, 2007).

Friedman, Jerome. "The Battle of the Frogs and Fairfold's Flies: Miracles and Popular Journalism during the English Revolution," *The Sixteenth Century Journal*, Vol. 23, No. 2, 1992, 419–42.

Friedman, Milton. *Capitalism and Freedom* (Chicago, IL: University of Chicago Press, 1962).

Friedman, Thomas. *The World Is Flat: A Brief History of the Twenty-first Century* (New York: Farrar, Straux and Giroux, 2006).

Friendly, Fred. *Due to Circumstances beyond Our Control* (New York: Random House, 1967).

Frontard, Raymond. "Standards Related Activities, The Global View," in *Friendship Among Equals* (Geneva, Switzerland: International Standards Organization, 1997), on the Web at: http://www.iso.org/iso/about/the_iso_story/friendship_equals.htm

Fukuyama, Francis. *The End of History and the Last Man* (New York: Free Press, 1992).

Garvin, Glen. "Walter Cronkite, 1916–2009," *Miami Herald*, July 19, 2009.

Gates, Bill. *The Road Ahead* (New York: Viking, 1995).

Gavin, Clark. *Famous Libel and Slander Cases of History* (New York: Collier Books, 1962).

—. "Content is King," January 3, 1996; on the Web at: http://www.craigbailey.net/content-is-king-by-bill-gates

Giles, Jim. "Internet Encyclopedias go Head to Head," *Nature*, 438:7070, December 15, 2005, pp. 900–01.

Gilliam, Terry. "The Ten Best Animated Films of All Time," *The Guardian*, April 27, 2001.

Ginzburg, Carlo, John Tedeschi and Anne C. Tedeschi. *The Cheese and the Worms* (Baltimore, MD: Johns Hopkins University Press, 1992).

Godin, Seth. *Tribes: We Need You to Lead Us* (New York: Portfolio, 2008).

Goff, Leslie. "Univac Predicts Winner of 1952 Election," *CNNTech*, April 30, 1999, on the Web at: http://articles.cnn.com/1999–04-30/tech/9904_30_1952.idg_1_election-returns-election-night-machine?_s=PM:TECH

Goldberg, Vicki. "Introducing the Poor to the Middle Class," *The New York Times*, November 3, 1991, p. H35.

Goodman, Amy. "Media Giant John H. Johnson Paved the Way for Black-Owned Press," *Democracy Now*, August 16, 2005, on the Web at: http://www.democracy-now.org/2005/8/16/media_giant_john_h_johnson_paved

—. "The FCC & Censorship: Legendary Media Activist Everett Parker on the Revocation of WLBT's TV License in the 1960s for Shutting Out Voices of the Civil Rights Movement," *Democracy Now*, March 6, 2008, on the Web at: http://www.democracynow.org/2008/3/6/the_fcc_censorship_legendary_media_activist

Gordon, John Steele. "The Public Be Damned," *American Heritage* magazine, September/October 1989, 40:6.

Gosling, John. *Waging the War of the Worlds: A History of the 1938 Radio Broadcast and Resulting Panic* (Jefferson, NC: McFarland, 2009).

Gottlieb, Agnes Hooper et al. *1,000 Years, 1,000 People: Ranking the Men and Women Who Shaped the Millennium* (New York: Barnes & Noble, 2006).

Greeley, Horace. "The Philosophy of Advertising," *The Merchant's Magazine and Commercial Review,* November 1, 1850, p. 580.

—. *An Overland Journey from New York to San Francisco in the Summer of 1859* (New York: C. M. Saxton, Barker & Co., 1860).

Green, Abigail. "Intervening in the Public Sphere: German Governments and the Press, 1815–1860," *The Historical Journal*, 44, I (2001), 155–75.

Greenberger, Martin. "The Computers of Tomorrow," *Atlantic Monthly*, May 1964.

Griese, Noel L. "AT&T: 1908 Origins of the Nation's Oldest Continuous Institutional Advertising Campaign," *Journal of Advertising*, Vol. 6, No. 3 (Summer, 1977), 18–23.

Gronow, Pekka. "The Record Industry: The Growth of a Mass Medium," *Popular Music*, Vol. 3, Producers and Markets, 1983.

Grunig, James. "Symmetrical Presuppositions as a Framework for Public Relations Theory," in C. H. Botan and V. Hazleton, Jr (eds), *Public Relations Theory* (Hillsdale, NJ: Lawrence Erlbaum Associates, 1989).

Guha, Ramachandra. "Gandhi the Journalist," *The Hindu*, June 8, 2003, on the Web at: http://www.hindu.com/thehindu/mag/2003/06/08/stories/2003060800320300.htm

Habermas, Jürgen. *The Structural Transformation of the Public Sphere*, trans. Thomas Burger (Boston, MA: MIT Press, 1991).

Haberstich, David. "Photography and the Plastic Arts," *Leonardo*, Vol. 6 (1973), 113–19, Pergamon Press.

Halberstam, David. *The Making of a Quagmire: America and Vietnam during the Kennedy Era* (New York: McGraw-Hill, 1965).

—. *The Best and the Brightest* (New York: Random House, 1973).

—. *The Powers That Be* (New York: Knopf, 1979).

Haley, Alex. *Roots: The Saga of an American Family* (New York: Doubleday, 1976).

Hallin, Daniel C. *The "Uncensored War": The Media and Vietnam* (New York: Oxford University Press, 1986).

Hammond, William M. *Reporting Vietnam: Media and Military at War* (Lawrence, KS: University of Kansas Press, 2007).

Hand, Richard J. *Terror on the Air!: Horror Radio in America, 1931–1952* (Jefferson, NC: Mcfarland & Company, 2006).

Hannavy, John. *Encyclopedia of Nineteenth-century Photography* (London: Routledge, 2007).

Hart, Roderick P. and Mary Triece, "US Presidency and Television," Museum of Broadcast Communication Encyclopedia of Television, on the Web at: http://www.museum.tv/debateweb/html/equalizer/essay_usprestv.htm

Hauben, Ronda. "From the ARPANET to the Internet," online paper, Columbia University, on the Web at: http://www.columbia.edu/~rh120/other/tcpdigest_paper.txt

Hedges, Chris. *Empire of Illusion: The End of Literacy and the Triumph of Spectacle* (New York: Nation Books, 2009).

Hemingway, Ernest. *Men at War* (New York: Crown Publishers, 1942).

Herschthal, Eric. "The Other Guy with That Mustache," *Nitrateville*, July 31, 2008, on the Web at: http://www.nitrateville.com

Hiebert, Ray. *Courtier To the Crowd: The Story of Ivy Lee and the Development of Public Relations* (Sioux City, IO: Iowa State University Press, 1966).

Higgins, Marguerite. *Our Vietnam Nightmare* (New York: Harper & Row, 1965).

Hilmes, Michelle. *Only Connect: A Cultural History of Broadcasting in the United States* (New York: Wadsworth, 2006).

Hiltzik, Michael. *Dealers of Lightning: Xerox PARC and the Dawn of the Computer Age* (New York: Harper, 2000).

Hind, Arthur M. *A Short History of Engraving and Etching* (Boston, MA: Houghton Mifflin, 1908).

Hippler, Fritz. "Film as a Weapon," *Unser Wille und Weg*, 7 (1937), 21–3, on the Web at: http://www.calvin.edu/academic/cas/gpa/hippler1.htm Also see Fritz Hippler, Internet Movie Database (IMDb), August 2010.

Hirshberg, Peter. "On TV and the Web," *TED Talks*, 2007, on the Web at: http://www.ted.com/talks/peter_hirshberg_on_tv_and_the_web.html

History of Computing Project, on the Web at: http://www.thocp.net/, accessed May 2010.

Holt, Debra J. et al., "Children's Exposure to TV Advertising in 1977 and 2004: Information for the Obesity Debate," Federal Trade Commission, June 1, 2007.

Holtzberg-Call, Maggie. *The Lost World of the Craft Printer* (Urbana, IL: University of Illinois Press, 1992).

Horan, James. *Mathew Brady: Historian with a Camera* (New York: Crown Publishers, 1955).

Horwitz, Robert B. "Broadcast Reform Revisited: Reverend Everett C. Parker and the 'Standing' Case (Office of Communication of the United Church of Christ v. Federal Communication Commission)," *The Communication Review*, 2:3 (1997).

Houseman, John. "The Men from Mars," *Harper's Magazine*, December 1948.

Howe, Daniel Walker. *What Hath God Wrought: The Transformation of America, 1815–1848* (New York: Oxford University Press, 2007).

Hsü, Immanuel C. Y. *The Rise of Modern China* (New York: Oxford University Press, 1970).

Hudson, Frederic. *Journalism in the United States, from 1690–1872* (New York: Harper & Brothers, 1873).

Hume, David. "Of the Liberty of the Press; Essays Moral, Political and Literary, 1742," The Founders Constitution (Chicago: University of Chicago Press, published on the Web at: http://press-pubs.uchicago.edu/founders/)

Hutchins, Robert M. Chair, the Commission on Freedom of the Press. A Free and Responsible Press: A General Report on Mass Communication: Newspapers, Radio,

Motion Pictures, Magazines, and Books, University of Chicago, 1947. Full report on the Web at: http://www.archive.org/details/freeandresponsib029216mbp

Huws, Ursula. *The Making of a Cybertariat: Virtual Work in a Real World* (New York: Monthly Review Press, 2003).

Illinois Inter-ocean Publishing Co. v. Associated Press, 184 Ill. 438, 1900.

Innis, Harold. *Empire and Communication* (New York: Oxford University Press, 1950).

International Telecommunications Union, History of the ITU, on the Web at: http://www.itu.int/en/history/ accessed August 2010.

Internet Advertising Bureau, "IAB Internet Advertising Report," 2010, on the Web at: http://www.iab.net/insights_research

Irwin, Will. "The American Newspaper," *Collier's Magazine*, January 1911 (Series republished by Iowa State University, 1969).

Israel, Shel. *Twitterville* (New York: Penguin, 2009).

Jefferson, Thomas to John Tyler, 1804, E-text, University of Virginia, ME 11:33, on the Web at: http://etext.virginia.edu/jefferson/quotations/jeff1600.htm

Johnson, Paul. *Birth of the Modern* (New York: HarperCollins, 1991).

Jung, Carl and Marie-Luise von Franz. *Man and His Symbols* (New York: Doubleday, 1964).

Kahn, David. *The Codebreakers: The Story of Secret Writing* (New York: Macmillan, 1967).

Kane, Yukari and Russell Adams, "Apple Opens Door, Keeps Keys," *Wall Street Journal,* February 16, 2011.

Katz, John. "Bulletin Boards: News From Cyberspace," *Rolling Stone*, April 15, 1993, pp. 35–77.

Kellner, Douglas. "Jean Baudrillard," *The Stanford Encyclopedia of Philosophy (Winter 2009 Edition)*, Edward N. Zalta (ed.), on the Web at: http://plato.stanford.edu/archives/win2009/entries/baudrillard

Kelloway, Lucy. "BP Is the Company We All Love to Hate," *Financial Times*, June 18, 2010, on the Web at: http://www.ft.com/cms/s/0/9c732c98–7b01–11df-8935–00144feabdc0.html

Kennan, George Frost. *Russia Leaves the War: Soviet-American Relations, 1917–1920* (Princeton, NJ: Princeton University Press, 1989 [originally published in 1956]).

Kennedy, Robert F. *Crimes against Nature* (New York: HarperCollins, 2004).

Kershaw, Alex. *Blood and Champagne: The Life and Times of Robert Capa* (New York: St. Martins, 2002).

Kesterson, W. H. *A History of Journalism in Canada* (Ottawa, Canada: Carlton University Press, 1984).

Kielbowicz, Richard B. *News in the Mail: The Press, Post Office, and Public Information, 1700–1860s* (New York: Greenwood Press, 1989).

Kiplinger magazine, "Radio Listeners be Damned," February 1947, p. 7.

Klein, David and Scott Donaton. "The Advertising Century, Advertising Age, 1999," on the Web at: http://adage.com/century/

Kluger, Richard. *The Paper: The Life and Death of the* New York Herald Tribune (New York: Knopf, 1986).

Knight, Charles, ed. *London* (London: Henry G. Bohn, 1851).

Knightly, Phillip. *The First Casualty: The War Correspondent as Hero and Myth-maker from the Crimea to Iraq* (Baltimore, MD: Johns Hopkins University Press, 2004).

Kochersberger, Jr, Robert C. *More than a Muckraker: Ida Tarbell's Lifetime Journalism* (Knoxville, TN: University of Tennessee Press, 1996).

Kohut, Andrew. "Internet News Audience Highly Critical of News Organizations: Views of Press Values and Performance: 1985–2007," Pew Research Center for People and the Press, August 9, 2007, on the Web at: http://people-press.org/report/348/internet-news-audience-highly-critical-of-news-organizations Also see: Gallup Polls, "In U.S., Confidence in Newspapers, TV News Remains a Rarity," August 13, 2010, on the Web at: http://www.gallup.com/poll/142133/confidence-newspapers-news-remains-rarity.aspx

Kovarik, Bill. "Publishing technologies for Eastern Europe," memo to the Center for Foreign Journalists, July, 1990.

—. "To Avoid the Coming Storm: Hezekiah Niles Weekly Register as a Voice of North-South Moderation, 1811–1836," *American Journalism*, Summer, 1992.

—. *Web Design for Mass Media* (New York: Pearson, 2001).

Kroeger, Brooke. *Nellie Bly: Daredevil, Reporter, Feminist* (New York: Three Rivers Press, 1995).

Kulash, Jr, Damian. "Whose Tube?" *The New York Times*, February 19, 2010, A17, on the Web at: http://www.nytimes.com/2010/02/20/opinion/20kulash.html?th&emc=th

—. "OK Go on Net Neutrality: A Lesson from the Music Industry," *Washington Post*, August 29, 2010.

Kurtz, Howard. "In Lean Times, TV Reporters Must Be Jacks of All Trades," *Washington Post*, March 8, 2010.

Kurzweil, Ray. *The Singularity is Near* (New York: Viking, 2005).

Lacy, Stephen and Hugh J. Martin. "Profits Up, Circulation Down for Thomson Papers in 80s," *Newspaper Research Journal*, Vol. 19, 1998.

Lange, Dorothea. "The Assignment I'll Never Forget: Migrant Mother," *Popular Photography*, February 1960.

Leadbeater, Charles and Paul Miller, "The Pro-Am Revolution," *Demos*, November 24, 2004, on the Web at http://www.demos.co.uk/publications/proameconomy

Leary, Kevin. "Joe Rosenthal: 1911–2006; Photo Was His Fame—His Pride 'My Marines,'" *San Francisco Chronicle*, August 21, 2006, p. A1.

Lembcke, Jerry. *Spitting Image: Myth, Memory and the Legacy of Vietnam* (New York: New York University Press, 1998).

Lenin, V. I. "Where to Begin," *Iskra*, No. 4, May 1901; in *Collected Works*, trans. Joe Fineberg and George Hanna (Moscow: Foreign Language Publishing House, 1964).

—. Speech at the Opening Session of the First Congress of the Communist International, March 2–6, 1919, Marxist Internet Archive, accessed August 2010, on the Web at: http://www.marxists.org/archive/lenin/works/1919/mar/comintern.htm

Leonard, Andrew. "BSD Unix: Power to the People, from the Code," *Salon*, May 16, 2000, on the Web at: http://www.salon.com/technology/fsp/2000/05/16/chapter_2_part_one

Lessig, Lawrence. *Free Culture: The Nature and Future of Creativity* (London: Penguin, 2005). Also see TED 2007 talk: "Larry Lessig on laws that choke creativity," on the Web at: http://www.ted.com/talks/larry_lessig_says_the_law_is_strangling_creativity.html

Lester, Paul Martin, ed. *Images That Injure: Pictorial Stereotypes in the Media* (New York: Praeger, 1996).

Leuf, Bo and Ward Cunningham. *The Wiki Way* (Boston: Addison-Wesley, 2001).

Liebling, A. J. *The Press* (New York: Pantheon, 1981).

Life magazine. "Speaking of Pictures," April 21, 1951, p. 19.

Linder, Doug. "The Trial of John Peter Zenger: An Account," Famous Trials, on the Web at: http://www.law.umkc.edu/faculty/projects/ftrials/ftrials.htm

Linzmayer, Owen W. *Apple Confidential 2.0: The Definitive History of the World's Most Colorful Company* (San Francisco, CA: No Starch Press, 2004).

Lippmann, Walter. *Public Opinion* (New York: Harcourt Brace, 1922).

Litchfield, Richard Buckley. *Tom Wedgwood, the First Photographer* (London: Duckworth, 1903).

Lloyd, Caro. *Henry Demaerest Lloyd, 1847–1903* (New York: Knickerbocker Press, 1912).

Lord, Walter. *A Night to Remember* (New York: Holt, 2004 [originally published in 1955]).

Low, A. M. "Wireless to Rule Our Lives, British Professor Predicts," *The New York Times*, August 30, 1925, p. XX7.

Lowen, James W. *Lies My Teacher Told Me: Everything Your American History Textbook Got Wrong* (New York: Touchstone 1996).

Luxon, Norval Neil. *Niles Weekly Register: News Magazine of the Nineteenth Century* (Baton Rouge, LA: Louisiana State University Press, 1947).

Manchester, William. *The Glory and the Dream* (New York: Bantam Books, 1974).

Marchand, Roland. *Creating the Corporate Soul: The Rise of Public Relations and Corporate Imagery in American Big Business* (Los Angeles, CA: University of California Press, 1998).

Markoff, John. *What the Doormouse Said: How the 60s Counterculture Shaped the Personal Computer* (New York: Viking 2005).

—. "When Big Blue Got a Glimpse of the Future," *The New York Times*, December 11, 2007, on the Web at: http://bits.blogs.nytimes.com/2007/12/11/when-big-blue-got-a-glimpse-of-the-future/

Marshack, Alexander, "The Art and Symbols of Ice Age Man," in David Crowley and Paul Heyer (eds), *Communication in History*, 4th edition (Boston, MA: Allyn & Bacon, 2003).

Martin, James B. *Mass Media: A Bibliography with Indexes* (New York: Nova Science, 2002).

Martin, Kirsten E. "Google Inc., in China," *Business Roundtable* (Washington D.C.: Catholic University, 2007).

McCabe, Charles, ed. *Damned Old Crank: A Self-Portrait of EW Scripps from His Unpublished Writings* (New York: Harpers, 1951).

McCauley, Anne. " 'Merely Mechanical': On the Origins of Photographic Copyright in France and Great Britain," *Art History*, Vol. 31, No. 1 (February 2008), 57–78.

McChesney, Robert. *Telecommunications, Mass Media and Democracy: The Battle for Control of US Broadcasting, 1928–1935* (New York: Oxford University Press, 1994).

—. *The Death and Life of American Journalism: The Media Revolution That Will Begin the World Again* (New York: Nation Books, 2010).

McChesney, Robert and Victor Pickard. *Will the Last Reporter Please Turn Out the Lights: The Collapse of Journalism and What Can Be Done to Fix It* (New York: The New Press, 2011).

McDonald, Hamish. "Freedom of Speech Is Still Something of a Trial in China," *The Melbourne Australia Age*, November 2, 2005.

McLeod, Elizabeth. *The Original Amos 'n Andy: Freeman Gosden, Charles Correll, and the 1928–1943 Radio Serial* (Jefferson, NC: McFarland & Co., 2005).

McLuhan, Marshall. *The Gutenberg Galaxy* (London: Routledge, 1962).

—. *The Global Village: Transformations in World Life and Media in the 21st Century* (New York: Oxford, 1992).

—. *Laws of Media: The New Science* (Toronto: University of Toronto Press, 1992).

—. *Understanding Media* (Cambridge, MA: The MIT Press, 1994).

McMahon, Michael. "Public Service versus Man's Properties: Dock Creek and the Origins of Urban Technology in Eighteenth Century Philadelphia," in Judith A. McGaw (ed.), *Early American Technology: Making and Doing things from the Colonial Era to 1850* (Chapel Hill, NC: University of North Carolina Press, 1994).

Melvern, Linda. *Conspiracy to Murder: The Rwandan Genocide* (London, New York: Verso, 2004).

Mercado III, E., L. M. Herman and A. A. Pack. "Song Copying by Humpback Whales: Themes and Variations," *Animal Cognition* 8 (2005), 93–102.

Meyer, Philip. *The Vanishing Newspaper: Saving Journalism in the Information Age* (Columbia, MO: University of Missouri Press, 2009).

Miller Center, Project on Media and Governance. *Old Media, New Media and the Challenge to Democratic Governance* (Charlottesville, VA: University of Virginia, 2010), accessed December 2010 on the Web at: http://millercenter.org/public/debates/internet

Miraldi, Robert. "Scaring Off Muckrakers with the Threat of Libel," *Journalism Quarterly*, 65:3 (Fall 1988), 609–14.

Mitgang, Herbert, ed. *Spectator of America: A Classic Document about Lincoln and Civil War America by a Contemporary English Correspondent, Edward Dicey* (Athens, GA: University of Georgia Press, 1989), on the Web at: http://www.mrlincolnandnewyork.org/inside.asp?ID=38&subjectID=3

Moore, Gordon E. "Cramming More Components onto Integrated Circuits," *Electronics Magazine*, April 19, 1965, 4.

Morison, Stanley. *The English Newspaper* (Cambridge, UK: Cambridge University Press, 1932).

Moritz, Scott. "How Yellow Colored an Era," *Editor & Publisher*, September 28, 1996.

Morris, Roger. *Richard Milhous Nixon: The Rise of an American Politician* (New York: Henry Holt, 1991).

Morse, Samuel Finley Breese and Edward Lind Morse. *Samuel F.B. Morse: His Letters and Journals* (New York: Houghton Mifflin Company, 1914).

Mott, Frank Luther. *American Journalism, a History: 1690–1960* (New York: Macmillan, 1966).

Moxon, Joseph. *Mechanick Exercises: Or, the Doctrine of Handy-Works Applied to the Art of Printing* (London: Atlas, 1683).

Munro, John. *Heroes of the Telegraph* (London: The Religious Tract Society, 1891).

Murray, Michael D. *Encyclopedia of Television News* (Phoenix, AZ: Oryx Press, 1999).

Murrow, Edward R. Speech to the Radio TV News Directors Association, 1958, on the Web at: http://www.rtdna.org/pages/media_items/edward-r.-murrow-speech998.php

Museum of Broadcast Communications (MBC). "Civil Rights and Television," on the Web at: http://www.museum.tv/eotvsection.php?entrycode=civilrights

Nassaw, David. *The Chief: The Life of William Randolph Hearst* (New York: Houghton Mifflin, 2001).

National Academy of Engineering (NAE). "Greatest Achievements: Computer History," 2010, on the Web at: http://www.greatachievements.org/?id=3985

Neiva, Elizabeth M. "Money Technology, Tax Law and Trouble, Chain Building: The Consolidation of the American Newspaper Industry,1955–1980," *Business and Economic History*, 24:1 (Fall 1995).

Nelson, D. L., U. S. Reed and J. R. Walling. "Pictorial Superiority Effect," *Journal of Experimental Psychology: Human Learning & Memory*, 2 (1976), 523–8.

Nelson, Ted. *Literary Machines* (San Antonio, TX: Project Xanadu, 1981).

—. *Computer Lib/Dream Machines* [1974] (Redmond, WA: Tempus Books of Microsoft Press, 1987).

Neuzil, Mark. *The Environment and the Press: From Adventure Writing to Advocacy* (Chicago, IL: Northwestern University Press, 2008).

Neuzil, Mark and Bill Kovarik. *Mass Media and Environmental Conflict* (Thousand Oaks, CA: Sage, 1997).

Nevins, Allan. *The Gateway to History* (New York: D. Appleton-Century, 1938).

New Republic, "A Woman in History—The Wonderful, Horrible Life of Leni Riefenstahl," 210: 11, March 14, 1994, 30.

Newspaper Association of America (NAA). "Advertising Expenditures," on the Web at: http://www.naa.org/TrendsandNumbers/Advertising-Expenditures.aspx

Newth, Mette. "The Long History of Censorship, 2001," on the Web at: http://www.beaconforfreedom.org/about_project/history.html

New York Magazine, "Is 'The Golden Compass' Too Anti-Christian, or Not Anti-Christian Enough?" October 16, 2007, on the Web at: http://nymag.com/daily/entertainment/2007/10/is_the_golden_compass_too_anti.html

New York Times, "Ivy Lee, as Advisor to Nazis, Paid $25,000 by Dye Trust," July 12, 1934.

—, "The Pentagon Papers," 1971, on the Web at: http://topics.nytimes.com/top/reference/timestopics/subjects/p/pentagon_papers/

New York Times Co. v. United States, 403 U.S. 713, June 30, 1971.

Niemi, Robert. *History in the Media: Film and Television* (Santa Barbara, CA: ABC-Clio, 2006).

Novik, Peter. *That Noble Dream: The Objectivity Question and the American Historical Profession* (Cambridge: Cambridge University Press, 1988).

O'Brien, Frank. *The Story of the Sun* (New York: Doran Co., 1918).

Office of Communication of the United Church of Christ v. FCC, 359 F. 2nd 994; 1, 1966.

Olasky, Marvin. *Corporate Public Relations: A New Historical Perspective* (Mahwah, NJ: Lawrence Earlbaum Associates, 1987).

Ong, Walter. *Orality and Literacy* (London: Routledge, 2002).

Outlook, "Birth of a Nation," April 14, 1915, p. 854.

Paivio, A. *Mental Representations: A Dual Coding Approach* (Oxford, UK: Oxford University Press, 1986).

Parish, James Robert and Gregory Mark. *The Best of M-G-M, The Golden Years: 1928-1959* (Westport, CT: Arlington House Publishers, 1981), p. 143.

Parliamentary Reform. February 26, 1785, p. 3, issue 49, col. A.

Parsons, Frank. *The Telegraph Monopoly* (Philadelphia, PA: Equity, 1899). Also see Arthur Mann, "Frank Parsons, the Professor as Crusader," *Mississippi Valley Historical Review*, Vol. 37, No. 3 (December, 1950), 471–90.

Parton, James. *The Life of Horace Greeley* (New York: Mason Brothers, 1855).

—. "Samuel F.B. Morse," *Scientific American*, December 3, 1870.

—. "The Battle of New Orleans," in Rossiter Johnson (ed.), *Great Events by Famous Historians, The National Alumni*, Vol. XV, 1905, p. 343.

Pauly, Philip J. *Biologists and the Promise of American Life: From Meriwether Lewis to Alfred Kinsey* (Princeton, NJ: Princeton University Press, 2000).

Pearson, Drew. Washington Merry-Go-Round, December 8, 1943 (Washington, D.C.: American University, Drew Pearson online archive: http://www.library.american.edu/pearson/).

Pershing, Ginny. "Cybertelecom Project", on the Web at: http://www.cybertelecom.org/notes/att.htm

Petersen-Perlman, Deborah. "Texaco's Support of the Metropolitan Opera Broadcasts," *Journal of the Northwest Communication Association*, Spring 1994, 65–90.

Peterson, Iver. "Newspapers End Network for Web Sites," *New York Times*, March 11, 1998, p. D-6.

Pew Project for Excellence in Journalism, "State of the news media," on the Web at: http://www.stateofthemedia.org/2010/index.php

Pew Research Center for People & the Press, "Internet Overtakes Newspapers as News Outlet," December 23, 2008, on the Web at: http://people-press.org/report/479/internet-overtakes-newspapers-as-news-outlet

Photographic Times, "A Bit of History," December 1910, 483.

Plattner, Steven W. *The Standard Oil N.J. Photography Project* (Austin, TX: University of Texas Press, 1983).

Playboy Interview: "Marshall McLuhan, A Candid Conversation with the High Priest of Popcult and Metaphysician of Media," *Playboy* magazine, March 1969.

Polk, Ralph. *The Practice of Printing* (Peoria, IL: Charles A Bennett Publishers, 1926; Rev. edition, 1964).

Popkin, Jeremy D. "The Press and the French Revolution after Two Hundred Years," *French Historical Studies*, Vol. 16, No. 3, Spring 1990.

—. "Pictures in a Revolution: Recent Publications on Graphic Art in France, 1789-1799." *Eighteenth-Century Studies*, Vol. 24, No. 2, Winter 1990–91, 251–9.

—. *Media and Revolution* (Lexington, KY: University of Kentucky Press, 1995).

Postman, Neil. *Amusing Ourselves to Death: Public Discourse in the Age of Show Business* (New York: Penguin, 1985).

President's Commission on the Accident at Three Mile Island, US Government Printing Office, 052–003-00734–7, 1979.

Press, Bill. "Progressive Radio is Alive and Well," *Huffington Post*, on the Web at: http://www.huffingtonpost.com/bill-press/progressive-radio-is-aliv_b_432621.html

Price, Derek J. de Solla. "An Ancient Greek Computer," *Scientific American*, 1959, 60–7.

Princeton University Library, Mudd Manuscript Library, Ivy Lee collection, Biography of Ivy Lee, accessed June 2010 on the Web at: http://diglib.princeton.edu/ead/getEad?id=ark:/88435/m039k489x#bioghist

Pyle, Ernie. *Home Country* (New York: Wm. Sloane & Associates, 1935).

—. *Brave Men* (New York: Henry Holt, 1944).

—. *Ernie's War: The Best of Ernie Pyle's World War II Dispatches*, edited by David Nichols (Norwalk, CT: Easton Press, 2000).

Pyle, Richard. "19th-century Papers Shed New Light on Origin of the Associated Press," *AP News Release*, January 31, 2005.

Radio France International (RFI). "Minitel Lives On," February 11, 2009, on the Web at: http://www.rfi.fr/actuen/articles/110/article_2851.asp

Ramo, Joshua. "Jeffrey Preston Bezos: 1999 Person of the Year," *Time* magazine, December 27, 1999.

Read, William. *America's Mass Media Merchants* (Baltimore, MD and London: Johns Hopkins University Press, 1976).

Recording Industry Association of America (RIAA), "Piracy: Online and on the Street," on the Web at: http://www.riaa.com/physicalpiracy.php

Reed, Harry. "My Life with the ENIAC—a Worm's Eye View," in *Fifty Years of Army Computing: From ENIAC to MSRC*, Symposium Proceedings, Aberdeen Proving Ground, US Army Research Laboratory, November 13–14, 1996.

Reed, John. *Ten Days that Shook the World* (New York: Penguin Books, 1977 [originally published 1919]).

Rehak, Joan. "Tylenol Made a Hero of Johnson & Johnson: The Recall That Started Them All," *The New York Times*, March 23, 2002.

Reichardt, Rolf. "Die stadtische Revolution als politisch-kultureller Prozess," in *Die fran- zosische Revolution*, ed. Rolf Reichardt (Frankfurt, 1988).

Reid, T. R. *The Chip: How Two Americans Invented the Microchip and Launched a Revolution* (New York: Random House, 2001).

Reid, Whitelaw. "Newspapers," *Encyclopedia Britannica* (London, New York: 1911), p. 546.

Rhees, David J. "A New Voice for Science: Science Service under Edward Slosson, 1921–29," Master's Thesis, University of North Carolina, 1979.

—. "The Chemists Crusade," Ph.D. Dissertation, University of Pennsylvania, 1987.

Rheingold, Howard. The Virtual Community, *Homesteading on the Electronic Frontier*, 1993, on the Web at: http://www.rheingold.com/

—. Testimony, *Reno v ACLU*, April 1, 1996, on the Web at: http://www.ciec.org/transcripts/April_1_Rheingold.html

—. *Smart Mobs: The Next Social Revolution* (New York: Basic Books, 2002).

Roberts, Gene and Hank Klibanoff. *The Race Beat: The Press, the Civil Rights Struggle and the Awakening of a Nation* (New York: Vintage, 2007).

Robinson, Eugene. "Lena Horne: A Glamorous Revolutionary," *Washington Post,* May 11, 2010.

Rokicki, John. "Advertising in the Roman Empire," *Whole Earth Review*, Spring 1987, on the Web at: http://findarticles.com/p/articles/mi_m1510/is_1987_Spring/ai_4806053/

Roosevelt, Theodore. "Reform through Social Work: Some Forces That Tell for Decency in New York City," *McClure's Magazine*, March 1901.

Roselle, Mike. "Dragline: The CGZ Interview," *Appalachia Watch*, January 26, 2010, on the Web at: http://www.appalachiawatch.org/2010/01/dragline_25.html

Ross, Corey. *Media and the Making of Modern Germany* (New York, London: Oxford University Press, 2008).

Rossetto, Louis. "Cyberpunks Anticipate a New Digital Culture," *Wired* magazine, September/October, 1993.

—. "In a Letter to His Kids, *Wired*'s Founding Editor Recalls the Dawn of the Digital Revolution," *Wired* magazine, May 19, 2008, on the Web at: http://www.wired.com/techbiz/media/magazine/16–06/ff_15th_rossetto

Rothenberg, Randall. "The Advertising century," *Advertising Age*, Crain Communications, 1999, on the Web at: http://adage.com/century/index.html

Royal Commission on Newspapers (Canada), Ministry of Supply and Services, 1981.

Rusbridger, Alan. "I Was Shown the Media's Future 16 Years Ago: Now with the iPad, It's Here," *The Guardian*, April 11, 2010.

Saerchinger, Cesar. "Radio, Censorship and Neutrality," *Foreign Affairs*, January 1940, 337.

Saffo, Paul. "Farewell Information, it's a Media Age," December 2005, published on the Web at: http://www.saffo.com/essays/index.php

Sagan, Carl. *Cosmos* (New York: Random House, 1980).

—. *The Demon-haunted World: Science as a Candle in the Dark* (New York: Random House, 1995).

Saleh, Basel. "Tunisia: IMF 'Economic Medicine' has resulted in Mass Poverty and Unemployment; Protest by Suicide as a Symbol of Resistance," Center for Research on Globalization, December 31, 2010, on the Web at: http://www.globalresearch.ca/index.php?context=va&aid=22587

Sampson, Anthony. *The Seven Sisters* (New York: Viking, 1975)

Sampson, Henry. *A History of Advertising from the Earliest Times* (London: Chatto and Windus, 1875)

Sarnoff, David. The Birth of Television, Address at New York World's Fair, Flushing Meadows, New York, April 20, 1939, *Looking Ahead: The Papers of David Sarnoff* (New York: McGraw Hill, 1968)

Savage, William. *A Dictionary of the Art of Printing* (London: Longman, Brown, Green and Longmans, 1841)

Scheeres, Julia. "Lech Walesa: Tech Freedom Fighter," *Wired*, June 19, 2002, on the Web at: http://www.wired.com/politics/law/news/2002/06/53299

Schickel, Richard. "Charlie: The Life and Art of Charles Chaplin," 2003, Warner Brothers video.

—. *The Essential Chaplin: Perspectives on the Life and Art of the Great Comedian* (Lanham, MD: Ivan R. Dee, 2006).

Schrage, Elliot. "Testimony before the House Committee on International Relations Subcommittee on Asia and the Pacific and Subcommittee on Africa, Global Human Rights, and International Operations," February 15, 2006.

Schramm, Wilbur. *The Story of Human Communication, from Cave Painting to Microchip* (New York: Harper and Row, 1988).

Schudson, Michael. *Discovering the News: A Social History of American Newspapers* (New York : Basic Books, 1978).

—. *Advertising, the Uneasy Persuasion: Its Dubious Impact on American Society* (New York: Basic books, 1986).

Segaller, Stephen. *Nerds 2.0.1: A Brief History of the Internet* (New York: TV Books, 1998).

Seigenthaler, John. "A False Wikipedia Biography," *USA Today*, November 29, 2005.

Seldes, George. *Witness to a Century* (New York: Ballantine Books, 1987).

Shafer, Jack. "Newspaper Death Foretold by Warren Buffett," *Slate,* Monday, April 27, 2009, on the Web at: http://www.slate.com/id/2217014/

Shannon, Warren. "Confronting the Nazis: Americans and German Propaganda," Ph.D. Dissertation, Washington State University, 1995.

Sharf, A. *Art and Photography* (London, Penguin Press, 1968).

Sheehan, Neil. *A Bright Shining Lie: John Paul Vann and America in Vietnam* (New York: Vantage Press, 1988).

Shein, Edgar H. *DEC is Dead* (San Francisco, CA: Berrett-Koehler Publishers, 2004).

Shirer, William L., *The Rise and Fall of the Third Reich : A History of Nazi Germany* (New York: Simon and Schuster, 1960).

—. *Gandhi: A Memoir* (New York: Pocket Books, 1986).

Shirkey, Clay. "Institutions versus Collaboration," July 2005, TED Video.

—. *Here Comes Everybody: The Power of Organizing without Organizations* (New York: Penguin Press, 2008).

—. "How Social Media Can Make History," June 2009, TED Video.

Siebert, Frederick. *Theodore Pederson, Wilbur Schramm, Four Theories of the Press* (Urbana, IL: University of Illinois Press, 1963).

Sinclair, Upton. *The Jungle* (New York: Doubleday, Page & Co., 1906).

—. *The Brass Check: A Study of American Journalism* (Pasadena, CA: Published by the author, 1920).

Sinha, Shall. "Mahatma Gandhi the Journalist," 2010, on the Web at: http://gandhi4peace.com/journalist.htm

Smiles, Samuel. The *Huguenots* (New York: Harper, 1867).

Smith, Jeffrey A. *Printers and Press Freedom: The Ideology of Early American Journalism* (New York, London: Oxford University Press, 1988).

Smith, Sally Bevell. *In All His Glory: The Life and Times of William S. Paley and the Birth of Modern Broadcasting* (New York: Simon & Schuster, 1990).

Smith, W. E. and A. M. Smith. *Minamata* (London: Chatto & Windus, Ltd., 1975).

Snyder, Louis L. and Richard B. Morris. *A Treasury of Great Reporting* (New York: Simon & Schuster, 1962).

Softky, Marion. "Building the Internet: Bob Taylor Won the National Medal of Technology for Visionary Leadership in the Development of Modern Computing Technology," *The Almanac*, October 11, 2000, on the Web at: http://www.almanacnews.com/morgue/2000/2000_10_11.taylor.html

Sontag, Susan. *Regarding the Pain of Others* (New York: Picador/Farrar, Straus and Giroux, 2003).

Sperber, A. M. *Murrow: His Life and Times* (New York: Fordham University Press, 1998).

Sriramesh, K., James Grunig and David Dozier, "Observation and Measurement of Two Dimensions of Organizational Culture and Their Relationship to Public Relations," *Journal of Public Relations Research*, 8(4) (1996), 229–61, Lawrence Erlbaum Associates.

Standage, Tom. *The Victorian Internet: The Remarkable Story of the Telegraph and the Nineteenth Century's On-Line Pioneers* (New York: Walker & Company, 1998).

Starr, Paul. *The Creation of the Media: Political Origins of Modern Communications* (New York: Basic Books, 2004).

Stephens, Mitchell. *The Rise of the Image* (New York: Oxford University Press, 1998).

—. *A History of News* (New York: Oxford University Press, 2007).

—. "A Call for an International History of Journalism," accessed 2010 on the Web at: http://www.nyu.edu/classes/stephens/International%20History%20page.htm

Stevenson, Robert Louis. *Essays* (London: Charles Scribner's Sons, 1890).

Stevenson, William. *A Man Called Intrepid* (New York: Ballantine Books, 1978).

Stone, I. F. *The Best of I.F. Stone* (New York: Public Affairs, 2007).

Strauss, Neil. "The MP3 revolution," *The New York Times*, July 18, 1999.

Streible, Dan. *Fight Pictures: A History of Boxing and Early Cinema* (Los Angeles, CA: University of California Press, 2008).

Story, Louise. "New Advertising Outlet: Your Life," *The New York Times*, October 14, 2007.

Stverak, Jason. "The pros and pros of 'Citizen Journalism,'" *Online Journalism Review*, March 12, 2010, on the Web at: http://www.ojr.org/ojr/people/stverak/201003/1830/

Suite101, "The Communications Revolution in Early America," on the Web at: http://americanhistory.suite101.com/article.cfm/the-communications-revolution-in-early-america#ixzz0tJxp7d9a

Surowiecki, James. *The Wisdom of Crowds: Why the Many Are Smarter Than the Few and How Collective Wisdom Shapes Business, Economies, Societies and Nations* (New York: Little, Brown, 2004).

Swanberg, W. A. *Luce and His Empire* (London: Scribners, 1972).

SXSW 2010. Richard Rosenblatt Interview: "Content On Demand," on the Web at: http://www.youtube.com/watch?v=8diEYt-g0xY

Tallentyre, S. G. aka Evelyn Beatrice Hall, *The Friends of Voltaire* (New York: G. P. Putnam's Sons, 1907). Also see *Saturday Review* (May 11, 1935), p. 13 and accessed August 2010 on the Web at: http://en.wikiquote.org/wiki/Evelyn_Beatrice_Hall

Tate, Ryan. "Five Ways Newspapers Botched the Web," *Gawker*, accessed August 2010 on the Web at: http://valleywag.gawker.com/5039619/5-ways-the-newspapers-botched-the-web

Tebbel, John and Mary Ellen Zuckerman. *The Magazine in America* (New York, London: Oxford University Press, 1991).

Telephony, "The Kellogg Company: Dismal Failure of Five Years' Strenuous Efforts to Deceive Independents," *Telephony*, Vol. XIV, September, 1907, p. 136.

Thomas, Isaiah. *The History of Printing in America* (Worcester, MA: The Press of Isaiah Thomas, 1810).

Thomas, Nigel J. T. "Founders of Experimental Psychology: Wilhelm Wundt and William James," *Stanford Encyclopedia of Philosophy*, accessed May 2010, on the Web at: http://plato.stanford.edu/entries/mental-imagery/founders-experimental-psychology.html

Thompson, E. P. *The Making of the English Working Class* (London: Penguin, 1972).

Thoreau, Henry David. *Walden: Or, a Life in the Woods* (Boston, MA: Beacon Press, 2004 [originally published in 1854]).

Timberg, Bernard. *Television Talk* (Austin, TX: University of Texas Press, 2002).

Time, "The Formula Flap," July 12, 1976.

Time-Warner, "America Online and Time Warner Will Merge to Create World's First Internet-Age Media and Communications Company," Press Release, January 10, 2000, on the Web at: http://www.timewarner.com/corp/newsroom/pr/0,20812,667602,00.html

Toops, Diane. *Food Processing*, July 01, 2005.

Tosh, John. *The Pursuit of History: Aims, Methods, and New Directions in the Study of Modern History* (Toronto: Longman, 2000).

Trenchard, John and Thomas Gordon. "NO. 15. Of Freedom of Speech; That the same is inseparable from publick Liberty," February 15, 1721, *Cato's Letters: Essays on Liberty, Civil and Religious, and Other Important Subjects* (London: London Journal, 1720–1723).

Tuchman, Barbara. *The Guns of August* (New York: Macmillan, 1962).

Tuney, Michael. Online Readings in Public Relations, Northern Kentucky University, accessed June 2010, on the Web at: http://www.nku.edu/~turney/prclass/readings/3eras2x.html

Twain, Mark. *A Tramp Abroad* (Hartford, TC: American Publishing Co., 1880).

—. *Mark Twain's Speeches* (Ithaca, NY: Cornell University Press, 2009 [originally published 1920]).

United States Holocaust Memorial Museum. "The Press in the Third Reich," *Holocaust Encyclopedia*, accessed August 2010, on the Web at: http://www.ushmm.org/wlc/en/?ModuleId=10005143

United States House of Representatives, "The Transmission of Telegrams," Hearing on HB 3010, May 24, 1912.

Usborne, David. "Entrepreneur Taps Mistrust of Media for New Venture," *Sunday Independent*, November 23, 2005, on the Web at: http://www.independent.co.uk/news/world/americas/entrepreneur-taps-mistrust-of-media-for-new-venture-516533.html

Van Doren, Carl. *Benjamin Franklin* (New York: Viking Press, 1938).

Varian, Hal. *Newspaper Economics Online and Offline* (Palo Alto, CA: Google, 2010), on the Web at: http://www.scribd.com/doc/28084224/030910-Hal-Varian-FTC-Preso

Vaughn, Stephen L. *Encyclopedia of American Journalism* (London and New York: Taylor & Francis, 2008).

Voltaire. *Lettres Philosophiques*, c.1778, Modern History Sourcebook, on the Web at: http://www.fordham.edu/halsall/mod/1778voltaire-lettres.html

Waldrop, M. Mitchell. *The Dream Machine: J. C. R. Licklider and the Revolution That Made Computing Personal* (New York: Viking Penguin, 2001).

Ward, Hiley. *Mainstreams of American Media History* (Boston, MA: Allyn & Bacon, 1996).

Warren, Donald. *Radio Priest: Charles Coughlin, The Father of Hate Radio* (New York: The Free Press, 1996).

Washburn, Patrick Scott. *A Question of Sedition: The Federal Government's Investigation of the Black Press during World War II* (New York: Oxford University Press, 1986).

Washington Post, "JW Mack Under Fire," February 28, 1928, p. 1.

—. "Crisis at Three Mile Island, 1999," on the Web at: http://www.washingtonpost. com/wp-srv/national/longterm/tmi/whathappened.htm

Watson, Thomas. *Exploring Life, the Autobiography of Thomas A. Watson* (New York: D. Appleton and Co., 1926).

Waugh, Alec. *The Lipton Story* (New York: Doubleday, 1950).

Weber, Eugen. *Europe since 1715: A Modern History* (New York: Norton, 1972).

Weber, Johannes. "Strassburg, 1605. The Origins of the Newspaper in Europe," *German History*, 24, 2006, 387–412.

Weiser, Philip J. "The Ghost of Telecommunications Past," *Michigan Law Review,* 103:6, May 2005.

Wells, H. G. *The Sleeper Awakes* (London: *The Graphic*, Illustrated Newspapers Ltd. 1898), on the Web at: http://www.gutenberg.org/files/775/775-h/775-h. htm#2HCH0009

—. "World Brain: The Idea of a Permanent World Encyclopedia," *Encyclopédie Fran-çaise,* August 1937.

Whelan, Richard. *Aperture* magazine, Spring 2002, accessed May 2010, on the Web at: http://www.pbs.org/wnet/americanmasters/episodes/robert-capa/in-love-and-war/47/

White, Thomas A. *United States Early Radio History*, accessed in 2010 on the Web at: http://earlyradiohistory.us

Wikinvest, "Decline in Television Advertising," on the Web at: http://www.wikinvest. com/concept/Decline_in_Television_Advertising (accessed in 2010).

Wildstrom, Steve. "Apple Crushes Clone Maker in Court," *Bloomberg Business Week,* November 14, 2009.

Williams, Keith. *The English Newspaper: An Illustrated History to 1900* (London: Springwood Books, 1977).

Winston, Brian. *Media Technology and Society* (New York: Routledge, 1998).

—. *Technologies of Seeing: Photography, Cinematography and Television* (London: British Film Institute, 2008).

Wolf, Gary. "The Tragedy of Craigslist," *Wired*, September 2009.

Wolf, Maryanne. *Proust and the Squid: The Story and Science of the Reading Brain* (New York: Harper, 2008).

Wolfe, Tom. *The New Journalism* (New York: Pan, 1975).

Wood, James. *The Story of Advertising* (New York: Ronald Press Co., 1958).

Woods, Oliver and James Bishop. *The Story of the Times* (London: Michael Joseph, 1985).

Wright, B. E. and John M. Lavine. *The Constant Dollar Newspaper: An Economic Analysis Covering the Last Two Decades* (Chicago, IL: Inland Press Association, 1982).

Zinn, Howard. *A People's History of the United States* (New York: HarperCollins, 1980), on the Web at: http://www.historyisaweapon.com/defcon1/zinncol1.html

Zittrain, Jonathan. *The Future of the Internet and How to Stop It* (New Haven, CT: Yale University Press, 2006).

Zoglin, Richard and Elaine Dutka. "Cinema: Lights, Camera, Special Effects!" *Time* magazine, June 16, 1986, on the Web at: http://www.time.com/time/magazine/ article/0,9171,961611,00.html

Index